Patrons, clients and friends

Themes in the Social Sciences

Editors: Jack Goody & Geoffrey Hawthorn

The aim of this series is to publish books which will focus on topics of general and interdisciplinary interest in the social sciences. They will be concerned with non-European cultures and with developing countries, as well as with industrial societies. The emphasis will be on comparative sociology and, initially, on sociological, anthropological and demographic topics. These books are intended for undergraduate teaching, but not as basic introductions to the subjects they cover. Authors have been asked to write on central aspects of current interest which have a wide appeal to teachers and research students, as well as to undergraduates.

Patrons, clients and friends

Interpersonal relations and the structure of trust in society

S. N. EISENSTADT

and

L. RONIGER

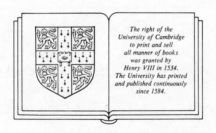

The right of the
University of Cambridge
to print and sell
all manner of books
was granted by
Henry VIII in 1534.
The University has printed
and published continuously
since 1584.

CAMBRIDGE UNIVERSITY PRESS

Cambridge
London   New York   New Rochelle
Melbourne   Sydney

Published by the Press Syndicate of the University of Cambridge
The Pitt Building, Trumpington Street, Cambridge CB2 1RP
32 East 57th Street, New York, NY 10022, USA
296 Beaconsfield Parade, Middle Park, Melbourne 3206, Australia

First published 1984

Printed in Great Britain at the University Press, Cambridge

Library of Congress catalogue card number: 83-26333

British Library Cataloguing in Publication Data
Eisenstadt, S. N.
Patrons, clients and friends – (Themes
in the social sciences)
1. Interpersonal relations
I. Title   II. Roniger, L.
III. Series
302   HM132

ISBN 0 521 24687 3
ISBN 0 521 28890 8 Pbk

Contents

Contents

Contents

Preface

The origins of this book go far back to the article on 'Ritualized Personal Relations' which I published in 1956 in *Man*, as an outgrowth of the comparative studies of age groups and youth movements published the same year in *From Generation to Generation*. For many years after that, while I followed the literature on friendship and interpersonal relations, it was not at the centre of my attention. In 1970 the invitation of Professor E. Leyton to contribute to the volume on Friendship which was based on the colloquium held on the theme at the Memorial University of Newfoundland gave me the first opportunity to rethink some of the theoretical problems involved in these phenomena, and my preliminary musings on these problems were published in the volume of the Symposium.[1]

In the meantime I have become very much interested, as an outgrowth of comparative studies of modernisation, in the analysis of patron–client relations – becoming more and more convinced that such relations are a sign not just of underdevelopment, but of special types of social formations closely related to specific types of cultural orientations.

These problems were analysed in great detail in an inter-disciplinary seminar which I conducted together with Dr Yael Azmon in 1974/5 within the framework of seminars on comparative civilisations at the Hebrew University. One of the major themes worked out in that seminar was that the development of patron–client relations is very closely related to the structure of trust in society; its relevance to the study of interpersonal relations was thus highlighted and many of the assumptions of the earlier works were made explicit. Interestingly enough this work brought this study close to some of the major works of my teacher, the late Martin Buber, especially his work on *I and Thou*.

It is the explication of these assumptions that, in a comparative analytical framework, constitutes the focus of this book.

Luis Roniger participated in the 1974/5 seminar, and has developed his own interest around the study of patron–client relations in the

Preface

Mediterranean and Latin American societies. Already in 1975 we had started to cooperate in the comparative study of patron–client relations, publishing several papers on the subject.[2] As a result of this cooperation, we have undertaken to prepare this book together; it thus constitutes a common venture in every sense of the word.

The research on which this work is based has been undertaken within the framework of the Unit on Comparative Civilizations and Modernization of the Truman Research Institute of the Hebrew University. Large parts of this research have been supported by a grant from the Volkswagen Foundation.

We should like to thank Professor R. Paine for very useful critical remarks on parts of the manuscripts which he made during his visit to Jerusalem in the spring of 1982, as well as to Esther Sass for her superb editorial work and to Morris Levy who typed most efficiently the greatest part of our manuscript.

The Hebrew University   S. N. EISENSTADT
Jersusalem

1

vvvvvvvvvvvvvvvvvvvvvvvvvvvvvvvvvvvvvvvvvvvvvvvvvvvvvvvvvvvvvvvvvvvvvvvv

Personal relations, trust and ambivalence in relation to the institutional order

I

This book is about some special types of interpersonal relations – above all about friendship, ritual personal and patron–client relationships – and their connections to the institutional matrix in which they develop.

The most important illustrations of such relations are blood brotherhood and affine relationships of covenanted comradeship or sacrosanct amity initiated through some ritual exchange of personal substance (blood, saliva, semen, etc.) as reported in the Muslim Middle East, in Africa (for instance, among the Zande studied by E.E. Evans-Pritchard), in Caucasian tribes and among North American Indians; practices of 'fictive' kinship, as found for instance among slaves of warlike African tribes who were adopted into the lineages of their captors, or in the Japanese practices of adoption of strangers into families (*mukoyōshi*) and into rural kinship units (*dozoku*); patterns of ritual kinship, such as the various Christian forms of co–parenthood (*compadrazgo, comparaggio*, etc.) reported in Latin America, southern Europe, the Balkans, Yugoslavia, and other eastern European settings; patron–client relations as found typically in Latin America, southeast Asia and the Mediterranean areas; ritualised bonds of friendship such as blood-friendship or 'best' friendship links of some African peoples and cultures of the Pacific such as the Tikopia; and the numerous forms of less formalised friendships reported in many, above all complex, societies in general and modern societies in particular.

These interpersonal relations, although in part seemingly informal, and which in one way or another are found in almost all human societies, are yet very often defined in very articulated symbolic and institutional terms. Within most of these relations, several themes are emphasised, which more or less intensively or articulatedly are

1

common to many – if not all – types of informal interpersonal relations that develop in human societies.

These relations are usually defined in terms of mutual intimacy, of moral and emotional obligations, stressing above all trust and empathy, and sometimes the sharing of common 'pure' pristine values, as well as some equality. In the relations of friendship, this mutual trust is consistently based on the relative equality of the participants in this relationship, while patron–client relations entail hierarchial differences between the patron and his protégé, his 'client'. Even then a moral equality of the different participants is implied, as J. Pitt–Rivers has rightly pointed out.[1]

Some ambivalence is also common to most of these relationships – sometimes weak, sometimes very strong – towards the more formalised organised structure of the society in which they develop.

These themes are probably common to numerous types of informal interpersonal relations that develop in human societies, but they are more fully articulated in the special types of interpersonal relations with which we are concerned in this study, namely in patron–client relations, ritual personal links, and friendship.

II

These interpersonal relations touch on some basic aspects of the construction of social order and of the tensions and ambivalences which such construction entails.

In order better to understand the characteristics of such relations and their institutional significance it might be worthwhile first of all to examine the way in which they were analysed in the social sciences, in the 'classical' traditions of sociology and social anthropology. These traditions dealt, above all, with highly structured entities such as groups, social structures and institutions.

Interpersonal relations were not on the whole part of this analysis. In some cases, as in the work of Georg Simmel, or in a different vein in social psychology, they formed a distinct mode and subject of analysis, with but little connection to more central analyses of social structures and institutions. It was only the study of primary groups and relations, which developed especially in American sociology in the forties, that constituted any exception to this. But even this was only a partial exception, because most of these studies mainly pointed out the importance of such relations or groups in the life of their members and in the structure of society, but did not analyse their distinct characteristics as types of interpersonal relations.[2]

It was above all in the anthropological and – to a smaller degree – in the sociological literature that, already in the late forties and early fifties, some types of rather exceptional interpersonal relations, such as different types of friendship, of ritual friendship and of patron–client relations, were noted. But until the late fifties and early sixties, the study of these kinds of relations was in most of the social sciences – anthropology, sociology and political science – in a rather marginal position. Patron–client relations as well as relations of ritual or informal friendship – although fascinating – were seen as rather marginal in societies and were studied in the framework of the concepts, approaches and concerns which were predominant in these disciplines. They were usually treated as (sometimes negative) illustrations of the principles of organisation of macrosocietal complexes, and they were above all seen as greatly differing or deviating from the 'corporate' kinship and territorial groups so strongly emphasised in anthropological literature and from universalistic–bureaucratic or market frameworks which were usually portrayed in sociology or in political science as epitomes of modernity and rationality.[3]

This picture has changed since about the late fifties, especially with respect to the study of patron–client relations, which became more central to sociological and anthropological analysis.[4] Thus, in this area, the change was connected with the shift in the objects of these studies from relatively limited, dyadic, interpersonal, semi-institutionalised relations between a single patron and usually one or at most a few clients to a much greater variety of types of social relations and organisations. These ranged from semi-institutionalised personal dyadic or tryadic relations in more organised settings (such as various bureaucratic agencies) to relatively loose, less rigidly prescribed social relations, often organised in complex networks and connected by different types of brokers, as well as to loose cliques and factions in political machines.

Second, this change was connected with the spread of these studies over a very wide range of societies throughout the world – in the Mediterranean, the Near East, Latin America, India, southeast Asia and other parts of the world.[5]

Third, the centrality of these studies became connected with the growing awareness that patron–client relations were not destined to remain on the outskirts of society or to disappear with the development and establishment of democratic or authoritarian regimes or with economic development and modernisation or with the development of class consciousness among the lower strata; and that, while any single type of patronage, as for instance the personal semi-institutionalised kinship-like personal dyadic patron–client relationship, may disappear under such conditions, new types of such relations may appear, and may be found, in a great variety of forms, in different societies, cutting across different levels of economic development and types of political regimes, and seemingly performing important functions within such more developed modern frameworks.[6]

III

The various types of such interpersonal relations as blood brotherhood, ritual kinship or pseudo-kinship, and different types of less formal or institutional friendship have been studied even since the fifties much less systematically and continuously than patron–client relations.

The study of the more fully institutionalised types of such interpersonal relations was mostly undertaken within tribal and peasant societies, within the framework of systematic anthropological analysis. In these studies, structural variables such as the character of kinship and of territorial and other groups were stressed initially as explaining the development of such relations. In later anthropological studies, from about the mid-sixties onwards, with the growing stress in the social sciences in general (and in anthropology in particular) on the autonomy of the symbolic dimension, there did develop also the interpretation of these different types of interpersonal relations as part of the symbolic domain of the structuring of human relations.[7]

The study of the more informal types of interpersonal relations in general and of friendship in particular in more complex societies – and especially in modern ones – was discontinuous, even if undertaken from various perspectives by socio-metric and psychosociological analyses, as well as by sociological and to a smaller degree anthropological ones.[8]

The psychosociological and socio-metric approaches have naturally stressed in particular the element of choice and of mutual attraction in the constitution of such relationships and the possible importance, in such choices, of compatible or incompatible but complementary personal attributes.[9]

Lately several studies of friendship have also been undertaken from the point of view of developmental psychology, either from an ethological–developmental point of view or from a developmental–structural vantage point greatly influenced by Piaget.[10]

The more specifically sociological analyses – best exemplified in the works of Parsons and White, of Naegele and of James Coleman [11] – stressed the importance of such interpersonal relations in general and of friendship in particular in structuring or facilitating the transition, in American society at least, from the world of childhood into that of adulthood, from the seemingly secure solidary world of the family and of childhood into the world of 'adult' competition.

In the same vein S.N. Eisenstadt's analysis of age groups [12] has stressed the importance of formalised age groups – as well as of less formalised youth groups, movements and the like – as providing such interlinking mechanisms in those societies in which the broader macrosocietal institutional principles differ from those of the family structure, i.e. are universalistic and specialised. Although in this work no special emphasis was laid on purely interpersonal relations as such, yet it was those characteristics of the age groups and youth movements – above all their strong stress on ascriptive criteria and on solidary relations, which stood close to the traits of such interpersonal relations – that were stressed in this study. Hence Eisenstadt's somewhat later analysis of ritualised interpersonal relations [13] was a natural offshoot of this more comprehensive analysis.

IV

Side by side with these studies there have also been, in the last three decades, several attempts to bring these various studies of friendship, ritual kinship and the like into somewhat more comprehensive frameworks. The first such attempt at bringing the various studies of friendship into a systematic comparative framework was probably the Harvard Seminar on Friendship conducted in 1955 and 1956 by Cora Du Bois – the proceedings of which were however never published. In 1956 Eisenstadt presented one of the first published comparative analyses of these relationships. In 1961 Y. Cohen published another such broad survey, basing himself on a wider range of data.[14]

In 1966 E. Wolf presented, already in close relationship with the study of patronage, a classification stemming to some degree from Aristotle's work on different types of friendship, stressing mainly the difference between emotional and instrumental friendship. In 1969 a Symposium on Friendship was conducted by R. Paine and E. Leyton in the University of Newfoundland and parts of its proceedings, with some additional materials, were published in 1974.[15]

The systematic analysis of ritual kinship of pseudo-kinship has been, since the fifties, most continuously pursued by Julian Pitt-Rivers while the literature on friendship has been analysed by Odd Ramsøy in the *International Encyclopaedia of Social Sciences* and more recently by R. Paine and C. Du Bois in the Newfoundland Symposium.[16]

In these various analytical summaries of the field – especially in the later ones – some attempts were made to connect the disparate analytical or theoretical approaches to the study of these various types

5

of interpersonal relations; yet very often these very attempts have highlighted the lack of direct connection between these approaches. Thus, to give only one illustration, Ramsøy's article in the *International Encyclopaedia of Social Sciences* does not contain reference to most of the anthropological studies, while Pitt-Rivers' article on pseudo-kinship in the same work does not refer to the more psychological or sociological analyses of friendship. It is perhaps only in the Newfoundland Symposium that at last an attempt has been made to combine these various strands of analysis.

V

Despite the relative discontinuity and the great disparity of the approaches in the study of these different types of interpersonal relations and between them and patron–client relations, some common themes can indeed be discerned in most of them. These can be identified with respect to the definition of the most salient features of such interpersonal relations in general and of friendship in particular; with respect to the broader conditions which generate them or within the context of which they develop, as well as with respect to attempts to classify them. Among these themes stand out, first of all, the (most voluntary) construction of a realm of solidarity and trust, and, second and to a smaller degree, the problematics of emotional affinity, intimacy and participation in a realm of pristine spiritual values. Most of the definitions and descriptions of the patterns of these interpersonal relations have emphasised very strongly at least part of these themes as constituting the central core of these interpersonal relations.

Thus for instance in 1956 Eisenstadt proposed – albeit referring only to more fully institutionalised types of such relations – the following definitions of their basic analytical characteristics:

they are particularistic, personal, voluntary and fully institutionalized (usually in ritual terms). By particularistic I mean that the incumbents of the relationship act towards one another in terms of their respective personal properties and not in terms of general universal categories. In this they are very close to kinship relations and groups (which are also predominantly particularistic) but unlike the latter in that they are incurred in a voluntary way.

... In order to understand more fully the nature of these relationships, we should also inquire into the contents and nature of the obligations that they incur. The fact that these relations are both voluntary (hence to some extent contractual) and also particularistic and personal indicates that we have some interrelation between solidary and instrumental obligations. In all such relations there exists a set of mutual obligations in the instrumental and economic fields. Some such obligations seem to recur in most of these cases – e.g. mutual help in cases of economic hardship, illness or other calamities – some sort of mutual insurance in common economic enterprises, participation in funeral expenses, participation in some costs of educating children, etc. ...

... these mutual (or, as sometimes in cases of godparent–godchild relations, unilateral) instrumental obligations are set within a framework of diffuse solidarity. These obligations are not defined as stemming from some specific, limited contractual, market-type commitments and relations, nor are they set in terms of universalistic categories of people.[17]

A similar strong emphasis on trust or on solidarity can be found in the more psychosociological or sociological definitions of these relations. Thus the relative importance and strength of such dimensions of solidarity in these relations has been also a major starting point for most of the attempts at classification of them. Y. Cohen distinguished between inalienable, close, casual and expedient friendship, while Wolf differentiated between emotional and instrumental friendship; similarly Cora Du Bois presented in the Newfoundland Symposium several basic dimensions according to which different types of interpersonal relations can be distinguished.[18] Common to all of them, according to her, is that they are voluntary and preferential, and they differ as to whether they are expressive or instrumental, dyadic or polyadic, as well as in the degree of intimacy they entail and in their mutability and duration. She then distinguishes between three major categories of friends – exclusive, close and casual, which differ in these dimensions – and summarises the dimensions and types of friendship as shown in table 1:[19]

Table 1. Dimensions and types of friendship

	Exclusive	Close	Casual
Expressive–instrumental	Primarily expressive	Expressive–instrumental	Largely instrumental
Dyadic–polyadic	Dyadic/exclusive	Multiple dyads	Polyadic
Intimacy (confidence, responsibility)	Inclusive	Selective	Incidental
Mutability	Assumed permanent	Hoped durable	Not stressed

Similarly, K. Naegele[20] identified as the most prominent feature of friendship that connected with trust and personal choice, and as complementary the elements of dependability, mutual understanding and general acceptance and a varying presence of interest considerations and positive emotions. These emphases were found to different degrees among the various categories of friendship identified by high school students in that study: namely just friends, a gang, people one knows, people one hangs around with, people who are close, people who are one's best friends.

VI

The theme of trust, of solidarity and of the search for pristine values has also been central in the attempts to explain the conditions which generate these various types of interpersonal relations, and which themselves changed in their emphasis with developments in sociological theory and analysis which have developed since the late fifties or early sixties. Thus in 1956 Eisenstadt propounded an analysis of the conditions which give rise to such – especially institutionalised – relations, stressing the functions of social control.

Such conditions arise mostly in some types of predominantly particularistic societies and are related to some tensions and strains inherent in the societies.
     ... It seems to me that in such societies there exist two main areas of strains and consequent problems of integration. The first are strains which exist within the basic constituent groups of such societies (lineages, clans, castes, some territorial groups, etc.) and which are inherent in the structure of these groups. Second are the various strains and tensions between the main groups and categories of people of which such societies are composed, and the consequent problems of their integration ... Most of these tensions can be related to the fact that in such groups, by the very nature of their organization, there usually is but little specification of the allocation of the various major obligations within the group or category. These are left – at least on many occasions – to the internal arrangements of the particular group. Sometimes these relations may be structured and clearly defined – quite often in ways which may increase the tensions (as in the right prescription of seniority rights) – but quite often they may be left to some internal unspecified arrangements of the group involved. These may enable the exercise of many pressures, of bargaining and of illegitimate power, etc. Moreover, it is not always specified, and in many cases cannot be specified by the very nature of the case, which of the members of a group will start a chain of activities or become involved in some problems or conflicts, which may then affect the whole group. Thus it can never be known who will start a particular feud which may involve the group or some of its members, or who will engage in various commercial or economic activities with other groups, etc., or who will show more initiative or ambition in any field of organization, etc. While it may perhaps be easy to identify such persons in terms of individual idiosyncrasies and characteristics, these do not necessarily coincide with any definite structural positions within the group or within a broad category of people. Thus the very nature of such particularistic groups, with their emphasis on diffuse solidarity (sometimes

8

also on seniority, etc.), lends itself to easy manipulation by certain people who may easily go beyond what seem to other persons to be their legitimate rights. This is especially so in those areas of life and in those enterprises which involve not fully structured intergroup relations, which are not entirely contained within the group and regulated by it, and which yet may easily involve the group itself and many of the members by the very existence of clear definition of situation.

An additional factor of strain in such societies is the possibility of conflicting claims and pressures from different groups or categories of people or any persons, and the limiting of the area of the individual's choice or private life through such pressures. This seems to be especially important in problems of inheritance, the amount and type of property that one can bequeath according to his own wish, etc. . . .

. . . It seems to be characteristic of most of these relations and obligations, especially in the instrumental field or in political relations (as, for example, among the Azande), that they are not entirely 'contained' and regulated by the particularistic criteria and relations of each of these groups and by what may be called their routine interrelations. Many of these mutual obligations are not clearly and concretely defined simply because they are not stated in general, universalistic and specific ways but rather in more diffuse and particularistic terms, and are limited within the framework of diffuse solidary relations. Thus the exact demands that a noble can make of a commoner among the Azande, or a member of a superior caste among the Tanala towards a member of a lower one, are not usually clearly defined and may give rise to a lot of 'private' interpretations and extortions. The same seems to be true of the demands of members of senior age groups towards younger ones or of the demands between certain family groups in the spheres of intermarriage, etc. This is especially so in cases of eruption, or continuous existence, of hostile relations between such groups or their members. In such cases the exact definition of mutual obligations, compensation, etc. may be a very vexing and uncertain problem . . .

. . . In other words, it seems that the very kind of social organization existing in such societies creates some types of undefined situations or types of situations of potential conflict malintegration. These situations may be of either of the two main types mentioned earlier. They may arise in those cases wherein the internal solidarity of each of such sub-groups may come into conflict with various exigencies of cooperation and interrelationships between such groups. Or the extent of interrelationship between such different sub-groups may be so loose and small that it is difficult to maintain any regulated relations between them or their members.

. . . It is our basic hypothesis that the various forms of ritualized personal relationships constitute also a mechanism of social control which tends to mitigate some of the tensions and strains of predominantly particularistic societies analysed above.

. . . What seems common to most of them is that some incompatibility develops between an individual's instrumental obligations, his solidary obligations, and his predispositions in these spheres. His solidary relations to

9

some groups or categories of people may become strained because of conflicting or illegitimate claims in the instrumental field made by members of such solidary groups, and/or he may be incapable of fulfilling his instrumental obligations and aspirations because of such solidary claims or because of lack of what to him seems adequate support from his solidary groups. It may therefore be a plausible suggestion that this type of strain is most likely to occur in those situations in which both problems of intra-group solidarity and of intergroup relations arise. In other words, in such situations there arise problems both of societal integration and of individual tension and adjustment.

. . . It is because of these various characteristics of situations of strain that the different types of ritualized personal relations are so closely related to them. The basic characteristics of ritualized personal relations, analysed in the first part of this paper, enable these relations to mitigate precisely these types of conflicts. In order to avoid imputation of any teleological implications in this argument it should be stated at the outset that we do not assume that, whenever such tensions exist, these (or any other) mechanisms of social control always develop, nor that these are necessarily the only types of such mechanisms which could perform this function.

. . . A closer analysis of the different types of obligations incurred through relationships of ritual kinship, as well as of its voluntary and personal nature, will illustrate the way in which these relations tend to mitigate the above-analysed tensions, from the point of view of both the individual and the social structure.

. . . As has already been indicated, most of these obligations contain some element of insurance against unexpected risks and calamities. These may be the cases of illness, of death, of unexpected sudden economic demands, hardship, etc. In still other cases we find some sort of assurance of safe ways in strange and hostile parts of the country . . .

. . . But in all these relations there exists an additional basic element – namely, that the performance of these obligations is assured through a special personal bond which transcends the usual existing groupings and categories of people and cuts across them. This bond is usually seen as no less binding – sometimes even more – than that with the categories and groups. In some cases, this bond is more or less expressly oriented to assuring the individual's will as against possible pressures from different groups . . .

. . . Their ability to perform these functions of social control and alleviation of tensions that arise under the conditions specified above is made possible because the very nature of these relationships is set firmly within the basic structural principles of these societies. As has been pointed out above, they are particularistic, diffuse, and are sanctioned in terms of the most important values and symbols of their respective societies . . .

. . . Moreover, it is the fact that they are sanctioned by the highest ritual sanctions that enables these relationships to 'compete,' as it were, with the usual kinship, etc., relations which are also related to the ultimate values of these societies . . .

. . . This is especially seen in the organization of instrumental and solidary relations on the one hand and of personal and particularistic relations on the other. Thus while in these situations in which the strains are generated the instrumental obligations are set within the framework of ascribed, non-voluntary, solidary groups which limit the area of individual choice, in the ritualized personal relations the instrumental relations are also set within a solidary and ritual framework – but one that is personal and voluntary, and that cuts across existing solidary groups. Thus these relations provide a new type of solidary framework for instrumental relations which is different from that of the main groups of the society and yet complements them. In this way they seem to conform to some general characteristics of mechanisms of social control.

Because of this it can also be understood that these types of relationships do not usually arise or exist under different structural conditions and in different types of societies. The tensions analysed here seem to be peculiar to the type of predominantly particularistic societies discussed here.[21]

VII

In 1961 Cohen continued the analysis of this theme of solidarity, albeit with a stronger psychological emphasis. He has proposed that the different types of friendship he designated – inalienable, close, casual, and expedient – vary according to the nature of the significant solidary grouping to which the individual is attached. He expected (in Ramsøy's wording) inalienable friendship to coincide with the maximally solidary community (generally, localised descent groups where nuclear families and households are socially, physically, and emotionally close as a societal nucleus sharply distinguished from other groupings). Close friendship was expected to be associated with the solidary–fissible community (where solidarity is split between kinship group and community). The non-nucleated society (where isolated, solidary nuclear families are tied loosely together) is expected to be associated with casual friendship. Finally, an expedient type of friendship institution is expected to occur in individuated social structures (where there is emphasis on individual amassing of wealth and relatively little solidarity even in the nuclear family).

Cohen's interpretation of this finding has been made, as Ramsøy has put it, in terms of holistic compatibility in culture and personality. A dimension of personal generosity versus withholding seems to be the basic variable that unites community structure with friendship structure. There is a correlation between childhood gratification versus deprivation, on the one hand, and adult food sharing versus individual amassment of food or money on the other.

VIII

Two major shifts have taken place in the comparative analyses of these types of interpersonal relations since the early sixties: from the

11

structural–functional or psychosociological modes of explanation which characterised these two first attempts at such analysis.

The first such shift – mainly from the stress on the integrative functions of such interpersonal relations – can perhaps best be illustrated by Burridge's criticism of Eisenstadt's earlier exposition:

In what way does friendship in Tangu 'mitigate some of the tensions and strains' to be found in Tangu society? Taking the sentence at its face value, and without examining too deeply what is meant by 'mitigate', 'tension' and 'strain', 'tension' may be predicated of any relationship and more especially of one that makes any explicit demands. We have seen how the presence of a friend within the community resulted in breaking it; it is also clear that having a friend in another community both facilitates the expression of an issue or dispute, and at the same time provides a channel for settling the dispute within terms of certain conventions. If a friend were called upon to perform what was properly the task of a kinsman, friendship would be put to an unendurable strain; so that one might say with equal aplomb that kinship mitigates the tensions in friendship.What Tangu do when they feel uneasy about a particular relationship is to avoid it. They go out to their hunting lodges, or to their garden shelters; they visit a friend, or, as the luluai did, they found a new settlement. But none of these expedients necessarily prevents them from expressing a 'tension' in mystical ways – sorcery and the like. In the same way, no number of friends releases a man from his obligations to co-operate with his brothers or make food exchanges with the households and his brothers-in-law – though, of course, it may well be that he feels more ready for toil after a day with his friend. And yet, if he loiters with a friend in front of his brothers, the latter may call on him, or wish to call on him, and at once he is confronted with a conflict of claims. In short, to say that friendships 'mitigate tension' is not to say anything of friendship in particular . . .

To conclude. We have seen that friendship inTangu is different from other kinds of 'lateral' relationship; that brothers and brothers-in-law were deeply involved in economic and political matters whereas it was characteristic of friends not to be so involved. Second, the chief significances of friendship emerge in the context of inter-community relations, and the normal marriage under kinship rules; the nexus between both sets of facts is that while inter-community relations are, or are thought to be, desirable or necessary, the basic and preferred lines of communication follow the kin links. Friendship is here centrally placed, either to provide of itself a form of communication – particularly if no kin links exist – or to create the kin links through which Tangu normally prefer to communicate. Finally, while friendship only indirectly – and from outside as it were – serves ad hoc economic ends, these ends in themselves have only a small significance in relation to the overall economic process; at the same time, friendship may be the seed-bed of prestige and useful in scoring political points without involving oneself or another in political alliances.[22]

IX

A second shift in the analytical explanation of these relations – first continuously elaborated by Pitt-Rivers and later by, among others, Gudeman in his works on *compadrazgo*[23] – was characterised by a growing emphasis on the symbolic dimensions, as against the purely structural ones, of these relations. Those analyses were focused on the tension between these bonds and kinship relationships. Maurice Bloch and S. Guggenheim have extended this focus and combined it with a stress on power relations in a way which has been characteristic of many of the new theoretical approaches:

Gudeman convincingly argues that the foundation of the institution lies in the conception of man's dual nature as a natural and spiritual being. This is the starting point on which a variety of institutional links are built. In this case, baptism is a second birth negating the earlier one. It creates the 'juridic' person, with all the rights and obligations belonging to a member of the moral religious community. This, Gudeman maintains, is the continuing ideological core of the historical and geographical transformations which the institution undergoes . . .

. . . The ideological core of compadrazgo and baptism consists in the denial of biological birth and of the ability of women to produce 'legitimate' children by first declaring childbirth to be polluting and then by replacing it with a ritual re-enactment of birth which involves giving other parents. Indeed, it should be noted that the one categorical rule governing the choice of sponsors is that the biological parents cannot sponsor their own children. This creating of godparenthood is, however, only the first step in the making of a spiritual and ideological society of which the compadrazgo links are the second.

The role of the godparent or the sponsor is not simply that of substitute parent. We are not dealing with a situation where the power of creativity is handed over to these persons. What is stressed equally in all the examples, but is especially clear in the case of the Christian godparents, is that the substitute parents are but an intermediary with no creative power of their own but who have been given the power to be parents from on high, whether from the Church, the State or the ancestors. The denial of parenthood becomes the basis of an ideological insertion, not so much of the godparents themselves, but that which makes them godparents. Because what is inserted by the denial of the creativity of childbirth can be understood as 'authority', unlike the denigrated entity, motherhood, the substituted entity is extremely varied, as varied as the political and economic structures of the societies that use the idiom, and this is reflected in the variety of people who can be godparents. The creativity made available by second birth rituals can be used to legitimate all kinds of situations. Yet it always legitimates in the same way: by making these other people, or the entities they represent, the repository of the ability to create social/spiritual people. In fact, this notion has been extended so that other aspects of creativity such as the acquisition of wealth or profit (Taussig 1977) may similarly be recovered through analogies with baptism and compadrazgo. It has been witnessed in Mexico that the acquisition of cars, refrigerators, blenders and other goods is marked by the giving of godparents to the object, and the new compadres may even go so far as to have a priest officiate. Here too, creativity cannot be left to an extra-communal source; it must be recovered by legitimate authorities who then 'make' these things be born again through sanctified creativity. In this light we can see why the links established through baptism are so often used to mystify class relations, by giving them a pseudo-sanctity, ideologically transforming domination into the gift of creation.

Presented as such, the problem we have been considering is not specifically concerned with gender but might be described as generally ideological. Yet the use of gender symbolism to resolve it is both present in and unites the various examples. The reason for this conflation seems to lie at the root of the dialectic of symbolic domination, and can be represented as a three-stage argument. The first stage consists of the symbolic focusing of the process of people production on the actual moment of birth, thereby overemphasizing the role of women. The second consists in the declaration that the first state of affairs (symbolically acted though it is) is impure, subversive, evil (associated with evil spirits in the Christian case). In the third stage another birth, pure, legitimate, authorised, holy, is necessary and this is performed by the legitimate authorities through the power invested in them by God. By the argument of the ritual, by the need for a second birth created from the denial of the first, the authority of the power-holders is represented as beneficial and creative in the most fundamental way possible.

In the cases we have looked at, the legitimation of domination, whether of gender or of class, is anchored in the same symbolic use of sexual dimorphism. This explains our original puzzle, the fact of the generality of the symbolism and the specificity of its use. On the common humiliation of mothers are built the varied and many symbolic constructions of power.[24]

We therefore see that there were wide shifts in the explanation of personal relations in the psychosociological, sociological and anthropological literature. These shifts point out the crucial fact that all such relations tend to construct a realm of intimacy, trust and of, usually equal, participation in the spiritual sphere beyond those major institutionalised sectors of a society – above all, but not only, that of kinship – in which trust and meaningful participation appear to be fully institutionalised. The construction of such a realm of interpersonal relations is often connected with the search for participation in pure, pristine, spiritual values. These relations are usually considered to be based on general human or spiritual virtues, as conceived in any given culture, in the purest form, detached from the more concrete attributes of institutionalised collectivities and considerations and conflicts of power and interests necessarily involved.

Such different relations seem to be based on attributes of solidarity and trust beyond the primordial, the sacred, and the civil types,[25] with their strong tendency to institutionalisation. Friendship and cognate types of behaviour ideally embody the purely personal values and not just 'psychological' attributes and attachments or 'primary' relations or 'simple' intimacy. Rather a combination of these is involved with spiritual qualities, trust and virtues which can only be fully embodied in individuals, as moral beings, and hence they entail a very strong element of equality.

Thus, as Pitt-Rivers emphasised, even when dimensions of friendship or honour are added to some hierarchical, unequal relationships like those between patron and client, such an addition implies, beyond the difference in power, an element of moral equality between the two individuals involved.

X

Most of the studies of such relationships also indicate that the very attempts to construct such a realm of trust or solidarity entail some basic tensions or contradictions which are focused above all on the ambivalence to the institutional order in which they develop and to their own institutionalisation.

The most important tensions inherent in these relations are, first, those between the emphasis on purely solidary or spiritual relations and concrete – power and instrumental – obligations; second, those entailed in the tendency to institutionalise such relations as against seemingly taking them out of the institutional order; and, third, the one existing between the tendency inherent in these relations to uphold the pristine values which stand at the basis of any social order as against a 'subversive orientation' to this order (that is, a departure from it), and a paradoxical concomitant ambivalence in relation to other types of subversive orientations or activities that develop in any society.

The most central is perhaps the first tension between the stress on pure trust and pristine values as against the more formalised, institutionalised relations contaminated, as it were, with power and instrumental orientations. It is manifest in the fact that, on the one hand, the most intensive interpersonal friendship or comradeship is very often defined as 'totally' unconditional, overriding even the most powerful institutional obligations. On the other hand, in most cases, these personal relationships involve relatively circumscribed and limited patterns of obligations. But above all, it is the pristine, moral basis of these obligations that is characteristic of relationships of friendship and of cognate types of behaviour. Hence, while the moral obligations implied in these relations may not be more encompassing in their scope or legally more forceful than those of kinship, they often seem to be 'purer', not only because the obligation is voluntarily undertaken but also because it is seemingly disconnected from specific group membership or ascriptive bases, from identification with clear interests, institutional boundaries, rights to property and institutional power.

The strong tension between such pure attributes of these relations, especially of friendship, and the claims to uphold clearly defined obligations is evident above all in the fact that the upholding of the more instrumental or political duties of friendship is beset with severe difficulties. Claims to fulfil such obligations may be considered as negating the pure elements of friendship, or extrapolating this personal relationship into the very areas from which it seemingly provides an escape; or, in other words, involving it with those elements of power and economic relations seemingly alien to it into the realm of friendship. Hence such a claim may be seen as exploitative, while a refusal to accept it can be conceived as a betrayal of friendship.

Closely related to this first, central, tension is the second one, between the tendency of such relations to become institutionalised and the desire to escape from such institutionalisation. When such relationships are established, this tension is first of all evident – as stressed by K.D. Naegele and developed by R. Paine and implicit in much of the psychosociological and socio-metric literature – in the search for some privacy, for seeking some niches beyond and often in opposition to the formal institutional matrix of society. This theme apparently stands in contradiction to the tendency of such relationships to exhibit a high degree of institutionalisation, as can be seen in blood-brotherhood, ritual kinship or pseudo-kinship.

These problematic dynamics are evident in the tension, already alluded to above and relatively well documented in the social sciences, between the more formalised interpersonal relations, such as blood-brotherhood or *compadrazgo*, and kinship ties proper, as well as between them and the more informal ties which can be found by their side, and which will be discussed later on.

This tension is thus focused on the search for 'pure' trust, intimacy or pristine values as against the more institutionalised relations contaminated by power and instrumental considerations.

Closely related to the tensions mentioned is the one focused on the ambivalent attitude to the established order. This tension, connected to the dimension of trust and of sharing in some common pristine values or meaning, is manifest in the following situations. First, in the recognition, on the one hand, of the necessity for and the ubiquity of trust in human relations and the impossibility of building continuing social relations without some element of trust and common meaning; and, on the other hand, in the awareness of the fragility of this dimension, when it is interwoven with the exigencies of organised social relations.

Second, this ambivalence is rooted in the recognition that the search for pure trustful or meaningful relationships – unencumbered by organisational, instrumental and power considerations – transcends any institutional order and epitomises its incompleteness. But, at the same time, the fragility of any such relationships is unwillingly recognised as well as their almost imperious tendency to become interwoven with the institutional order.

Most of these relations tend therefore to emphasise the spiritual and moral qualities without which no institutional order can function, but which at the same time are considered as beyond any such order.

This ambivalence is thus manifest in such interpersonal relations being oriented to the more formalised, organised institutional structure of the society and its basic premises. These relations are usually defined on the one hand as transcending and even opposed to any institutional order. The emphasis on pure trust or empathy and intimacy, based on common characteristics or on sharing in pristine values, is usually seen as opposed, to some degree at least, to the more routine institutional life exigencies which can lead to the possible contamination of trust. On the other hand, however, all these relationships exhibit a certain tendency to formalisation and to become interwoven in the institutional matrix of their respective societies.

Accordingly, the ambivalence expressed towards the social order through many of these relations is often paradoxically – but significantly enough – oriented not just against purely instrumental or power relations, but against the interweaving of the more interpersonal elements with such relations. This is evident in the tension between informal and even ritualised friendship on the one hand, and, on the other, the kinship order. This tension exists in many tribal and peasant societies and also to some degree in modern ones and is noted there in the interweaving of instrumental and power dimensions of social action with 'pure' trust and with the provision of pristine meaning which occurs in the sphere of kinship.

Thus the crux of the paradoxical and ambivalent relations between friendship and kinship lies in their sharing many characteristics while, symbolically and organisationally, friendship appears distinct from kinship and even potentially opposed to it.

Yet, even in cases of formalisation, such relations – be they those of friendship, ritual kinship or patron–client relations – tend to retain that emphasis on pure trust or empathy as against the exigencies of organised social life. Also, a concomitant strong ambivalence to some of the basic aspects and premises of the central institutional matrix of the society is evident. The more formalised such relations become, hence entailing also a structuring of instrumental and power relations, the more often other less formalised and sometimes even clandestine relations (defined as 'pure' or 'real' friendship) seem to develop within such societies. These ties are seen as distinct not only from the general institutional matrix but also from those more formalised, interpersonal relations.

Because of all these orientations, the tendency develops in many societies to perceive such interpersonal relations in general and friendship in particular as slightly subversive to the institutionalised order, to fully institutionalised relationships or to membership of collectivities.

Indeed, very often these relationships exhibit characteristics of what Victor Turner has designated 'liminal' phenomena,[26] that is, phenomena at the boundaries of institutional life, with potential antinomian tendencies, often also exhibiting a strong emphasis on the attempt to build *communitas*, unrestricted by the social division of labour and of power.

And yet a tension tends to develop between the liminary or subversive spirit of such interpersonal relations and that of religious or political sects or of movements of change which, by their very nature, also succumb to the exigencies of organisation of power. This tension is indeed of great importance to our analysis.

The construction of trust in the social order and its ambivalences: viewed from the development of sociological theory

I

The preceding discussion indicates that a clue to the understanding of the links between the interpersonal relations studied here and the institutional matrix within which they develop can be found in the analysis of the place of trust and meaning in society, as well as in the connections of social relations with some higher, ultimate meaning in the construction of social order.

This has indeed been among the basic problems of classical as well as of contemporary sociological theory, but it was not connected – with the partial exception of the analyses of primary groups that developed from the 1940s onwards – with the study of interpersonal relations. It was only from the mid-sixties, as we have indicated above, that the study of such relationships – especially patron–client links – was connected with central problems of sociological theory, and with those controversies which developed around the functional school in anthropology and the structural–functional school in sociology.

The institutional significance of interpersonal relations is better understood within the context of these developments in sociological theory. Accordingly, in the following sections, we shall review briefly the way in which the place of trust in the construction of social order was analysed in classical sociological theory and in the functional school in sociology. We shall then proceed to analyse some of the major controversies in sociological theory which have developed since about the sixties and which have focused particularly on the criticism of these schools and the connection of the study of interpersonal relations in general, and of patron–client relations in particular, to these controversies.

We shall first go back to basic themes and insights of classic sociological theory, which in a sense constructed the parameters of the sociological tradition.[1]

This tradition developed around two seemingly opposed yet complementary themes. One was the recognition, closely following the insights of the first political economists like Adam Smith, of the importance of the 'social division of labour' in explaining the working of the social order and the institutional contours of any society. Second, and in seeming contrast to the first, was the recognition that such organisation cannot explain fully the nature, working and continuity of the social order in general and of any specific institutional order in particular.[2]

As is well known, these basic insights have been fully developed by the Founding Fathers of sociology – E. Durkheim, M. Weber and, to some extent, K. Marx[3] – who have not accepted the assumption, implicit in utilitarian ethics and in classic economics, of the predominance and sufficiency of the major mechanism of social division of labour in general, and of the market in particular, as the regulator of social order and as a mechanism which assures the maintenance of such order.

The Founding Fathers did not deny the importance of the market as such a mechanism – or of other mechanisms of social division of labour. Indeed, in many ways, they elaborated the analyses of such mechanisms far beyond what had been done by the political economists. But they all questioned whether such mechanisms were sufficient to explain the very structure, reproduction and continuity of any concrete social or institutional order. In different ways, they all showed how the very construction of social division of labour in general, and of the market in particular, cannot assure the continuity of any such concrete order. Indeed, they stressed that the very organisation of social division of labour, of social exchange in general, and of market relations in particular, generates several problems which render problematic the working of social division of labour in general and of any concrete social division in particular. The Founding Fathers stressed in their writings, in different degrees, three aspects of the social order which cannot be explained by an analysis of such an organisational mechanism of social division of labour as the market.

These aspects of social order have been, first, the construction of trust and solidarity, stressed above all by Durkheim and to some degree by Tönnies;[4] second, the aspects of regulation of power and the overcoming of the feelings of exploitation attendant on them stressed above all by Marx and Weber; and, third, the provision of meaning and of legitimation to different social activities, stressed in different ways by all the Founding Fathers, but perhaps especially by Weber.

Construction of trust in the social order

All the Founding Fathers insisted that the very construction of the social division of labour generated uncertainties with respect to each of these dimensions of social order, but at the same time, and because of this, no social division of labour could be maintained without these dimensions or problems being implemented or resolved through institutional arrangements. They all stressed, however, that the provision of institutional arrangements which would take care of these dimensions is a crucial aspect of the organisation of social order. Also that the construction and maintenance of social order are conditioned on the development of some combination between the organisational structure of division of labour and the institutional construction of trust, meaning and legitimation.

And yet the Founding Fathers did not – with the exception of Weber, especially in his analysis of charisma, and of Durkheim, in his analysis of ritual – analyse systematically the organisation of structural mechanisms through which these dimensions of social order were institutionalised. They did, of course, point to some of the most important areas of social life – especially those of legitimation, ideology and ritual which bear on such construction. But their analysis of these dimensions was, on the whole, much weaker than that of the working of market or of direct power relations.

This was partially due to the fact that the conceptual apparatus available at that time was relatively underdeveloped. But it was also probably related to the fact that the Founding Fathers were strongly aware of the great tension between the organisation of social division of labour, on the one hand, and the regulation and legitimation of power and the construction of trust and meaning on the other. The stress on such tension has probably been one of the most important heritages of the classical period of sociological theory.

II

The analysis of the place of trust (solidarity) and of meaning in the construction of social order took on a new direction with the emerging predominance of the functional school in anthropology[5] and especially of the structural–functional school in sociology, developed by Talcott Parsons, Edward Shils, N. Smelser, Robert K. Merton, K. Davis, W.E. Moore and others,[6] which since the late forties has provided the most important analytical map for sociological work. The development of the contemporary controversies in sociology, which were focused from the fifties on the premises of this school,[7] provided a further step in this analysis.

The structural–functional school or approach addressed itself

21

squarely to the problem of how the dimension of solidarity (trust), meaning, and – to a smaller degree – power is institutionalised in the construction (or 'production') of social order. These dimensions of social life were defined as needs which every social system (and in a different way also personalities and cultures) has to cope with, or as prerequisites of the inherent working of such systems. In one version of this approach – probably the best known – these dimensions were defined as follows: the need for solidarity (integration), which can be seen as equivalent to trust; the need for pattern maintenance (meaning); the need for maintenance of instrumental orientations (closely related to, but not entirely identical with, regulation of power); and the adaptive need – that is, the need for adaptation to the respective systems' environment, which is taken care of through the organisation of social division of labour. In this conception, pattern maintenance and integration were seen by Parsons as having a higher cybernetic role in the regulation of social activities than the instrumental or adaptive needs. Thus, using the terminology of cybernetic theory, Parsons indicated that the last two provide the actors or the systems with energy while the first two supply them with the information which 'moulds' such energy. This higher cybernetic role of the construction of meaning (and to a smaller degree of trust) was evident in the central place in the social systems which Parsons allocated to value-consensus – a point which became very early the subject of continual criticism.

Thus, by defining the construction of trust, the provision of meaning and, to some degree, the regulation of power in such a way, and by analysing them systematically, Parsons – as well as Merton and many others – was able to achieve systematically what the Founding Fathers were able to do only tangentially: namely to specify the institutional processes through which these dimensions of construction of social order are interwoven in the structure of society.

This specification was greatly facilitated by the important achievement of this school or approach – namely its restructuring of certain central concepts which, hitherto, had been widely accepted in sociology and social anthropology. Many concepts – such as role, status, role-sets and institutions, prestige, power and solidarity, which were common to both sociological and anthropological research – underwent a far-reaching analytical transformation in the structural– functional school. Instead of being used in a descriptive or classificatory manner, they became conceptual tools specifying how different systems of action and different social settings are related to one another and to the broader macrosocietal settings. New conceptual refinements, like role-sets and status-sets, were also developed.[8] All such analytical refinements of concepts were very closely connected – although certainly not fully identical – with the analysis of the structuring of power, trust and meaning discussed above.

The research influenced by these conceptions became widespread, and hardly an area was left untouched. The structural–functional approach provided, for almost all the fields of sociological research, a general view, image or map of the social system as well as analytic guidelines which led to far-reaching research programmes, the likes of which had not been seen hitherto in the history of sociology.[9]

The single most distinctive feature of many of these studies was the indication provided, through the use of these new conceptual and analytical tools, of how the concrete institutional structure researched – be it a hospital, factory, professional organisation or broader macro-societal settings, or the structure of roles and status that is prevalent within them – could be explained in terms of the manner in which these basic needs of any social system were defined and taken care of within it. These researches – especially those influenced by Merton – showed also how different configurations of social structure generate different institutional contours and different patterns of individual behaviour. It was these orientations that provided the new core common to many of these researches, and which attested the strength and influence of the structural–functional school.

One of the most interesting developments in this context, from the point of view of our discussion, was the reinterpretation of the many studies of primary groups and relations that have developed, especially in American sociology. These researches have shown the importance of such relations, whether in the army or work place, or in the processes of communication, or in absorption of immigrants, in maintaining the formal structure of organisations.[10]

This importance was interpreted – above all by Shils – as indicating the crucial importance of primary relations, of solidarity and of trust as a basic component of any social interaction or any social system – thus bringing these studies into the basic analytical framework of the structural–functional school.

III

The predominance of the structural–functional school did not, as is well known, go unchallenged.[11] The more general criticism of this focused upon several different but interconnected themes. First, this model – because it assumed a basic social consensus based on central societal values and goals, and because it emphasised the boundary-maintaining mechanisms of social control, and implicitly minimised the importance of power and coercion as a means of social integration – was considered to be unable to explain social conflicts and social change.

Closely connected with these criticisms was the charge that the structural–functional model was necessarily ahistorical. More specifically, the accusation was that in their explanation of concrete historical situations or phenomena, the supporters of this school neglected past influence and processes in favour of a 'static' or 'circular' explanatory theory. They were said to explain social phenomena as functionally adjusted to one another through their contribution to societal needs, and to assume that equilibrating mechanisms existed in the social system which counteract functional maladjustments or inconsistencies.

But perhaps the most general and substantial accusation against the structural–functional school – and, indeed, the most closely related to our subject – was that, because it defined the problems of trust (solidarity), meaning and power as needs of the social system, it joined them with the organisation of social division of labour. As a result, the tension between these dimensions of social order, so strongly emphasised by the sociological classics, disappeared.

Thus, what was initially seen as the strength of the structural–functional approach – namely the analysis of the manner in which meaning and trust were institutionalised and, above all, the definition in terms of needs of these dimensions of social order as of social systems – began to be perceived as its major weakness.

This impression was reinforced, of course, by the fact that the functional school in anthropology and the structural–functional school in sociology analysed all these aspects of the social order in systemic terms as well as in terms of their contribution to the maintenance of the boundaries of respective social (or personality and even cultural) systems – seemingly taking their very emergence and crystallisation for granted. Because of this, the structural–functional school was seen, both by its opponents and by some scholars who had initially at least been connected with it,[12] as negating the creative autonomy of groups or individuals in the very construction of such order. This school was also considered as denying that within any such construction a strong tension necessarily develops between, on the one hand, the organisation of social division of labour and, on the other, the regulation of power and the construction of trust and meaning.

IV

The criticisms of the structural–functional school converged around a common theme – namely the rejection of the 'natural' givenness of any single institutional arrangement in terms of the needs or systemic prerequisites of the social system in which they develop.

Any given institutional arrangement – be it the formal structure of a school or a factory, the division of labour in the family, the official definition of deviant behaviour, or the place of a ritual in a given social setting – was no longer taken for granted as given, and derivable from its functional place in the social system. The patterns of behaviour that developed in connection with these were no longer examined solely or mainly in terms of their contribution to the working of the institution or of deviation within it. Instead, the very setting up of institutional arrangements was viewed as constituting a problem for analysis, and many of these approaches stressed that every institutional structure or order develops, is maintained and is changed through a process of continuous interaction, negotiation and struggle among those who participate in it.

Several themes, closely related to the problem of the place of trust and meaning in the construction of social order, were stressed in many of the attempts to explain the construction of institutional settings and arrangements that developed in connection with these theoretical controversies. First, an explanation was attempted in terms of the power relations and the power coalitions which were developed in the course of such relations. Second, the importance of coercive as well as of conflict elements in the construction of any institutional setting was emphasised. Third, a strong emphasis was placed on the manipulation of symbols – symbols of solidarity and/or of transcendental meaning – on attachment to them, and on combinations of symbolic and power orientations in the crystallisation of patterns of interaction and institutional arrangements. Fourth, there developed a strong emphasis on the autonomy of sub-groups, or sub-systems, which defined goals differing from those of the broader organisation or institutional setting.Fifth, it was stressed that participants in any such interaction may attach different meanings and definitions to such situations, and also that these definitions are related to perceptions emerging from the occupation of different roles. Sixth, it was often stressed – especially but not only in the symbolic interactionist and ethnomethodologic approaches – that it is in daily micro-situations (such as encounters, forced or occasional meetings or other social gatherings, based on face-to-face interaction) that the basic cognitive rules and meanings of social life, the grammar of the language of social interaction, are constructed and often also articulated. Of special importance here are the various works of Erving Goffman, who has developed since the late fifties a line of research focused on the dynamics and processes of construction of interpersonal relations in situations of daily interaction organised by norms of commingling. In his work, Goffman often points out the problematic and continuous character of building trustful relations in these situations.[13] Seventh, a growing emphasis developed on the 'environments' within which institutions and organisations operate – and even more broadly on the importance of the international system for the analysis of 'total' societies or macrosocietal orders.

All these formulations have necessarily reopened the problem of the place of trust and construction of meaning in setting up any institutional arrangement. It could no longer be assumed that such a place is naturally assured by the very process of construction of any organisational institutional setting. Such a reopening became closely related to the studies of interpersonal relations.

Thus, one of the most interesting developments that took place, in close relation with these controversies, was the reinterpretation of many of the informal primary relations and groups which had earlier mainly been interpreted as supportive of existing institutional frameworks, as a form of potential dissensus, protest and change.[14]

This development was closely related to the more general recognition of the possibility of development of strong institutional contradictions between the construction of social division of labour on the one hand and the regulation of power, construction of trust and provision of meaning on the other, as well as between these last three dimensions.

V

All these themes became – for the first time in the history of sociological and anthropological analysis – continuously and systematically connected with the study of interpersonal relations in general and patron–client relations in particular. We have already above briefly noted some of the shifts in the analytical explanations of the development of the types of interpersonal relations – shifts which were closely connected with the theoretical discussions already analysed. It was above all in the study of patron–client relationships and of different types of friendship that the revision of the place of the construction of trust in the social order, derived from the major theoretical controversies analysed above, became systematically connected with the study of interpersonal relations.

Since then, the study of such relations in general, and of patronage and patron–client relations in particular, has come to occupy a very central place in most social sciences – especially in social anthropology, sociology and political science. On the most general theoretical level, the analysis of these relations has become, in all these disciplines, closely connected with the major outcries against prevalent 'functionalist', systemic and 'developmentalist'–evolutionary emphases in anthropology, sociology and political science, and against the assumptions of the 'classical' studies of modernisation and development which, as is well known, were very closely related to the structural–functional school in sociology.

This connection with the major theoretical controversies could most clearly be seen in the major themes that developed in the studies of patron–client relations and in the attempts to define precisely their central distinguishing core. The first such theme was the stress on the importance of personal and interpersonal relations, quasi-groups, networks and power relations as against the strong emphasis found both in 'classical' functionalistic anthropology and in the structural–functional school of sociology on groups and their needs and boundary-maintaining mechanisms.[15]

The second topic was that this stress on interpersonal relations and exchange became connected in the study of patron–client relations and friendship with the emphasis on several aspects of social structure and action which were seen as having been neglected both in classical functional anthropology and in the structural–functional approaches in sociology, as well as in the prevalent studies of modernisation. Those were the very aspects which were also stressed, as we have seen above, in the major theoretical controversies in the social sciences. These aspects were, first, those of the autonomous dynamic of power within society; and the concomitant stress on the relations between the distribution of power, the flow of resources and the structure of social relations in society; and the stress on several aspects of the structure of interpersonal relations such as hierarchy, asymmetry and inequality. Second, there was a strong stress on the autonomy of some aspects of the symbolic dimension of human activity in general and on symbols of trust – and of transcendental meaning – in particular. These aspects were seen as manifest in the close links between patron–client bonds, pseudo-kinship, ritual kinship or friendship relations on the one hand, and such concepts as 'honour' or other spiritual dimensions of interpersonal links on the other. They were also seen in the ties to some specific perceptions of social order, as, for instance, in such terms as that of 'limited good' which G.M. Foster claimed to be characteristic of peasant societies.[16]

VI

The studies of patron–client relations, and to a smaller degree those of ritual friendship, have also, at the same time, brought to the fore another central theoretical problem which has become very visible since the mid-sixties or seventies and which is also closely related to our starting point, namely the different levels of continuity, or discontinuity, in the construction of the institutional order.[17]

Thus, these studies have shown that some of these relationships tend to persist beyond changes in levels of economic development or political organisation. For instance, contrary to what has been assumed in some of the earlier studies of patronage, as we have already indicated above, patron–client relations do not necessarily disappear with economic development or political modernisation. True enough, many aspects of their organisation do change. In some countries, like Italy or Spain, the more traditional limited dyadic patron–client relations yield to complex clientelistic networks, as will later be shown. But the centrality of patron–client relationships as a major mode of social control and of regulating institutional relations persists. Similarly some patterns of ritual kinship such as those of different types of *compadrazgo* or the type of friendship so fully depicted in classical Russian literature,[18] seem to persist in the 'same' societies across different periods of their history, in spite of changes in levels of economic development, structural differentiation or political organisation.

These facts indicate that different aspects of the institutional order evince different levels of continuity or discontinuity. Above all, they indicate that the tempo and direction of change in some crucial aspects of social division of labour – as manifest above all in levels of technological and economic development – may differ from those that develop in the construction of trust and meaning, and in the regulation of power – thus bringing us back to the starting point of this chapter.

vvv

The structuring of trust in society: unconditionalities, generalised exchange and the development of interpersonal relations

I

These developments in the explanation of the basic traits and the conditions generating different interpersonal relations point out a crucial fact, already mentioned at the end of the first chapter, that all such relations tend to construct a realm of intimacy, trust or participation in a spiritual realm beyond the major institutionalised spheres of a society – particularly, but not only, that of kinship – in which trust is seemingly most fully articulated. Such construction is based on the search for participation in the realm of pure, pristine, spiritual significance, and on the tensions between such search and the 'mundane' institutional realm. These tensions are indeed central not only to the definition of these relations, but also with respect to the explanation of the contexts within which the construction of such relations takes place and of the conditions which lead people to engage in such relations.

Thus, from all the vantage points, the central problem at the core of the analysis of friendship, ritual personal and clientelistic relations is the one of the construction and institutionalisation of trust and meaning in the social order and the ambivalent attitude to such institutionalisation that pervades these relationships.

The combination of the classical and the more recent theoretical discussions as well as the abundant new research data enables us to understand not only the fundamental importance of trust in social relations but also the possible roots of the ambivalence of the inter-weaving of trust with the institutional structure as well as the concrete mechanisms through which such interweaving is effected.

The roots of the search for trust and of the ambivalence to the institutionalisation of trust in the social order are found in the very process of socialisation of human beings within the family, of their going out of the familial and kinship settings into the broader society and in some of the major problems of the broader institutional order.

The crucial potential contradiction here is between the conditions which generate the construction of trust between different members of a group or society, on the one hand, and those which assure the availability of resources and entrepreneurs for the formation of broader institutional complexes, on the other hand.

Trust, which assumes the maintenance of mutual obligations, tends to be sustained to a greater degree, other conditions being equal (such as, for instance, the extent of coercion employed in such situations), insofar as criteria of ascription in general and of primordial particularistic ascription in particular predominate. These criteria define membership in solidary communities and a degree of unconditional relations between the members and clear criteria of mutual obligation on their part.

Thus, almost by definition, the conditions which lead to maintenance of trust are best ensured in relatively limited ranges of 'social' activity or interaction. Such limited ranges of interaction seem to constitute at least the necessary conditions for the generation of such trust, even if they may not be enough to ensure it. At the same time, however, these very conditions are inimical to the development of resources and activities needed for broader institutional creativity, for the construction of broader institutional complexes based on more variegated and differentiated orientations and criteria.

The conditions which generate resources potentially available for broader institution building also tend to undermine the simple settings of potential trust which may prevail unless counteracted by other forces in the more restricted types of social relations. Hence the very ability to institutionalise such resources along some long-range stable patterns, beyond those embedded in relatively narrow units or sets of social relations, remains problematic.

Indeed, such ability is, above all, dependent on the effective construction of broader ranges of meaning, on the extension of the symbolism of trust beyond the narrow minimal range of ascriptive primordial units, and on the connection of such trust with the organisation of broader scopes of more differentiated activities and free resources generated through the extension of instrumental and power activities.

II

The various problems bearing on the possibility of the breakdown of basic trust through the generation of new levels of resources, power and meaning are evident already in family and kinship settings and in the structuring of the different patterns of interaction and 'coalitions' that develop within such settings.

In almost all family and kinship settings, the set of interaction of mother and child, which, in fact, constitutes the initial 'coalition' from the point of view of the life cycle of the individual, is usually based on a high (although varying in different settings) degree of unconditional trust in which other more conditional elements are at most usually secondary. This coalition is also obviously based on unequal asymmetric relations.

Psychological studies[1] have shown that the failure to experience such a degree of unconditional trust in the early stages of life through an intimate mother–child relationship has enduring consequences on the development of what A. Aichhorn and C. Frankenstein have defined as the syndrome of 'neglected' youth. Such personalities, growing up in conditions of impersonal treatment – as the nursery children studied by John Bowlby – or indifference, develop attitudes of wholly instrumental orientations towards other human beings. They have an 'externalised' character-formation, i.e. they lack the ability to develop value orientations and are therefore defined as asocial. They see themselves as objects rather than as subjects in interactions within society and develop a reactive, magic-oriented stand towards the world. These consequences of a 'maternal withdrawal' point out the singular importance of the unconditionality inherent in the early interactions for the development of sociability and the possibility of transference of trust at later phases.

But even in most of the family and kinship settings in which this degree of unconditional trust is present, its totality is broken up by the progressive separation of the growing child from the mother and through the extension of the patterns of interaction. This process entails several tendencies, partially mutually reinforcing and partially contradictory: first, the growing autonomy of the instrumental and power dimensions of interaction, as well as that of construction of meaning in the structuring of social activities; second, the growing diversification of such activities and their organisation in different constellations; third, a growing search for some degree of greater equality and symmetry in social interaction; fourth, the breaking down of whatever balance has been attained in any situation between trust, meaning, instrumental activities and power, and attempts at their recrystallisation into new patterns in which orientations to equality become more sharply confronted with those of hierarchisation; fifth, the articulation, in the discontinuities entailed in such processes, of the tension between the distributive and the more

31

investment-oriented implications of different activities and use of resources.

Such processes of breaking up and reorganisation of trust in connection with other activities may be repeated several times within the family and kinship setting, as well as in the structuring of its relations with the broader institutional setting beyond it.

Several aspects of the structuring of the institutional order tend to exacerbate these problems of the breaking up and reorganisation of trust.

One such aspect is the tendency to structural differentiation, related to the organisation of the social division of labour. A second, closely connected but not identical, is the tendency to symbolic differentiation between institutional spheres and activities, that is the extent to which such a distinction is recognised in the symbolic realm of a society. A third aspect is the possibility that different institutional spheres of a society will be structured according to somewhat dissimilar principles, especially universalistic versus particularistic and egalitarian as against hierarchical ones. The fourth is the existence of different degrees of clarity in such principles and in their application to different institutional spheres in general, and in particular in the specification of the degree of autonomous, as against mediated (i.e. vested in various mediators), access of the different groups to major societal, political and cultural (usually religious) power.[2]

It is the various combinations of these dimensions that generate in human societies different areas and situations of breakdown of the extension of trust.

In all such areas and situations uninhibited, unregulated, instrumental and power relations may develop among individuals and groups. Accordingly, the problem of the possible extension of trust and of recombining such extended trust with broader, instrumental power relations as well as with broader meanings becomes crucial.

III

In all human societies there develop different ways of interweaving trust and meaning with instrumental and power relations in special types of institutional formations; and yet it is such interweaving that permeates the very ambivalent attitudes which are at the roots of the basic development of interpersonal relations and the tensions inherent in them which were analysed above.

In order to analyse the nature of the problems inherent in the institutionalisation of trust, we have to examine in greater detail those types of social activities or collectivities in which the interweaving of trust or solidarity is strongest within the institutional structure, namely the major 'ascriptive' solidary collectivities, such as kinship groups, communities, strata, nations and the like.

As kinship is accepted to be the most primordial of such settings, and is often seen as their model, it might be worthwhile to start with the analysis of its basic characteristics. Recent analyses of kinship have indicated that its core lies in the symbolic–ideological emphasis on relatively unconditional relations rooted in basic components of personal and collective identity. These entail mutual obligations between the people participating in such relations, obligations which are based on what Meyer Fortes has designated the core of kinship, amity.[3]

These obligations entail a combination of, on the one hand, the construction of symbols and frameworks of solidarity, trust, meaning and information on the basic premises of the social order and their symbolisation and legitimation, and, on the other hand, the regulation of the flow of instrumental and power resources.

Such a combination is shared by kinship with other ascriptive solidary communities and entails a specific mode of structuring the flow of resources in society, contrasting but not denying the purely conditional – instrumental or power – relations. It creates, rather, a certain type of connection between the instrumental and power relations and the solidary relations and construction of meaning. This connection is focused on the development of a pattern of long-range, relatively unconditional interaction or exchange expressed in terms of basic trust or solidarity and sharing a common meaning regarding the fundamental premises of social and cultural order.

IV

This special mode of structuring of the flow of resources shared by kinship with different ascriptive solidarities, but also with friendship and patron–client relations, and entailing unconditional relations, has been identified as generalised exchange in the classical sociological and anthropological literature. Such generalised exchange is in contrast to the simple, specific, market-like or power exchange given in the construction of social division of labour, which has been systematically explored and analysed in the theories of individualistic exchange best represented in the work of George C. Homans and Peter M. Blau.[4]

The problems with which the term generalised exchange is concerned were first defined in Marcel Mauss' analysis of the gift.[5] As is well known, he has in this analysis shown that gift-giving constitutes an exchange having rather special highly structured characteristics. The exchange of gifts is distinct from the usual 'specific' market exchange, in that, seemingly, it is non-utilitarian and disinterested. At the same time, it is highly structured and based on relatively elaborated and specified rules of reciprocity.

This concept of generalised exchange has been elaborated and somewhat modified by C. Lévi-Strauss* in his earlier works on kinship, and is also related to the analysis of generalised media of exchange undertaken, from a structural–functional perspective, by Parsons and, from an individualistic one, by J.S. Coleman.[6]

These differences are most closely related to the various 'purposes' or 'functions' of these two types of exchange. The latent 'function' or 'purpose' of the exchange of gifts is to establish the obligation to engage in social interaction and to uphold those obligations entailed in such interaction. In other words, if successful, generalised exchange helps to establish conditions of basic trust and solidarity in society and to uphold what Durkheim has called the 'pre-contractual elements of social life'.[7]

From the point of view of the individuals participating in any social activity, the various mechanisms of generalised exchange assume the functions of security or insurance systems against the risks and uncertainties of the 'open' market or power interchange or struggle.

V

These basic functions of generalised exchange have indeed been recognised in the classical statements – above all in Mauss' *The Gift*, as well as in some of the later expositions mentioned above. The more recent theoretical controversies and advances in research have provided some very important indications about the ways in which the institutionalisation of generalised exchange is effected in any society. The crux of such processes is found in the institutionalisation of limitations on the free exchange of resources in social interaction, and in the concomitant structuring of the flow of resources and social relations in society in ways which differ from such 'free' – market or

---

* The difference between specific and generalised exchange as presented here is not identical to the one between restricted and generalised exchange indicated above all by C. Lévi-Strauss. The latter distinction mostly refers to the scope and 'directedness' of restricted exchange as against the indirectedness of the other type of exchange. Specific exchange can, however, be both direct (barter) and indirect, and the more indirect it is the more it is dependent on generalised media of exchange, such as money, political loyalties or broader influence. The proper functioning of such media does, in a way, exacerbate the problem of trust and the importance of appropriate mechanisms of generalised exchange. Generalised exchange is, almost always, less direct, but its scope, i.e. the scope of the persons or spheres involved, may greatly vary between the different societies or sectors thereof.

power – exchange. First, this structuring entails the normative specification of the range of goals or desiderata available or permitted to the members of a certain group or socio-cultural category – sex, age, occupation, membership in territorial proximity. Second, it defines the basic attributes of social and cultural similarity which constitute the criteria of becoming a member of these sets or collectivities. Such a member is entitled to claim such rights unconditionally as well as participation in the rules of distributive justice, while being subject to certain rules of exchange. In addition, such structuring defines the duties which are interlinked with these rights in the processes of interaction, clearly distinguishing between a member's rights to participation as against non-members'. Third, side by side with the specification of attributes of membership and of solidarity, the designation of the obligations incumbent on the members specifies the general principles of distribution of power between them. Fourth, such structuring implies the provision of some higher, transcendental, meaning to these collectivities and to the social activities entailed.

The different types of ascriptive relations and collectivities provide, in all these ways, some of the rules defining the boundaries of any given collectivity or social interaction vis-à-vis its internal and external environments.

VI

The most important institutional mechanisms by means of which are set up all such unconditionalities and the various limitations on pure exchange entailed are applied, first, through the institutionalisation of various 'titles' or entitlements – i.e. ascriptive (often hierarchical, power-based) specifications of limitations on institutional interaction or exchange and on access to positions.[8] The best examples of such entitlements can be found in the various hierarchical privileges of the upper social strata in most traditional societies, and in the various social benefits, such as universal education granted in many modern welfare states to all their citizens.

Second, such limitation on exchange of resources is effected through the provision of 'public goods' by the collectivity (e.g. the government), such as defence or health services, which are so set up that, if one member of a collectivity obtains them, they cannot be denied to the others. Such limitation is also effected through the arrangement of the variable prices taken – directly or, through taxation, indirectly – from different groups for the arrangement of such public goods.[9]

Third, such structuring of the flow of resources is manifest in the public distribution of private goods, i.e. in the direct allocation of various services and benefits to different groups of the population according to criteria which greatly differ from those of pure exchange.

Fourth, and closely related to the definition of public goods, is the determination of the degree to which institutional credit will be enjoyed by the different groups, organisations, and institutional spheres – the degree to which the resources provided to any group are not intended for use in immediate exchange or in direct consumption, but are provided somewhat unconditionally, granting what may be called 'credit autonomy' to that group or institution. This autonomy provides the base for long-range functioning of the institution. The process of granting institutional credit also involves the definition of the range and the long-term conditions of such credit.

The flow of resources is structured in all these ways along the specific patterns of generalised exchange which distinguish it from the 'market' or power type of 'specific' interpersonal or institutional inter-relations and exchange.

Generalised exchange is also institutionalised in patterns of inter-action and in situations which symbolise and legitimise the very process of setting up such unconditionalities and entitlements and the concomitant arrangement of the conditions of trust and of the precon-tractual element in social life.

The gift, as analysed by Mauss, constitutes one such mechanism. Similar functions are performed, above all in primitive or 'traditional' societies, but probably also in more modern ones, by relations of hospitality, which were recently studied, significantly enough, by scholars in close relation with those researching patron–client relations.[10] But such mechanisms as gifts or hospitality, which are more visible in primitive societies or in 'small', often informal, sectors of more complex societies, are not, of course, the only ones in any society through which are structured the precontractual bases of social order, the conditions and frameworks of generalised exchange.

Even in the smaller, 'primitive', 'tribal', pre-literate or 'traditional' societies, the exchange of gifts is, as Lévi-Strauss and Fortes have shown, very closely interwoven with the whole process of inter-marriage and of exchange of brides, through which some of the basic solidary relations between the basic units of the society are main-tained.[11]

In more differentiated or complex societies many of these functions are, as has been shown by, among others, Parsons or Mayhew,[12] fulfilled on the macrosocietal level by such social mechanisms as the symbols of citizenship, and by various legal frameworks in which conceptions of basic entitlements and rights are upheld.

In all types of societies, all these mechanisms are very closely related

36

to the major ritual and communicative occasions in which basic symbols of societal identity and social order are upheld and legitimised. They are also upheld, to some degree at least, by the more informal, yet very pervasive, networks of solidary relations which have been studied in the literature dealing with primary groups.

VII

It is therefore through the institutionalisation of generalised exchange that the problems (analysed above) inherent in the possibility of breakdown of extension of trust are seemingly solved in different ways.

The construction of principles of generalised exchange – and of its major institutional derivatives of entitlements, public goods and the like, and their connection with specific exchange and the inequalities they engender – is common to all societies. However, the concrete details of such structuring (i.e. the criteria of entitlements and of public goods, and of the concomitant regulation of the flow of resources in society) greatly vary between the different societies, according to several conditions to be analysed below.

Such modes of institutionalisation of generalised exchange are based on different ways of articulating the major aspects of institutional structure – ways which are closely connected with the problems of extension of trust. These aspects are: the structural and symbolic differentiation of different institutional spheres; the similarity or dissimilarity in the principles structuring different institutional spheres; the relative clarity of such principles in general and of access to centres of power in particular.

VIII

While such institutionalisation of generalised exchange seemingly provides the solution to the problem of possible breakdown of extension of trust, yet, in fact, every such construction, every such institutionalisation of generalised exchange, entails several basic tensions that are inherent in the ways in which trust (solidarity), meaning and power combine with each other and with the social division of labour.

These tensions centre in the fact that in all societies the setting up of generalised exchange entails some contradictions inherent in the very process of interweaving and institutionalisation of trust and meaning in the social order, in close relation with the social division of labour in society. Given the contradictions and tensions, rooted in the close relations between the institutionalisation of generalised exchange and the control, by the major elites, over the flow of resources in a society, such institutionalisation need not be egalitarian.

The specification of the principles of generalised exchange and of its relations with specific exchange, and the institutionalisation of those principles through the setting up of public goods and titles, are effected in all societies by institutional entrepreneurs or elites. They attempt, in collaboration or in competition, to mobilise and structure the major resources available in a society. Such undertakings are influenced by the nature of the conceptions or 'visions' which inform the activities of these elites, derived above all from the major cultural orientations or codes prevalent in that society. Through these, they combine the structuring of trust, provision of meaning, and regulation of power with the division of labour in society.

In other words, the various types of elites are carriers of different cultural orientations prevalent in a society. In connection with these visions and orientations, the various elites tend to exercise different modes of control over the production and allocation of the basic resources existing in any society.

It is through the exercise of this control that such elites combine the structuring of trust, provision of meaning, and regulation of power with the division of labour in society, i.e. the definition of the principles of generalised exchange in a society and of its relations to specific exchange.

Such control is effected by a combination of organisational and coercive measures, together with the structuring of the cognitive imagery of the social order and of the major reference orientations available in society.

More specifically, such control is exercised by these elites (or rather by the coalitions of elites) primarily through regulating the access to the major institutional markets (economic, political, cultural, etc.), as well as through the conversion of the major resources between these markets; also, by controlling the production and distribution of that information which is central in structuring the cognitive maps of the members of a society, their perception of the nature of their society in general and their reference orientations and reference groups in particular.

Thus the institutionalisation of generalised exchange necessarily contains very strong elements of power and hierarchy, even if because of their strong interweaving with long-range solidarity and provisions of meaning such elements of power and hierarchy are structured here in ways which differ from direct power relations or market-like exchange. These non-egalitarian and power elements which are inherent in the institutionalisation of generalised exchange can be seen most clearly in the fact that one of the most crucial aspects of the institutionalisation of generalised exchange is the linkage first between membership in major ascriptive categories and sectors of a society on the one hand and access to the centres of power, to positions of control of production, and to the major markets on the other; second, between such access and the relative standing of different groups or categories in the major institutional markets – i.e. between ownership of resources and the ability to control their use in broader settings. Accordingly, such linkages generate different types of relations between inequalities in the major spheres of the institutional order and, in this way, shape the structuring of crucial aspects of social hierarchies in a society.

Different modes of institutionalisation of generalised exchange, by organising the major dimensions of the institutional order most closely related to the possibility of breakdown of extension of trust, also structure the various types of linkages between the different inequalities.

IX

It is because of such close interweaving of generalised exchange with power that while every specification of the details of generalised exchange, as set up by the different elites, entails different solutions, as it were, to the tensions inherent in the interweaving of trust with regulation of power, the construction of meaning and social division of labour, yet such a solution does not suppress these tensions. Therefore the pure pristine dimensions of trust or solidarity and of equality are, as it were, weakened or contaminated by the exigencies of power and instrumental relations. Hence, every such solution leads to the search for areas of pure trust and generates different types of interpersonal relations, in which such search becomes epitomised.

From the point of view of the individual, this search is rooted in the process of maturing, of socialisation, and in the separation, initially from attachment to the mother, and later from other relatively narrow coalitions in the concomitant attempt to combine trust with equality. In fact the process of growing up, and later of acting as an adult entails the interweaving of such extended trust with the realm of power and instrumental relations, thus diminishing, as it were, the realm of pure trust and pristine values.

It is out of the combination of, on the one hand, the separation and loss of the security of attachment and the concomitant search for the restoration of trust and for recombining it with some dimensions of equality, with, on the other hand, the tensions inherent in the institutionalisation of trust, through the specification of generalised exchange, that there evolves, among all human societies, the tendency to form new attachments in which the aims of pure trust and equal participation in pristine meaning could seemingly be attained.

Ethological studies have demonstrated that such a search seems to develop among primates, and even more among human toddlers, and, significantly enough, is usually closely connected to the tendency to engage in play, in a combination of explorative and imaginary behaviour, which takes them beyond the given situation.[13]

But it is only among humans beyond toddler stage, in close connection with all the vicissitudes of institutionalisation of trust, that the search for such an attachment becomes combined with the search for meaning or, to use Gregory Bateson's expression, for 'metameaning'. It is only then that this search becomes endowed with the special symbols of pure trust and pristine meaning and in the search for the pure dialogue between man and man and man and God, for the 'I and Thou', to use Martin Buber's expression. In his words

in every sphere, in every relational act, through everything that becomes present to us, we gaze toward the train of the eternal You; in each we perceive a breath of it; in every You we address the eternal You; in every sphere according to its manner. All spheres are included in it, while it is included in none . . . When the perfect encounter is to occur, the gates are unified into the one gate of actual life, and you no longer know through which one you have entered.[14]

X

The search for such pure pristine trust and intimacy and for equal participation in pristine meaning, for the pure dialogue, becomes most fully articulated in situations in which the potential for breakdown of the extension of trust develops, and in situations of transition from one institutional realm to another. In turn, as has been indicated in sociological studies of friendship and in the comparative study of age groups and youth movements,[15] this potentiality develops especially when such realms are structured according to different principles and entail dissimilar ways of interweaving of trust, meaning and instrumental and power relations.

It is in such situations that the contradictions inherent in the institutionalisation of trust and meaning in their relations to power and social division of labour become especially visible. Accordingly, it is in these situations that the tendencies develop also to construct new, different types of relations, in which, seemingly at least, trust, mutual empathy and sharing in common meaning will be maintained in their pure, pristine meaning. Friendship, ritual kinship and pseudo-kinship or patron–client relations, are probably the most important illustrations of such bonds.

The development of such relations, however, is but one aspect of a more general tendency to the construction of alternative types of interaction, of alternative systems of social relations, of antisystems and processes of conflict, change and possible transformations. Yet, the various interpersonal links analysed here develop in dialectic relation not only to the very institutionalisation of trust but also to the various movements of social change, rebellion or heterodoxy.

XI

These different types of interpersonal relations attempt to establish new areas of trust, whereby the participants in the relationship ensure to some degree at least that the struggle over power or resources, between the respective groups or networks to which they belong, will not go beyond certain limits and will not become anarchic or anomic. However, these participants may indeed become oriented to changes in the basic institutional premises of a society. Yet, in all such areas, the construction of trust is combined with the various tensions which are inherent in such attempts – above all, the tensions between the emphasis on purely solidary or spiritual relations as against concrete obligations; between the tendency to institutionalise such relations as against the propensity to take them out of the institutional order; and between the tendency to uphold the pristine values of the social order as against a subversive orientation to this order.

The ways in which the different interpersonal relations cope with these tensions vary, first of all, in the degree of their institutionalisation, and second, in the scope of the concrete obligations entailed. Third, they differ in the degree to which they are couched in highly ideological terms, above all in terms of symbolism of solidarity (trust) or of participation in some pristine spiritual values. Fourth, they vary in the degree and mode of ambivalence with which such relations are imbued against the basic premise of the institutional order in general and in particular against the specific ways of the institutionalisation of trust within it. Lastly, they differ in the degree – which is much more difficult to assess but which can still be identified to some extent, at least in its extreme manifestations – of the strength of the emotional, moral or spiritual bond between the people engaged in such informal relationships.

XII

While the search for pristine trust and meaning through such interpersonal relations is indeed to be found in all human societies, the institutional placement of such different types of interpersonal relations, the links between them, as well as their symbolic definition, greatly differ in the various societies, in each of which develop not just one but several types of interpersonal relations.

Thus, it is indeed impossible to understand these seemingly 'a-institutional' or anti-institutional relations, except in the context of the institutional setting within which they develop and in close relation to some central aspects of its institutional structure and the shaping of trust and of generalised exchange within them.

Given the ambivalence to the institutional structure which is inherent in these interpersonal relations, the understanding of the links between them and of the institutional structure in which they develop throws some light on some of the central aspects, problems, exigencies and uncertainties of the social order.

In the following chapters we shall attempt to explore the relationship between these types of interpersonal relations and the social structure, as well as the construction of trust and of generalised exchange in which they develop, in a systematic way and shall analyse these various types of relations in detail. We shall start with the most researched and relatively most institutionalised such ties – patron–client relations.

4

vvvvvvvvvvvvvvvvvvvvvvvvvvvvvvvvvvvvvvvvvvvvvvvvvvvvvvvvvvvvvvvvvvvvvvvvvvvvvv

The basic characteristics and variety of patron–client relations

THE CORE CHARACTERISTICS OF PATRON–CLIENT RELATIONS

I

What is meant by patron–client relations? Which types of relations are so defined?

Let us first give a few preliminary illustrations of such relations, taken from the abundant literature on the subject.

In Sicily, a student, interested in getting an introduction to a professor from whom he needs a favour, approaches a local small-town politician who owes him a favour. The politician puts him in contact with a cousin at the regional urban centre and the latter contacts an assistant to the professor who then arranges the appointment. The favour sought is granted and in return the student promises to campaign for the politician at election times.[1]

In an Umbrian community of Italy during the period 1860–1945, patrons lent money or guaranteed loans, gave employment, helped to provide dowries for the daughters of the client families, provided medicines and helped to obtain medical services. They filled out the papers which were required for civil or administrative purposes, spoke to bureaucrats on their clients' behalf. As government benefits were introduced, the patron was needed to obtain them. Signora M., whose husband was killed during the First World War, tried in vain for months to collect a government pension for war widows; only after her patron spoke of her case to the appropriate officials did she succeed in getting it. The patron interpreted the law to his client and offered advice. If there were troubles with the authorities, the patron intervened. Persons arrested by the *carabinieri* were released after intervention by their patrons; others sentenced to prison were pardoned

43

through their actions. When people had to go out of the community for any purpose, they persisted in trying to get a recommendation from a respected contact through their patrons. When M.'s grandmother tried to get the local tobacco concession, when R. applied to a military specialists' school, when F. took his dear sister to a physician in Rome, when P. as a young man went periodically to the coastal plain to seek work, when T. took his bride to Perugia to choose a coral necklace, they all secured for themselves such personal recommendations. As jobs in the national institutions expanded, access to them was also a matter of recommendation, and this remained true even after the adoption of the *concorso* system, an open competition for available jobs based on examinations.[2]

In Egypt, in Cairene quarters, a local strongman (*futuwwa*) was recognised as the patron of the neighbourhood, commanding a wide network of followers related to him as employees in traditional jobs. He mobilised his network in order to protect the quarter against central political forces or to fight competing *futuwwat*; if someone acted improperly with another person in the locality, he intervened immediately. In cases of police harassment, he beat the policemen. He upheld values of manliness and bravery, the quarter and its inhabitants being symbolically identified with him. Another type of *futuwwa*, such as G.D., abuses local people by imposing higher prices on monopolistic products, by taking goods without paying for them; he agrees to beat an opponent for a fee, spoils ceremonies or closes shops and clubs, to assert his image of power. If the school principal punishes the son of one of his clients, he blocks his way back from school and compels him to go home naked. He does not refrain from obliging a person to divorce his wife so that he can marry her, nor does he regard locally accepted values. He launches attacks on neighbouring *futuwwat* with the help of his network of followers.[3]

In the Sunni quarters of Beirut, Lebanon, the I. family has controlled since the 1950s about 4000 voters. Traditionally, they have supported the politicians of the S. family. In order to prevent other politicians from influencing them, and so as to maintain his hold on the I., S.S. has chosen a number of members of the I. family with support among their kin and has built them a position of monopolistic leadership as intermediaries to him. S.S. has let it be known that any I. who wants a service from him should first see these *qabadayat*, his 'official' representatives in the quarters. In 1958 one of these, H.I., was a minor *qabaday* or 'strongman', fighting under S.S.'s leadership. Over the years, he increased his local influence; and when S.S., recognised this strength he gave him considerable economic assistance. From being the owner of a small coffee shop he became part-owner of two of

Beirut's biggest cinemas, and one of the directors of a company that owns restaurants, bars and cafés in a fashionable quarter. S.S. seems also to have helped him to find capital and expertise, and in doing so he created an indebted ally.[4]

Among Cyrenaican bedouins, political status is anchored in proprietary rights over lands, and these are the prerogative of only that part of the population which has supposed noble ancestors and which is organised in corporations of agnates. Other sectors accede to lands by being attached to a patron, and, even if they can prosper economically to become wealthier than their patrons (in animals for instance), they cannot convert this wealth into political assets for the purpose of power advancement. In spite of this, clients are often as interested as patrons in maintaining the integrity of a corporate group's natural resources; they fight with them and work alongside them in maintaining wells and tending animals.[5]

In Thailand, some landless villagers employed as hired workers may not only work in the fields but also cook meals, tend children and eventually even bury the family gold. In return, they may be treated as members of the family, who not only feed and shelter them, and provide money when needed, but also help them to find a suitable wife and defray the costs of cremating a grandmother.[6]

P.D., a sub-district headman in Kedah, Malaysia, was, in the 1960s and early 1970s, one of the largest landholders of the district and had augmented his wealth with substantial interests in local logging operations. He employed forty or fifty families on his lands and many seasonal workers in his logging operations. In part his wealth was reinvested in land and equipment, but he also assisted others in need with loans or gifts. He was able to 'make ashamed' anyone violating public decorum and had a reputation for fair and harsh justice. While he was leader of an opposition party, he successfully sought government development projects with regard to roads, schools, mosques, etc. Such assistance from the government was provided in exchange for an active popular participation (by providing unskilled labour, etc.) in formal and informal official projects.[7]

In western Maharashtra, India, M.N. established a cooperative sugar factory in 1959, when he was still a member of the Bombay Cabinet; he has maintained control of it ever since. He retained the support of the labourers especially by paying them bonuses which the opposition directors, courting the support of the producer shareholders, claimed were too high. When his son campaigned for a legislative position in the State Assembly in 1967 he was helped by the labourers; they were often heard marching home from the factory chanting his election slogans. During the period many were given leave from work to help in the surrounding villages in the campaign. They gathered at the father's palace where B., the union leader and M.N.'s right-hand man, gave them handbills and campaign instructions. They were then driven in trucks, normally hired by the factory to transport cane, to villages, where they distributed the handbills from door to door.[8]

N., E., T. and G. are Colombian local leaders. Some of them are said to know a lot of people at the more important urban centres, a fact supposed to be very useful 'if things are going to be done'. Thus, they can arrange a scholarship for the daughter of a local resident, loans of cash, seeds, fertilisers and tools; they can get a son of a follower out of jail through the intervention of some official. In return, they are able to aggregate political party followings and mobilise local support for the national political parties they decide to back.[9]

Until 1952, the Bolivian *hacendado* of the Yungas region demanded from his debt-peonage Aymara peasants agricultural and domestic services in return for a strip of land to work or a job on the estate; at the same time, he mediated any contact they had to maintain with outside social and institutional frameworks. Peasants of any age were addressed by the landowner as *yocalla* (boy), in a demeaning, condescending sense, while landowners were addressed, hat in hand, as *tata* (father).[10]

In a Mexican village, the municipal authorities decided to build a new school on the land of J.D. Initially he agreed on a certain purchase price; later on, he decided he did not want to sell at that price. J.D. was a peasant not involved until that moment in community politics; he had neither patrons nor clients; nor did he have political contacts. By aligning himself with several local patrons, two union leaders and a teacher, he managed to fight the sale for several years. Although he eventually lost, his patrons helped him by getting the new municipal president (whom they had put in office) to delay the building of the school. When the opposition brought the issue to court, his local patrons secured him a lawyer through their state union and party contacts, advised him on bureaucratic procedures, and informally spoke to state officials. He in return provided financial resources for them in political contests and supported them in local politics. Eventually, this issue developed into a dispute, involving local leaders, over the location of the projected school within their own neighbourhoods. Whereas the leaders' choice coincided with their residence, factory workers and other followers made their choice according not to where they lived but to where their leaders lived.[11]

N.S., a practising Brazilian rural physician, had once been a member of the Partido Republicano (P.R.) party. When offered (by representatives of the party then in power at the national level) campaign funds and a series of promises to be fulfilled later, S. agreed to oppose his former associates (and kinsmen) of the local ruling party; he stood for election as mayor of his town on behalf of the Partido Trabalhista Brasileiro (P.T.B.), was elected by an overwhelming majority, and remained in office for years. He arranged to have a clinic built by the state government in his town and was supplied with medicines for its health-post pharmacy. As the only physician in the country, he was in great demand for his professional services, which he provided to poor people generously even if they could not pay for the visit, as well as giving them medicines gratis from the health-post pharmacy. As the son of a landowner and as a landowner in his own right, he was a member of the local elites. Those belonging to his network or faction knew that, in case of need, they could write a note to him, and their dependent workers and clients would be ushered by the nurse to the front of the queue and treated without delay and even without having to pay for examinations and medicines. In such and in other ways, he came to know many of the residents of the town and the countryside, who became indebted to him. Thus it was that, even if he supported the political forces deposed in 1964 by the military takeover, the new central government – eager to demonstrate its popular support – chose to back him at the local level, and not the opposite local faction, which was more sympathetic to the policies of the centre.[12]

An American city boss sought to control the key legislative and financial officials – from supervisors and eldermen to comptrollers and the mayor. He did it by arranging jobs for most of them. This allowed him to manipulate warrants charged against the city treasury, to the advantage of favoured businessmen, who in turn were expected to augment their bills and pass back to the boss sizeable portions of their profits. Often the boss operated as lobby-broker for those businessmen seeking to pass or to kill legislation vital to their interests. The machine boss had power as he could gather the votes of the immigrants who were uprooted in the city, living at marginal levels of subsistence and lacking elementary services or welfare assistance. To these people, the boss offered patronage, counsel and help in their immediate short-term needs of eating, finding employment, protecting the young in an alien environment. His rewards were votes and loyalty.[13]

The illustrations presented above highlight two important points. On the one hand they indicate that the different types of interpersonal relations designated as patron–client relations exhibit certain basic common characteristics. On the other hand, however, it is quite clear that beyond these basic characteristics, different patron–client relations evince a very great variety of concrete forms.

II

What, then, first of all, are the basic characteristics of patron–client relations common to all of them? What kind of areas of trust do they construct? The illustrations presented above, as well as the fuller and more systematic materials which will be presented later, indicate that the most important of these core analytical characteristics of patron–client relations are:

(a) Patron–client relations are usually particularistic and diffuse.

(b) The interaction on which these relations are based is characterised by the simultaneous exchange of different types of resources – above all, instrumental and economic as well as political ones (support, loyalty, votes, protection) on the one hand, and promises of reciprocity, solidarity and loyalty on the other.

(c) The exchange of these resources is usually arranged in some sort of 'package-deal' – i.e. none of these resources can be exchanged separately, but only in some combination which includes each type.

(d) Ideally, a strong element of unconditionality and of long-range credit is built into these relations.

(e) Closely related to the preceding is the strong element of interpersonal obligation that is prevalent in these relations – an element often couched in terms of personal loyalty or reciprocity and attachment between patrons and clients – even if these relations are often very ambivalent. This element of solidarity may be, as in the restricted primary relationship of the classical type of patronage, very strong or, as in many of the more modern political machines, very weak – but to some degree it is to be found in all of them. It is often very strongly related to conceptions of personal identity, (above all of personal honour, personal value or face-saving) and of obligations, and it is also evident in the presumed existence in such relations of some, even if very ambivalent, personal 'spiritual' attachment between patron and clients.

(f) At the same time, relations established between patron and clients are not fully legal or contractual; they are often opposed to the official laws of the country and they are based much more on 'informal' – although very strongly binding – understandings.

(g) Despite their seemingly binding, long-range, almost (in their ideal portrayal) life-long, endurance, patron–client relations are entered into, at least in principle, voluntarily, and can, officially at least, be abandoned voluntarily.

(h) These relations are undertaken between individuals or networks of individuals in a vertical fashion (the simplest manifestation of which is a strong dyadic one) rather than between organised corporate groups; and they seem to undermine the horizontal group organisation and solidarity of clients and patrons alike – but especially of the clients.

(i) Last and not least patron–client relations are based on a very strong element of inequality and of differences in power between patrons and clients. Even at this stage of our discussion it ought to be evident that the most crucial element of this inequality is the monopolisation, by the patrons, of certain positions which are of crucial importance for the clients – above all, as we shall see in greater detail later, of the access to the means of production, major markets and centres of the society.

The combination of these characteristics indicates that the exchange that is effected in patron–client relations usually takes place on several levels; that it creates several paradoxical contradictions which constitute one of the major features of the patron–client nexus – the most important among which are, first, a rather peculiar combination of inequality and asymmetry in power with seeming mutual solidarity expressed in terms of personal identity and interpersonal sentiments and obligations; second, a combination of potential coercion and exploitation with voluntary relations and mutual obligations; third, a combination of emphasis on such mutual obligations and solidarity or reciprocity betweeen patrons and clients with the somewhat illegal or semi-legal aspect of these relations.

These core characteristics are indeed common to the various types of patron–client relations. But beyond these common characteristics, different patron–client relations evince – as even the preliminary illustrations presented above indicate – a very great variety of concrete forms.

As we shall see in greater detail later on, the various types of patron–client relations can be distinguished in two contexts. One such context is the organisational one, the different concrete forms which these relations evince. A second is the place of these relations in the broader institutional contexts of their respective societies – and especially the extent to which they constitute a basic aspect of the central institutional matrix of a society, of the mode of structuring generalised exchange within it; or the extent to which, while not actually constituting such a basic aspect or dimension of the central institutional matrix of the society, they yet constitute a recognised part of its institutional structure; or, last, the extent to which they constitute mainly what C. Landé has defined as an (often informal) 'addendum' to such central institutional context. To quote him:

formal, explicit, institutionalized contracts do not offer an adequate explanation of the way a community works because they do not provide for all of the needs of a community or of the individuals who enter into such contracts.

Some of these must be enlivened by the superimposition upon them of voluntary relations of a more selective, flexible, intermittent and emotional sort that can give them a vigor not found in conventional institutionalized contracts when these stand alone. This need is met by the addition of dyadic alliances.[14]

While in some cases there may exist, as we shall see, some overlap between these different types of patron–client relations, especially between the last two, on the whole it is not difficult to distinguish between them.

Accordingly, we shall now proceed in a more systematic way to present a varied panorama of such different forms of patron–client relations, as well as of the social contexts in which they develop.

We shall present here cases from several cultural regions and societies: first of all those like southern Europe, Latin America, southeast Asia, the Middle East, in which these relations are part of the central institutional context; second Japan, classical India, Rwanda and Cyrenaica, where they constitute, on the whole, a relatively recognised part, a legitimate addendum to the institutional fabric of society; and, third, the U.S.A., the U.S.S.R. and modern India, in which, just as in most modern democratic societies, they constitute above all an addendum to the institutional centre of the society.

PATRON–CLIENT RELATIONS IN SOUTHERN EUROPE

The Mediterranean areas of southern Europe – namely southern Italy, certain parts of Spain, Greece, Cyprus and Malta (as also Ireland in Northern Europe) – have been at the periphery of Western Europe, since the seventeenth century, both economically and politically.

Even though these countries have undergone wide transformations and modernisation of their political and economic structures since the early nineteenth century – and though most of them have relatively long-established traditions as political entities and as diversified economic structures, especially when compared to other areas of the world – they have been the areas of least development within Western Europe. For instance, compared to other countries there, they are only moderately industrialised, and, to this day, a relatively high percentage of their economically active population (ranging from 20·7% in Spain and 23·1% in Ireland to 28·4% in Greece and 32·5% in Portugal) is engaged in agricultural and related activities. Although they have long been integrated within the capitalistic world system, some being members of the European Economic Community – with the constraints that this fact imposes on their economic functioning – by most economic indicators, such as internal composition by sectors, gross-national product per capita, per-capita energy consumption, economically they still lag behind other members of that organisation.

Politically, both Mediterranean and non-Mediterranean countries bear today formal similarities. Constitutionally, most are parliamentary democracies that abide by some form of representative institutions and competitive party systems, hold contested elections and, generally, maintain unrestricted party activities. Behind this formal façade, however, there are many strong political and societal differences between the Mediterranean area and most other Western European settings.

Among these, in broad outline, stand out, first, the fact that Portugal, Spain and Greece, for instance, have only recently moved from years and, in the case of the first two countries, even decades of authoritarian rule to parliamentary democracy. There is also the fact that in some of these countries, like Italy or Cyprus, the political regimes lack widespread legitimacy among broad sectors of their own population – leading, as in the case of Cyprus, to separatist trends in their political structuring. Second, the political centres of these societies do not command a strong commitment among their citizenry or even among part of the elites. Third, and especially important from the point of view of our subject, the Mediterranean areas are also the main regions in which, to this day, clientelism flourished and was more salient.

Indeed, it was in these areas that clientelistic ego-centred networks were extensively found from the ancient Republican period in the second century B.C. In modern times, these societies evince great variations in the concrete expression of these ties. Thus, clientelistic clusters of dyadic ties were found between landholders and people short of land or landless strata involved in sharecropping and labour arrangements; in the agrotowns of Italian latifundist Mezzogiorno; in central Italy, in the mezzadrian *signori* and *mezzadri* paternalistic brokerage; in Spain, where the links were either normatively anchored in the values of the *pueblos*, and were often coterminous with a 'lopsided' friendship, or were oppressive and labelled as *caciquismo*.

With the process of national integration, individual localised patron–client attachments evolved into more complex networks linked to wider institutional frameworks such as parties or bureaucracies. In southern Italy, *clientelismo* and party-directed bosses were strengthened under conditions of continuing political competition, widening distribution of wealth and the transference of the locus of political articulation to higher levels of political contest. Such a pyramidal chain-to-centre structure also characterised Spanish *caciquismo* after the 1874 Restoration. Relations were then more instrumental and impersonal and less dependent on ideological prescriptions of solidarity than in the traditional settings. Connections with ruling parties and state bureaucracies, office-holding and control of marketing processes became connected – for instance in Greece and in Spain – with the emergence of clientelistic networks. The Sicilian *mafiosi* brokerage, between urban absentee landlords and the western Sicilian hinterland, has been characterised by a high degree of coercion; *mafiosi* competed among themselves vis-à-vis lower-standing sectors for a greater share of wealth, while related to landlords and powerful persons and at the same time attempting to undermine their control.

Several traits seem to have been particularly strong in these clientelistic relationships occurring in southern Europe. Among them stands out, first, a tendency to emphasise highly elaborated cultural codes of behaviour (such as honour, generosity, *omerta*) in establishing and maintaining clientelistic relations. This emphasis has been related to the broad meaning and personal involvement that social actors have attributed to these hierarchical attachments, which were not expected to be reduced to power differentials. Second, a wide range of organisational variants of clientelism has existed in this area, from dyadic and localised to more complex pyramidal networks. Third, patrons had to assert their positions through clientelistic networks without being able to manipulate emic images of broader kin support (as found, for instance, in the Middle East). Fourth, images of clientelism have existed in the spiritual realm, especially in the Catholic areas. Thus, mainly among lower strata, there was a widespread popular faith that the intercession of the Virgin and the saints with the ultimate source of patronage – God – was needed in order to pursue any enterprise or activity. Ecclesiastical authorities did, accordingly, assume the role of patrons through their own channels of access to, for instance, administrative and judicial machineries. But, while their patronage and intermediation in spiritual and material matters was indeed sought, a too large degree of interference in political activities was usually resented by temporal patrons.

We shall describe below some of these patterns of clientelism in detail.

Ancient Republican Rome[15]

I

In late Republican Rome, *patrocinium* and *clientelae* denoted various and different clusters of relationships: first, the *patronus–libertus* link (the oldest relationship and the most open to coercion, established between a former master and his freedman, created by *manumissio* and subject to inheritance for several generations); second, the ties contracted by a distinguished Roman as patron: (a) to individuals of lower social standing such as the urban plebs, or the soldiers after Marius' reform in the army. The Roman formula of *applicatio* was widely used to establish such relations. This type of *clientela* was expected to be characterised by a more exclusive commitment than the two forms that follow. Within this type there was a variant of links which people interested in advancing political positions maintained with 'machine' men acting in their service; (b) to provinces, *municipia, colonia*. Based mainly on *deditio* and on the representation of the client by the patron before the institutions of the Roman State; and (c) to members of those communities, particularly men of distinction such as the knights (*equites*). Ties of *hospitium* were typical of such relation.

Third, there were ties of *amicitia*. It was characteristic of ties established between members of the ruling class and other powerful sub-elites. When fading into clientelism, its main forms were the following: (a) the attachment of a prospective upward mobile person as a follower and *amicus* to an active general or politician as a way to learn the practical and procedural aspects of the state machinery, or to get power and influence, and to advance the interests of both partners in public affairs; (b) the commendation of a client to *amici*. This act reinforced an established link between *amici*, and the commendation was accepted and the client became attached to both patrons, especially when he provided useful services to his new patron; and (c) pleading in courts. As political struggle was often conducted in criminal courts, the pleader in court acted sometimes as patron to his *clients*. Fourth were the foreign *clientelae* that the Roman State maintained with *civitates liberae*.

The core of such relations of *patrocinium* or *clientelae* was the long-term *fides* which permeated them and which people recognised as the moral element that held together relations which in many cases were legally unstructured, ambiguous from a conventional point of view and open to conflicting interpretations and to instrumental manipulations.[16]

In what follows, these patterns of patron–client relations are described in detail.

II

The relationship maintained between Roman patricians and their freedmen[17] was historically the most persistent of *clientelae* links. Seemingly, it was derived from the patrimonial authority of the Roman *pater* in his condition of 'master, magistrate and priest' over his freed servants, his *clientes*, which remained attached hereditarily to family or *gens.* T. Mommsen characterised the *clientes* as those individuals 'who while they are not free burgesses of any commonwealth, yet lived within one in a condition of protected freedom. These included refugees who had found a reception with a foreign protector, and those slaves in respect of whom their master had for the time being waived the exercise of his rights, and so conferred on them practical freedom.'[18]

The manumission was granted to slaves under different circumstances. First, it was granted to slaves who had been able to accumulate wealth (by practising some industry for example) and hence could buy their freedom or the freedom of their beloved. Second, *manumissio* was used as a means to reward faithful services done by domestic slaves. Third, it was also used in harsh economic times by owners who tried to shift their economic obligations onto the shoulders of the freedman (*libertus*), while still enjoying some of the services of the latter. Such a trend was perhaps especially popular after grain distributions were sanctioned to freedmen who could then still be required to work for the patrician while obtaining their rations from the State.

The *patronus* was thus the granter of freedom and hence he was considered to be entitled to exercise coercion or *potestas* over his *libertus*. The relationship had not properly the character of a relation *de jure* like the links that tied a man to his guests or to his slaves; the client remained non-free, although good faith and use and wont alleviated in his case the condition of non-freedom. In early times, the patron was entitled to reassume property over his client, to reduce him in emergency to the state of slavery, and even to inflict capital punishment on him. However, re-enslavement remained only a possibility; it did not occur as the natural outcome to the breaking of obligations by the *libertus*. Even if *potestas* had no defined limits, cruelty was considered contrary to consuetudinary practices.

But even when cruelty occurred, the freedman could not leave one patron for another; the established attachment was in principle unseverable and was transmitted in the *gens* of the *patronus* from father to son. After freedom had been enjoyed for several generations, the *dominium* of the heirs of the releaser over the descendants of the released could not be claimed without flagrant impiety.

As can be seen, the *clientes* had only a kind of 'dependent freedom', that is they enjoyed rights only by being related to a *patronus*. A certain degree of *coertio* and minor punishment was allowed, and legally the freedmen had no guarantees against it save to turn a patron's good faith and goodwill to themselves.

From ancient times, freedmen were required to perform economic services and prestations for their patrons. Ancient laws for instance required the client to endow the daughter of the patron, to pay the patron's fine, to furnish his ransom, or to contribute to the expenses of his magistracy.[19] In late Republican times, freedmen had to show their patrons *obsequium*, i.e. give them some services whose exact content changed over time, and give them *operae*, that is a certain number of days labour. A failure to provide *obsequium*, or its breach, led to the admission of patron in *societas* with the freedman, that is it entitled him to share the harvest of the latter. If the freedman did not give *operae*, he had to pay for the damage he caused. The rights that a patron had – such as inheritance, *tutela*, *obsequium* and also *reverentia* or outward signs of gratitude – were also protected by the extralegal coercive capability of the patron referred to as his *potestas*. A *libertus* was unqualified to hold property, or to act independently from the *patronus*, who bore a legal character in the State as a member of the city. Thus freedmen only held in trust the lands they cultivated, and these could return to the patron at their death; they could not engage in entrepreneurial activities such as tax-farming and commerce but only in representation of the *patronus*.

Even more, they could not contract marriage before asking the permission of their patron; they were subject to the *patronus*, who was entitled to judge them; they could not perform ceremonies of worship by themselves but were related to the gods through the intercession of the patron, who was the chief of domestic worship.

This pattern of clients 'shut up' in families changed over time. With the passing of generations, the condition of unfree birth was replaced by that of *ingenuus* and dependence became attenuated, exchange less lopsided and less oppressive, while the links of *clientelae* continued to be recognised until the patron's or the client's family died out. With time, descendants of freedmen were probably found among the 'political workers' of a patron, and among those who carried arms in the midst of late Republican Roman rivalries.

III

Another form of patron–client relation emerged between distinguished Romans and individuals of lower social standing, during the period of bitter partisan strife in late Republican Rome.[20]

By that time, Rome had annexed or maintained in vassalage or unequal alliance vast territories. The Empire's growth produced the enrichment and corruption of senators and *equites*, the former as governors of provinces or members of their staffs, and the latter as capitalists who brought resources and slaves from the provinces; senators commanded more and more the treasury and the right to assign provinces and armies to magistrates.

At the same time, this process was conducive to the impoverishment of the common people, who, if they had not perished in wars, when they returned from them were unable to retain their small farms, because their property had suffered during their absence or because their crops could not compete with the cheap grain of the provinces. The land around Rome was swallowed up into large estates worked by slave labour. The population was increasingly composed of well-to-do and poor. Freedmen as well as freeborn were ready to hire themselves to anyone.

In the centre of that state, senatorial aristocrats dominated both the popular assembly and the access to positions of power such as the consulship and tried to avoid the entrance of newmen, even of the elite, to the higher offices of public life; ancestry and heredity were important conditions for access to office. Citizens were divided according to possession of landed property, which determined differential military service and power and weighted the votes of citizens in the *comitia centuriata* which assigned the high senatorial ranks of consuls and praetors and dictated the most important laws.

In the second half of the second century B.C., political strife became more intense. The Senate had an ever stronger hold on the State, which provided opportunities and spoils in the frame of a mighty empire. Therefore, the contest for high offices (open in small numbers annually) became bitter and was no longer maintained within the ranks of noble and senatorial families (called *optimates* in Cicero's times); instead, it came to include newmen who had for the first time gained admission to legislative bodies such as *comitia tributa*. *Optimates* (aristocrats) in control of the Senate prevented people of lower pedigree from getting the endorsement of the Senate for their measures; the defeated turned with the aid of tribunes to the *comitia tributa*, the tribal assembly, where they procured the enactment of laws which accorded with their own schemes. Such men were described as *popularii* (demagogues) by their opponents. *Popularii*, the patrons of the urban plebs, were not a corporate group; each one sought his own advancement, but by relying on popular support instead of manipulating the popular will, as the *optimates* used to do.

Besides this, Republican Rome knew the emergence of great generals strengthened by their bands of loyal soldiers. Until Marius (c. 155–86 B.C.), 'Roman soldiers had in general been recruited from the small landholders of Roman territories, but the normal levies failed after the supply of these landholders had been depleted by Rome's long and costly wars.'[21] Marius instituted the recruitment of landless poor and marginals of Rome and the Italian municipalities, who remained under arms for years instead of short periods.

Basic characteristics of patron–client relations

Thus, the clients were found among

the urban plebs, especially after it had been increased by men evicted from their lands, by vagrants who came to the city to enjoy the games and to benefit from the grain dole, and by the steady manumission of slaves ... a large group of people who possessed no means of livelihood except what could be had from attachment to nobles of the great houses and to popular leaders.[22]

Clients hoped to derive some advantage from submission in a society in which low-standing social strata had no lands and no protection before the courts. As for the nobles, when contest for office became bitter and acquired violent features, family–blood, affinity or adoption relations came to be insufficient to master this situation and they opted to add the popular support of clients, adherents and *amici* in Rome and elsewhere, and/or of their soldiers and veterans of war.

A conglomeration of clients was a valuable resource for a patron as long as clients lacked categorial consciousness or at least did not attempt to present collective demands. In fact, for instance, people entered the army in the hope of personal gains such as the acquisition of land, *bonum*. Generals stayed in politics after their victories were won and procured resources for distribution among their followings, whose support was of primary significance in intra-categorial contests for power among potential and actual powerholders.

The duties of clients were stated in a diffuse manner; they were required to be ready to support their patron in any way he demanded: in times of turmoil, going to war, exercising violence and giving an 'impression of power', either by peaceful means or through display of force, which was necessary for contesting politicians. This was so because, besides instrumental political services, clients showed by their support and through their number the trust placed on the patron's *fides*, demonstrating his valuable character and virtue and promoting his image in public life.

The patron provided for his clients protection, assistance when in need and land, mainly acquired through his sponsorship of laws that regarded the interests of his clients. Thus, besides getting in the *comitia tributa* personal gains (such as assignations to offices, military commands, prerogatives), patrons also got rewards for their followers; such rewards included the distribution of state-subsidised food for the urban plebs, agrarian laws providing lands for the landless, the extension of citizenship, the opening of offices for newmen.

When in the army, soldiers looked to a patron for rewards, in return for allegiance and support. To win elections, generals began to send their armies to Rome to vote or, if necessary (that is, if constitutional means were insufficient), to use violence. Soldiers' knowledge of war-making was a relevant symbolic and instrumental source of bargaining power, in a society in which political contest was strongly associated with the impression of power. After they were established in colonies with grants of lands, soldiers continued as veterans to regard their former general as their patron, to look to him for aid while responding to his call when needed. This was made possible by their settlement in colonies following military divisions' lines: they could be called out for service in their old formations.

The more or less exclusive character of clusters was a consequence of mutual interests in defining limits to loyalty and in the rewards both partners derived from the relationship rather than a result of the use of coercive power.

The established relationship was considered to be a close one, based on a moral base: partners were assumed to be related morally (*in fide esse, in fidem venire*). Obligations could be then loosely defined, and it was a matter of *fides* to state their scope; clients had no legal claims in law. Loyalty was considered essential to the link. To accuse each other in law suits or to act against each other or to abuse of the patron's position of power and of his trust were considered acts of treason, impious and 'unlawful' behaviour.

In addition, the link was reinforced by some measure of ritualisation. Clients were expected to come in the morning for the daily *salutatio* and/or to appear on the Forum. By the time of Cicero, the ratio of followings grew and patrons began, according to Gelzer's evaluation of Quintus' letters to Cicero, to divide their friends and clients into classes: those of the first were admitted to the house singly, those of the second class in groups and those of the third *en masse*. Gelzer affirms that the latter comprised the clients we are referring to here.[23] The first and second categories of followers will be discussed below as forms of *amicitia*; the second group refers mainly to close adherents and political workers who were necessary for the manipulation of the plebs by nobles.

This form of clientelism was established mainly through *applicatio*; that is, a free-born prospective client approached a patron appealing for help and willing to give him his support and to follow the man he approached. The latter could accept or reject the *applicatio*. The oath of allegiance to a general was the institutionalised equivalent in a military context. Another procedure was commendation, which took the form of introduction of prospective clients to a patron by one of his other clients or *amici*; however, this form was usually reserved for clients of higher social standing and therefore will be discussed below.

With the elimination of the Republic, and even before with the growth of the ratio of followers to patron, the market positions of partners changed in favour of the bargaining power of the patron. However, the link remained present during the Empire.

IV

Distinguished Roman individuals maintained also personal client-elistic ties with non-Roman families and individuals and with whole communities in need of representation before the Roman centre.[24] Typically, Roman magistrates in the allied cities became the representatives of conquering power among their subjects. Prospective clients lacked the power to influence decisions and avoid exploitation except through the establishment of links with Roman influentials. Furthermore, communities could lose autonomy if they had not enough influential senators attached to their interests. Also professional associations such as the *publicani* had to have their interests represented at Rome by powerful senators. Notwithstanding such a position, the ruling class in the centre of the Republic lacked categorial unity, and intestine strife was common, as we described in detail above. The fear of an accusation in court as a means of ending the political career of an enemy also made connections a highly valuable resource for Romans (charges were usually of extortion in the provinces, embezzlement of funds, treason against the State, malpractice in candidacy).

During the Republic, there were many forms of contracts between leading Romans and foreign communities that could lead to the establishment of *clientelae*. First, there was victory in war: this tie had no permanent character and ended usually with the transference of the consul to another province or to Rome. Second, there were administrative contacts: during his time in office, every governor acquired positions of patronage in the province under his control, and after he left that office he tried to maintain relations with local people, mainly with prominent individuals. Third, the initiative could be taken by the community concerned or by the Roman Senate; in the second case, by assignation at the request of the community, to protect the interests of foreigners by prosecuting at Rome someone who had oppressed them. In the first half of the second century B.C., the complaining community could also nominate its own prosecutor. Entry was formalised through *applicatio* in the case of individuals and *deditio* in the case of a surrendered community. Fourth, such ties could be promoted by some Roman notable interested in the sanction of citizenship and enfranchisement laws in order to strengthen his power networks in foreign communities.

In the case of ties between distinguished Romans and client communities, the patron provided mediation, facilitated diplomatic contacts; maintained relations of hospitality (*hospitium*) with envoys, entertaining them at Rome and introducing them to the Senate; he would support pleas and would use his influence to obtain a favourable settlement; he would arbitrate internal problems in the foreign community (his arbitration could not be rejected); he informed the community about decrees and laws that could affect it. As can be seen, a patron's resources were mainly political representation, support, and protection from extortion or oppression; communities as well as leading families of foreign chieftains, kings, etc., had to rely on Roman patrons. Thus, the decisive source of bargaining power for a patron was his full citizen rights and his access to the political centre, evinced in his connections at Rome.

In return, the Roman patron got support in his private difficulties, protection from his Roman enemies, a place of refuge and assistance if condemned or in adversity, the provision of the necessary means for capturing popular favour in Rome (by paying for circus exhibitions, the distribution of cheap crops, etc.). A noble's foreign *clientelae* gave him *dignitas*, leading to concrete advantages in his political advancement. In Rome, his foreign *clientelae* had indirect influence in his political career, through the provision of means for electioneering and their symbolic support and, later, through fostering the formation of personal armies to serve those Romans to whom knights and other prominent non-Romans were attached. Colonies of Roman and later Latin and other Italian citizens deserve a special mention, as they had a supplementary resource, the vote, which was essential to the political advancement of the patron; municipal leaders were helpful in 'swinging' electoral districts for the noble and his *amici*. Italian leaders were important after their enfranchisement in the frame of the 'rural tribes', as they were a majority in the Roman tribal legislative system and could travel to Rome to decide the outcome of elections of higher magistrates. Another important resource was the symbolic significance of backing for the reputation of a Roman politician, for power in Rome was indissolubly linked with standing and prestige.

The content of the relationship was highly personalised; clients were expected to consult their patrons before taking decisions.[25] With the consolidation of Rome, this became less significant, as few decisions were left to clients, and less feasible with the multiplication of patrons. Clients were expected also to show devotion. The morning *salutatio* and the acceptance of claims to *hospitium* could confer 'visibility' to personal reliability. However, the way in which patrons and clients regarded their rights and duties was a matter of moral commitment.

With the increase in internal strife after 133 B.C., these links of *clientelae* were used in political contest.

V

Roman *amicitia* was highly unstructured. That is, it had in P. Brunt's words 'imperceptible gradations in quality and degree',[26] either linking people who were social equals in some sort of alliance or holding together social actors by mutual interest and a clientelistic provision of services (*officia*).

Links of *amicitia* were widely established by Roman notables and Italian *equites* and were used to promote different interests, to ward off attacks or to gain access to some administrative office. Nevertheless, the core characteristic of *amicitia* was the moral element or *fides* that people recognised and that brought *amici* to repay services even in circumstances when it was no longer in their short-term interest to do so. Thus, by maintaining links of *amicitia* people recognised a sort of obligation that might transcend the bonds of political friendship, either by obliterating recent obligations or by solidifying them through the conferring of an aura of *familiaritas*, closeness and seeming cordiality.

Although there was seldom a clearcut line of demarcation between ties framed in the idiom of *amicitia* and links that fell outside its scope, the first were in late Republican Rome characterised by a greater similarity in social status of the *amici* than was found in personalistic relations framed according to other idioms of interaction.

In the framework of clientelism, it seems that *amicitia* was present in the following cases:[27]

(a) Serving as the *amicus* of an active general or politician. The *amicus* was supposed to be a close adherent, a political worker. Such were the members of a noble's voting group or ward, that is his *tribules*, who assisted him in his own elections or in those of his friends. Among the *tribules* were found those who kept up what can be called the political machines; such men were in constant contact with local communities, tribal officers, men below the knights, and people like the *divisores* who distributed gifts to members of the electoral tribes in Rome.

The obligation of patrons to explain the law to their clients was probably characteristic of this kind of link. In Quintus' classification of clients,[28] the *deductores* who accompanied a patron to the Forum and the clients who followed a candidate when he asked for votes, probably fell into this relationship.

Later in his political life, the noble used *amici* to keep his own influence at Rome when he was away (assuming a public duty that the Senate assigned him and that was instrumental for his career at Rome) and in the provinces when he was at Rome.

For followers from patrician families interested in pursuing a political career at Rome, to serve as the *amicus* of an active politician or general was the natural way to know the working of the State, the relation of subjects and allies to Rome, the rules of senatorial procedure and the cases of precedent.

(b) The commendation of a client to *amici*. When the commendation was accepted, it reinforced an established link between the *amici*, especially when the client provided useful services to his new patron. In addition, the friend in the provinces gained contacts at Rome in return for accepting the commendation of the client of the Roman notable. It is highly improbable therefore that the status of clients was humble in this case. However, not all recommended people were of high senatorial rank, and *tribules* for instance were also commended.

(c) Pleading in courts was particularly institutionalised as an important form of establishing or cementing ties of interpersonal dependence and mutual obligations. On the other side, a contracted obligation could impose the pleading of *amici* at courts, even when the motivation to do so was lacking or minimal. For the defendant (the *patronus*), the defence of an *amicus* added to a public image of being reliable, i.e. it was a device for getting informal and electoral support and helped to maintain a position he had won, or to challenge that of established politicians. Such relations arose in a socio-political context in which political struggle was conducted frequently in criminal courts and endless prosecutions were brought for political motives by personal enemies who contested the politicians' right to the holding of office and to the manifold rewards of public life. Under such conditions, even when both pleader and prosecuted referred to each other as *amici*, the advocate was customarily designated *patronus*, even if he stood in lower position than the accused according to criteria such as wealth and birth. Indeed, patronage in the courts served as a channel of mobility for newmen such as Cicero, who came to be 'courted' by distinguished Romans and who acquired fame and acceded to offices and to special distinctions and honour, on account of his eloquence.

VI

From the fourth century B.C., Rome claimed and successfully exercised the right to extend its alliance to free states situated beyond Latium, on the fringes of its area of influence, and to protect them against their enemies, even when an attack on them preceded the alliance.

The relationship between those *civitates liberae* and the Roman state has been described as a case of 'extralegal dependence of the weak on a strong protector, founded on gratitude, piety, reverence and all the scared emotions and patron's power to enforce them'.[29] It was the weakness of the client states that allowed Rome to respect their political freedom, enabling it to control its ever widening area of influence and to exact submission and allegiance while being able to interpret flexibly its obligations to the *civitates liberae* in accordance with its own needs and policies.

Civitates liberae were mainly small states, mostly in Sicily and Greece, that appealed to Rome when in danger and put themselves in her *fides* (made *applicatio in fidem populi Romani*), were declared *liberae et immunes* (i.e. they were not obliged to make specified contributions to the armed forces led by Rome) and were accepted as allies. If they were attacked and war followed, the client state was defended and well treated after victory. The *applicatio* of a client was prompted by the desire to maintain freedom and perhaps by the will to avoid payments and specific contributions (*foedera*) for the Roman armies. The acceptance of *applicatio* depended on the interests of Rome. Rome was looking first, not so much for services such as active support in war, but rather for a means of guarding frontiers without wasting its own forces in territories in which control could be assured without using them. Second, Rome was interested in using the *civitates liberae* as a means to absorb the first shock in the case of an armed collision with external powers. Third, a supplementary gain could be derived from the reputation of Rome as the protector to which weak states could appeal when in danger; this was useful in the case of Sicily, which 'was destined to be the stepping stone to the conquest of the West', or in the Greek *patrocinium libertatis Graecorum*, which had, according to Badian, 'a propagandistic task to suit their traditions'.[30]

Even under such conditions, patronage was not granted to troublesome, 'ingrate' or treasonary states, or to states that would not accept for long a submissive role. Thus, Rome could afford to be generous and refrain from imposing formal obligations when she knew she would have a strong moral claim on the state concerned along with the power to enforce her interests in case of need.

The relationship was loosely formulated and was open to manipulative interpretations. *Civitates liberae* had no legal link with Rome; they were bound by her moral obligations and power relations. The client state conserved political internal freedom and got a loosely defined guarantee of protection, and of advice and assistance against external threats, which were interpreted according to the interests and priorities of the patron state. The patron state received submissiveness and *reverentia*, allegiance, and services such as information. The client state had not to forget its status, that is, that it was free as long as Rome did not care. When Rome wished to intervene, formal pretexts were not lacking, above all charges of ingratitude. The loose terms of Roman *fides* allowed Rome to decide how much help to accord, and at the same time the interpretation of the client's obligations rested largely with her. That is, Roman *amicitia* was no guarantee save if it suited Rome.

After the mid-second century B.C. Rome intervened directly in the territories under its influence, partly because the links of foreign *clientelae* were seen as unreliable. Such was the conclusion the Senate drew from the first Mithriadic war and from the intrigues of the generals in the provinces. Former *civitates liberae* were no longer of little direct concern to Rome while they could intrigue with her potential enemies. The imminence of civil war made it dangerous, in the view of the Senate, to respect the formerly accorded freedom. By 74 B.C. clientelism in public international affairs became merged with individual clientelism.

Southern Italy[31]

In the agrarian isolated agrotowns of latifundist southern Italy (the Mezzogiorno), many clientelistic ties between landowners and land-less strata developed in the nineteenth century. The Mezzogiorno was a zone known for its fragmented landownership, the precariousness of its agricultural contracts and its overpopulation. It was, consequently, further characterised by unemployment and underemployment and the sub-letting of small strips of land belonging to latifundists to peasants, who experienced a lack of capital investment and credit facilities, and by conditions of conflictive competitive relations among the peasants themselves. Save for some coastal towns, market centres were absent. The hinterland was not penetrated by roads or by the administrative machinery of centres which, since antiquity, were foreign, considered alien, and did not inspire commitment and institu-tional trust among the peripheral strata. These centres failed not only to monopolise the use of physical force and violence but even to control and tax the flow of economic resources in these 'frontier' areas. Society was organised according to bilateral kinship, and the nuclear family was the only effective kinship aggregate.

Under these conditions, primary producers were separated from a secure hold on the means of production (land and the essentials for cultivation), the work assignments were fragmented, scarcity was endemic in the area and class cohesion was feeble. The channels of upward mobility were, in the main, closed to all but a minority of peasants, who either acceded to estate stewardship or employed methods of banditry or followed a *mafiosi* style of behaviour to achieve advancement.

These factors, along with the fragmentation of power and its uncertain distribution, led people to depend, first, on the understanding of dyadic arrangements outside the nuclear family in order to gain access to economic and political security, and, second, on codes of honour and on their *sa fare* ('know how') ability to obtain access to resources and to a greater share of power through personal contacts.

The large landowners (the *latifondisti*), the would-be patrons, were engaged in grain speculation, in buying and selling estates, in owning shares in mills, etc. Peasants, shepherds, artisans, depended on leaseholders (*gabellotti*) and on the landowners' administrators (*soprastanti*) as well as on the landowners themselves for their livelihood. They were in close contact with the latter in the agrotowns and tried to establish special relations of clientelism with them in order to soften the otherwise hard terms of agricultural contracts. For their part, landowners were involved in strife among themselves and built up followings as a means of obtaining a successful outcome in contestation of resources.

Occupation of patron–client relations was mainly individual and was set up through an informal, tacit agreement, but it could sometimes be formalised through the links of co-godparenthood, known as *comparaggio*. In reality, power differentiations between the partners were very great and the client was socially isolated and depended on the patron for access to sources of livelihood and to minimal security. No alternative means were found, and while overpopulation was a threat, migration was still uncommon. The ability of the landholder to grant or refuse a sharecropping contract (*mezzadria*) or to provide work on a daily basis to labourers (*braccianti*) gave him power over the rural population.

Patrons needed the submission and obedience of clients in their struggles with peers over land and influence and as a means to outdo outside interference in the latifundist area. In addition, clients provided labour and personal services. Under non-contractual conditions, the obligations of the peasants were diffuse, undetermined and capable of being manipulated by the patrons. Before harvests, the peasants had to borrow money from usurers or wheat from their *padrone* and, in return, owed unconditional support. The centres' attempts at penetration in the nineteenth century (through reforms, opening of markets, etc.) were countered by the *padroni's* use of *mafiosi*, *soprastanti* and *campieri* in order to maintain intact their power domains. In such a setting, violence was endemic and impersonal guarantees of security were lacking. In these capitalist latifundist settlements, highly diffuse – although no less hierarchical – links with a *padrone* could serve as a means of protection and life insurance, and of softening the otherwise harsh terms of an unequal relationship. The role of the patron is reported to have been given constant and authoritative validation by the Church through the widespread cult of patron-saints and by the delivery of sermons dealing with the divine origin of social order. Indeed, a patron was sometimes called a *santo*.

The region retained those characteristics until the Piedmontese unifiers made use of the Napoleonic traditions of centralised administration, according to which regionalism was a danger to the structure of the State. Even then, however, integration was achieved by encapsulating southern Italy's power domains following the access of the 'Historical Left' to parliamentary power in 1876 (replacing the northern-based 'Historical Right''s sole control of the new national State).* Nevertheless, as L. Graziano pointed out, 'the division of *domanio communale*, purchases of Church lands, and a greater erosion of ex-baronial property on the part of a rising middle class, had created a greater degree of commercialisation of the economy and a far greater social stratification'[32] in continental Mezzogiorno and, later, also in Sicily. Peasants underwent proletarianisation processes. The workers, peasants and petty bourgeoisie depended on notables for their sources of livelihood and achievement of instrumental aims. Overpopulation, competition over resources and the existence of conflicting orientations and identification among these strata allowed for the continuity of a pattern of individualistic pursuit of interests. Access to authority existed only through vertical *clientela* links. The notables, even if in strong economic positions, had to recognise the growing relevance of political control and had to enter formal office in order to retain their power domains. In close connection with these processes, an important transformation of the clientelistic ties took place. There developed a tendency among these dispersed networks of local clienteles to become transformed into political *clientelae*, i.e. to become related to formal institutional channels of organisation, such as governmental agencies, municipal organisations and the like, depending thereafter on the control of governmental and municipal power and resources to maintain themselves.

* The cooperation between the northern bourgeoisie and the southern landed (rental) capitalistic forces entailed a lack of direct impingement of the southern periphery by the centre which, only through recognition of the notables' political control and by allocating them the newly created administrative functions and roles, succeeded in penetrating this peripheral area.

Basic characteristics of patron–client relations

Progressively, *padroni* had to compete for positions in the formal administrative machinery. They transferred their control over peripheral followings into the political sphere: votes were given on a *preferenza* or optimal preference base to candidates rather than to parties. The patrons' qualifications as intellectual bourgeois of high *massari* (rich peasant) origins in the continental south allowed them to control the channels of allocation of municipal resources and the links between town and national community. In Sicily, the patrons' position as notables with economic supremacy allowed them to convert their local power into political leverage. Their support was indeed sought by nation-oriented politicians. The political centre – the ministries, parliament and the like – was penetrated by conflicting factions, and the ties of local municipal members through provincial deputies led hierarchically to national deputies to the parliament, among whom the most powerful were elected ministers. Their incumbency was utilised to compensate their supporters by a particularistic allocation of resources.

The southern Italian 'political single *clientelismo*' was then based on economic supremacy, or on that together with professional capabilities, which were transferred to a wider frame of political contest in order to gain control over state and municipal resources as a means of further patronage. As S. Tarrow has stated, '*Clientelismo*, as a pattern of political integration, allocates key political roles to those who, through control of the land, have a network of vertical relations with numerous individuals.'[33] On the other hand, the control of the flow of resources derived from higher levels (State, prefecture, funds such as the Cassa per il Mezzogiorno) became critical for the maintenance of the control of local affairs by the notables. Through their holding of office, they controlled the fixing of local taxes, a large number of formal positions, the assignment of communal lands, the awarding of public contracts and employment, the enforcement of health and security regulations, the granting of licences, etc. The 'opening' of these resources, however, depended on the political support notables needed and received from their followers among broader strata. The personal and/or economic ties of the leader's core of high-standing supporters brought him votes, but this support was based more on short-term interests than was that of his personal *clientela*.

Internal stresses in the relationship appeared as the political contest developed in a more democratic idiom, as the traditional bases of economic supremacy became one among the many sources of livelihood, the distribution of wealth widened, and it was perceived that the notables were blocking the access to valuable (state) resources. According to the statements of the state administration, these resources could be claimed as a right by wide sectors of the population. The undermining of traditional economic sources of control was, in some cases, accompanied by a growing uncertainty as to the outcome of electoral acts. The introduction of a proportional representation electoral system in the late 1950s in Sicilian municipal elections – instead of a single majority system – was conducive to the same effects. Politicians began to rely on party organisational support. In other cases, the inability of political machines to dominate local notables with their own sources of patronage was one of the main factors which fostered the emergence of party-directed bosses at the local and regional levels. Thus, new methods of party-directed patronage flourished, characterised by a pyramidal clustering of linked networks of *clientelismo*, which were related to formal organisations within the context of political competition. Thus, the growing relevance of state funds and administrative allocation of resources was paralleled by the emergence of such linked networks of electoral articulation, in which party-directed bosses gained ascendancy. Their strength depended on party connections, on the control they had over the organs of the State and its resources and on their ability to manipulate these resources in order to gain electoral support.

Western Sicily[34]

The networks of *mafiosi* were typical of western Sicily. The *mafiosi* were violent political middlemen competing among themselves for the control of a greater share of wealth and valuable scarce resources. They gained tactical power in latifundist areas by acting as mediators between cities and the western Sicilian hinterland, between peripheral social strata and the more central political forces, as well as between absentee landlords and their clients.

To some degree, the *mafiosi* were the creation of landowners. From the beginning of the nineteenth century, *padroni* used *mafiosi* as brokers to offset the impact of the State and its policies on the one hand and, on the other, the rising demands of the peasantry. 'They checked open rebellions, and sustained revolts in several ways: by force; by keeping a hold on mobile peasants, and by turning outlaws and bandits into allies.'[35] In this manner, the *mafiosi* reinforced the existing patron–client relations between *padroni* and the peasants of the clustered agrotowns, who depended on the large landowners for access to strips of land (often dispersed and not contiguous), or who worked for the large estates as sharecroppers, day labourers, herdsmen, ploughmen, watchmen, etc.

Basic characteristics of patron–client relations

At the same time, they created new clientelistic ties around themselves, by giving 'protection' to people in independent positions in the
agrarian structure and intimidating and bringing pressure to bear on
others. Indeed, they were usually the instigators of the same troubles
they were called upon to solve in return for money or a gain for
themselves or for their *amici*. Their social 'visibility' was, itself, a
prerequisite for attaining economic mobility and for maintaining successfully economic occupations that involved, together with a high
risk, the possibility of rapid socio-economic advancement. Most of the
mafiosi had their roots in the middle peasantry, mainly among those
people who owned some land and cattle or who had once been
employed by the landowners to keep law and order and supervise their
estates – such as the *gabellotti* and *soprastanti*. They strove to build a
reputation for themselves of violent self-assertion in order to control
the resources leased by other – usually bigger – landholders and
padroni, or to increase their local sphere of power.

Their local power networks enabled the *mafiosi* to gain influence at
higher levels of national activity. They were, for instance, instrumental
in 'fixing' elections for politicians and, thus, eventually, added to their
assets connections with powerful outsiders. At the same time, these
higher-level contacts enabled them to use violent means locally – in the
form of theft, extortion, ransom and shooting – without fear of outside
punishment. These activities, though involving minor economic gains,
assured the *mafiosi* a monopoly on opportunities in certain gainful
occupations, influence on market conditions – since the *piazza*, location
of the labour market, was protected by them – economic supremacy,
intervention in land transaction and mediation in debtor–creditor
relations, as well as power to intervene in interpersonal matters.

These networks were characterised by a dispersed structure, in
which different opposed *cosche* (*cosca* was the quasi-group performing
mafiosi actions) used violent means to oust each other and enlarge their
own power domains in a countryside thus characterised by endemic
insecurity. At the same time, these networks developed at a period
when the Italian State was in the process of being formed and small-
scale communities were being integrated into larger institutional structures. Under such conditions, *mafiosi* were usually contacted by
regional politicians and gained tactical power from these outside
connections. Accordingly, their networks were linked, even if only
slightly and in an unstable manner, to wider institutional and organisational frames such as political parties and sectors of the administration.

Exchanges between *mafiosi* and members of broader strata usually
contained strong instrumental and power elements combined with

trust, and relations were expressed in diffuse – friendship-or kinship-like – models. In many instances, *mafiosi* were considered as simple men (perhaps because of their peasant origin), who nevertheless acted as spokesmen for everybody. Peasants often attached to the behaviour of the *mafioso* a 'Robin Hood' interpretation even when, in fact, the latter was connected to the wealthy.

Under conditions of environmental insecurity and abuse, a man who was able to settle affairs and resolve problems by a glance, a word or a gesture, i.e. by a show of 'authority', had prestige, honour and justification in his actions. The *uomo di rispetto* or *d'onore* (terms used when addressing or referring to a *mafioso*) and the *gentiluomo* who is not compelled to undertake manual work for a livelihood,* constituted the core of the Sicilian ideal for human existence.

Central Italy[36]

In the central Italian mezzadrian zone, patron-client relations were, until the 1950s, focused around patrons whose local base of power, derived from landlordship, was strengthened by the monopolisation of contacts with the regional and national system within which the agricultural communities were incorporated in 1860. Most patrons were locally resident *mezzadria* landlords (*signori*) who maintained close personal and regular contacts with their peasant partners. Other patrons occupied professional administrative local positions of authority as schoolteachers, pharmacists and tax collectors. Most of these bureaucrats and professionals were unlanded members of landed families. Locally, patrons were a source of economic assistance, protection and information about the outside world. They provided medicines, helped clients to obtain medical services and rendered collective services such as the derivation of funds and charities to groups of followers arranged in organisations sponsored by the patrons. In the first stages of the unification of Italy, these mezzadrian landlords controlled access to the administration and the resources it commanded. Patrons interpreted the law, offered advice, intervened on the client's behalf through their contacts with officials, and gave *raccomandazioni* so that clients could contact someone in higher circles of power. Direct participation in national political life was often reserved for patrons. The mayors and the administrative councils of the communities were selected from this stratum and they controlled the access to local bureaucratic jobs, as representatives of the State, and were the

---

* The Sicilians disliked manual work, and the people engaged in it – such as the *contadini* and the *viddari* – were regarded as lacking *civiltà*, in contrast with the high-ranking persons who did not need to work for their livelihood.

priests and the leaders of the local Church. The bargaining power of the lower strata increased as the concentration of lands disappeared and new sources of livelihood were opened up to wider sectors of the population. The *mezzadri* were fully incorporated into the market economy, large landowners became absentees, and universal suffrage gave rise to quite widespread political activity. With the rise in the levels of literacy and education, the development of modern means of communication and transportation and the establishment of relatives in urban centres, the members of the various social strata in small communities became increasingly aware of their participation in the national system and open to its impact. Many of the services which had been rendered by patrons were now handled and distributed by the State, in the form of credits, a national health plan, assistance for mothers and babies, special allotments during agricultural crises, etc., and by charitable organisations. At the same time, unions as well as political and religious organisations now offered assistance to their members on a limited scale.

Yet, the clientelistic patterns persisted in a changed organisational form. Specific forms of brokerage came to replace the traditional broadly comprehensive and monopolistic mediation of *padroni*. Brokers, drawn from different social strata, appeared within the administration and the formal organisations. As S. Silverman has pointed out, 'the national society is known and participated in not primarily through an upper-class landlord, but through the mayor who is also a peasant, the labor union confined to *mezzadri*, other formal organizations composed of lower-class persons, and relatives and friends who life in other towns'.[37]

Spain[38]

I

From the completion of the process of *reconquista* from the Moors, in the late fifteenth century, of the lands of what was to become Spain, and the discovery and conquest of the American territories, the Spanish centre embodied the ideal of universal Catholic monarchy colonising and converting the world. With its developed bureaucracy, its strong army and the close relation between its drive of power and a sense of mission, the monarchy early succeeded in breaking up the political strength of the nobility. It encouraged, however, or at least did not hamper, the aristocracy's attempts to monopolise basic sources of livelihood, such as lands in southern Spain or commerce with the Latin American colonies. The scarcity of people from other regions ready to settle in southern Spain, together with the grant of inalienable rights to individual nobles who had participated in the reconquest, led to the establishment of latifundiae, to extensive agriculture and sheep pastures which, with the passing of time, encroached on the common lands of the *pueblos* (communities) south of the Tajo, and to non-capitalised traditional methods of cultivation which exhausted the soil in the eighteenth and nineteenth centuries. The centre, weakened and 'decadent' since the seventeenth century, penetrated the periphery with bureaucratic demands for political order and taxation. Even if symbolically strong, it in fact conducted policies of encapsulation and adaptive relations with some sectors of the periphery – that is, recognition of the power domains of upper strata members, who acknowledged the primacy of the centre – and strong extractive policies in the areas of more active development, as in nineteenth-century Cataluña.

The short-lived attempts of the Bourbon rulers to reshape the policies of national integration in the late eighteenth century, and the subsequent French occupation followed by the war of liberation in the early nineteenth century, led to deep changes in the centre's legitimation criteria. Struggles also broke out among sectors of the elites (Royalists versus Carlists, etc.) attempting to take over power, and liberalist political institutions were formally established in that century, with intermittent periods of unrest on the one hand, and centralisation and order on the other.

Under these conditions, and especially in the less developed regions of Andalusia and Castile, until the mid-nineteenth century, local men of power known as *caciques* controlled unlanded peasants and the growing rural proletariat of *braceros* by the grant of land leases for sharecropping and of employment opportunities. These very limited and localised networks were used by the landed elite to counter the attempts of different administrations whose policies were seen as a threat to their predominance, as well as to subdue class revolt, at least until the creation of the armed corps of Guardia Civil in 1841. With the expansion of the liberal regime from the 1840s and the increased conflicts within the civil and military political elites, local *caciques* competed for effective vertical connections with higher-ranking politicians. There emerged patterns of linked networks in which patrons at the local and regional level gathered support and votes for the central political actors and, in return, received protection and immunity in taking 'spoils' in their power domains. This kind of clientelistic network, which developed in its full form – and beyond the boundaries of Andalusia and Castile – from the 1874 Restoration to the advent of the regime of Primo de Rivera in 1923, assumed a pyramidal structure: from the Ministry of the Interior or the two great parties, through provincial *caciques* acting as civil governors, deputies and wealthy members of the elite, to district and local politicians such as mayors and men of wealth, and, from them, to local *caciques* in the towns and villages. Thus, the centre gained control over the periphery by surrendering its direct influence, and the gap widened between its image of parliamentarism and effective control on the one hand, and reality on the other. Finally, the liberal regime collapsed as a result of its 'abuses'. This was accompanied by a strong distrust of the social policies initiated from above and led to the presentation of radical demands, to anarchic movements and to the subsequent polarisation of society. In the authoritarian Franco regime that emerged after the Spanish Civil War, instances of intercession and sponsorship (the well-known *enchufe*) and the delivery of particularistic favours by holders of power in the administration remained of great importance when approaching bureaucratic loci of decision-making. Of special significance was the securing of certificates of residence, social benefits, commercial activities, entrance to certain schools, import and export licences, permits for migration, etc. Bureaucratic delays could not be overcome through legal impersonal means because, as M. Kenny has colourfully indicated, 'it is not a question here of considering that one may be entitled to these things by right, for between what is one's right and what is possible lie a thousand indifferent shrugs of the shoulder'.[39]

II

At times merging with the political clientelism of the *caciques* described above, and at times clearly separated from it, there also developed in the villages and towns of the countryside other types of diffuse patron–client relations contracted between members of the local and regional leadership and local labourers (*braceros*, etc.), tenants and other small landholders and residents. Through these relations, the powerful persons assumed the role of patron by accepting (often only tacitly) a commitment to the moral codes of 'friendship' towards the community and to the needs of their poor *vecinos*, whom they agreed to help or sponsor.

Thus, mayors, priests, doctors and other professionals, legal and municipal bureaucrats, and landowners became focal points of clientelistic networks at the local level, while they themselves might, as clients, be attached to more powerful patrons in towns and cities. Among these powerful persons, some in particular tended to become foci of clientelistic approaches as, for instance, first, the mayor of the village – especially if he was a big landowner or had connections with bureaucrats and outsiders in general, and also if he was native born –

and, second, the priest, in his capacity as chairman of committees administering foundations and trust funds and as president of the local religious sodalities (*cofradías*). To be able to count on the friendship, assistance, influence and benevolence of these persons could be of great importance in case of need or difficulty. Through the establishment of such particularistic links, clients hoped to obtain instrumental resources such as employment, assistance, protection, loans or other benefits from the state organs, a means of contacting outside powers in an 'honourable way', by means of letters of recommendation, the testimonial of the patron being essential for this purpose. At the same time, the clients enjoyed being identified with their patron's social visibility and manliness (*hombría*). Those people who succeeded in becoming patrons were assured of several forms of services: the loyalty of employees, interested in looking after their protector's assets; symbolic–relational gains, as signs of esteem and recognition of prestige; political support as, for instance, against other members of the ruling group, and the provision of information on local affairs.

This last service was highly valued in situations of distrust and contest between members of the same social stratum. It confirmed, on the one hand, the loyalty of the dependants who 'do not keep anything hidden' from the patron, as the Spanish proverb goes, establishing relations of trust between the partners to the relationship, while, on the other hand, making it possible to cement the patron's position vis-à-vis other powerful persons at the local level. Similarly, the advice given by a patron was highly appreciated, not only because of its instrumental value but also as a sign of friendship and close personal links. The *pueblos*, where these relationships were contracted, were highly stratified communities. Political power and, usually, wealth were intensely concentrated there and large-scale property of latifundia was supplemented by small-scale peasant techniques and labour arrangements. The peasantry was increasingly short of land, 'proletarised' and cross-cutting occupational commitments were usual, and the latifundists let very small plots to peasants for cultivation on a wide variety of terms. Violence and social strife were common in the *pueblos*, but class rebellion was infrequent. Thus, occupational identities and stratification did not become the basis either for internal cleavage or for the organisation of clubs or parties. This trend was common to both the lower strata and the ruling group. Even if some standards of conduct were shared, the power group was divided and involved in struggles to maintain control and wealth. People were prone to conceptualise the members of their society in terms of the degree to which they were abiding by the local codes of moral behaviour, such as the generosity that was expected from responsible wealthy members of the community. Thus, the *pueblo* was seen as a moral community which comprised the local (often native) inhabitants as opposed to other *pueblos* (or even the 'people' of the nation–state as opposed to other nations).

Kinship ties were reckoned bilaterally and were strong only within the nuclear family. Beyond it, ties were optional and usually too weak to foster cooperation and allegiance, except in the cases of cousin marriages among both tenants and landowners, where property sometimes provided such an incentive.

These networks of clientelism at the local level were mobilised in the countryside during the Franco period, when the government had a highly centralised bureaucratic structure and applied authoritarian policies demanding submission to regulative and taxing measures. In parts of central and southern Spain, the political centre was looked upon with distrust and regarded as predatory. Its policies were seen as favouring a parasitic hierarchy of functionaries or, at least, as exceeding the capabilities (of tax payment, etc.) of the local communities. Political authority derived from the centre was viewed as dangerous and immoral because of its impersonality and its lack of commitment to the moral values of the *pueblo*.* Accordingly, the so-called 'parallel power structure'[40] of patrons and brokers induced the ordinary *vecino* to call upon them for assistance in evading or softening the impact of these policies.

Under such conditions, people tended to approach potential patrons in an attempt to establish a 'friendship-like' relationship. The poor were often precluded from entertaining such a diffuse relationship with powerful local leaders. If the patron was successfully approached, an informal link was contracted that involved mutual liking (*simpatía*) and mutual service, and was said to constitute also a source of emotional and economic security. The lack of formality often induced constant public declarations and demonstrations to the effect that the link was alive, to obviate any doubts that might otherwise arise.

At the same time, these networks characterised by clusters of dyadic relations were increasingly linked to wider institutional frameworks, such as the bureaucracy. In the mountain communities, which were more isolated, some of these networks retained their dispersed structure, especially when the central political forces did not need the wide support of the inhabitants and – as during the Franco period – chose

---

* The local people expressed these attitudes by romanticising, for instance, the figure of the bandit who, by being the helper of the poor to the detriment of the wealthy, symbolised defiance to the State in spite of the fact that bandits in rural areas were often, indeed, associated with landowners.

merely to coopt the local patrons as part of the administrative organisation of the government in these peripheral areas. Such policies, which
we may describe as encapsulative, did not lead to the reshaping of the
dispersed structure of these networks. In other, more central, areas,
such as urban settings, the clusters were linked to clientelistic networks
close to the centre. In such cases, the authoritarian policies of the
Franco centre attempted to modify the dynamics of the political sphere,
where allegiance was demanded, as well as of the economic sphere,
where strong developmental pressures were fostered, even if no
attempt was made to implement such policies at the expense of the
traditional elites. In these spheres or institutional markets, attempts
were made, especially by members of the bureaucratic officialdom, to
control and mediate. In this case, the proximity of potential patrons to
loci of power – and especially to the head of the State, the so-called *Jefe
máximo*, and his ministers and to the reflection of their authority on
lower levels – was a central factor in building power domains.

III

These relations were reinforced, particularly in the rural areas, by local
conceptions of appropriate social behaviour. In Spain, where to submit
one's will to the commands of another person might be interpreted as a
humiliation, the fact of being related to a powerful and socially
outstanding patron obviated this dishonour and added to the dependant's social prestige when he manipulated some of the power derived
from his patron vis-à-vis other poor people to his advantage. Generosity on the part of the patron became a point of honour. In addition,
clients felt obliged to voice and demonstrate their loyalty to their
patron, and this created goodwill among the partners and added to the
latter's social prestige.

Similarly, such relations were established with the Virgin or patron
saints, who were supposed to be empowered to grant favours to
believers who asked for them and promised repayment should their
requests be granted. The favours asked might have been to find and
keep a loved one, for success in economic enterprises and activities, for
recovery from illness, etc. Pilgrimages, penances, donations or the
placing of ex-votos and candles at shrines of the patron saint were some
of the forms taken by the believers' gratitude for a granted favour or for
the intercession of the saint before God the Father.

This parallelism of patron–client relations in the secular and religious
spheres was further evident in the intermingling of clientelistic with
ritual spiritual relations, namely *compadrazgo*, sanctioned by the Catholic Church and implying a sacred duty. Thus, patrons were asked by a

dependant or a 'friend' (once it was known that the ties between them were 'reliable') to agree to sponsor the baptism of the client's son, which symbolised the entrance of the child's soul into the Church. By acting as godparent, the *padrino* endorsed responsibility for the spiritual and social welfare of the *ahijado*. This imposed on him the obligation to give presents at ritual occasions as, for instance, at the First Communion, to care for and guide the child during his school years, to help him to enter a career or job, to give him advice when he contemplated marriage, etc. These deeds were considered as an act of grace, adding to the social prestige of the patron. At the same time, spiritual and natural parents became *compadres* – that is, ritual kin committed to helping each other, being joined in an unalienable relationship of absolute trust. These egalitarian potentialities of the relationship, however, were not automatically realised. Often, the basic relationship of say a landowner and his worker did not change but the ritual link added a moral base either to the submissiveness of the client or to the superiority of the patron, cementing a reliable and respectful relationship. This was evidenced in patterns of interpersonal address, the granting and repayment of loans, peaceful compliance with each other's demands, etc.

These moral overtones of such *compadrazgo* ties led, perhaps, to the use of the terms of address and reference of *compadrazgo* in the secular forms of clientelism, in which a ritual commitment was not contracted. Thus, the term *padrino* in Andalusia also meant any powerful person who was prepared either himself to adopt the role of patron to a poor man or to *apadrinar* him in contacting governmental offices, by giving him, for instance, a letter of recommendation or his personal card on which he would express the high personal interest he had in the bearer and his greetings and assurances of friendship to the addressee of the card. Similarly, in Old Castile, protectors or benefactors have often been referred to as *compadres*.

Greece[41]

Under the multisecular Ottoman rule of Greek territories, the language and the Orthodox Christian faith remained the central elements defining membership of the Hellenic community, which was spread over the Empire and specialised in commerce. The Turkish rulers were unable to enforce public peace within the actual boundaries of Greece, and unrest and violence plagued the agricultural plains, carried on by bands of fighters (*klefts*) living in impoverished, sheep- and goat-breeding mountain villages. Even though life in these villages was difficult because of the scarcity of fertile land and the pressures on the local resources in order to secure livelihood, they still attracted a steady flow of peasants. These were seeking the relative security the villages provided, especially during periods of banditry in the eighteenth century and the subsequent wars of revolt and independence.

In the 1820s, Greece emerged as an independent state. It progressively added to its territories, and for the first time the majority of Greeks lived within its boundaries. The characteristics of the new nation comprised: a high rate of mobility in the economic and political spheres; a lack of commitment and of deference and obedience generally due to official position and rank; and a prevalence of mistrust towards the formal government. The nation was furthermore constituted by an agricultural society with great differences in its stratification but lacking a landed aristocracy (if only because the majority of the Greek soil was poor and had for long been unsuited to large-scale production of cereals), the dominant feature being a peasantry organised in tightly-knit nuclear families striving to produce for the market and competing with one another for the most profitable exchanges with outsiders.

The adoption of Western European forms of government and the long-standing cultural dependence of local elites on outside models of administration moulded the formal rules of contest over the access to positions of power even if it did not affect the realities of power itself. Thus, from that point, Greece came to be characterised by a centre which tended to avoid the formal delegation of authority, by a bureaucracy lacking effective power at low levels of the administration, by a tendency to interpret flexibly the law, as well as by the control of distant communities through complex, overlapping and often conflicting agencies and regulations, and by the weak impingement of peripheral social forces mostly through extractive policies of taxation and military recruiting.

Networks of politicians and their followings competed for the particularistic appropriation of state jobs and resources. These networks were headed by party patrons and their close clients in the rural areas, such as local lawyers and politicians, heads of prominent 'notable' families or merchants with influence among the villagers. The parties and other organisations were regarded by the people as a means to gain particularistic access to resources rather than as an instrument of articulation or aggregation.

In this connection, the bureaucracy was and still is penetrated by political clientelistic networks. Administrative requests could be granted through intercession with top political leaders or through connections with bureaucrats, either direct or mediated by urban 'expeditors', that is, by people who specialised in obtaining routine decisions from governmental offices, where they knew the 'right' persons and the steps to be taken to beat the intricacies of the administration.

To abide by the rules and let officialdom work its will unassisted seems to most Greeks a mark of stupidity or laziness. Things just do not get done that way, and everybody knows it. It is up to each man to make his mark by activating the network of friends and acquaintances he has been able to create, to get the services and permissions needed for whatever business he wishes to pursue. Anything else is simply self-defeating. Such behaviour, well enough attuned to a village or small town in which everybody knows everybody else . . . successfully survived Athens' tremendous growth and showed no signs of faltering in 1976. No one who has lived there for any length of time doubts that the most important transactions of everyday life occur at this personalized level, and are only registered and ratified by official, formal enactment afterwards.[42]

In Athens and Salonika, underemployment and unemployment are common; there is intensive competition for the available positions in the service sector, as Greek industrial plants cannot absorb the great flow of rural migrants, and because the short working hours in the bureaucracy permit the seeking of spare-time occupations; but, even if granted a governmental position in the bureaucracy, the public servant has grounds (perhaps due to the precarious financial returns from such positions) for manipulating his role in order to add other sources of income to his recognised salary. In such a manner, the State and its organs have come to be perceived as unresponsive to universalistic demands. Allocation of resources is carried out without regard to programmatic priorities, and the broader strata consider that to deceive the State is evidence of 'cleverness'. As indicated by W.H. McNeill, 'from a Greek point of view, such regulations [i.e. the regulations of the State], whenever they happened to interfere with individual and family self-interest, were obstacles to be overcome, not rules to be obeyed'.[43] Accordingly, for a long time, authority was not challenged but avoided, or was approached through a local patron or broker with access to party and governmental leaders, and thereby exemptions, personal favours, etc., were obtained. At the same time, government leaders saw legislation as a means of increasing or creating political resources, which were useful for the satisfaction of particularistic demands.

Competing political networks of 'cliques, clubs, and small groups of notables' have been found not only along party lines but also across them, and changes of allegiance have been usual. Parties were coalitions of factions interested in securing a ministerial position, especially until the Second World War but also thereafter. Unless a leader succeeded in this attempt, his personal power was suddenly diminished as his supporters deserted him for more auspicious and successful brokers and patrons. At such higher political and administrative levels, volatility of support and sudden shifts of alignment have been the rule. Disappointments and defections also characterised the relations of deputies and ministers with heads of government and political patrons, over the question of the granting of favours and preferential access to positions.

Despite the huge process or urbanisation of Greece, a great part of the active population lived and still lives on agriculture, pastoralism and fishing, mostly at subsistence levels. Peasants and communities of shepherds, such as the Sarakatsani of the Epirus region studied by J.K. Campbell, have been only marginally incorporated in the national polity. Internally, they lacked corporate organisations and categorial representative institutions. A deep distrust and moral indifference characterised the relations between people unrelated by kinship or affinity, preventing the setting up of effective cooperation. While competing for social prestige in terms of a shared value system concerned with ideas of honour, pride and toughness, social actors saw the interests of unrelated families as opposed and mutually destructive. Shepherds such as the Sarakatsani owned no land, and the numbers of head of sheep owned by single households rendered it uneconomic for them to set up their own cheese-making stations. They therefore engaged in associations with specific merchants. Those merchants were the source of credit for the landless shepherds, who needed advances in cash to obtain administrative certificates that gave them the right to keep their flocks and produce. They also needed small loans to enable them to face their family emergencies, to improve their individual holdings, to purchase manufactured goods and to repay officially granted loans. To obtain those loans as well as support in their dealings with government officials and the village authorities, Sarakatsani tried to enter into special relationships with merchants and to reinforce these relations in terms of spiritual kinship (*kumbaros*), friendship, or at least the provision of gifts. To achieve this aim, they had to command a following in their own community, i.e. they had to be *tselingas*, leaders of kith-and-kin networks, to which end they competed among themselves. They became so indebted to merchants that they were discouraged from borrowing the sums necessary to pay the rent or to purchase equipment to turn their own milk into marketable cheese. Furthermore, products had to be sold in urban markets, mainly in Athens, and shepherds lacked the facilities and knowledge to do so, and this strengthened the merchants' monopoly on the marketing of produce of a certain area. The dependence of the *tselingatos* had consequences for the conversion of social power within the political market. Local patrons were 'supported' by the voting allegiance of the

Basic characteristics of patron–client relations

tselingas, their families and kinsmen, affines and friends. This allowed the patron to command in a monopolistic manner contacts with civil servants, members of parliament, and other politicians.[44]

PATRON–CLIENT RELATIONS IN THE MUSLIM MIDDLE EAST

The Middle East is characterised by several singular developments and traits. First, until relatively recently, it has retained its traditional economic and political structures despite its being located in geopolitical proximity to Europe; second, the region had a long-established predominance of Islamic and Arabic traits and culture; and, third, only in the last decades has it attained political independence both from Ottoman rule and from the subsequent Western domination and engaged in an accelerated process of nation-building, partly generated by Arab nationalist intellectuals and political elites inspired by or revolting against the European concepts of nation–state building.

These common traits are supplemented by strong national and transnational, religious, ethnic and cultural splits and tensions, as evident, for instance, in the struggle of the Sunni Kurds in Shiite Iran and in Iraq or of the Alevis in Turkey, or in war-torn Lebanon. The transnational character of Islam also poses peculiar problems for the states of this area, while at the same time the economic and political structuring of these countries has changed considerably in the nineteenth and twentieth centuries, above all under the impact of incorporation into the European economic system.

From an economic perspective, cash crops (such as cotton, tobacco and opium) have, since the early nineteenth century, replaced subsistence agriculture and, instead of extensive methods, intensive farming has been progressively used. The existence of greater agricultural surpluses had induced the emergence of new forms of commerce, banking and services. Barter has been replaced by a widening use of money in exchanges, and markets have been enlarged. Population has grown as a result of the introduction of Western medical knowledge and facilities, and the region has been increasingly incorporated within the traditional world division of labour. This fact has contributed to the decadence of traditional crafts and to their replacement by imported manufactured products from Europe, to a widened differentiation and stratification, and to the rise of urban centres and the transfer of nomadic populations there. Nevertheless, these changes have not altered the predominantly agricultural (and, later, extractive – when relating to oil production) character of the economies until relatively recent times. Indeed, save for the partial exception of Iran and Turkey, which industrialised their economies after the First World War under

81

the impulse of their central elites, most countries initiated such processes of diversification of their economies only after the Second World War period. Most of these countries show, even today, the predominance of primary sector activities in their occupational and productive structure, along with the more recent development of the tertiary sector. Thus, while declining, the proportion of the population engaged in agricultural activities was, in the mid-1970s about 56% in Egypt, Turkey and Iran and 48% and 40% in Algeria and Lebanon respectively.*

Urbanisation was unplanned and was mainly the result of a stagnant agrarian structure. It was not accompanied by the opening of new occupational opportunities in the overpopulated cities, where services to the growing population were, and to a considerable degree are still, lacking. The rate of illiteracy is very high up to the present time, ranging from about 35% in Lebanon and Turkey to about 60% in Iran and Egypt, and approaching 80% to 90% in Saudi Arabia, North Yemen, Libya and Sudan.

These countries also differ widely in their political structure, ranging from electoral polities (some of them multi-party as in Turkey or Lebanon, where this fact coincides with religious and other partisan splits) to parliamentary authoritarian regimes as in Egypt and Tunisia, and to autocratic polities as in Libya, Kuwait and Saudi Arabia. In fact, during the greater part of their existence, most have been independent states with single-party polities. In most countries, military officers have been major political actors either participating directly in the centre, as in Libya or Algeria, or constituting the main support of the regime, as in Jordan or Saudi Arabia. Beyond these and other differences, the force of 'personalism' (that is, the relevance of the personal traits of the rulers and main political actors – from eloquence to courage to the Arab *baraka* or especial grace, charisma) was long recognised and still remains a major trait of Middle Eastern life. This is paralleled, at

* There are differences in the economic–demographic balance in the countries of this area. Some, like Saudi Arabia, have sparse populations and oil-rich desert resources, and are trying to modernise their economic structures – mainly by attracting foreign specialised, as well as unqualified, labour force, while attempting to withstand the pressures towards political modernisation. Other nations, like Iran, Algeria and Iraq, have dualistic economic structures, in which a sophisticated oil-producing sector generates the major part of the national revenues while employing only a limited labour force. The agricultural and industrial sectors, which offer most of the occupational opportunities, lag behind in their development and modernisation. A third pattern is evident in Egypt, Turkey and Sudan where strong population pressure is brought to bear on the economic resources and which opted for development based on foreign investments (due to their lack of oil reserves), industrialisation and rural change. Finally, countries such as Syria, Jordan, Lebanon, Tunisia and Morocco are not densely populated and have industrialised their economies at various rates.

Basic characteristics of patron–client relations

various levels of society, by the widespread existence in this area of different forms of clientelistic relations.

Thus, a kind of *smiyya* (reputational), paternalistic and protective relationship was found in the case of the Egyptian *futuwwa as ibn-el-balad*, who protected the neighbourhood from external powers and threats. In the case of the Lebanese, it was the *muqata'ji*, whose power, strength and traditional position were sustained by the support and loyalty of his followers, or *atba'*. In northern Iraq, networks known as *al-taba'iyya* predominated, clusters of clients (*ra'iyya*) and their families being linked to patrons in order to obtain protection, benefits and social standing. In all these cases, there was a social and political identification of clients with the social position of the patron, which was 'reflected' in them.

Instrumentally oriented patterns of such relations were reported for the links existing between Iraqi *Sa'adi* landowners and Shabak tribesmen, and for the Jordanian *murabi* link, whereby individuals of very different status were related in a manner that lacked moral overtones. Politically oriented patterns have been described in the case of the patronage by appointed notables (*a'yan*) in Ottoman Iltizam, in which warlords, aristocratic chiefs and notables were invested with governmental authority to apply the law and to be the representatives of the formal government at the village level. More closely associated with the patron's patronymic group's reputation (and less oppressive, though instrumentally biased) were the patron–client relations that emerged around Turkish *aghas* in eastern Turkey.

In other cases, there were brokers whose power depended on their close relationship to powerful political entrepreneurs, as the *makhātir* in relation to the *zu'ama* leaders in Lebanon. Violent entrepreneurship characterised the Egyptian *futuwwat as baltagi*, who exploited and abused the people of some Cairo quarters by the use of force and by inducing fear, and the Lebanese *qabadayat* who were used by *zu'ama* to demonstrate muscle in political meetings, campaigning activities and in the guarding of quarters and who tended to maintain their own followings.

Shillal circles of friends seem to proliferate in the bureaucratic authoritarian polities of Egypt and Tunisia. These circles involve multiple actors who act intermittently as sponsors and sponsored in order to advance or to be promoted in the bureaucracy.

Lebanese *zu'ama* seem sometimes to have acted as traditional patrons. They were generous with their time, influence and wealth towards the people of their districts and provided minor administrative and judicial services. Beyond this level, they may have played central roles in the election of candidates to political offices and fostered the

83

establishment of complex organisational networks of clientelism within the framework of the modern Lebanese state.

But even in traditional settings the relations of patronage and clientelistic networks have not been confined to a single institutional level but have rather pervaded the whole structure of society, as is evident in the case of Morocco. There, the sultans and later the kings acted as 'great patrons', balancing opposed actors, arbitrating, mediating and fostering factionalism and personal allegiance among elites and their followers.

Several traits seem to have been particularly emphasised in the clientelistic relationships found in the Middle East. Among them stands out, first, a relatively strong stress on patrons' personal identity and personal abilities and on individual actions rather than on the patrons' capability as incumbents of administrative offices. This was even evident when their performance was primarily related to such incumbency. Second, a similarly strong emphasis was placed on force and its potential for 'good' and 'bad' uses, these being defined in terms of ties of the solidarity or non-solidarity which patrons and brokers were willing to maintain with their followings. Third, in many instances, and especially in traditional settings, patrons manipulated images of potential (real or assumed) reliance on broader kinship groups based on patronymy, etc. Fourth, religious prestige or activities tended to be a source of clientelistic power domains, when political 'native' secular power was weak, as in the case of *marabout*, in pre-protectorate Morocco, or of members of the ʿulamā in eighteenth-century Cairo.

Some of these instances of clientelism are presented in detail below.

Turkey[45]

Within the Ottoman Empire, clientelistic networks were found at the local level around the 'great family' *aghas* (chiefs) in the rural districts, especially in the eastern part of Turkey. The *aghas* were powerful local leaders who controlled such basic sources of livelihood as land, and maintained a hold over such offices as village headmen (*mukhtar*) and over the few associations that existed in the countryside, such as agricultural cooperative action-groups or mosque-building projects. At the same time, their power and influence depended on their ability to consolidate extensive networks of followers comprising kinsmen and allies. The efforts of the Ottoman rulers, after 1850, to undermine their power and replace them by appointed bureaucrats were unsuccessful, especially in the eastern agrarian areas around the Black Sea.

These leaders derived their influence from the support of their respective large patronymic groups, and their power was associated with the latter's reputation and prestige. The *aghas*, however, were not the incumbents of an institutionalised office of leadership in a system of clear-cut corporate descent groups, but were, rather, leaders of unstable and informal alliances, largely but not exclusively composed of people accepting real or fictive (*kivrelik*) ties. Indeed, the patronymic groups of the area were not corporate units, in the sense of controlling property, of being associated to a specific territory or of being exclus- ively involved in marriage exchanges and blood vengeance and pay- ments. Moreover, they did not participate in common ritual ceremonies, nor did they assemble regularly for any purpose. The boundaries between these groups and their alliances were ill defined and were established and redefined ever anew. The *aghas* were the leaders who, through their activities, eventually led to the emergence and mobilisation of these quasi-groups, with a kith-and-kin character, and including kinsmen, related by patronymic ties, together with non-kin followings.

Within their power domains, *aghas* performed a wide variety of services for the villagers, such as interceding on their behalf with the administration, protecting them from police harassment, lending them sums of money to be repaid in kind or in seeds, giving them oxen, flour or tools, allowing them credit facilities in their shops in the neighbour- ing towns, and acting as guarantors for them when they were granted agricultural credits, etc. In return, the *aghas* benefited by instrumental and political gains, mainly through using the clientelistic support of kith and kin to increase their holdings at the expense of opposing networks.

In assessing the content of the relationship, people differentiated between 'good' and 'bad' *aghas*. A good *agha* was one who was concerned with protecting the local people, with maintaining order and religion, honour and piety, while abiding by the rules of hospitality and generosity. A bad *agha* relied more heavily on coercion. Tradi- tionally, these types of patron–client relations assumed, in some cases, religious or 'saintly' connotations, as in the case of *sheikhs* with control over lands. Their relations with followers were similar to those described for other *aghas*, though a strong emphasis was placed on salvation, as an integral part of the package deal. Elements of loyalty and obedience were prerequisites in these ties, as well as rendering instrumental services to the *sheikh*, such as collecting funds or donating labour.

During the one-party Kemalist regime, *aghas* enjoyed a monopolistic control over public offices in eastern Turkey but, as they were not an extension of the central government, their hold was weakened with the introduction of national policies and the strengthening of the formal organisation of the district administration, and people increasingly thought that new forms of leadership were possible. This control was further transformed by the transition to a multi-party electoral system in 1946, and with the introduction of cash crops, government investments, the establishment of new sources of livelihood – such as employment in governmental factories – and the organisation of agricultural cooperatives, as well as the possibility of migration to urban centres.

These processes brought about, first, a change in the market positions of patrons and clients. Thus, while the 'great family' *aghas* continued – until the recent banning of electoral politics – effectively to mobilise popular support in the countryside, they had to employ new strategies in their power domains. *Aghas* began to 'consult' with their followers on different matters and presented themselves as the spokesmen for the 'little' men, notwithstanding the fact that they continued to rely also on force and threats. Thus, clients gained some bargaining power, even in the less developed regions, such as eastern Turkey, and more balanced terms of trade tended to emerge.

Second, with the transition to the competitive multi-party system, political connections came to play a more significant role in building local power domains. Clientelistic networks on the periphery were increasingly related to parties and wider institutional frames, and the resources controlled by the administration were more extensively used to build networks at the local level. Some governmental programmes – such as making roads, drilling drinking-water wells, building schools and mosques, electricity or irrigation projects – became available as 'pork-barrel inducements'. Others, such as agricultural credits, employment, official contracts or preferential administrative treatment, were open to individual particularistic access through patrons or brokers.

Clientelistic networks became less localised and more linked to wider institutional frames. Thus, existing local factions were transformed into local sections of the national party, and the existing clientelistic networks were politicised. To the national party leaders, the relevance of local patrons was greatly increased, as they were necessary in order to gather votes at elections. Many local patrons were given office as mayors and municipal council members, while others became members of parliament.

In the more developed regions, the clientelistic networks of notables were replaced by party-directed clientelism. Thus, networks became more mutually related and integrated in a chain-to-centre structure, and more dependent on the hold that the different political organisations – the power of which was enhanced by patrons – had over the resources controlled and derived by the administrative organs of the Turkish centre. Businessmen, traders and professionals became brokers within the framework of such modern parties as the Democratic Party (D.P.), besides the more bureaucratic cadres of the rival Republicans.

In urban settings, party activists of the D.P. or the Justice Party (J.P.) helped the new rural-born migrants to settle down, to deal with the authorities, to find employment and even to marry. 'A particularly powerful weapon in the hands of the party controlling the municipal government is to tolerate, or even legalise, the illegal squatter houses (*gacekondu*) of the new urban migrants, or to demolish them by strictly implementing the laws.'[46]

In the eastern provinces, while the clientelistic ties were based on similar linkages to wider institutional frames, the networks retained their dispersed character, and the influential patrons the allegiance of their personal followings. These patrons often transferred their followings at will, as they switched parties in the political sphere. Such patterns, therefore, differed in their structure from the more organisationally based brokerage described above, in which networks became related by chain-to-centre links to these formal organisational frames. In both cases, however, a majority of the rural voters expected legislators to render them local or personal services in a particularistic manner.

The country's economic difficulties, along with the greater importance attached to broader political and economic issues – contrasting with the popular cynicism and distrust of the politicians' clientelism as a coherent policy – recently induced the military officers to take the power into their own hands in order to implement more developmental priorities.

But it is, as yet, too early to determine whether these changes will undermine the widespread presence of clientelistic intercession and mediation in Turkey.

Indeed, such forms of mediation are also found in other Middle Eastern areas such as northern Iraq, Lebanon and Jordan.

Jordan[47]

In contemporary Jordan, a *wastah* ('go-between') is sought in order to obtain such instrumental benefits and services as not to be cheated in the market place, locating or securing a job, resolving conflicts and legal litigations, winning a lawsuit, speeding up administrative decisions and bureaucratic procedures, finding a bride, etc. A *wastah* act by a mayor can aim at gaining gratitude which, eventually, will be translated into votes during the municipal elections. *Wastah* activities can be motivated by a sense of obligation to repay favours or to meet a moral commitment, as well as by the desire to create a sense of obligation in the receivers of the benefits. Mostly, *wastahs* do not have control over primary resources but have connections and knowledge of the relational and procedural rules for dealing with the administration or other institutional frameworks.

The *wastahs'* effective control over situations depends on their position within the broader system. Therefore, a concentration of *wastahs* at the village level is found among the members of the *majlis*, or municipal council, whose function is to promote road construction, electricity and water services, control food prices, inspect merchandise, ensure that taxes are paid and, in fact, act as mediators to broader institutional frameworks.

As the intercessions of *wastahs* do not create an enduring tie between the seeker and the granter of mediation, no assurances are offered or sanctions imposed to enforce repayment of assistance in the future. In the social hierarchy, the need to rely on a mediator is differently present. For instance, if a peasant wanted to approach a mayor, he would have to present an introduction by a *wastah* or to appear in the company of his mediator in order to have his request dealt with. An officer or soldier does not have to be accompanied by a *wastah*. Opters-out of the security forces, especially the educated ones, do not usually ask the rural mayor or another member of the *majlis* to act on their behalf as they have more useful contacts in town. But if they must ask for a favour, they will need a *wastah* in order to approach the mayor. Indeed, these people criticise the *majlis*'s members for their particularistic use of the municipal funds and want changes to be brought about in the traditional structure. Nevertheless, they often continue to rely on *wastah* intercessions, even if these are used mainly beyond the village level.

Northern Iraq[48]

In northern Iraq, these forms of intercession are related to the functioning of clientelistic networks around notables in the cities (*wajahas*) or the *aghawat* chiefs of nomadic or semi-nomadic tribes who live in Mosul for the greater part of the year. Patrons protect their clients (*taba'iyyat*), serve as mediators between them and the agents of the State, or any other potential exploiter, influence high-level decisions that may affect their clients, etc. In return, they obtain personal services and goods, free domestic labour or seasonal gifts and are assured of loyal voting and general support. Patrons belong to the traditional urban upper class, which is referred to collectively as *wujaha* – those who have 'social visibility'. The patron, accordingly, is the *wajh* of his client as 'it is [he] who confers social recognition and visibility on the faceless and socially insignificant client'.[49] Patrons can perform such mediation since, at the weekly *mājlis* (open house), they exchange information, gossip and solve with other notables, merchants, friends, followers, etc., problems of common interest.

Over a period of time, this relationship has changed from an all-comprehensive, religiously sanctioned dependency. It has become more specific and instrumental and commitments are more tenuous, involving a freer selection of patrons and intercessors. But these changes were not a simple consequence of economic transformations. Thus, in rural northern Iraq, landless peasants became independent farmers, encouraged by land reform laws (1958 and 1963) and by agrarian cooperatives. They continued, however, to rely on their former landlords for obtaining credit, guidance and help, and looked upon government agents with caution. Dependency was increased and patrons were favoured vis-à-vis clients in their market positions.

The rapid environmental transformations and the shifting policies of the centre accentuated the clients' feeling of helplessness. They turned to the *Sada* and other prominent families for assistance, on the assumption that the latter commanded influence with the government. The pattern, however, changed, bringing its brokerage character into relief. The educated members of the *muftis'* families helped *Shabaks* to cope with the new bureaucratic administration's needs and demands, such as getting a son into high school or registering a plot of land, etc.

Particular stresses existed in this and other ethnically complex areas, when cultural ethnic cleavages occurred due to the patrons' or the clients' identities. When this was the case, as with Christian peasants and Muslim landowners in northern Iraq, the cleavages formed a source of strain that turned into violent strife, in conditions of change and mobilisation.

Egypt[50]

I

The patterns already described contrast with some of the links found in Egypt or Tunisia. In Ottoman Cairo, some members of the ʿ*ulamā* seem to have been *sheikhs* who dominated patron–client networks among specific groups of the population. They had material wealth and, what was more important, strong social ties both with the rulers and with specific portions of the population. They arbitrated their clients' disputes and protected them from the oppression of the Mameluk and Ottoman rulers and their soldiers. At the same time, clients conferred social 'visibility' upon patrons and were used by them to gain political predominance over their peers. The more extensive and stronger their clientele network was, the greater became the importance of the *ʿālim* (patron) in the eyes of the Mameluk or Ottoman ruler.

Similar ties were also maintained by more secular leaders of Cairo neighbourhoods, who became known as *futuwwat*. The *futuwwat* were leaders, arbitrators and patrons in the different *hitta* (quarters) of Cairo. They flourished when the state controls over market conditions or working services were weak, and the central power was not legitimised as it had been during the French, non-Muslim, occupation.

Futuwwat held traditional, profitable jobs as butchers, coffee-house owners, dealers in foodstuffs or soap merchants. Their closer supporters (the *subim* or 'boys') were often their apprentices or dependants. Other clients relied on them for arbitration and access to scarce commodities such as oil and petrol in the *hitta*, for protection from thieves, and as guardians of ceremonials from attacks by outsiders or from quarrels. A *futuwwa* was accorded prestige and recognition as the leader of a quarter or *hitta*. He enforced decisions by coercion, broke up or temporarily closed shops and streets and his *gadaʿ* (manliness and bravery) was praised and given mythical lyric form in the literature. The term *futuwwa* became a synonym of generosity, courage and protection of the weak and the poor. The *futuwwat* were in constant opposition to each other in order to assert their supremacy. They maintained antagonistic relations, and conflict was common as a means of eliminating each other from their power domains.

Futuwwat were considered to be part of the population (*ibn el-balad*), associated with the common people. Their image was that of men maintaining the social structures and of guardians of morality, creating as well minimal conditions of trust in the neighbourhood. The protective character of their links with the population was modified under the existing conditions of migration to Cairo, overpopulation and poverty, together with the changes occurring in the wage-earning capacity of traditional occupations.

Futuwwat became known as *baltagi*, brutal men who based their power more on the support of jobless people, and used force or induced fear, accepted payment for beating-up an opponent, spoiling a ceremony or closing a shop. These new forms of brokerage were no longer based on local ties of solidarity and legitimation.

II

Under the bureaucratic authoritarian political system of modern Egypt (as also in Tunisia), government offices were valuable sources of personal security and steady income. Capability alone did not ensure access to office, nor bureaucratic seniority; this created a need to rely on powerful protectors and personal connections 'to beat the seniority system'. However, once these objectives were reached, the employees kept their ranks and salaries even if they were eventually dismissed or prevented from working in their offices. Thus, tenured offices were converted into some kind of private domain. Clients became no more than 'clients of the system', in C.H. Moore's words. Instead of vertical intra-bureaucratic clientelistic networks, the relative lack of vulnerability of officials seems to have fostered the emergence of *shillal*, transient circles of friends who were placed in different ministries and public companies (especially in the lucrative fields of contracting), which provided their employees and members with bureaucratic support and economic revenue from public funds at the expense of the public.

Lebanon[51]

The Ottoman principality (*imārah*) of Mount Lebanon was ruled in the late eighteenth and early nineteenth centuries by *muqataʿji* families. These held political authority over districts in which they collected taxes, maintained peace and order, implemented the Ottoman labour exactions from the peasantry and acted as judges. They depended formally on the local ruler known as *Amir el-Hakim*, who arbitrated among the *muqataʿji* and satisfied the demands of the *pasha* who was the Ottoman representative. On the other hand, the *muqataʿji* based their legitimacy on personal allegiance on the part of the peasantry, rather than on coercive obedience or impersonal military duties. They lived among the villagers and their power and wealth depended on their followings of *atbaʿ* or *ʿuhda* (clients), whose support was mobilised to ward off Ottoman rulers from their traditional jurisdictions. Hereditary patrilineal ascendancy reinforced the sovereignty of these *muqataʿji*, because patrons who were known to be backed by numerous kin members gained credibility as protectors of the local residents. Relative ecological isolation, linguistic and social divisions and local village loyalties led people to rely on *muqataʿji* to obtain protection from the distant *pashas* and *amirs*, who exacted corvée labour and taxes or 'arbitrary' conscription.

Indeed, the main obligation of the *muqataʿji* towards their *ʿuhda* was defined as 'to tend and protect' them, while the strength of their followings was the means by which integrity and position could be maintained in the *imārah*, especially as the *muqataʿji* were involved in contests over power or over the rulers' favour during the nineteenth century. *Muqataʿji* also gained ceremonial deference and gifts; and, when collecting taxes for the Ottoman rulers, they extracted additional sums for their own benefit. For their part, the *muqataʿji* armed followers and maintained them during war periods. The link existing between *muqataʿji* and followers was defined as *amiyyah*, that is, 'taking another man's name'. The name of the *muqataʿji's* house was used to define the dependent's place in society and, socially and politically, the resident was identified as an adherent of a certain *muqataʿji*; this conferred upon the relation a high degree of exclusivity in comparison with other clientelistic networks. *Muqataʿji* referred to followers as *nāsunā* ('our men'). These power domains were not established on a religious basis.

Several efforts were made, after 1820, to undermine the localised power domains of such *sheikhs*; these either failed or were used by the latter to strengthen their position, as in the case of the organisation of local councils of *majlis*.

The *mutasarrifyah* administration (1860–1920) divided Lebanon into districts and introduced the election of councils, the members of which were the notables with whom the authorities entered into agreements, granting them administrative positions. Accordingly, clientelistic networks became centred on linkages with the bureaucratic realm, and some patrons became political leaders. Lawyers and governmental officials, closest to the formal administration, became increasingly important as foci for clientelistic approaches. Under the electoral political system and the development of a democratic urban society, the people were either partially unemployed or employed in the service sector and in commercial and financial capitalism. Patrons holding an administrative position and/or having commercial and financial contacts were helpful in interceding with public officials. These intercessions on behalf of their clients were made with a view to obtaining government concessions, public works contracts, employment in governmental and private sectors, promotion in professional careers and within the civil service, the grant of free or cheap public education, medical treatment, or special protection from implementation of the law. Within the framework of the Lebanese State, these resources were mostly derived from the holding by patrons or by their close clients of offices such as a seat in the Lebanese Chamber of Deputies, or as ministers, and through these offices, their gaining control over civil service appointments, jurisdictive competence and allocation of public funds.

Basic characteristics of patron–client relations

These high-level political leaders, known as *zuʿama* (plural of *zaʿim*), struggled bitterly among themselves, mainly in the urban areas, for a hold on the state resources, and their position depended on the extension of their clientelistic support.

At the local level, *zuʿama* relied on the political brokerage of *makhātir*, or on powerful bosses in urban quarters, known as *qabadayat*. *Makhātir* were political agents who sought out the needs of people of the middle and lower strata (the higher stratum approaching *zuʿama* without intermediaries). The *makhātir* offered these people a means of access to a certain *zaʿim* who could resolve their problems, or persuaded them to consult the *zaʿim* by themselves. *Qabadayat* were local strongmen, often of humble background and connected with traditional occupations involving entrepreneurial activities (often semi-legal or illegal), with a reputation for manliness and fearlessness and commanding influence in the neighbourhood. Occupationally, they were shop-keepers, butchers, taxi-drivers, petrol station owners, small businessmen, port workers, contractors or bodyguards. Many were involved in such activities as protection, racketeering or hashish smuggling. The people had a proclivity to idealise the role of the *qabadayat*, affirming that the latter only wished to protect the local residents, to guard their honour and to defend the poor. Indeed, the *qabadayat's* main interest was to assert their position of power vis-à-vis the other local bosses and aspirants. Due to their tendency to use force and coercion, to their ability to influence the electorate, and to their intimate knowledge of local solidarities, they were sought by *zuʿama* to serve as their political brokers. As such, they recruited supporters and organised armed bands of youngsters (*shabab*) to impose the *zaʿim's* will, channelled requests for favours from clients, supervised the participation of people at the polls, protected political meetings and campaign processions, guarded the streets and the quarters to keep out other politicians' campaigners and organised mass support demonstrations on behalf of their patrons. In return, the *zuʿama* might allow them financial benefits, but mostly they protected their brokers from punishment for infractions of the legal regulations and backed them in offensive actions against other *qabadayat* for control of such resources as governmental concessions and permits (for instance, for the transport of cargoes from ships to shore).

Through the activities of these and other assistants and clients, ritual demonstrations of loyalty were organised on public occasions such as feasts or receptions or the return of the *zaʿim* from a journey. Such expressions of loyalty at the 'right time' and in a fashion suitable to the clients' position, were expected to demonstrate that these clients and assistants were at the disposal of the *zaʿim* and belonged to his party;

93

also that the clients and assistants expected the *za'im* to be at their disposal as well.

In order to gather support, the *zu'ama* (especially the ones at higher political levels) also organised their own parties and parliamentary blocs. They patronised labour organisations and sponsored voluntary organisations which, while fostering narrow identities in an already fragmented (religiously, etc.) social setting, served to promote their interests, or those of their allies, in obtaining power and control over public positions and resources. Often, they promoted to political office candidates who thus remained indebted to them and who, once in office, attended to their requests for services and favours in the allocation of public funds, and facilitated bureaucratic contracts for the *zu'ama's* clients. Through such clients, who often manipulated their bureaucratic functions in such a manner as to build their own clientelistic networks, patrons gained access both to public funds for developmental projects for loyal villages and urban constituencies (such as electrification, expansion of telephone and postal services, better public health and educational services) and to public resources, including positions, which could be handed to followers as personal favours. Such resources could vary, from employment in minor administrative positions to the issue of traffic licences to favoured clients, shortening of prison terms and granting of licences, exemptions from regulatory demands, scholarships, etc.

At one time, the *zu'ama* could rely heavily on their own assets as landowners, investors, owners of companies involved in international trade, etc.; but, even if these resources were instrumental in providing services for clients, the pre-eminence of the resources commanded by the State endangered the position of those *zu'ama* who persistently failed to gain access to the centres of political power. While, in the short term, a *za'im's* indebted 'friends' (such as a judge who owed him his original appointment, or a contractor who had benefited from the favours that he had granted him) could still provide services to their patron's clients, in the long run his clientele would be limited to his close associates and followers only.

Patrons and brokers contributed to the widespread belief that a *wastah* (an intermediary) was the necessary means to contact and deal with public and private bureaucracy. The *za'im's* own political machine, through which clients of high status contacted the patron directly – while poor clients, needing to funnel their demands through political agents, and unfranchised people were denied the role of clients – reinforced such a belief.

Attempts to modernise the state bureaucracy in the late 1950s and the 1960s were only partially successful. People could not be discharged easily from the bureaucracy, and this conferred upon them leverage and autonomy vis-à-vis the political patrons. The latter, however, could still have the bureaucrat transferred and/or effectively demoted, especially in district towns, but even more so in smaller villages.

Criticisms of the use of clientelism were expressed by religious sects and intellectuals but did not have the effect of neutralising altogether the power of such networks. While economic changes have led to the virtual elimination of the localised power domains of resident land-owners in the rural areas and to the decline of their networks of followers depending on them for their livelihood because of the lack of alternative employment, other forms of clientelism have replaced them, as we have already seen. The proliferation of clientelistically dominated parties, militia groups and sponsored labour unions, under conditions of weak central power and strong (ethnic, religious, etc.) fragmentation, led in the 1970s to violent strife over power and control in Lebanon.

Morocco[52]

I

Among the various organisational principles found in traditional Moroccan society in the eighteenth and nineteenth centuries – such as various blood relationships, residence patterns, Islamic institutions – kinship and geographical proximity have often been reported to be primary, from the point of view of emic significance. As far as the first-mentioned principle is concerned, the inclusion of social actors in households, extended families, lineages, sections of tribes, tribes and confederations was supposed to be regulated by rules of patrilineality and real or assumed descent from a common ancestor. Patterns of residence varied from diffused hamlets to concentrated villages, for-tress towns (*ksour*), nomadic camps and larger cities having administrative, social and political functions.

Until the twentieth century, the territories were assumed to be divided into the *Bled es-Siba*, or 'Land of Insolence', inhabited by feuding nomadic Berber tribes, and, mainly in the plains and steppes, the *Bled el-Makhzan*, or 'Land of Government', which the Sultanate controlled and which was organised in a more hierarchical fashion. In nineteenth-century pre-protectorate Morocco, the Sultan's administration (known as *makhzan*, or 'storehouse') collected taxes in cash and kind and maintained an army to levy them and repress stubborn tribes. The objective of these hostile tribes and of the alliances they established was seldom to overthrow the Sultan or even his *makhzan*, but rather to escape from his secular arm and avoid the payment of taxes and the control of the local officials. While the tribes viewed the Sultan with religious veneration, they regarded the administration with contempt. In addition, the tribes were connected by marketing relations to urban centres (where the administrative seats were based), and factional disputes existed within the tribes and confederations of the *Bled es-Siba*. These were often encouraged and even promoted by the *makhzan* through the recognition of certain tribal leaders at the expense of others, thus often rendering the tribal rebellions uncoordinated and ineffective. Even if remote, the *makhzan* was able to manipulate local politics and localised power domains by means of intrigues, promises, the grant or withholding of favours, and by arbitrating in regional struggles. Such a strategy was even more evident in the late nineteenth century, when, with the diffusion of gunpowder in tribal areas and the commercial as well as the direct and indirect political penetration of North Africa by the Europeans, the *makhzan* lost its superiority.

In the rural areas, tribesmen conceptualised and explained the nature of the socio-political relations they maintained according to emic representations of 'segmentary lineage' loyalties and agnatic descent and of *elfuf* (plural of *leff*) alliances and factions. Such arguments were indeed used when attempting to recruit support and when forming and dissolving political alliances. In fact, social actors used these and other principles in order to gather a large following, through which they tried to gain power and control over sources of wealth. In order to build such a power domain, these people had to manipulate and control their closest agnates, as these were the most prone to quarrel over rights to land, water-holes and wells, over inheritance of positions of power and wealth, as well as over questions of honour and social recognition. They were also the ones most prone to oppose the building of a political career or wealth by their agnate kin, since they thought that this would be achieved at their own expense.

In order to be in a position to oppose his close agnates, a social actor usually established a following among persons who were related to him by economic ties or to whom he had provided refuge and protection. This involved the creation of links of indebtedness and obligation among the poor, as well as of friendship with persons of similar social standing living far away, who would not, therefore, compete over the same human and material sources of wealth and power. Control over marriages and political alliances, between leaders of lineages, were the main means used when contracting links with persons of similar social standing. Such links created what has been described as the 'chequerboard' of Moroccan alliances. These alliances were generally temporary and contracted under conditions of precarious distribution of power and wealth and of collective responsibility to promote or defend honour in a forceful manner. Local patrons tried to remain unaffected by the fall of their own patrons. There were, therefore, frequent shifts of allegiance, the local patrons hoping that, by these means, their market positions would be advanced and that they would reach positions of greater strength. On the other hand, even when changing sides, the lower-level patrons sought to gain recognition as local or regional leaders from some patrons at higher government levels. This was achieved with greatest success in the areas closer to the political centre, when the patron was recognised by important leaders in the *makhzan* or by the Sultan himself as *caid* (chief) of one or more tribes, that is, as representative of the *makhzan*. In this case, he was invested with a share of the Sultan's temporal power, with such functions as military chief, civil governor, tax collector or criminal judge. Once that eminent position was reached, the patron continued to foster the search for clients, allies and patrons. These were needed to control the tribes and tribal notables and to prevent ambitious *cuwwad* (plural of *caid*), or local pretenders, from seizing power, as well as to prevent the *makhzan* from weakening the patron, in case he became too influential, by waiving or reformulating previous directions.

The clientelistic alliances could be established through the use of religious share-compulsion (ʿ*ar*) and covenant (ʿ*ahd*). The first implied the transference of a conditional curse for the purpose of compelling somebody to grant a request, while the second indicated a solemn oath by which parties agreed to act together or to suffer the unforeseen consequences of their acts.

Some of the local patrons were assisted by, or were themselves, prestigious *shurfa* (descendants of the prophets) or *murabitin* (saints), with *baraka* (a blessing of God, sanctity) and followers. These assistants could transform feuds with rival patrons and *murabitin* into holy wars, and acted, in periods of established power domains and peace, as local arbitrators, as guarantors of pacts and agreements in cases of minor disputes.

The problems facing local patrons were duplicated at higher levels and in the *makhzan* itself. Sultans could not inherit loyalties and had to build tribal alliances anew with their accession to the throne, being constantly engaged in buying off or reconciling dissident tribes while repressing and resettling others. Challenges directed at the Sultan often originated from members of the dynastic family. The strongholds of support for the Sultanate were constituted by the urban elites and by the mercenary Guich tribes.

Through their links with the Sultan and the *makhzan*, as well as through the intercession of officials and individuals who were close to the Sultan, members of the urban elite often acceded to offices and received appointments, or obtained such privileges as ownership of real estate, tax farming, the use of government property, revenues from the tomb of a saint or the lodge of a religious order, and exemption from duties and taxes. Lands, especially those situated away from the centre, were subject to the depredations of nomadic tribes and were, therefore, less favoured as sources of wealth and authority. Once in office, the members of the elite could redistribute wealth, confer employment, intercede with the administration on behalf of clients and give them protection and assistance.

II

The Spanish occupation of northeast Morocco (1909–55), and the French Protectorate over the rest of the country (1912–56), helped to create a more effective and centralised administration, aimed at expanding economic revenues and promoting economic market activities. Accordingly, the importance of informal leaders (*murabitin*) in local affairs declined, and power was granted to such local officials as *sheikhs, miqaddims* and *qā'ids*, under the strict supervision of local foreign officers. But clientelistic networks did not disappear, and clients continued to present gifts and favours to patrons in return for protection or a share of spoils. Networks retained their tendency to disaggregation and reaffiliation around members of the urban bourgeoisie and the rural notables. When political parties emerged in the 1930s and 1940s, they were centred on personalities close to the centre, designated simply 'the friends of such and such a' patron. Following the struggle for independence, the monarchy emerged as a prestigious national symbol of unity and as the major distributor of spoils and patronage, which were augmented considerably in comparison to earlier times. The King manipulated rewards such as governmental positions, export–import licences, exemptions from customs duties, sources of credit, spoils and real estate acquisitions and non-competitive contracts, and distributed them to the elite factions attempting to win his favour. The King avoided compromises and concessions under pressure but gave unilateral gifts which attested his munificence, creating an obligation by his 'generosity'. He also retained control over a wide range of administrative appointments, as well as over commissions and promotions in the armed forces and over contractual arrangements chanelled through the Secretary-General of the government, by means of which a large number of middle-and low-level bureaucrats were able to supplement their salaries and to obtain special promotion beyond that possible through the normal Civil Service procedures.

Basic characteristics of patron–client relations

The shifting of allegiances and commitments still remained evident during the period of political independence, except in the case of clients of ministers and high-ranking officials, who often followed their patrons in their ups and downs. As indicated above, the main breeding ground of clientelistic networks was, in this period, the administration (and especially the Ministry of the Interior), the palace, and urban patrons with access to the King and his immediate counsellors.

The centrality of the resources commanded by the centre was reflected in the periphery where, as clients, officials and local patrons approached either such other locally powerful persons as governors and *qā'ids*, or patrons in the Court and central administration. In these cases, the clients used their positions and contacts to demand that the government should become more active in their areas, instead of trying to prevent its interference, as was typical of the pre-Protectorate period.

PATRON–CLIENT RELATIONS IN LATIN AMERICA[53]

The Iberian heritage, bequeathed by three centuries of colonial rule, and the formal political independence enjoyed during one and a half centuries, have greatly influenced Latin American societies. These emerged as the result of the Spanish and Portuguese imperial expansion in the late fifteenth and early sixteenth centuries, into the territories extending from the southern United States to Cape Horn.

The conquest of the Indian territories and the establishment of colonial societies in Central and South America combined national and personal, spiritual and material purposes, which can be synthesised in the formula 'gold, Catholic gospel and personal glory'.

The Spaniards settled in centres of native population which contained mineral wealth, and soon established political–ecclesiastical hierarchical control and sophisticated urban administrative and cultural centres in their colonies. The Portuguese colonisation was, from the beginning, more centralised and less militantly religious, more rural and commercially and agriculturally oriented. The absence of densely settled, highly civilised Indian populations in the territories which would later constitute Brazil necessitated the importation of African slaves to work the fields.

During the eighteenth century, the similarity between the two areas became more marked with, on the one hand, the discovery of gems and minerals in central Brazil; and in the Spanish realm, on the other, the reduction of the Indian population and the exhaustion of the mines brought about the shift of the economic primary from mining to agriculture and cattle-rearing. The eighteenth century was also an era of far-reaching administrative changes for the Spanish colonies, induced by the Bourbon rulers who had replaced the Habsburgs on the throne of Spain.

In the early nineteenth century, the Spanish domains broke up into some twenty separate states, while in the Portuguese regions a peaceful transition to independence was effected under the monarchical rule of the House of Braganza. This house succeeded in precluding the establishment of separatist trends, especially in north and south Brazil, in the first half of the nineteenth century.

Differing in their ethnic, demographic and ecological characteristics, the nations – especially the Spanish-speaking ones – shared basic structures and institutions inherited from the colonial period, such as the large landholding system, strong strata differentials and the parallel hierarchies of church and political power. Liberal principles were adopted as models for the governments, which were torn by internal power struggles, and the nations maintained relations of cultural and economic dependence with the European – and later the American – centre of Western metropolitan hegemonic powers.

Patron–client relations emerged in Latin America as a result of two processes. They arose, on the one hand, out of the conquest and colonial rule that set up a societal order built on a strong element of power relations between the strata and a pervasive preoccupation with hierarchical standing and its concomitant and estamental prestige and honour. On the other hand, they arose out of the weakening of the central institutions' control, and the localisation of power domains.

Hierarchical clientelistic arrangements were established by social forces in widely differing settings. In Spanish American *haciendas* and Brazilian *fazendas*, they were set up between landlords and labourers. The latter obtained access to land and other basic sources of livelihood as well as a relative insurance in times of crisis, and in return they provided services as a steady and personally loyal labour force. They recognised, at the same time, the right of the landholder to control their contacts with outsiders and to exercise a quasi-monopolistic control over access to markets. Spanish American *caudillos* typically maintained such relationships with their followings within the framework of violent entrepreneurships, which flourished subsequently to the breakdown of the colonial administration in the early nineteenth century.

Brazilian northeast *fazendeiros* opted to rely on paternalistic links with dependants and marginal sectors, in the absence of other means of avoiding encroachment on their domains by other rural plantations.

From the mid-nineteenth century, the machinery of the new states penetrated peripheral areas, and the development of parliamentary politics, based on a slowly but continually expanding franchise, induced the emergence of political patron–client networks on a wide scale. Rural and urban periphery *caciques*, in Mexico, or their Brazilian equivalents, the *coronéis*, bargained with political forces located at the regional, state or national capital level. They offered the votes they commanded in exchange for the control of resources related to the holding of administrative positions in the locality or at higher levels in the hierarchy.

Alongside the enhanced regulative and distributive activities of the State, the manipulation of contacts with ruling parties or promising opposition parties, or with the state bureaucratic powerholders, was instrumental in gathering a following at the local level. This capability was commonly used to gain greater access to loci of power, to advance personal position or to obtain vacancies in administrative offices, which would be filled with loyal clients. Such activities were increasingly regulated by forces placed at the centre of the society. This was evident in the case of Brazil – in the activities of the *pelegos* ('activists') during the populistic corporative organisation of workers, or in those of the *cabos eleitorais* who gathered votes during the period 1945–64 – and in the case of the Colombian *gamonales*, at least until the establishment of the National Front in 1957, as well as in the Venezuelan clienteles, where peasant-organised support was given to political forces struggling for office at the centre of society.

More localised dyadic relationships emerged (and still flourish), linking urban and rural marginals and poor people with professionals such as lawyers and physicians, whose unpaid services created personal indebtedness which could be turned into political support – as was the case in rural Brazil – or with merchants possessing a more intimate knowledge of market devices and practices than peasants – as occurred for instance in Bolivia and northern Argentina.

Economic changes and a growing political awareness drew potential and actual clients to revolt in some cases, and former patrons to exert more coercive means of social control, as happened in Mexico, with the *cacicazgos drásticos*, and also in the Brazilian northeast. In a parallel way, strong urban middlemen and *caciques* appeared in modern squatter areas and *barrios*, exploiting the need to legitimate the illegal invasion of lands and the allocation of parcels in their contacts with politicians and bureaucrats, so that the urban slum dwellers were transformed into politicised passive clienteles of politicians, parties and regimes.

Several traits seem to be particularly emphasised in the clientelistic relations existing in Latin America. Among these stands out, first, the fact that, while sharing with Catholic southern Europe a basic recognition of crystallised cultural codes of honour, the Latin American settings seem to put a greater emphasis on power differentials and have traditionally evinced a greater degree of coalescence of primordial (ethnic) identities and positions of control over access to markets and centres of power. At the same time, this linkage between primordial identities and market positions has been weakened by the basic Catholic orientations of equality and by the liberal principles adopted by the independent states, and, in some cases, by such political developments as the Mexican revolution. But, in some areas – as, for instance, in Bolivia – this coalescence has been maintained to a greater extent by the differing abilities of strata to participate in the national culture and by the limited possibilities of structural change. Where changes in the structuring of power domains have been forthcoming, they have often tended to assume radical overtones.

Second, a wide range of organisational forms of clientelistic networks has developed in the region, ranging from dyadic and localised to more complex pyramidal networks.

Third, clientelistic relations have often been related to the manipulation of broad kinship ties by patrons, who either supplemented them or utilised them in struggles with kin-related and other members of the elite stratum.

Fourth, and in common with instances of clientelism in Catholic southern Europe, strong similarities have existed between temporal clientelism and the image of dependency on the spiritual realm. In addition, the ecclesiastical authorities have long supported temporal patterns of clientelistic mediation.

We will describe below some of these patterns of clientelism in detail.

Colombia[54]

The territory of Colombia presented strong regional, ethnic and economic–ecologic cleavages already in the colonial period, when it was known as Nueva Granada. Regionalism burst out in the early nineteenth century with the end of Spanish rule, and following the brief attempt of Simón Bolívar to integrate Venezuela, Colombia and the presidency of Quito (Ecuador) into a single political unit to be called Gran Colombia. Local notables such as priests and *caudillos* became involved with their followings in violent strife over regional spheres of influence and power. Towards the mid-nineteenth century, these struggles became galvanised by the opposition that crystallised within the elites, between a centralising Conservative Party and a federalist Liberal Party.

The measures taken by the administration of either of the two parties were, as a rule, reversed by the succeeding administration. The struggle was complicated by bitter religious controversy resulting in the expulsion of Jesuits and in other measures taken against the Church, as well as by the loss of authority of the central government. The parties incorporated regional *caudillos* who had control over departments (provinces), and local political leaders, known as *gamonales*, who were dependants and supporters of the *caudillos*. The *gamonales* were either public officials, *hacienda* owners and overseers, or priests and other influential rural figures, who organised local power domains and occasionally mobilised large armies of followers in order to perpetuate their own powerful positions as well as those of higher-ranking *caudillos*. Control over formal positions in the government and over its budget and bureaucratic machinery was assured to *caudillos* and *gamonales*, through support at the polls, by people who aspired to fill central political positions.

Thus, Colombian politics came to be described as being negotiated in 'secret dialogues' between the departmental capitals and the municipal *gamonales*. Once in power, the holders of office considered the bureaucracy as a source of pay-offs and a provider of incentives to followers and party supporters. The party in power, be it the Liberal or the Conservative, purged the bureaucracy of members of and sympathisers with the opposition and, in order to strengthen itself, distributed jobs and public funds, thus supplying *gamonales* with resources in return for the electoral support of their constituencies. At the regional level, factions followed the national cleavages and the political aims, and were pushed into violent clashes and attempts to terrorise their opponents. Local networks of *caudillos* and *gamonales* became involved in endless uprisings against holders of power, in wars of retaliation and defence and in attempts to widen their spheres of domain and influence.

One of these wars (the 'War of the Thousand Days'), in the late nineteenth century, exhausted both parties and enabled the Conservatives to dominate politics, under the coffee export 'boom', until 1930, when the Liberals returned to office. Purges of Conservatives from office then followed, especially in the Conservative-dominated hinterland areas, as well as attacks on Liberals by Conservative authorities, and retaliatory actions by Liberal guerrilla bands, which initiated a period of about thirty years of what became known as 'La Violencia'. This unrest claimed thousands of lives, and caused massive displacements of populations fleeing to more secure settings (to the cities, for instance), throughout most of rural Colombia, except for the Atlantic coast and the extreme southwest.

In the 1950s, the central government still exercised no authoritative control over most of the country. Local notables and peasant village leaders maintained order, being (themselves or their relatives) close clients of the guerrilla leaders, who provided protection and arms to loyal peasant followers. In such periods of turmoil and violence, protection was secured by becoming a member of the party in power or by banding together in large groups so as to discourage attacks by contesting factions.

Liberals and Conservatives expected partisan treatment by the bureaucracy, and the bureaucrats came to be regarded by broader strata as potential patrons and brokers.

The National Front then established endured for a period of seventeen years (1957–74, and extended to 1978) and provided an alternation of presidents from either party, who thus came to agree on a common candidate who ran alone and received bipartisan support. The understanding also decreed a parity rule for the holding of both the elective and the non-elective positions in the administration. This compromise devalued the position of *gamonales* as providers of valuable resources and services to political followers, as well as reducing in the administration the number of vacancies open to contest between the parties.

The competition for office was transferred from the inter-party arena to intra-party factionalism. People continued to regard bureaucrats as a whole as potential patrons, but public services came to be considered as depoliticised. The maintenance of peaceful relations between contending political forces, together with the rapid expansion of the bureaucracy, led, however, to other consequences. It allowed the introduction of technocrats to high positions in the national bureaucracy, and the centre was enabled to distribute the resources at its command in order to enhance the legitimacy of the regime in accordance with a rhetoric of development and provision of resources given as citizenship rights rather than as pay-offs for partisan support.

Gamonales became less necessary than hitherto for gathering electoral support. The National Front was not further extended after 1978 and the elected Liberal President could return to the old practice of appointing party members to the administration. In fact, due to the narrow margin of the Liberal electoral victory, Conservative incumbents were able to retain their positions.

Brazil[55]

During the colonial period, and more broadly after the abolition of slavery in the second half of the nineteenth century, localised dyadic patron–client relations were established between *fazendeiros* and rural workers and tenants (*agregados*) in the northeast sugar cane zones of

Bahia and Pernambuco and, later, in the coffee-growing area of São Paulo. Such paternalistic relations were fostered by the relative isolation of the *fazendas*, the weak effective control of the centre and the blurred boundaries of influence of contesting landowners. Under such conditions, plantation owners held full control over the rural population and the sources of livelihood in their areas, as well as over contacts with regional, state, and national governments and markets. The local priests were subordinated to the landowners and officiated in the plantation chapels, preaching a sort of popular Catholicism which emphasised the natural helplessness of mankind and the need to rely on divine and human protectors and benefactors. These same conditions of rural unrest and categorial contest for wealth and power among the upper strata led *fazendeiros* to establish rather large networks of loyal dependants, with whom they maintained relations expressed in idioms of paternalism, deference and prestige.

As the northeast lost its former economic prosperity and value, and later became more integrated into the sphere of influence of the national forces, as administrators replaced absentee landowners and the lower stratum sought alternative employment, the relations of debt-peonage, sharecropping (*parceria*) and *cambão* (unpaid labour in lieu of rent for land use) assumed a more instrumental and coercive character.

In the southern region, with its centre in Rio Grande do Sul, the clientelistic networks that emerged under the conditions of sparse population, cattle-rearing economy and frontier spirit, closely resembled in character the loyal, personal, military and 'egalitarian' patterns of clientelism existing in the Argentinian and Uruguayan ranch-complex area, which will be described below.

With the adoption of liberal institutions by the government during the 'Old' Republic (1889–1930) and the development of parliamentary politics based on a very narrow but expanding franchise, political clientelistic networks emerged around the so-called *coronéis*. These *coronéis* bargained with political forces at the regional and especially the state capital level for their support and for the handing over of the votes they controlled locally in exchange for access to office-holding and to the benefits attached to it, such as employment opportunities, health or credit facilities and exemptions from regulations. In such ways, the *coronéis* were able to offer a great variety of services and commodities to foster positions of social and political authority and to establish diffuse relationships with followers at the municipal and regional level. They could arrange employment, lend money, secure lawyers and influence judges, 'persuade' witnesses and prevent the police from confiscating their clients' weapons, collaborate in the legalisation of land rights, be *padrinhos* to the sons of servants, employees and other dependants, grant fiscal exemptions in their capacity of local authority, settle interpersonal problems and disputes, write letters, receipts, contracts and give written recommendations, as well as, among other things, patronising the work of lawyers, doctors, etc., within their sphere of influence.

The crisis of the agricultural export economy of the 1930s affected the large landowners' power domains at the national level and in the southern states. The national government enhanced its distributive and regulative activities, and the networks of clientelism became linked to wider institutional frames. Contacts with politicians and bureaucrats at the centre were used to gather local followings. The ability to do so was used by patrons to gain greater access to loci of power and to positions of control over the flow of resources, either for themselves or in order to place in them a loyal client. While a similar situation existed until 1930, mainly at the regional level, within the states, such activities were increasingly fostered and promoted by social actors – whether individuals or collectivities – related to the institutional centre of society. Such was the case of the union activists and leaders known as *pelegos* during the period of populistic corporative organisation of workers under Vargas (until 1945).

Rural power domains then remained largely untouched and the Vargas regime fostered the emergence of forms of mediation within the urban workers' unions, whereby the *pelegos* reconciled the interests of workers, employers and the government. At other levels, the central regime intervened in the Brazilian states and had loyal supporters appointed governors. The bureaucracy was no longer under the control and influence of an elected parliament, and the extensive nationalisation of resources and economic enterprises transformed the bureaucracy and the executive power of the centre into the main dispenser of resources in the society. Accordingly, clientelistic networks came to be linked to such foci of power. Similar in structure to the *pelegos'* chains of clientelistic brokerage were those networks induced through the electoral gathering of votes by the *cabos eleitorais* during the multi-party period that followed, from 1945 to 1964. During those years, people could, through giving electoral and other forms of support, extract the particularistic grant of some favour or help in dealing with the administration.

Within the administration – and related to influential persons outside it – there existed political–administrative cliques concerned with the advancement of the interests of their members, and with seeking a 'flexible', favouritist implementation and advantages also outside the realm of the administration.

In such cliques, known as *panelinhas*, local entrepreneurs and officials were linked to influential lawyers, bureaucrats, ministry officials, federal deputies and senators and, through them, to the centre and, in some cases, even to the President. Through such *panelinhas*, the centre obtained support in the elections and in implementing administrative decisions at the state and municipal levels. In turn, the *panelinhas* acquired access to information and to avenues of influence to and within the administration. Members of these *panelinhas*, such as customs officials, insurance men, lawyers, businessmen, accountants, municipal and federal deputies, bankers, formed as it were pools of information on government contracts or licences, and on credit and sources, in order to take advantage of such opportunities. They were also granted exemptions from laws, immunity in speculations and smuggling, etc.

The military coup of 1964 attempted, initially, to remove the clientelistic networks from the administration. Indeed, it led to a temporary centralisation of personalistic intercession, whereby the state organs came to be regarded and approached as surrogate patrons.

Nevertheless, the huge rural migration to the cities, especially to the centre–east and southeast regions, together with industrialisation and high rates of unemployment and underemployment, produced strong strata differentiation and distance between the *favela*-dwelling population of such cities as Rio de Janeiro and São Paulo and other urban sectors. It also reduced the possibility of establishing patron–client relations and hence the proneness of broad strata to seek such relations anywhere save in domestic and auxiliary services. From the 1960s, urban violence and disorganisation became acute there.

In the rural areas, however, lawyers and physicians, among others, continued to gather dispersed followings and to enjoy prestige by offering services to the rural and peripheral urban poor without obtaining significant immediate returns, thus creating ties of indebtedness that were turned into political support when these powerholders ran for office. Similarly, within the political realm, politicians maintained, as before, clientelistic networks.

Peru[56]

I

Peru was one of the main centres of pre-Colombian civilisation, of concentration of Indian population and later, until the late eighteenth century, of Spanish colonial mining, commerce and administration. It then lost its monopolistic, commercial and administrative hold over

South American contacts and transactions with the metropolitan forces, and still retained a strong rural character despite its position within the Spanish American colonies.

In the rural areas, the private appropriation of lands was prevalent from the eighteenth century, and *haciendas* emerged on lands bought or seized from Quechuan communities, whose members became tenants and labourers (*colonos*) on those lands. The *colonos* were allowed to farm small plots on a subsistence basis, and were sometimes also given housing, tools and seeds. In return, they were required to work the *hacendado's* lands for a specific number of days, planting and harvesting cash crops produced for local and regional markets, as well as to provide household personal services in the *hacendado's* house. The landholder controlled the marketing of the produce and the purchase of goods at outside markets. He mediated in cases of encroachment by the police and the administration on his *colonos*, protecting the latter, when in trouble, from government officials. He also resolved interpersonal disputes that arose within his realm. *Colonos* were expected to be thoroughly loyal to their patron and to support him in his disputes with other *hacendados* and officials and, if necessary, to become part of his private militia. Constant rearrangements of personal allegiances were made between *hacendados* and officials, priests, policemen, mineowners and other landowners.

Similar dyadic and diffuse relations were found at the national level in the nineteenth century. The *caudillos* managed to control the presidential seal from 1826 to 1895 with the help of their armed followers and upper-class government officials and struggled among themselves to obtain a greater share of wealth and power for distribution among their clients.

In the rural areas the members of the 'independent' egalitarian Quechuan communities who controlled lands increasingly encroached upon by the *haciendas*, had to supplement their subsistence farming gradually by undertaking seasonal work at neighbouring *haciendas*. Some of them were given guarantees of employment through the establishment of patron–client relations with the landowners of the Sierra *haciendas*.

From the first half of the nineteenth century, the coastal cash-crop (mainly cotton and sugar) plantations, and holdings producing guano and nitrates for the international market, acquired increased importance, and the *hacendados* of the Sierra were relegated to a secondary position within the elites. This situation was only tempered by intermarriage and 'friendship' relations between the landowners of both regions. However, the *hacendados* of the Sierra maintained their positions as regional patrons, much as the colonial *hacendados* had done, until the mid-twentieth century. Thus, local power domains continued to be based on their control over the appointment of local government officials and judges; they prevented the enactment of government decisions which they opposed. They also commanded influence at higher levels of government by having some of their clients or even themselves elected to the national legislature, which over-represented the departments of the Sierra.

In the twentieth century, the Sierra was opened up to growing marketisation, to new networks of transport and communications, and a shift in the economic sphere developed, from the centrality of primary products to the secondary and tertiary sectors. Through the emergence of more radical urban parties such as the A.P.R.A., from the 1920s at the national level, relations in the Sierra contained more elements of stress. Peasant unrest, from the 1950s, was repressed but led the modern elite sectors and the military to a growing conviction that land reforms and the replacement of the Sierra *gamonales* were essential.

In the coastal plantations, the *colono–hacendado* relationship became more commercialised and was based upon wage-cash payments. In the sugar plantations, until their expropriation in 1970, the permanent workers were given housing, medical care, food, soap, clothes, in addition to low cash wages, in return for their labour. In the rice plantations, some of the permanent workers were given small plots of land to farm but had to sell their produce to the plantation, whose managers marketed it or sold it to outside merchants. In this region, the land was held by absentee owners who had moved to the cities and entered the fields of banking, credit, insurance, real estate and manufacture, mining or oil enterprises. Workers were in contact with the managers or foremen with whom they attempted to establish informal and *compadrazgo* relations.*

The expansion of markets in the Sierra also gave rise to the privatisation of communally held lands, to increased migration to the cities and the coastal region and to the direct participation of the peasants in domestic commercial markets. The communities tended to break up with the emergence of great internal stratification, and commercial and government forces pervaded local networks. The more wealthy residents, familiar with avenues of marketing and with a rudimentary knowledge of Spanish, came to dominate other people and to mediate in contacts with government agencies. At the same time, the resources controlled by these agencies considerably expanded in the 1960s, with the introduction into the subsistence farming areas of programmes of

---

* The patterns of traditional patron–client relations described for the Peruvian coastal plantations or the *haciendas serranas* seem to typify other areas of Latin America, such as the Bolivian *yungas*, which will accordingly be described in less detail below.

agricultural aid, in the form of seeds, fertilisers, credit, technical knowledge, etc., from Alliance for Progress and International Agency of Development funds. Local leaders sought to establish particularistic relations with government officials in charge of the implementation of these programmes, and thus local power networks were increasingly related to the links which local patrons and brokers could establish with wider institutional frames, such as the national bureaucracy. From the late 1950s and until the military take-over of 1968, patron–client relations with bureaucrats at regional levels were in demand as a means of gaining information about laws and procedures before approaching the administration formally. Initial introductions to some of the bureaucrats in charge of the relevant offices thus had to be obtained. In return, the officials – who, themselves, were brokers for higher-level politicians and officials – were able to entertain influential and friendly relations with local people. These relations could, with widened enfranchisement, be turned into political support. As a favour to the patrons to whom they were attached, the bureaucrats sometimes acceded to the requests of these local leaders.

In the cities, only a minority of the working class was unionised. The protective social legislation, enacted nationally in the early 1920s, was less a response to the organisational strength of unions than a paternalistic legislative measure taken by the presidents and their clients to deflect class conflict and mobilise urban workers under the aegis of middle-class parties. Links of clientelism flourished between union leaders and politicians and government functionaries, and bosses had the power to hire and recommend people for positions in the public sector and in the organised union enterprises.

Similarly, access to bureaucratic offices and successful careers was afforded to people of the middle stratum through the intercession of politicians and high-level officials. In other words, in pre-1968 Peru the clientelistic networks structured the political parties, the national bureaucracy and the regional and local arenas.

II

The military authoritarian and developmental regime which ruled Peru from 1968 brought some changes in the system. This regime attempted to reorient foreign investment and local capital to the secondary sectors of the economy. An agrarian reform was implemented in the coastal sugar plantations and in a large number of Sierra *haciendas*. Their owners were, nevertheless, compensated for the expropriation and encouraged to shift – if they had not already done so – their capital to industrial investments and to finance. The bases of the upper sectors' economic strength, which were closely related to foreign capital (such as banking and manufacturing industries using plantation crops), were left untouched. Landholding, however, was restructured, and *haciendas* of the Sierra, for instance, were converted into cooperatives. Nevertheless, former managers often continued to dominate their local power domains, having been appointed administrators of the new enterprises.

Besides eliminating elections and ousting the civilian political parties from their traditional hold on the bureaucracy, the military regime condemned and tried to undermine the clientelistic system of preferential treatment in governmental agencies. As the primary task of industrialisation of the economy was assigned to the national centralised bureaucracy, the centre attempted to rationalise the bureaucratic realm, in order that resources should be allocated efficiently. A careful examination of the personnel was conducted, employing technically trained candidates. Increased checks of bureaucratic activities were made. 'Moralising' campaigns were launched to change the bureaucrats' attitudes, and the impersonal enforcement of laws and regulations was emphasised in the requirements and demands of the administration officials. Clientelistic allocation of resources was equated with corruption, and various pressures were brought to bear to end personalistic behaviour.

It will be possible to evaluate fully the effects of these recent measures only in the future, but there are indications that, among the changes effected, such a policy has made it harder for persons of lower standing and community rural leaders to approach the administration, and has removed the search for mediators to fields outside the bureaucracy, without undermining as a whole the clientelistic forms of access to resources and to loci of decision-making.

Bolivia[57]

Bolivia was once the demographic and economic mining nucleus of the territories of the Spanish South American vice-royalty of the Rio de la Plata, but has since become sparsely populated and one of the most impoverished countries of Latin America. The subjugation of Aymara and Quechuan Indians, who were forced to work in the mines, was part of its colonial history. Bolivia gained its independence with the help of outside sources.

After a short-lived Peruvian–Bolivian confederation, the country was torn by the struggles of *caudillos* striving to seize power, but the changes meant little to the Indian population as, since the 1870s, they had lost their lands to white and mestizo (*cholo*) landlords.

Patrons, clients and friends

The participation of Bolivia in the Pacific War of 1879 led to its loss to Chile of the Atacama lands on the Pacific. In 1899, its rubber-producing area of Acre was annexed by Brazil and, between 1932 and 1935, its territory was further reduced, following the Chaco War with Paraguay. The defeat was attributed by young officers to the under-developed and unequal social structure of the country, and labour legislation and unionisation were fostered by the succeeding military presidents. From the 1940s, new political parties emerged, which appealed to the urban working and middle classes. The Conservative political forces lost ground before the National Revolutionary Movement, which consolidated these sectors, gaining power in 1952. The new regime embarked on a programme of agrarian reform which returned to the Indians most of their lands in the Altiplano and nationalised key economic sectors, as, for instance, tin-mining. It also attempted to develop eastern Bolivia and tried to democratise the polity and mobilise workers in support of the regime. This government was, however, overthrown in 1964 by the military forces, which have retained power up to the present time supported by 'right-wing' political factors.

Until the early fifties, traditional patron–client relations were maintained between landowners and the Aymara-speaking peasants in the isolated *haciendas* of the *yungas* region. The *hacendados* had their *colonos* under their power and could demand agricultural and domestic services from them. The *hacendados* could decide in which realms they would abide by the ideal image of benevolent and paternalistic *patrones*. *Colonos* were virtually allowed no freedom in choosing protectors; and, in retrospect (after the agrarian reforms of the Bolivian Revolution of 1952), clients emphasised the limitation imposed on them by clientelistic attachments, while former patrons tended to consider only the benevolent side of the relationship. The administration showed indifference towards the Indian peasants, and patrons mediated the latter's every contact with outsiders within their *haciendas*, provided means of subsistence during crises and settled and arranged the reaching of agreements, in public as in private affairs (weddings, divorces, etc.).

With the 1952 reforms, lands were granted to former *peones*. The patrons sold their own produce to wholesalers and exporters of coffee and cocoa in the city of La Paz, while the *campesinos* were forced to rely on middlemen in provincial towns, because not only did they not know the wholesalers, but they could not gather sufficient quantities of the commodities that could be meaningful to those merchants. The middlemen, who were frequently former *hacendados*, often lent money to their *campesino* suppliers during lean months between harvests, and

112

thus held the sole option on buying the latter's produce. These middlemen also served as *compadres* (ritual godparents) to the *campesinos'* children, helped them with the authorities, or provided them with counsel and first aid, if necessary. Minor gifts and loyalty were given them in return by the peasants. New patrons thus emerged, who happened to fulfil ancient roles. Syndicate leaders were appointed to oversee the public works projects undertaken in the name of the union, in a manner closely resembling that of the *mayordomo* of the landlord, who supervised the agricultural work.

Argentina[58]

Contrasting with some of the forms of clientelism described above are the relations maintained between patrons and their *gauchos* in the nineteenth and early twentieth centuries in the *pampas* ranch complex of Argentina and Uruguay. Sparsely populated and, until the mid-nineteenth century, torn by *caudillo* wars and under attack by nomadic tribal Indians, the Argentinian *pampas* provided agricultural and cattle resources for the international trade. These constituted the main source of revenue for the new state. In these regions, as well as in the Uruguayan and southern Brazilian plains, extensive labour operations requiring high expertise were required from workers (*gauchos* and *vaqueros*) in cattle-rearing. These were physically dangerous jobs demanding a high degree of courage. Personal independence and honour, competitiveness and egalitarianism were valued and related to professional competence. In fact, manpower was plentiful but there was a shortage in competent and reliable labour force. Foremen and section chiefs (*puesteros*) came to act as patrons to junior workers, to whom they provided job referrals in return for help in social and economic activities. These people remained dependent on the ranch owners for access to land parcels and to credit facilities, for the use of machines to raise commercial crops, etc. Through these clientelistic networks, the landowners gained informal control over a labour force whose values were against the formal (on-the-job) discipline, as well as access to a large and only indirectly known labour force in the region. Last but not least, the patrons gained the ability to gather political support (though this was restrained under Perón's rule).

Under these conditions, patrons and clients maintained relations which were assumed to emphasise mutual respect, independence, intimacy and the loyalty of the *gauchos* to their employers, who were supposed to be as competent as the former in cattle-raising activities and skills.

Networks were dispersed, not being linked to wider institutional frameworks, except in those cases – especially in the earlier periods – where patrons attempted to dominate the embryonic states and moved to the capital cities which centralised the flow of international trade.

In other areas of Argentina, there have been found traditional patron–client relations which resemble closely the networks described above for Bolivia and Peru. In consequence, such patterns are not analysed here.

Mexico[59]

I

Mexico was the centre of the first Spanish viceroyalty in America, in an area of highly developed pre-Colombian Indian civilisations and of concentrated Indian populations. These dwindled in contact with the Europeans and under the harsh labour conditions to which they were submitted. Until the nineteenth century, however, many Indian communities succeeded in insulating themselves, somehow, from outside interference, owing in part to the crown policies. Some of these communities produced in general only enough food to subsist, but also one or several commodities for marketing. Others were corporate communities with communal rights over lands located in marginal areas and participated in local marketing systems, being only partially integrated into national and international economic circuits.

The first period of independent political life (1821–55) was characterised by anarchy, rivalry among political leaders and *caudillos*, and corruption and incompetence in matters of government. From the mid-nineteenth century, liberalist forces gained control of the government and implemented policies involving the alienation of communal corporate Indian and Church-owned landed property. The Law of Sales and Expropriation (Ley de desamortización) of 1857 provided that communal corporate Indian property be granted to individual Indians cultivating plots at the time. The Indians were easily exploited by speculators and *hacendados* who tended to consider the *haciendas* as profit-making ventures to supply agricultural products for the changing national and international markets. Villagers partially or completely lost ownership of the soil and became tenants or farm labourers in the encroaching *haciendas*. By 1910, less than 1% of Mexican families controlled 80% of the total land, while 80% to 90% of the villagers and town-dwellers in central Mexico had almost no landed property. Political power continued to be greatly fragmented between powerful personages: the *caudillos* – regional and local military chieftains whose wealth had been amassed by the use of violence – and *caciques*, many of whom were descendants of the Indian patrician families. These men claimed loyalty and obedience from their followings in their domains in view of their control of military power and wealth and because they provided various services, especially means of protection and avenues of upward mobility and prestige.

During the so-called Porfirian era (1877–1910), an ordered structuring of these pyramidal networks was attempted by the supreme *caudillo*, Porfirio Díaz. He implemented policies inspired by positivist liberalism and based on compliance or repression (the renowned *pan o palo*, i.e. 'bread or stick', policy) and applied them to the broader strata of the population. This implied the backing of local power-holders and the use of coercion in relation to peasant demands and uprisings. In the 1910s, peasants who faced crises of population growth, loss of land and increasing difficulties in earning a livelihood, responded to chieftains who led them in a series of largely unconnec-ted revolts against the local political leaders, the plantation owners and the regime, at a time when the State was also challenged by political entrepreneurs from the elite sectors. The peasants who, in the preceding period, had benefited from the clientelism of land-owners (the *acomodados* or permanent workers) were one of the main targets of the landless peasants' uprisings. During the Mexican Revo-lution (1910–20) and the post-Revolutionary regime, Mexican society underwent rapid and far-reaching political and social trans-formations. The lands of the *haciendas* were distributed among com-munal *ejidos* and individual smallholders. The market economy and the network of communications were expanded, and the country was transformed into a modern and industrial state. At the same time, the patterns of clientelism that had prevailed during the periods of the *caudillos* and the Porfirian era were changed but did not altogether disappear.

II

Numerous powerholders replaced the ordered structure of the pyra-midal networks under the aegis of the supreme *caudillo*. In addition, the peasants were no longer considered unimportant in politics, and revolutionary leaders now competed for the leadership of the masses. Cooperation was rewarded by grants of money, jobs and status. With the 'institutionalisation' of the revolution and the reinforcement of the Institutional Revolutionary Party (P.R.I.) in the 1930s, the numer-ous locally entrenched regional *caudillos* – and the local *caciques* attached to them as *hombres de confianza* (literally, 'men of trust') – risked being displaced and therefore submitted to the authority of the new central system. Nomination to candidature within the framework of a single-party system and accession to office in the machinery of the State became attractive rewards for loyalty shown to a patron. After the Revolution, such accession to office involved a high degree of discretionary use of formal powerholding for personal enrichment, this creating the impression of uncoordinated corruption on the part of petty political activists and holders of formal office. In fact, the networks of clientelism became linked to wider institutional frameworks, such as the government bureaucracy, the ruling P.R.I., or the police.

The rule (introduced in the late 1920s) of democratic non-re-election of the supreme patron, the President of the Republic, resulted in a massive turnover of the personnel occupying positions at all levels of the political system at the end of the six years that the President spent in office. This factor induced flexible and dispersed loyalties on the part of clients, especially those occupying prominent positions.

A patron who is well placed in the current *sexenio* could just as easily be without a job in the subsequent one, if the 'wrong man' is chosen to be president. It is, therefore, important to show loyalty to one's patron, 'but not too much' . . . the goal is to maintain sufficient flexibility so that you can easily transfer your loyalty from downwardly mobile to upwardly mobile individuals.[60]

Political contacts in the form of clienteles or of *camarillas* (political cliques) are very profuse in the administrative realm, within the framework of such a system, in the same manner as *caciquismo* – although strained by new political trends – is used at the local level to control peasant populations, to attain to higher levels of decision-making, or to obtain preferential treatment in dealing with the administration. These contacts were also used by the ruling party, at least until the early 1970s, to gather support for the regime.

At the local level, formal powerholders, party (P.R.I.) representatives and politicians tried to monopolise the loyal support of the members of rural communities, of workers' and peasants' unions and of the population of urban squatter areas (*colonias proletarias, populares*) in order to retain power, to gain prestige and/or to advance their positions within the regime. They relied on verbal, ideological, revolutionary phraseology and on the recognition of the independence of supporters as citizens, union members, etc., while at the same time, employing various other means to achieve their aims. Thus, threats and repression were used against individuals and groups that were too autonomous; particularistic benefits were granted to loyal supporters, on whose behalf the powerholders also interceded before the organs of the single-party regime to which they had preferential access. Moreover, these powerholders manipulated concepts of paternalism and personal loyalty and honour as evinced in abiding by the requirements of superiors, to whom the people were tied by their *palabra de hombres* (literally, 'word of a man', which is to be respected).

A special case of clientelism – common to other urban marginal areas of Latin America, such as some of the Peruvian *barriadas*, the Brazilian *favelas* or the Venezuelan *barrios* – was found in the squatter *colonias*. There, urban dwellers in need either of legalisation of squatter settlements or of resources and contacts with government offices were mobilised as passive clienteles by politicians (and, in other areas of Latin America, by different parties) supported by squatters' leaders. These leaders, on their part, built up clienteles by proving they had connections with the decision-makers. This claim was corroborated by the power given to the squatter leaders to allocate land parcels, in the early phases of settlement, and, later, to provide employment, housing or communal services. The relations thereby created involved loose ties of mutual obligation and were based on bargaining and cross-cutting allegiance, but the leaders did try to foster their image as patrons concerned with the well-being of their followers and with maintaining close personal contacts with the dwellers and their problems.

Since the mid-1970s – and under increasing pressure through delegitimisation of the monolithic rule of the P.R.I. – the national elite has proclaimed its decision to end the rule of *caciques* and local strongmen at the periphery, but has not yet developed alternative means of wide participation for large sectors of the population. Mediation in social and political markets is still common, and the huge revenue from oil sales is applied to maintaining policies of wide government employment and distribution of resources by the State. These resources are, in fact, still appropriated – though in decreasing amounts – by the powerholders and their clients in the bureaucracy, and by sectors of the broader strata.

PATRON–CLIENT RELATIONS IN SOUTHEAST ASIA[61]

Southeast Asia is a highly diversified region, comprising the Theravada Buddhist countries of Burma, Thailand, Laos and Cambodia; the 'Sinitic' territories of Vietnam; Indonesia, mostly Islamic, but integrating Buddhist and other ancestral beliefs and practices; and, in the Pacific, the Christian Philippines. Some of the societies found in Malaya, Burma or Indonesia evince. cleavages but others – as in Thailand, the Philippines and Cambodia – are relatively homogeneous. Among the populations of this widespread region are mountain peoples living in tribal settings, structured according to descent groups united through exchange of wives and goods, while others – especially in the valleys, plateaux and plains – are integrated into wider institutional structures.

The period extending from the thirteenth to the nineteenth century, that is from the decline of the Pagan and Angkor civilisations to the impact of European colonialism, was one of fragmented power for the Indianised societies of southeast Asia. Of all the polities of the mainland area, only Siam, known today as Thailand, developed a strong centralised state.

In traditional Buddhist areas, the majority of the villagers produced rice to supply local needs and as 'merit-making activities' (i.e. as acts of benevolence and cooperation which would, according to popular perception, merit reward), as well as to pay the taxes levied by the local lords or by agents of the kings, who were believed to hold ultimate rights to the land. And, although there were slaves, either captives or indentured peasants, the villagers were traditionally also required to provide labour services. Because the polities were underpopulated, warfare was endemic and mostly conducted in order to gain control over the people (who were resettled) rather than over lands.

The traditional links of clientelism in southeast Asia evinced various characteristics. In the main, the ties were informal but, in such areas as the kingdoms of Siam, Burma or the independent and so-called *kraton* (literally, 'palace') states of Java, they were comparatively institutionalised, being embedded in the formal organisation of these polities. In the Malay states, Luzon and the coastal kingdoms of Indonesia, the claim to a position of district authority, for instance, was based on personal followings of local personalities who thereby gained recognition as the representatives of a more powerful regional leader. In the periphery of kingdoms, during periods of unrest or dynastic decline, clientelistic relations emerged centring around leaders of trading expeditions or around bandits.

The pace of change in southeast Asia became very much accelerated in the nineteenth and twentieth centuries. Direct or indirect (but effective) colonial control is relatively recent, beginning in the early nineteenth century and gaining intensity from the 1880s to the Second World War, when the Japanese dominated the area for a short period. In the late 1940s and the 1950s, a few years after the European postwar return, independence was granted to most southeast Asian colonies. The celerity of these processes brought profound changes in these societies but, at the same time, did not altogether do away with traditional patterns which, to this day, coexist with the modern sectors of society.

With the introduction of direct and indirect European (mainly

British, French and Dutch) rule, new concepts of bureaucratic administration were introduced, along with the redefinition of traditional personal relationships of subordinates and superordinates. These created tensions between alternative models of administrative behaviour, tensions which are still manifest to the present day. The colonial powers proceeded to effect economic transformations, centred in the promotion of export of foodstuffs and raw materials such as tin, rubber or teak from those colonies, and of import of manufactured goods. The major ports became 'primate' cities, growing far more rapidly than other cities or towns and even than the whole population. Investments in infrastructure (railways, waterways, irrigation canals, etc.) were also made. With commercialisation in the production of rice and other commodities, land, labour and capital came to be considered as market commodities, and land tenure practices and taxation changed, as well as interpersonal economic arrangements, especially in lower Burma, central Thailand and Java. Cambodia, and in particular Laos, were less affected by these market transformations, and alienation and sales of lands were less usual.

Within the first group were included social settings characterised by legitimised inequalities in status and wealth, the absence of impersonal guarantees for physical security, property and position and the inability of traditional village communities and of kinship units – built on principles of bilateral kinship and patterns of equal inheritance – to serve as means of advancement and social security, especially since the colonialist period. Then, outsiders such as absentee landlords, wealthy urban persons and members of minorities came to control many of the resources people valued and sought. When the intermittent authority of the centres reached the peripheral areas, it tended to legitimise local power domains as long as the powerful personalities were loyal to the centre and supplied taxes and corvées as required.

Patrons owed their positions to personal skills and wealth and occasionally to their connections with regional leaders. Concentration of landholdings, population pressures and the spread of state power usually gave strength to the patrons over their subordinates. The greater availability of alternative social mechanisms of security, such as kindred or closed corporate communities (as existed in Java), served to prevent the radical imbalance of power in favour of the patrons, in the same manner as the existence of unclaimed land (in Thailand for instance) or the absence of outside backing benefited the bargaining positions of would-be clients.

As colonialist rule and the commercialisation of agriculture narrowed the comprehensiveness and diffuse character of exchange, especially in lowland areas, separate ties with specialised elites appeared. On the other hand, the legal backing of the colonial administration encouraged local patrons to ignore local opinion and become more exploitative.

Under such circumstances, and especially during wars and crop failures, the peasants' claims to be granted subsistence needs clashed with the efforts of men of power to exact revenue and manpower. This induced reactions which were expressed by such means as passive resistance, petitioning and banditry – in areas such as central Luzon or lower Burma in the 1920s and 1930s – and extended to major uprisings such as the Sayasan rebellion in Burma, the Sakdal movement in the Philippines, and other such movements in post-Second World War Indonesia.

When, however, power domains were localised, patrons were under pressure to redistribute wealth – in the form of contributions, loans, etc. – in return for the prestigious position which their followers accorded them. Such practices were more effective in traditional villages than in directly ruled settlements such as lower Burma.

In addition, the commercialisation of crops induced social actors to undertake transport, crop-brokerage, money-lending and shop-keeping activities. They became foci of dependence for less favoured peasants and for the strata that were landless as a consequence of indebtedness. Under such conditions of increased vulnerability, due to the world market fluctuations and to the breaking up of levelling mechanisms in local societies, clientelism came to be appreciated among smallholders and tenants. Smallholders depended on large landowners for the purchase of seeds and tools, transportation and marketing, connections with officials and, occasionally, credit. Tenants in such places as east and central Java hoped to obtain, through relations of personal dependence, a minimal insurance until the crops were harvested. Workers were interested in securing employment as tied labourers to landowners, and a minimal livelihood.

Patrons might provide for clients resources such as steady employment, land for cultivation, equipment, marketing knowledge, technical advice and help during subsistence crises or in case of sickness and emergencies or during the year following a poor harvest. They could protect their clients against personal enemies, bandits or public dangers, ranging from courts and officials to tax-collectors and soldiers, and use their influence on their behalf. Patrons might also subsidise local charity and relief organisations, donate land for communal use, support local public services such as schools and roads. They might host visiting officials, sponsor village festivals and ceremonies and provide administrative favours, communal loans, etc. In return, clients were expected to supply goods and services according to the specifications of their patrons, such as field labour, firewood and water for the patron's household, personal domestic services, periodic gifts of food, and other services as members of the patron's local faction.

With the establishment of Western patterns of administration and rule, clientelistic networks emerged between peasant populations and politicians, office-holders and rural bosses. Local spheres were affected by wider institutional frameworks, which did not command the commitment of the people. Thus, in order to run elections and to rule, the political forces had to rely on material inducements provided through their own channels or through the existing dispersed clientelistic networks. Parties or the President – as in the Philippines – acceded to positions of power through the support of important local patrons. State welfare administrators, teachers, local traders, resident managers of foreign-owned plantations became potential foci for clientelistic approaches, in addition to the more traditional patrons of highland areas.

On the whole, followings became cross-cutting and less exclusive, and there were instances of multiple allegiances. Individual patrons and brokers had less control over resources than the traditional patrons had once had. Ties were contracted in specialised realms, such as the political sphere, the modern sector of employment, the administration. Package deals were arranged in a more specific and less diffuse manner. Resources were mainly those which were provided by or attained through the administration, and the contacts of brokers and patrons with the ruling coalitions and the bureaucracy became salient. The ability to gather votes in electoral systems or to dominate avenues of access to administration in presidential and military regimes was applied to development projects and jobs in the nationalised enterprises or in the bureaucracies, which were granted as favours to clients and dependants. Votes and other forms of support were given to those individuals who interceded on the patron's behalf.

Political instability which existed in Indonesia, Burma and the Philippines resulted from the need (the 'inflationary' need, to use J.C. Scott's term)[62] to increase the use of national budgets in order to distribute benefits to followings. This tendency, of what have been called the 'patron–client democracies', has threatened the basis of these regimes, especially during periods of economic stagnation, when criticisms of 'corruption' and 'inefficiency' have been voiced by social sectors not involved in clientelistic networks, such as students and part of the military forces. .

The high diversity found among southeast Asian settings makes especially difficult the task of detailing those traits which are particularly emphasised over the whole area, in the clientelistic patterns existing there. Nevertheless, we may indicate in a preliminary way the following features as especially prominent. First, there is an emphasis on reciprocity and mutually beneficial exchanges rather than on personal commitment and personal significance as basic constitutive elements of clientelistic attachments. Hence, the predominance of restive attitudes on the part of clients and the mutually conditional obligations entailed by such relations. In this connection, the Christian Philippines are somewhat exceptional in the stress, found in patron–client relations there, on personal gratitude and loyalty between the partners as expressive of expectations regarding each other.

Second, and related to this, is a tendency in Indonesia and the Buddhist areas towards personal inconstancy, and fragility of clientelistic relations as soon as there is no unmediated contact of patrons with clients and no danger of loss of face; and, consequently, there is a tendency towards limiting such attachments to face-to-face networks, save when these are fully formalised and regulated by the State, as they were in eighteenth- and nineteenth-century Thailand. This stands in contrast to the tendency towards complex organisational networks manifest in the Philippines.

Third, especially in Indonesia, engagement in ritualising, ceremonial behaviour is used as a means of advertising power as well as of concealment of disagreements and dissent between patrons and clients.

Fourth, particularly in Buddhist settings, there is ambivalence in attitudes towards authority – an ambivalence to be overcome only if superiors show merit, by being (however strong) benevolent and indulgent father-surrogates.

Fifth, the use of religious symbols by patrons as the basis of legitimacy has been more prominent in Indonesia than in the Buddhist or even the Philippine contexts, although in the latter patron–client relations have sometimes merged with ritual kinship ties.

We will now describe some of these patterns of southeast Asian clientelism in detail.

Indonesia[63]

I

Indonesia has long been the largest and most densely populated nation of southeast Asia. It is a fragmented archipelago, made up mainly of volcanic mountainous land, covered by dense tropical forests, and relying heavily on agriculture and on the export of plantation crops, timber and other products. Its population is highly heterogeneous –

ethnically, linguistically and religiously – while strong social and political differences have also been observed. Thus, the irrigated rice areas of Java were mostly integrated into the *kraton* states, to which peasants contributed tithes and compulsory services; the seaboard principalities of the coasts of Java, Sumatra and Malaya were linked to international trade, and the sparsely populated hinterland of the seaboard principalities of Sumatra and Borneo were engaged in shifting cultivation, turning, in the late nineteenth century, to plantation crops grown with debt-bond labour. The Javanese society, the most populous and culturally sophisticated of the area, broke up into mutually exclusive, ideological (religious) organisational clusters known as *alirans*. These comprised people of different social standings; that is to say that, while peers of different *alirans* could be opposed, social actors belonging to different strata were linked together. These *alirans* were traditionally those of the *santri* (or devout, orthodox Muslims), typical of traders; the *priyayi* (or more Hinduised people), originally associated with the Javanese aristocracy but later with the majority of the white-collar stratum; and *abangan*, strongly influenced by syncretism of Muslim and pre-Muslim elements, and mainly, but not exclusively, associated with peasants.

The Dutch influence on Java was felt from the eighteenth century and, in the nineteenth century, it increasingly gained direct control over the area. Dutch policies induced an expansion of commercial agricultural production for export, under the *cultuurstalsel* or forced cultivation system instituted in 1830. Indirectly, the Dutch policies caused the increase of the native and migrant population in Java and, with ups and downs, strengthened the establishment of a salaried administration. They also led to the growth of estate production through European capital, from the 1870s until the early twentieth century, and to attempts to expand the health services and educational facilities during the period of so-called 'ethical policy' in the early twentieth century.

District and village patrons became connected to administrative sources of power during the Dutch 'dual policy', until the 1870s or 1880s, and had to collect taxes, organise corvée labour, keep records and information regarding villagers and apply government regulations. As, from the nineteenth century, the criterion of landownership became an important basis for social stratification under the Dutch colonial rule, these patrons gained economic strength as landowners, especially in west Java. These developments, together with such other factors as the land taxes, and the rule of equal inheritance which precluded the departure of surplus manpower to the cities, stimulated the growth of a system of 'shared property'. The size of land assets decreased with successive generations and this accentuated the need to rely on people outside the villages in order to obtain critical resources. Traditionally, individual patrons supplied clients with access to land or agricultural employment, either as sharecroppers or as wage labourers, as well as help in such emergencies as droughts, and loans to pay off moneylenders. Clients perceived that this help induced a moral obligation (*hutang budi*) on their part, which might never be discharged. However, while the cash value of the favours granted by the patron might never be returned to him, instrumental debts were transformed into a long-term commitment. The patron's follower could be called upon to provide labour services, to pay respect, to attend ceremonies, to ask for the patron's advice when voting and to act according to his instructions, etc. The practice of asking a prominent person for his advice, in order to adopt his viewpoint on the issues of the day, was typical of village and urban poor neighbourhoods.

Accordingly, and from an emic perspective, Indonesian clientelism was ideally couched in familistic terms, being known as *bapakism*. The *bapak* (father) was the leader of a circle of clients (*anak buah*, or 'children') and was expected to take care of the material, spiritual and emotional needs of his followers. In return, the *anak buah* were expected to back him up, to defer him, to give him contributions, to participate in ceremonies testifying to the patron's social importance, to join or leave political parties according to his will and even to fight and defend him in physical clashes.

Some patrons used religious symbols to gain legitimacy, as did the *santri* (pious) landlords to whom the Muslim peasants of the *aliran* were attached by what seemed to be regarded as a privilege, supposedly enabling them to perform their religious duties better. In other instances, the landlords' sole control over resources did not lead to the acknowledgement of pre-eminence by village commoners, the so-called *abangan*. Even relatively recently, in the late sixties, clientelistic ties were the means through which *aliran* members could be mobilised in what were considered incipient signs of class struggle. Indeed, poor peasants and sharecroppers were mobilised by *santri* landowners to repress – with the support of the military authorities – those who tended to incite agrarian unrest or who (like the communist P.K.I. party) were sympathetic to movements of agrarian reform.

II

With its massive rural population, its few non-industrialised cities – which had mainly served as administrative, consumer and trading centres – and after two centuries of Dutch influence (especially in Java) and rule and a short period of Japanese occupation during the Second World War, Indonesia emerged as an independent state in the late 1940s. As a polity, the country was characterised by a multiple-party system comprising mostly elite parties (save for the P.K.I.) with regional and *aliran* strongholds, and distinguished by instability, with the president, the P.K.I. and the army emerging as the main political actors. Sukarno's Guided Democracy attempted to bring together primordial and political forces under a presidential corporative regime. He failed, however, to provide the political (party, etc.) structures to back it up and to deal with problems connected with economic processes, urbanisation and the growth of unorganised urban masses of unemployed *lumpen* (proletariat). The failure of this regime led, in the mid-1960s, to a centralised government under a military aegis.

The primary form of material help in the urban settings, at least from the time of independence, was to find employment (even a part-time job) for clients either in the administration, in private businesses or in the nationalised enterprises. Under conditions of high unemployment, securing a job carried, for the unemployed, long-term obligations both towards the person who found him the job and towards his immediate superior at work. Most jobs were underpaid, and multiple employment had become the rule. By granting such assistance, patrons felt assured that the work would not only be done but would be carried out in a relatively efficient manner.

Since the 1940s, the bureaucracy has become a main source of employment, growing from 82,000 to 600,000 employees from 1940 to 1953, and to 1,200,000 by 1972.

In the bureaucracy and in private business, the patrons have supplied clients with additional sources of income in different ways, by diverting to them part of their own extra job payments (*korupsi*), by allowing them to charge tariffs in excess of the legal rates for official services (*catut*) and by permitting them to use official equipment to supply unofficial services to customers (*ngompreng*). In return, they were assured that their orders would be carried out and that materials and products would not be stolen. Superiors who were not *bapaks* could not expect compliance with their instructions.

Patrons have also provided employment in crafts and trade, asking clients to supply services and goods at a set price, which the latter could not refuse to do even if the price offered would not cover the item's production cost. In return, *anak buah* expected the patron to furnish, in the future, additional help, cash, etc., if the need should arise.

Patron–client relations in the peripheral areas of cities were less directly tied to membership in *alirans* than in the villages, and the loyalty of the rank and file was more tenuous. The duration of attachments was more limited, i.e. ties were established on a short-term basis. Patrons dropped clients and clients left one patron for another. Urban *bapaks* could not be sure about what to expect from their clients in critical situations. Partners expected more instrumental, market-like considerations to figure in each other's behaviour. Recent migrants to cities were less tied to patron–client networks, which were no longer related to geographic boundaries. People were, accordingly, related to outsiders, to persons lacking a close association to them. Complexity of forces and factors in the urban scene have left patrons in a position of lesser control over environment than their rural peers.

Urban patrons could give emergency loans, in case of illness or when the client could not meet the terms of a deal; or, if the client was in jail, might bail him out. Repayment was an implicit part of any such understanding but cash returns might never be required.

Other patrons established relations with clients of various intellectual, social, administrative and financial statuses, thus constituting the vital connecting link in a network, which K. Jackson calls a 'heterogeneous entourage'.[64] Through these networks, clients might obtain medical, legal and other services at reduced prices or even free of charge. In return, the patrons gained reverence, respect, a position of social pre-eminence, and their advice was sought and mostly followed. A patron was shown respect in public, as for instance in the street. He was approached by the authorities if a need occurred to mobilise people for communal projects. He was flattered by followers who assumed that he was powerful enough to arrange things without a considerable effort. People followed his decisions in public affairs, since he was able to mobilise manpower for short-term activities – such as riots and violent actions – as well as in support of a particular political trend. In addition, each client added his skills and assets to the network, and diligent services, ranging from building a house to holding parties or tending a garden, were available at little or no cost.

In high-level politics, patrons and clients had more instrumental orientations and their relations were more fragile and unstable. Allegiances were switched as political conditions changed. This fragility, as well as the other characteristics of Indonesian clientelism, is related to some of the basic values of Javanese culture, such as indirectness, subtlety, the repression of open emotions and the concealment of signs of dissent as long as possible. The overt expression of disagreement with the plans of a superior was discouraged and motives were expected to be veiled in ritualised etiquette and 'civilised' manners, as activism and frankness were considered unrewarding.

In addition, ritualistic behaviour – in the form of ceremonials and rallies – was a means of advertising power. Political power was demonstrated by smooth ceremonial contacts and was conceived in zero-sum terms, as sharing a cosmic basis and not open to expansion through mass mobilisation and participation. 'Portions' of power were granted to actors by the ruler or by the patron in return for deference and loyalty.

A basic legitimacy was granted to inequality in income and in status, as well as standing in the market place, before the law and in dealing with the administration. People conceived social justice to be related to the fulfilment of responsibilities attached to unequal roles. Social injustice was felt only when patrons failed to redistribute (or did not wish to) and grant clients access to resources. Emotional satisfaction was reported to be felt by the clients when showing deference and respect to patrons, as well as by the latter upon receiving such marks from their clients.

University students formed a partial exception to these rules, as they considered *bapakism* as corruption.*

In some respects, these patterns resemble the forms assumed by clientelism in the Philippines, while in others there are some differences.

The Philippines[66]

The Pacific archipelago which comprises the Republic of the Philippines has been at the crossroads of international routes and trade since the fifteenth century. It was Christianised and strongly Hispanised during the Spanish colonial period, which lasted from the sixteenth to the end of the nineteenth century. In that period, localised patron–client relations emerged between large landowners (*hacenderos*) and tenant labourers and indebted peasants, in a manner similar to the one already described for Latin America. The Philippine fight for independence in the late nineteenth century drove the Spaniards out of many provinces, and with the cooperation of American armed forces from Manila a short-lived independent state was established, which was soon replaced by American rule. During the American period (1898–1946) – with a brief Japanese interregnum between 1941 and 1944 – the centralised character of the government was maintained to avoid geographic, cultural and linguistic fragmentation. It was incorporated

---

* K.D. Jackson indicates that 'it is as yet uncertain whether the vehemence of student criticism stems from their being partially excluded from the system because they are unable to obtain bureaucratic positions consonant with their educated status or whether it is from a thorough rejection of the system of their elders. Anti-corruption campaigns often are attempts by political "outs" to oust the "ins" rather than to change the system of selective distribution of the benefits of government.'[65]

into the 1935 Constitution and reinforced by the system of administration and taxation. The elite of wealthy, educated, mostly *mestizo*, plantation and real estate owners and learned *ilustrados* maintained itself and, for the first time, was given opportunities for political advancement under the system of restricted electoral contest. Since the elections to the first National Assembly in 1907, national politicians attempted to attract the support of the most powerful regional and village factions and leaders and, even if clientelistic networks remained dispersed as in the Spanish period, they thus became linked to the workings of such wider institutional frames as the Congress and the administration.

During this period, and particularly since independence, when the merit system deteriorated and there were increasing pressures for employment in governmental offices and agencies, politicians and other patrons and brokers wangled from the bureaucracy favours and services for their clients. Thus, congressmen and senators, the president and his close associates, influential businessmen, members of the press, bureau directors and office chiefs all made telephone calls, wrote letters of recommendation or personally accompanied their protégés to agencies where vacancies and new positions were available. Such protégés were, for the most part, loyal political supporters, relatives, *compadres* and godchildren and 'friends'. In the postwar period, congressmen and senators dominated all but the most powerful administrators, mainly through threats to cut departmental allocation of funds or promotions, as well as by placing their clients in civil service positions or in government-controlled enterprises. Departmental secretaries, bureau directors and office division chiefs – themselves recruited from among the party-faithful clients and political protégés, or clients of heavy financial contributors – mediated between their own clients and the more powerful politicians. In the 1950s and 1960s, it was usual for Congress members to have 'quotas' of positions and jobs in agencies reserved for them to fill according to their personal considerations. Members of minority parties were given only a few such jobs, or none at all, while members of the ruling coalition had great opportunities to control the distribution of positions in governmental agencies in a particularistic manner – either temporary employment (as during pre-election times) or jobs of a permanent nature. Senators and congressmen who were overtly critical found that 'their' allocations for development programmes in their districts had been cancelled or their payment delayed, that they were denied access to central banks, to the Customs Department or to executive agencies, and that they were experiencing great difficulty in fulfilling their role as representatives of constituencies. On the other hand, bureaucrats had to abide by the demands of those politicians who had elaborated in the line-item budget establishing the amounts each agency would receive. In this manner, informal networks progressively superseded formal organisational arrangements.

At the local level, clientelistic attachments in municipalities and rural areas made use of the sense of debt or of gratitude of an indebted client and of his feelings of shame, embarrassment and shyness if he could not settle such a debt, to ensure his loyalty. In addition, some of these relations were cemented by ritual kinship (*compadrazgo*) ties.

In the elite sectors, activists and leaders did not abide by such cultural definition of relations and changed sides easily, as there were no ideological splits between parties but only a bare contest for power and for control over avenues of access to resources. Cases were reported of old allies quickly becoming opponents in a struggle over the allotment of rewards earned during their earlier association. Despite the competitiveness and the particularistic behaviour of congressmen (until the disbanding of parliament by President Marcos in 1972–73) at the apex of clientelistic networks, there existed an awareness of a broader community-wide interest and yearning for communal harmony. None of the individuals or clientelistic factions would accept permanent exclusion from access to benefits, and peaceful conditions could only be ensured if no one was permanently excluded. Besides the American-type formal structure of politics (which until recently consisted of a two-party electoral contest for elective seats and presidential office) and administration (civil service examinations, etc.), dyadic alliances, mostly vertical, were used to link villages to the national government. Impartiality and favouritism were equally present. Many kinds of association were in existence in the Philippines. Ordinary members, however, derived little benefit from their membership unless they had special links with the leaders, whose interests received first attention. A patron–client relation with a politician willing to help might be more instrumental than joining a categorial group.

In elections, people voted for personalities rather than for a specific party. Candidates for office arranged their campaigns on a strictly personal level and sought the help of lower-level political leaders who had personal followings and hence votes they could deliver 'at will'. Also, the candidates courted people who were interested in financing their campaign in order to accede later on to high administrative offices. Strong allies were sought without regard to party lines. As votes were gathered in return for material benefits and promises of future support, electoral victory tended to be the lot of people with great personal wealth – such as landowners in regional and local rural levels – or of those who stood good chances of winning and therefore of gaining control over institutional resources.

During the electoral period that ended in 1973, clients exchanged their votes for instrumental benefits. Electoral support was obtained by the massive distribution of a broad range of rewards used as inducements for families and individuals. The ordinary voter traded his vote for either the promise of a job in the public works, free medical care in a government hospital, protection against harassment by a local policeman or exemption from tax payments.

Thus, during the independence period, the Philippine clientelistic networks have tended to become integrated and related to the administrative channels of societal organisation. In the first stage, this was mainly effected through politicians who were members of the Philippines' major 'cadre' parties, with non-ideological appeal to the population, rather than of the mass parties which addressed themselves to specific sectors of society.

This organisational character of clientelism was maintained even when, in the late 1960s, the locus of power changed and was transferred to the President of the Republic. It was then that President Marcos established administrative and military channels to link his office directly to the rural population, in order to bypass congressmen.

By the time of his re-election campaign in 1969, he was in a position of being able to work directly with provincial and municipal officials in the allocation of the large sums he had at his disposal. These he disbursed either directly – by handing out checks to *barrio* captains assembled in the presence of a municipal mayor – or through agencies clearly identified (like the Presidential Arm for Community Development) as belonging to him.[67]

This, together with the increasing cost of clientelistic mobilisation of political support by congressmen, explains the relative ease with which the president banned the Congress through his 1972 martial law. Nevertheless, overt protest and repression became widespread towards the early 1980s.

The above process also led to strengthening the administration vis-à-vis the parliamentary patrons. The administration became more integrated and the intrabureaucratic networks more salient. Accordingly, 'wise' officials created personal followings of their own among those of their subordinates who were willing to give them their primary loyalty in return for special favours and informal delegation of authority.

Thailand[68]

I

Until the late nineteenth century, the territory of what is today central Thailand was sparsely populated. Like other southeast Asian polities, before their consolidation in the eighteenth century, the patrimonial bureaucratic kingdom of Siam was mainly concerned with the control of its rural population living in agricultural, primarily rice-producing, communities, and working lands which, ideally, were vested in the ruling monarchy. The kingdom functioned through the (ideally voluntary) affiliation of sub-units and collectivities and resembled what L. Hanks has colourfully described as a 'chain store operating where it had affiliates'.[69] Indeed, contrasting with the notion of a Thai entity, modelled according to the cosmological principles of Theravada Buddhism, the territorial boundaries of Siam were fixed only when the French occupied Indo-China and the British controlled Burma and Malaya, and were mainly established to preserve Siamese sovereignty.

During the eighteenth and the first half of the nineteenth century the population had to be registered under a *nāi* noble who could use their corvée labour for about three months every year, making it available, at the King's request, for various tasks. This system of registration of peasant clients (*phrai*) made it possible to keep track of the precise size of the population and of its distribution among the various administrative units (*kroms*). At the same time, in the absence of sophisticated weapons and owing to the undeveloped transportation and communications systems, control of the manpower gave *nāis* the authority to exact gifts and services from the *phrais*. The King tried to curtail the emergence of such independent power domains by encouraging denunciations of illegal strengthening of high-ranking nobles by their peers. He attempted, more or less successfully, to retain the *nāis'* allegiance by applying a complicated hierarchical system of awards of rank, honorific names and elaborate 'dignity' (*sakdi na*), which extended from the highest official to the meanest landowner.

Clients were expected to obey, respect and comply with the wishes of their patron. They were said to be under the 'care and protection' of a superior (*faktua*) and, accordingly, had 'to remember and eventually reciprocate' (*katanyū kataũethi*). In practice, the clients provided gifts and such services as free manpower for farming or marketing agricultural produce, which were important to *nāis*, interested in maintaining their superior life style. For their part, *nāis* settled disputes, protected their dependents, avoided their being brought to trial, argued on their behalf when they became involved in litigation, helped them to obtain exemptions from tax payments and to avoid corvée assignments or to be given light ones.

Similar relations with their masters were also developed by slaves, by people who voluntarily entered bondage ties in order to avoid corvée service, or who sold themselves or their children into slavery to mitigate the harsh conditions under which they had to earn their livelihood in times of agricultural difficulty. Such links resembled the patron–client relations maintained by free people. Slaves, indeed, retained their former rights, such as starting a family and inheriting or passing on property, even if these rights could only be exercised through their master's mediation. They could change masters, if redeemed by another sponsor, and their children were automatically freed. Moreover, when they were freed, they could re-enter society with little or no stigma or disadvantage attached to them.

The evolution of these ties into informal clientelistic arrangements was further encouraged and reinforced by the various socio-economic changes which Thai society underwent from 1850 to 1932. Previously, as already indicated, rural central Thailand lacked an established stratum of rural landlords, as because of land surplus, there was no restriction on the use and marketing of lands, which did not become a symbol of status. This resulted in minimising the proportion of hired labour from the landless stratum as well as the prospects of tenancy arrangements. The rural elites were therefore mostly constituted by the priests of the local Buddhist temples, village headmen and a few well-to-do peasants, in addition to the government representatives, the merchants and the teachers in provincial towns.

On the other hand, common villagers had small farms and, while the rule of equal inheritance made those too tiny to provide a livelihood, the peasants could move to and claim uncleared tropical forest lands.

From the mid-nineteenth century, Thailand was opened to international trade. Commercial rice cultivation increasingly replaced its production for bare subsistence. The population grew rapidly, increasing sixfold from 1850 to 1950; slavery was abolished and replaced by free labour; rents and payments in cash and kind replaced corvée labour, and uncleared lands were progressively reduced. In a parallel manner, the centre relied no longer on *nāi–phrai* links, and wealth rather than control of men became the basis for establishing informal patron–client relations. Landowners kept increased liquid wealth at hand to be in a position to purchase services from the landless stratum, which had no lands to allow them to engage in reciprocal labour with neighbours or kin and no prospects of acquiring land. These people, therefore, could either be employed by landowners in the rural areas, move to new areas or migrate to Bangkok. Labour contracts seldom covered more than a year, but during that period the labourers lived with the landowners for weeks and were almost accepted as family members. By becoming the client of a well-to-do landed neighbour, such people tried to obtain recurrent employment, loans at low interest or even gifts and assistance in time of need. For his part, the patron could acquiesce, and allow the relationship to turn into a diffuse one encompassing numerous unpaid services. The partners, however, could only trust that their hopes and expectations would be realised at a critical time. Uncertainty prevailed in these relations, as such links were not formally established, and here, as in other forms of Thai clientelism, even overt signs of cooperation, compliance and responsiveness to verbal requests and orders could, later, be ignored, when a certain situation ended.

Similar relations pervaded other spheres in nineteenth-century Thailand. They existed between *nāis* striving for advancement, for career mobility, or to obtain an appointment to a lucrative office (such as that of judge). They were also established by *phrai*, with persons of higher rank than their traditional *nāi* (to escape, perhaps, the latter's oppressive terms when dealing with him), as well as by Chinese tax-collectors, who became clients of powerful Thai social actors.

At this stage, the Siamese centre impinged on the periphery through extractive demands without substantially changing the social relations and local 'traditional' power domains there, but rather by 'encapsulating' them. This was achieved through tacit coalitions with such local holders of power as landowners or by coopting local patrons as part of the lowest level of the administrative organs of the centre. In this case, patron–clientelism was built on linkages to the wider institutional frames of administration of the Thai society. This coopting, however, did not lead to the reorganisation of the dispersed structure of these networks, which merely resembled each other and the centre itself in their structure and in the functions they fulfilled.

Occupation of roles was individual, and relations were established either on an ideally long-term basis, as in the case of the more institutionalised *nāi–phrai* links, or, as in other ties, were more open to alterations induced by changes in the transactional actual positions of patrons and clients. The content of the relations was highly instrumental, even if phrased in the already-mentioned cultural idioms which, by enforcing hierarchical relations, reinforced the maintenance of clientelistic patterns in spite of the impermanence of specific arrangements with a particular patron. This is a characteristic typical also of other forms of clientelism which later occurred in this society and to which we shall return in greater detail below.

II

Thus, from the mid-nineteenth century, the Thai centre expanded its activities, adding the provision of various instrumental services to the traditional role of Buddhist rulers in the ceremonial and cosmological structuring of order and in securing the welfare of a society. Similarly, its regulative tasks were expanded and the administration became less localised, more functionally differentiated and centralised in the capital. However, the growing salience of resources ordered from the centre was combined with the penetration of the administrative frameworks by clientelistic networks, or 'circles' as they came to be designated in the literature on Thailand. These networks competed with each other for a greater share of public wealth. They tried to expand their hold, even if this led to overlapping of activities and to ill-defined distribution of functions among the various ministries and government departments. Accordingly, appointments to public enterprises, the details of implementation of rules and the grant or refusal of licences, permits, and the like, were usually a means of rewarding or creating followings and of expanding or reinforcing circles of bureaucratic power domains.

There was, thus, an overlapping of formally differentiated administrative structures and undifferentiated structures and orientations – which F.W. Riggs designated, a few decades ago, the 'sala' model of administration,[70] and which embodied contradictory behavioural patterns for people in the administration, sustaining a tension between their primordial (family, clientelistic) orientations and the official norms of behaviour.

It was usual for each agency to have separate rules of entrance to the civil service, and this made possible the use of such posts as rewards for partisan followings and particularistic services. Similarly, within the bureaucracy, personal forms of coordination came to matter more than staff relations and operational formal imperatives. Career advancement and preferred assignments could be fostered or hampered by the personal support of patrons or their reluctance to assist. In relation thereto, the employee's loyalty was not necessarily assured to his bureaucratic superior but may have been given to his patron. However, mainly in the past, but to some degree even recently, there was a tendency for patrons to move their clients to staff the offices to which they themselves had been transferred. This was related to the practice of discharging holders of office and replacing them by the followers of the new patron designated to head the department. This trend towards exclusivity was coupled with a low degree of commitment of clients to specific patrons and was reflected in the fact that, even in recent times, the latter strove to isolate the members of their cliques from contacts with other cliques, especially with those by whom those members could be coopted. Accordingly, clients were expected to proclaim the untrustworthiness of rival patrons, usually by complaining anonymously (as overt conflicts were avoided) against colleagues or even nominal superiors.

Usually, the administrative sections of government handled a wide range of activities supposed to be within the realm of other agencies. It was not unusual, for instance, for the police department to run a television broadcasting station, or for the department of religion to run its own hospital, for other branches of government to have their own banks or their own dance groups to entertain guests. Thus, a client's gains by being attached to such a circle were not limited to a single realm, but could range from free bus passes and reduced prices in different markets to bureaucratic particularistic treatment.

The establishment of a constitutional monarchy and of a formal democratic electoral system in 1932 did not alter the basic traits described above. The broad strata remained largely unchanged and the clientelistic patterns untouched. The new forms of government merely added new arenas – such as the electoral contest – for clientelistic exchanges and networks which have been ultimately oriented to the control of resources at the disposal of the administrative organs of the State. Accordingly, and especially during the periods of military rule and influence (such as the late fifties and early sixties), those clientelistic circles with bureaucratic office-holders attained a relatively long-lived existence, while those networks not having a hold over the access to resources and to foci of administrative decision-making were more ephemeral.

Thus, at this stage, the main clientelistic networks were developed as links to wider institutional frames, and especially to the bureaucracy – that is, around some quasi-monopolistic hold on public services and its allocation to clients in return for their support. Networks were mostly related to, and integrated into, large circles with a chain-to-centre structure. These structures might even go beyond the territorial boundaries of the country by linking patrons of high-level circles with sources of foreign (U.S.A., for instance) aid from which the resources used within their power domains were drawn, in return for allegiance, military bases, etc.* The peripheries of these circles were the most vulnerable areas and the first to suffer in hard times, when the resources basis for the patronage was severely reduced.

III

Besides these forms of organisational clientelistic brokerage, however, networks also developed which, while similarly built on linkages with wider institutional frames, showed a dispersed structure. Such, for instance, were the relations maintained with Siamese officials by economic entrepreneurs (until recently, mostly Chinese) who had

---

* The establishment of clientelistic links of dependence of heads of local power domains with foreigners across national boundaries is typical of many other 'developing countries' analysed here. The exact nature of interrelation between the two levels of dependence – i.e. the internal and the international – remains a main task for research in the future.[72]

become engaged in what Riggs has defined as *pariah* entrepreneurship.[71] Their activities could flourish if they were able to establish special relations with more or less influential officials and thereby obtain access to quotas, permits and licences. Irregularities would be ignored and special privileges granted them, provided they contributed to the private income of their protectors and patrons at the government level. From the 1950s, such officials were included in the Board of Directors of Chinese Thai firms to make them more 'interested' in the welfare of these organisations.

Similarly, beyond the realm of the bureaucracy, there have been smaller circles of patrons, brokers and clients in villages where they controlled access to markets and local productions and were engaged in robbery (of bus lines, etc.).

Among the intellectual groups, clienteles were established between leading intellectual patrons and students and disciples. The patron had trained these clients in the methods of the profession and, at the same time, helped them to find jobs, lent them money, sponsored their weddings or ordinations, published their writings, the students becoming the patron's men and advancing his interests.

Thai clientelism was defined and conceived in the framework of highly elaborate cultural idioms, which affected the behaviour of the social actors. Among these behavioural orientations stands out, first, the fact that even when Thais considered that relations should be friendly, congenial and correct, they undertook little personal commitment, or none at all. If reciprocity was not forthcoming, clients quietly ceased to follow their patron's directions. Without rudeness, discourtesy or public display of anger or show of conflict, they stopped fulfilling the demands of their partners in the relationship. Second, the Thai emphasised a strong sense of autonomy and individuality – unconnected however to the recognition of ontological conceptions of personal identity – which, at times, made it difficult for them to submit to those who wielded power. This emphasis was related to variegated features of Thai society: on a symbolic level, to the conception of freedom of individual choice in shaping the *dharma* and the social standing of a person which is so widely emphasised by Theravada Buddhism; on a structural level, to a high mobility of population, to the lack of long-term obligations in village life, to the loose definition of the responsibilities of kinsmen, and to the trend to educate children with leniency during the early phases of socialisation.

Third, there was an ambivalence in attitudes towards authority though this was supposed to be overcome if superiors showed merit (*bun*) and moral pre-eminence in accordance with societal expectations modelled primarily on Buddhist orientations. In our context, this means that while superiors deserved, in principle, to be obeyed and respected (a fact expressed in the term *kreng chai*, meaning respect for superiors and humility and obedience to authority), they were expected to act on behalf of clients in a benevolent and concerned fashion, as strong but indulgent father-surrogates. Patrons were expected to support clients and retain their allegiance by successfully advancing their mutual interests. At the village level, and also beyond it, personal advancement was believed to depend on finding an effective patron or entourage leader.

Fourth, the lack of deep personal commitment was related to a great emphasis on the personal presence of patrons, urging the limitation of fully-fledged clientelistic attachments to face-to-face networks and their widening only through friends of friends. Thus, there were pressures towards the close association of patrons and clients if the networks were to be effectively mobilised for specific tasks. For instance, it was believed that the presence of a superior was the only way to provide the proper moral support at work. It was claimed that the superior prevented the evils that would occur if only the inferiors were present. He made unity possible among fissiparous groups . . . The presence of a superior reduced the inferior's fear of failure. To the inferior, the superior's presence meant that the action that now appeared correct would not later backfire and turn out to be wrong or evil.[73]

Fifth, there was a strong sense of humility and fear (*kreng*) in concrete interactions with superiors. Similarly to what we have described for Indonesia, and especially in rural areas, an inferior here could fear a superior so much that he would not dare to talk back to him or disagree with him. In Thai clientelism – by contrast to the Javanese pattern – superiors expected their actions to go unquestioned and displayed power in order to reassert their position. But, in this case, they were referred to as *cao nāi*, meaning an outsider of superior social status and education who must be obeyed when circumstances so dictated but was, preferably, to be avoided.

Finally, this ambivalence rendered most attachments rather fragile under the conditions of change in institutional markets, referred to above. Scholars have reported that Thai patron–client relations involved an element of 'personal impermanency', especially in high-ranking circles. Clients did not hesitate to change their allegiance if their patrons were unable or unwilling to provide them with access to resources. Neither patrons nor clients were normally censured for terminating such relations and forming new ones.

Burma[74]

While sharing with Thailand similar ecological conditions and an agricultural village structure, involved in rice farming in the flooded tropical fields and, later, in the production of rubber and other commodities for export, Burma was, however, plagued by violence and ethnic–cultural and other internal cleavages. In the nineteenth century, it lost its dependence and territories to Britain. Since regaining its independence, Burma has experienced serious economic problems and inner political conflicts and has adopted an authoritarian military rule.

Burmese entourages closely resemble the clientelistic patterns described for central Thailand, with even more assertive authoritarian traits, especially in the self-restraint said to be essential when clients entertain connections with their patrons. The cultural prescription of humility is phrased in the concept of *anade* which is extensively used in Burma. According to S.M. Bekker, who analysed it,[75] its major elements are the observance of respectful behaviour, proper language and forms of address, the inability to express self-assertive needs, a reluctance to become an inconvenience to others, timidity, control and fear of aggression by oneself and others, observation of propriety of behaviour as formally defined by situation and status, the maintenance of a balance of obligations, and sharing with those in need, showing compassion and pity for them.

Some traits, already indicated in regard to Thai clientelism, are more emphasised here. Among these must be mentioned, first, the sense of restraint in self-assertiveness (especially among Burmese Buddhists), which might inhibit behaviour to such a degree as to make necessary the intercession and brokerage of third parties to bridge the gap between prospective partners to a clientelistic attachment; second, the emphasis on reciprocity and expedience instead of on expectations of deep loyalty and commitment, which has been salient in keeping networks alive; third, the trend towards impermanence of particular arrangements over time and changing of alliance; fourth, the emphasis on respect, deference, decorum and propriety of speech and approach between persons of unequal rank and the strong contest between social actors, such as leaders, of relatively equal social standing; fifth, the general recognition of customary rights and obligations, whereby the consequences of the authoritarian balance of power are limited. Thus, people have been reported as feeling ashamed when they were not able to provide the required help, or embarrassed if they had to ask a subordinate to do more than was usually requested.

PATRON–CLIENT RELATIONS IN CHINA, JAPAN, INDIA, RWANDA AND SOUTHWESTERN CYRENAICA

In the preceding sections we have presented detailed analyses of patron–client relations in societies in which they constitute a central aspect of the basic institutional matrix of a society. We will discuss in detail later the common dynamics and the variations in such patron–client relations.

We shall first proceed to describe the forms of patron–client relations in several societies (Imperial China, Japan, traditional India, Rwanda and Cyrenaica), in which, while not constituting such a central aspect of the institutional matrix of a society, they yet make up on the whole a recognised, even if relatively limited, part of the basic institutional matrix of a society – sometimes lapsing into what we shall later on designate the 'addendum' type of clientelistic relations.

China[76]

I

Until the early twentieth century and for a period of several centuries, the Chinese polity had a centralised bureaucratic imperial structure. It was sustained by rents and taxes paid by the masses of peasants and artisans who made up the bulk of the population in this agrarian society, characterised by landlordship and a low technological level. Recurrent popular revolts and invasions led to changes of dynasties, especially under circumstances of overpopulation, weakened government and widespread famines, when the population was inclined to believe that the reigning dynasty had lost its 'mandate from heaven' to rule for the welfare of society. Neither changes of dynasties, however, nor the shifts in the relative strength of families, cliques and regional forces, altered the basic social and political–administrative structures based on the gentry, the literati tradition and the primacy of the centre and its control over the competitive system of scholarly examinations to fill the administrative positions of the government.

In Ch'ing China (1644–1919) special relations of 'warmth and intensity' developed between persons of unequal social standing, frequently as a result of long acquaintance. These relations, referred to as *kan-ch'ing*, could be found in a variety of settings and could be set up between landlords and tenants. Through such relations, the landlord avoided being cheated of produce revenue, especially when he was an absentee owner or a scholar unfamiliar with farm conditions. He was also given some special services such as food gifts on holy days or was provided, at his request, with additional labour and domestic help. The tenant was thereby given an unwritten promise that his land tenure would be renewed in the future, and was secure in the knowledge that he would be helped in unforeseen emergencies, when *kan-ch'ing* ties could be invoked to obtain a reduction in rent, or in claiming the use and even the sublease of the landlord's animals.

The special treatment arising from such relations, which were supposed to be impregnated with goodwill, was particularly significant in that agricultural society, characterised by an abundant labour supply and simple technology. The people could not resort to the law for protection, even when the legal codes supported their claims. To resort to civil courts usually meant disaster (incarceration, financial ruin, etc.) for defendant, accuser and witnesses, especially if they were of low social standing and had no means of extra-legal influence over the court's decision. Magistrates themselves were unfamiliar with legal precedents and could lose jobs and even more for 'mistakes' made, and tried, therefore, to avoid delivering judgements. In addition, the legal emphasis on personal virtues and on humane treatment by officials was supplemented by a demand for docility from the broader strata, by the illegitimacy of categorial interest representation* and claims and by a particularistic treatment in courts. People did not trust justice and had to build up networks of alliances and friendships as a form of insurance against depredations, false accusations by enemies and officials and the extractive demands of the government and of its formal and informal representatives at the local level.

Kan-ch'ing relations could also be important in securing non-agricultural contacts or careers for persons with an agricultural background. Thus, a tenant involved in such ties, could, on his way to market, stop at the landlord's town house for a rest and advice on market conditions. The landlord could also exert his influence to obtain employment for a *kan-ch'ing* tenant turned artisan, or to give employment in service to a temporarily unemployed farmer or to the latter's son or daughter.

Similarly, such relations could be established with long-term workers in agricultural settings or with some of the employees in mercantile enterprises, where *kan-ch'ing* ties could reward an apprentice by promoting him to shop assistant, and later to clerk, and by allowing him increasingly to enjoy the delegated power of the owner. This employee could also be recommended for employment elsewhere when his apprenticeship was completed. Tenants and landowners were interested in maintaining good *kan-ch'ing* relations, on the local level, with government officials, who directed tax levies, labour and military drafts and maintained existing social relations, sanctioning by military authority the claims of landlords.

Merchants and urban employers also cultivated the goodwill of guilds, commercial and bureaucratic authorities through social intercourse and by giving gifts and doing favours. These relations were particularly important as the tax system allowed officials to exact, for

---

* In spite of this emphasis, massive peasant rebellions were endemic in China.[77]

their own benefit, extra-legal fees and taxes, over and above the quota required.

Kan-ch'ing ties were equally found between merchants and steady customers in pre-inflation commercial transactions based on credit, as well as between artisans and farmers, whereby the former ensured for themselves a steady supply of some commodity – such as good-quality bamboo, for instance – by the latter, even during periods of shortage, thus minimising the effects of competition and price rises.

Some peculiarities are brought out in this review of *kan-ch'ing* relations in China. First, under the conditions of bureaucratic Imperial rule and (ultimately military) support of agrarian class relations at the periphery, the basic means of protection and of the reduction of official and para-official extractive demands was, for the people who did not belong to the gentry or to the class of officials, to be attached to a representative of those strata able to pull wires. This was achieved by ensuring the mediation of a member of those representatives' families or lineages who had academic degrees and bureaucratic contacts.

Second, these *kan-ch'ing* relations – even if contracted outside official and formal bureaucratic spheres – were ultimately rooted in, and sometimes related to, the existence and demands of the formal power structure. This was evident, for instance, in the fact that access to bureaucratic foci of decisions and enforcement was sought by members of the gentry and that local leaders, even when powerful, lacked legitimacy among local strata and, under certain circumstances, could be affected by the attacks of enemies merging with representatives of the centre, or by those of local bandits.

Third, the clusters of *kan-ch'ing* relations did not become integrated into pyramidal networks, remaining accessory to the formal – legal and extra-legal – channels of widespread societal organisation based upon class, locality, kinship and bureaucratic institutional links. This was reflected in the way such factors as kinship and friendship were considered. Conversely – in a negative sense (in that positions were given to bureaucrats *outside* their homeland) – the territorial background was taken into account when granting bureaucratic positions and promotions and in evaluating job performance, while *kan-ch'ing* ties were only occasionally brought up for consideration.

Fourth, the existing gap (which was sanctioned by the State) between the different social strata – at the province and district levels – was related more to the predominance of kinship and friendship relations within the strata than to *kan-ch'ing* ties between members of different strata. This situation was used to ensure the smooth functioning of cooperative labour exchange teams, and the contacts among members of the upper stratum – as in the case of classmates' friendships – were used when securing positions or influencing bureaucratic decisions.

Fifth, while goodwill and propriety of interaction were stressed in *kan-ch'ing* ties, this emphasis was not peculiar to them but was also placed upon kinship and friendship, all this being derived from the codes of Chinese ethics sustained by the imperial centre and widely accepted in interpersonal relations. In this relation, there was no clear-cut distinction between friendship and clientelistic relations. This contrasted with the typical view, in the Japanese setting for instance, where such lines were clearly defined through the ritualisation of *oyabun–kobun* ties (see below). While, in the Chinese case, there may at some point have been a clear emphasis on the hierarchical standing of the partners, the nature of the relations may have changed over time from friendship to clientelism and vice versa, following modifications in the partners' positions within institutional markets.

II

This was particularly evident in the case of the *mu-fu* system of privately hired provincial advisers to officials, in the late Ch'ing period, from the second half of the nineteenth to the early twentieth century. These advisers – known as *mu-yu* – who were found from the late Ming period, were practical experts who gave professional advice to officials. The latter had mostly a broadly based moralistic and scholastic background in legalistic procedures and laws but were, generally, unable to cope with practical problems of government. The *mu-yu* thus had the means to lead a placid life in an environment where there were few opportunities for scholars who were either unemployed, had not obtained a satisfactory position or, while having a practical frame of mind, had failed in the examinations. A *mu-yu* could therefore engage in scholarly pursuits and gain power and wealth, spend time in studying and in sitting examinations, or wait for a worthwhile appointment without degrading himself by becoming a clerk. Through the official's intercession, the *mu-yu* could also obtain valuable resources. A scholar seeking to enter such a circle would usually be recommended by a mutual friend or a relative to an official or would be invited by the official himself to join him.

Such arrangements were entered into because the Imperial centre expected its officials to discharge their functions as administrators properly, even though they lacked technical and social knowledge of the district or province to which they had been appointed. On the other hand, the centre did not recognise the *mu-fu* system, and the *mu-yu* were hired and paid privately by the officials, their fee being commensurate with the officials' salaries.

The *mu-yu's* standing depended on his skills: *mu-yus* specialising in law and taxation were the most prominent, while skills in correspondence and account-registration were considered less important, and the inferior *mu-yu* had to rely on the support of the former type to enter a *mu-fu* circle.

The dependence of the officials on the *mu-yu's* skills was reflected in the rules for social intercourse and address that Chinese etiquette prescribed. Accordingly, the host (*chu*, in this case the official) assumed a lower position in relation to the guest. Thus, a *mu-yu* was assumed to hold an honourable and respectable position. It was not uncommon that the official went to a *mu-yu's* rooms to seek advice or teaching. In the case of a *mu-yu* teacher, he was referred to by his *tzu* name, which indicated respect due to equals and superiors. Members of a *mu-fu* were generally referred to by some of the following names: *mu-yu* (tent friends), *mu-pin* or *mu-k'e* (tent guests) or *mu-liao* (tent colleagues). Thus, the relationship was highly egalitarian and was particularly reinforced in times of internal turmoil or when international pressures became more acute, as from the mid-nineteenth century. To excel, then, in non-traditional skills came to be considered (together with military resources) as more useful than official nominations in maintaining and enhancing regional power domains. On the other hand, the adoption of Confucian principles and the dangers of a salient position in times of unrest led the *mu-yu* to remain in a subordinate position to the *chu*, and not to challenge his leadership. When, however, the *chu* of an influential *mu-fu* – like Li-Hung-Chang in the late Ch'ing period,[78] – commanded influence within the Chinese centre and controlled a wide range of resources, the pattern resembled a clientelistic relation in which the ratio of followers of the *chu* was increased and the market position of a particular *mu-yu* was lowered.

III

We have described the particular character of the clientelistic relations found in Chinese society. The emergence of such patterns seems related to some features of the society during the Imperial rule and, among them, stands out, first, the central role played by the bureaucratic Imperial centre in structuring the societal hierarchies and the ideological configuration of the traditional Chinese society. Related thereto were the widely recognised monopolisation of interest articulation and aggregation by the governing class and, in the eyes of the government, the illegitimacy of strata interest representation, except when such frameworks assisted individuals, or regulated internal relations, as in the case of clans, provincial associations or trade guilds. These elements heightened the tendency of medium- and lower-level bureaucrats and members of the gentry to become the focus of particularistic approaches.

Second, this situation might have been reinforced by the fact that there were no formal rules of separation between private and public realms in bureaucratic performance, and the officials' particularism was not only allowed but was even reinforced by Confucian prescriptions.

Third, obedience and respect for authority were demanded and expected even when cruelty and coercion were demonstrated. Since early socialisation, people were assured that self-restraint and proper conduct were necessary if security and protection were to be expected.

Nevertheless, the political administrative realm was supposed to be confined to the world of bureaucratic officials and this prevented *kan-ch'ing* relations established between 'patrons' and followers from achieving systematic impingement on the macro-societal structuring of society, save during periods of dynastic decline, unrest and the growth of 'independent kingdoms' at the local and regional levels. In this respect, a striking continuity can be observed in Communist China as compared to the imperial polity. In the post-revolutionary setting, contests for power were maintained for long periods within the confines of the political class. When they were opened to broader sectors, as during the Cultural Revolution, factional conflicts between leaders at the national level were intensified by the existence of relatively independent regional power domains in the provinces, as in Inner Mongolia for instance, or in bureaucratic realms, as in the field army systems of the People's Liberation Army or the state bureaucracy under Chou En-lai. These splits encouraged violent clashes between opposed Red Guard units at the local level. These confrontations of loosely structured movements, however, were conditioned by class and ideological orientations. In addition, the mobilisation of the Red Guard units was effected and controlled through the authority and the organs of the Communist Party, such as the party committees and the official press.[79]

Other societal features of Imperial China constrained, at the same time, the nature of *kan-ch'ing*. Thus, Chinese identity was modelled along primordial lines, and the relation of personal self-consciousness to the wider society was mainly effected through lineage mediation and ancestor worship. These traits conferred on the *kan-ch'ing* an instrumental significance, seemingly less strongly related than other patterns to conceptions of personal identity. The non-instrumental component of these relations was, as we have indicated above, not peculiar to them but was shared by other labour and social arrangements between people of both similar and dissimilar social standing.

Finally, various forms of friendship, stressing either common experiences, or a shared occupational and regional affinity, seem to have been more salient than *kan-ch'ing* ties in Chinese society. We shall deal with this point in greater detail below.

Japan

I

With its insular character, Japanese society has, over the centuries, developed an ethnic and cultural homogeneity shaped by the incorporation and modification of the Chinese ideographic script, the amalgamation of Shinto cults and Buddhism and the adoption, by the hereditary sovereigns of divine descent, of Confucian ideas of public morality and government.

In practice, the Tokugawa shoguns brought civil warfare and the rule of military overlords to an end and united the country through bureaucratic officialdom, the grant of strategic lands to faithful followers, etc. During the greater part of this period (1603–1868), the shoguns applied a policy of insulation while, internally, they envisaged a basic clear-cut social hierarchy, with merchants at the base and *samurai* warriors at the top. The social actors' standing was indicated and emphasised by personal contacts and by the terms of address and reference to superiors and to subordinates. From their early training, the *samurai* adopted a code of behaviour which stressed the importance of respect and loyalty to superiors, of dignity and decorum, of judging conduct by standards of morality, and of acting with justice towards subordinates. This code of behaviour was imposed on the other social classes and especially on the farmers.

The Meiji Restoration (1868) strengthened the power of the Emperor as head of the State and of the national Shinto cult. In order to counter Western expansion and threats, industrialisation was started and Japan adopted an active, expansionist role in international affairs, which culminated in its defeat, in the Second World War, by the U.S.A. The polity was then reformulated along the lines of a constitutional monarchy, a parliamentary democracy and a continued emphasis on the development of the economy.

Two main types of clientelistic relations are found in twentieth-

145

century Japan: the *oyabun–kobun* link and the political brokerage of *yuryokusha* (influential men), which will be discussed in another section.[80]

The *oyabun–kobun* link may be characterised as a highly emotional and diffuse dyadic arrangement. A 'superior' adopts an 'inferior', and the latter recognises the long-term authority of the former, both partners maintaining a long-term, personalised mutual concern with each other's public and private affairs.

This personal, long-lasting attachment can be found between masters and disciples in traditional professions and occupational groups living communally, between landowners and tenants, between labour contractors and workers in peripheral industries characterised by seasonal demands for labour supply, as well as in those trades where traditional skills and long periods of apprenticeship are required. At the place of work, the *oyabun* is usually a person in a senior position with whom a *kobun* has entered into a close personal relationship which has grown with time.

The concrete specification of such relations varied considerably according to the status of the social actors involved, to their relative mutual need and to personal capabilities and characteristics. In principle, however, there were clear-cut expectations regarding the behaviour implicit in the roles of *oyabun* and *kobun*. The *oyabun* was expected to give expressive and instrumental services, such as help in finding employment or in securing promotion or a stable career, protection, financial help during illness, or the teaching of technical skills and social customs related to a craft. *Kokata* (plural of *kobun*) drew additional related gains by being socially identified as the followers of a powerful *oyabun*.

The *kobun* was expected to turn to his *oyabun* for advice before taking important decisions, in private as in public affairs. He had to be ready to offer his services whenever and wherever they were required by the *oyabun*. He was, ideally, expected to reciprocate (by *ongaeshi*, or repayment) the favours he had received by showing exclusive deference and loyalty to his *oyabun* and (what is significant from our point of view) by working hard and in a responsible manner in fulfilling his duties at the workshop. Indeed, as in the case of foremen and labour contractors, 'good' workers thus proved their worth and vindicated their right to positions of trust and authority they occupied in society. Similarly, the headmaster of a high school might be under an obligation to a company for doing him the favour of accepting his graduates to fill job vacancies. The company could rest assured that the headmaster would instruct the newly recruited workers in the appropriate behaviour to be adopted at work, and in union and off-the-job activities. In return, the *oyabun* expected some services from his 'protégés' and their families together with prestige and, what is more important, the maintenance of his basis of power and efficiency.

The most long-lasting links were those established at the place of work. Thus, even if seniority relationships (*sempai–kohai* ties) existed at high-school level and the people involved kept in contact for a long time, the relations contracted in the occupational sphere – mainly in industry and business rather than in politics and in the administration – implied more far-reaching obligations.

People will sometimes affirm, in modern spheres, that a man does not merit the term *oyabun*, being no more than a senior (*sempai*).* Even then, however, it would be hard for a *kobun* to refuse either to provide the latter with some required service, or to be recognised as attached to this particular 'patron', unless the 'client' was willing to dissociate himself from the group sharing commitment to that *oyabun*.

Sometimes, the relationship may be formalised through a ceremonial act which involves symbolic motifs of birth and marriage, and terms of address and reference that are patterned on the kinship model.† The ritual kinship imagery then provides the model for the setting up of the link, whereby the client becomes, as it were, part of the *oyabun's* kin group, and the link is no longer subject to the actual transactional interests of the partners. Such a formalisation was typical, for instance, of the relationship known as *dozoku* ('common kin'),[81] which occurred in rural areas of northern Japan and in the southern frontier zone (Kyushu).

These areas were characterised by heavy population pressures, chronic stagnation of extensive agriculture on poor lands, isolation from marketing centres, and communal interaction in closed communities. *Dozoku* consisted of a hierarchy of households linked by kinship or fictive kinship ties, within which the households were allocated a fixed social standing, which was translated into access to arable lands, farm management and seniority rights, and was maintained through ties modelled on *oyabun–kobun* relations.

Arable land, virtually under the control of the *oya* ('senior household'), was thereby let to other members of the community. Households related by kinship ties to the *oya* received small plots of farmland with houses and, upon settling, furniture and tools from the *oya*. They

---

* Especially after the Second World War, when young workers condemned such relations and considered them inconsistent with the democratic ideals and practices fostered during the American occupation. Most workers, however, did not adopt this view, although more instrumental attitudes existed, which exerted some pressures on the traditional arrangements.

† Descendants sometimes use the professional or ritual names of their ancestors' *oyabun*, following a custom which originated in the system of apprenticeship in pre-industrial Japan.

were not obliged to pay rent or give services to the senior household, but only to recognise its pre-eminence and seniority and ask for its advice and consent. The tenant households having only assumed kinship relations to the *oya* were settled by former labourers, former independent farmers and former servants, to whom land was leased under sharecropping and labour–rent arrangements. The former servants also provided services of this kind and, at the same time, were linked by highly affective ties to the senior household, which had agreed to receive them as members of the community with the right to work its lands.

II

In common with patron–client relations typical of other societies, Japanese clientelism was based on the recognition by clients (*kokata*) of their patrons' right to control the avenues of exchange and flow of resources. In Japan, however, this recognition was deeply rooted in some of the cultural orientations of that society, which were reflected in the symbolism of trust pervading the *oyabun–kobun* relation. Among these orientations, and particularly important in this context, stand out the emphasis on harmonious contacts and on *giri* obligations, and the concepts of *onjō-shugi* (paternalism) and of *chuu* (loyalty, duty and obedience), which is equated to filial piety. I. Najita describes the *giri* obligations in the following terms:

In its idealistic sense, a *giri* is a humane feeling of obligation one feels or ought to feel in response to a pure 'blessing' (*on*) bestowed on him by another person. This reciprocation is understood as being pure and without selfish interest, as springing from one's spiritual self. Actually, it is assumed that a person rarely concedes or surrenders everything of himself. Thus, a kind act invites a reciprocal or *quid pro quo* recognition of a legitimate residuum of self-interest in the actor himself, although the relationship may be uneven. Still, it is clear that the primary ethical legitimation in *giri* relations is drawn directly from traditional idealistic ideas about true and humane feelings.[82]

This congruence between relations and cultural values crystallises, as we have seen, when the links are modelled in accordance with ritual kinship terms, whereby the transitory relative positions of control over avenues of exchange and conversion of resources in institutional markets are anchored, from the outset, in a permanent, quasi-'sacred' basis. This formalisation of links makes them no longer subject either to actual market positions or to changes in the transactional strategy of partners. As long as the principle of seniority is recognised, the *oyabun* only derives gains from improvements in the market positions of his subordinates. He is given social recognition, prestige and the ultimate right to make decisions; this allows him to confer instrumental and emotional gratification upon his *kokata* by performing supportive functions on their behalf. He thereby reinforces the acceptance of ranking societal order and of a personalised conception of society, according to which outsiders – whatever their rank – are considered as potential enemies and hostility, or at least indifference, must be shown them.

The importance of these conceptions as a force in structuring the *oyabun–kobun* links stands out in any review of the processes of continuity and change that such ties underwent in modern Japan. These relations were affected by such changes as the technological developments that made long training periods unnecessary and by the interest of large firms in building a permanent labour force within their realm, as well as by the fact that the standardisation of wages and the establishment of new institutional arrangements modified the forms that the pattern would take in modern society. The modern foreman does not wield the same degree of control as the labour contractor or the master craftsman had over his subordinates. Accordingly, *oyabun–kobun* links remain prominent in those places where the ladder of vertical mobility is longer, the rewards potentially great and the criteria of evaluation vague, as in unions or in management hierarchies; in which cases it may be in the *kobun's* interests to be attached to an *oyabun*.

Of no less importance, however, is the acceptance or rejection of the vertical arrangements. Ideally, the roles of the partners are fixed forever, even in the face of radical changes in their market positions. The acceptance of seniority is, therefore, decisive, even more so than the actual power of the leader. Accordingly, the main expressions of revolt against these relations of personal dependence occurred during the postwar period, particularly within the circles of young people influenced by Western ideas and working in modern industry, among whom the ideals of *giri* obligations somehow became discredited.

The occupational realm seems to be the main area for contracting *oyabun–kobun* ties. Vertical diffuse attachments are less commonly established within the bureaucratic realm in Japan. Appointments to the bureaucracy are made principally on the basis of merit, assessed by highly competitive written examinations and interviews, and favouritism in recruitment is far rarer than in southern Europe, Latin America or southeast Asia. Clientelistic relations seem to occur only within official circles, but are conceived in senior–junior terms and do not evince the semi-legal character of fully fledged clientelism.[83] In the political realm, on the other hand, relations are less reinforced by cultural conceptions and are, indeed, more instrumentally biased. Accordingly, ambivalent attitudes towards the political brokers are the norm in this sphere.

Another peculiarity of the Japanese patterns is that, despite their strong character, *oyabun–kobun* networks remained dispersed and are not, as a rule, integrated into wider chains. Indeed, personal links are very strong and exclusive, and demand a high level of personal trust and commitment. This trust, however, is not transferred to the political sphere, under conditions of political modernisation, but remains attached to the original network. Accordingly, Japanese relations lack a pyramidal tendency and do not become a form of society-wide social exchange and organisational articulation.

India[84]

I

India has developed as a very large, heterogeneous, densely populated and impoverished sub-continent, with a long history of warfare, change of rulers and mass movements. The Hindu *varna* caste scheme has provided throughout history a universal model, according to which *jatis* (traditional localised castes confined to a few neighbouring villages), tribes and groups have been rather flexibly incorporated and assimilated into a single socio-cosmic order. The social order was conceived in terms of the organic interdependence originating in the primordial division of labour between castes and the economic relations that members of different *jatis* maintained at the local level through *jajmani* (patronage) relations. As is well known and as has been emphasised by, among others, L. Dumont,[85] these interactions and exchanges were anchored and legitimised in a transcendental (all-India and universalistic) manner by the Hindu conceptions of purity and pollution and the *chatuvarna* ideal of society developed by Brahminic jurists and literary scholars. Some of the relations and interchanges between castes were indeed regulated by the exchange of services, ascriptively and continuously assured by the hierarchical model, as is usual, even today, between *jajmans* as patrons of Brahman priests, barbers or funeral priests. In such a case, localised clan segments are, throughout life and even hereditarily, mutually related by ritualised links involving a high degree of commitment. The ritual specialists thereby receive unsolicited gifts and instrumental help, while the patron gains merit and prestige generated by the impeccable status of his partners in the exchange. In such relations, the client has an unconditional obligation either to give ritual services to the *jajman's* household, or to provide a substitute for himself. The *jajman* is obliged to reward the client to the limit of his capacity and to utilise only 'his' priests in the performance of ritual services. These are conceived as a kind of *jaddi* or ancestral property (in some cases, can even be bought and sold).

In traditional India, similar arrangements were duplicated – as well as legitimised by the *varna* Hindu model – in the relations established between clusters of agricultural labourers and farmers and the *zamindars* (landowners). Such links flourished under various conditions – when, for instance, a high concentration of landownership together with village isolation made it almost impossible for servants to seek outside possibilities of employment (even if such opportunities as existed during the nineteenth century were still available), or when there was an abundant supply of relatively unskilled manpower, as also when the cultural premises condoned the low place that dependants held in the ritual hierarchy. Under such conditions, the grant of help, loans, etc., created relations of bondage, which implied the possibility of compulsory exchange based on unequal terms. The *jajman*, however, strove to increase his power and prestige and not merely his income. His initial aim was to give up agricultural work – perceived as being 'defiling' – and thus to suit his 'clean' status and life-style to those prescribed by his caste status. This could be achieved by his using the services of the farm servants. Some of these *kamins* became their patron's confidants, were consulted on agricultural issues, knew intimate details of their *jajman's* family and received help on different occasions, not as payment but as a grant, ideally related to the *jajman's* responsibility for his *kamins'* welfare. In fact, by adopting a servile attitude and behaviour, humility expressed by words and gesture and exaggerated deference, *kamins* tried to compel the *jajman* to live up to his ideal role. Loyalty figured importantly in the moral code of the *kamins*, who looked with contempt on those people who, in the traditional villages, withdrew from the relationship, relinquishing the security and social ties entailed in it. The exclusiveness of such arrangements became further anchored in ritual and ideological representations of caste rights and duties when, in the nineteenth century, the local officials were forbidden to assist runaway farm servants.

II

Less anchored in ritual considerations were the relations established between landowners and *kamin* craftsmen. In these cases, already in traditional India, *jajmani* orientations were used more flexibly, especially after the expansion of markets under British rule. Artisans such as blacksmiths, carpenters, weavers, basket- or shoe-makers, were paid in kind, according to agreements reformulated periodically rather than piece-work, and were expected to provide prompt service when requested, especially in periodic agricultural work. But these links were less stable than the ones between the agricultural labourers and the *zamindars* or between the ritual specialists and the *jajmans*. The details of exchange and payment could be negotiated according to short-term local considerations such as, for instance, the results of the annual harvest. Thus, disputes usually broke out between artisans, landowners and employers and, from the English period, the resulting instability was further accentuated by factory-made commodities flowing into the local markets and eliminating the need to rely on the services of members of artisan castes.

Thus the *kamins*, even if they ideally held a caste monopoly in their traditional crafts, could not withstand the competition of outside 'interlopers' or, what is more significant, the pressure of factory-made products available in the local market in modern India. This, together with the increase in the price of grain, and the difficulty of buying it even if cash was available, has largely eliminated from the *jajmani* system of customary rewards the artisan (potter, weaver, basket- and shoe-maker) castes that provided the required commodities.

Indeed, the occupational structure of modern India has changed to such a degree that large parts of the population are employed outside the villages – a fact that facilitates their access to 'free-caste' occupations and to higher educational opportunities. Among the remainder, only a small proportion earn their livelihood from the pursuit of specific caste occupations, while even full-time specialists draw additional gains from other sources of income. From an economic perspective, *jajmani* ties are affected by – and recede before – the relations modelled on class principles fully operative within the agrarian classes and the urban labour sector.

Since the gaining of independence in 1947, the Indian government has adopted democratic political institutions – such as the cabinet parliamentary system and the competitive electoral framework – and has attempted to transform some of the basic tenets of the ascriptive hierarchical system. Positions of formal authority have proliferated and are, in principle, open to all Indians, irrespective of caste or class considerations, or are reserved for low castes and tribes, such as the Untouchables, in accordance with the policies of 'affirmative discrimination' in the political and educational realms.

Wide areas of social interaction – especially important in rural locales – have, however, been passed over in such regulations of the 'secular' State as those controlling the exchange of food, greetings, tobacco, access to wells and temples, etc. In addition, since about 70% of the population are still illiterate, the policies of 'positive' discrimination in official positions indirectly reinforce, rather than undermine, in the short term at least, the caste identities. There are also countervailing social forces that preclude members of a minority and of low castes from succeeding in challenging the hold of the dominant castes' members over avenues of access to the centre and to the resources derived through government channels. Members of non-dominant castes – village leaders for instance – join the networks of higher-level politicians as dependants and clients and, in return for electoral support, are granted sources of patronage.

Thus, the openness of the modern Indian political sphere, together with the existence of strong hierarchical structures, has fostered the emergence of such networks of political clientelism. These are evident in the weak organisation of Indian constituencies, in the existence of unions patronised and subsidised by the parties (Congress or Communist) with low bargaining power in an economy contending with large surpluses of labour force, and in the people's low expectations from the bureaucratic and political formal institutions, which have largely been unresponsive to universalistic programmes and priorities.

We will return later to deal in detail with the dynamics and trends of *jajmani* relations and political clientelism in modern India.

Rwanda[86]

In pre-independence Rwanda, clientelistic relations emerged between persons of unequal standing either in terms of rank (as in the relations between Tutsi aristocrats and Hutu peasants) or in terms of political and economic assets (as in the relations between poor Tutsi and wealthier or powerful Tutsi). This relationship, known as *buhake*, tied a lord (*shebuja*) to clients (*umugaragu*) for a lifetime and often for some generations. It was established through the ceremonial receipt of a patron's cow. When reinforced by structural conditions, the relation might be maintained at a minimal level of exchange and cooperation, without this impairing its moral and jural potential. In fact, a client who was severely exploited by his patron could seek to end the relationship by looking for a new patron who would protect him from the anger of his former *shebuja*.

Through these links, a client obtained usufruct of cattle; protection against potential predation by other powerful Tutsi, or help in litigation; provision of food when needed; contributions to his bridewealth if he or his lineage could not meet their obligations, in case of death; support of his widow and children if they were left destitute; vengeance, in case he was murdered – if his lineage was too weak to exact it; payment of fines and, if the client committed an offence, the provision of shelter. In addition, the Hutu clients of a powerful Tutsi chief might exercise considerable informal authority and influence, and sometimes obtain political office. In return, clients provided patrons with instrumental resources, such as services and gifts of meat and beer (if they were Hutu peasants); also, the right to certain duties owed to the clients, in case they were Tutsi, by their own Hutu dependents. Such services could include attending to the patron's homestead, guarding its enclosure and giving the patron labour services in agriculture (Tutsi emphasised pastoral values and disdained agricultural tasks). Clients were expected to accord respect to their patron, accompanying him when he went to war or on visits to his allies and superiors.

The ceremonial establishment of the *buhake* link also imposed ideological constraints on the patron. A bad patron would lose his reputation as well as additional clients, thus leading to loss of power. The relationship was voluntarily entered into through the presentation of a request by the client and its eventual acceptance by the patron. In principle, it could also be severed by either partner, but in fact clients were prevented from ending such links, as this implied the return of cattle (which, even if increased in number during the period of attachment through the client's efforts, remained the 'legal' property of the patron) and consequently imposed a harsh burden on the *umugaragu*.

Southwestern Cyrenaica[87]

In southwestern Cyrenaica, Libya, clientelistic attachments among the Bedouins were entered into between *Sa'adi* families and the dispersed status category of *Mrabtin as-Sadgan*. The latter lacked jural rights to land and water, while their patrons held a monopolistic control of proprietary rights and political responsibility. In this setting, regulated by principles of corporate descent, there is a genealogical differentiation between patrons and clients. People can have either 'free' or 'tied' ancestors, and this fact conditions their quasi-legal supremacy or subordinate position in the social market. These positions are formally evidenced in the contracted personal links that sanction the virtual monopolisation of access to markets, and social representation of clients, by patrons.

The *Sa'adi* agnate corporations (tribal sections) own the land, and within their sections live a number of their clients, in groups of three to six tents. These sections seem collectively to occupy the role of patron. The landless people wander from one section to another, repeating ever anew their supplication for access to land use. They thus commend themselves to collective patrons, abdicate social and political

154

autonomy and, although they remain thereafter free in daily life and almost indistinguishable from the patrons, save on formal occasions, henceforth have no legal personality and are 'tied' to the decisions made by the patrons. In fact, since the 1920s, many of the 'tied' *Mrabtin* have acquired lands and, by tending herds, have become even wealthier than *Sa'*, but they can only convert their wealth through the patron–client link.

Clients only constitute a small proportion of the section's working force, and are dispersed in small nuclei among the patrons' tents. This dispersion ensures their remaining a status category, unable to amalgamate themselves into a single structure and to take a common stand vis-à-vis the patrons. Sometimes, the *Sa'adis* give their daughters or sisters to *Mrabtin* in marriage, in order to render the relationship more durable and stable (membership in the tribal corporations not being acquired through women).

PATRON–CLIENT RELATIONS IN THE U.S.A., THE U.S.S.R. AND MODERN JAPAN

We shall now proceed to describe succinctly the patron–client relationships in the U.S.A., the U.S.S.R. and modern Japan, where they tend, on the whole, to constitute addenda to the institutional context or contexts of the society.

Needless to say, such addenda-like types of patron–client relations do develop at many informal levels of social life. But they may also develop in much more crystallised ways – as the following analyses attest.

The U.S.A.[88]

The U.S.A. developed as the first fully modern polity based on premises of political equality, participation and equal access of the citizens – or at least of those granted the franchise – to the centres of power, and on the supervision of those centres by the citizenry and its elected representatives through the construction of institutional balances in the exercise of power and office holding. The basic ideology and these institutional premises were in principle inimical to the development of patron–client relations. Yet in the second half of the nineteenth century, the United States underwent great changes which gave rise to the widespread existence of such relations. The most important of these changes was the disappearance of small cities and the advent of the metropolis as the major ecological unit. This process of very rapid urbanisation was accompanied by a huge international and domestic migration. Within the American cities, the inhabitants' demands became more complex, owing to the need for services such as paved streets, sewers, garbage removal, school buildings, crime control, etc. Decisions regarding priorities in these fields were complicated by the mixture of different classes as well as by the different ethnic and religious backgrounds of the urban population. The traditional rule and, in principle, the voluntary and disinterested public service offered by the gentry, with its 'aristocratic' flavour and its distaste for contact with the masses, no longer fitted the variety of these demands.

Under these conditions, the political machine – whose main purpose was to win elections under universal suffrage and thereby to control key public offices and agencies – emerged, for the broad strata, as a 'way to get things done', that is, as an extra-legal organisation that could help solve the problems of newcomers. Among these problems were: finding work, securing food and fuel in hard times, learning the language, and obtaining advice and assistance in unforeseeable cases of bureaucratic impersonal rule application or interpersonal troubles. Assistance might be offered in speeding up official treatment, helping people to obtain pardons or bail in criminal courts, or settling disputes between tenants and landlords. In addition, the boss, often himself of humble origin, by invoking a rhetoric of personal–communal commitment and support, could assume the character of spokesman for the people and give the newcomers a feeling of mastering their new situation and of becoming integrated.

In return, the 'machine' (or political) boss who succeeded in presenting his deeds as personal acts of grace or generosity, elicited a sense of obligation that bound the poor to him as his followers. At election time, he mobilised these loyalties to obtain votes either for himself, for his people, or – in his role of the neighbourhood wardleader – for a higher-level candidate. By winning the elections, he held direct control over, or indirect access to, public and party offices and therefore access to thousands of jobs that could be distributed as rewards to followers or as inducement to the creation of ties of allegiance among the poor population sectors. Indeed, such access to and intimate knowledge of the municipal, country or state agencies were very important to allow the 'boss' to proffer his help only to the 'right' (i.e. reliable) people of his constituency.

In addition, his control of, or preferential access to, key legislative and financial officials, such as supervisors, aldermen or mayors, enabled him, at the same time, to mobilise the support or collaboration of businessmen, bankers, contractors or corporations (and even of gangsters). These social actors were interested in the award of contracts and in obtaining approval of plans related to real estate speculations, the grant of licences, the obviation of rule enforcement, or the reduction of tax assessments. Some of these 'favours' could represent a concrete material gain for the boss, either through the receipt of bribes or of a share of the benefits, or through practices of 'honest graft', such as those described by G.W. Plunkitt.[89]

The close collaborators of the boss and the party activists also enjoyed some of the benefits described above, from jobs to material inducements, as well as participation in the social recreation and fellowship entailed by membership of political clubs.

Thus, numerous instances of clientelistic short-term bargaining emerged within, and in relation to the functioning of, the political machines, in the efforts made to mobilise votes and to gain support in a system where electoral success was essential for obtaining control of government resources and sources of employment. These relationships were constrained by other features of American society and, from the 1930s onwards, underwent far-reaching changes which will be detailed below.

The U.S.S.R.[90]

Until the mid-nineteenth century, Russia was a monolithic state in which about 80% of the population were serfs tied to the soil, and depending either on the monarch or on the nobles. The tsar provided the legal underpinning of the system, and the nobility drew privileges from it and depended on the ruler. The polity was characterised by an absolute executive rule, censorship and the use of the secret police for political purposes. Attempts made by the tsars in the nineteenth century to develop the economy changed the rigid class structure. New middle-class strata emerged that, under the influence of liberal and radical European ideas, criticised the inegalitarianism of the society and the wide powers wielded by the monarchy. The Bolshevik regime that finally acceded to power late in 1917 ruled a country which, despite the impact of the sequence of wars in the early twentieth century, included masses of peasants hardly affected by the values of the small Russian bourgeoisie. The Bolsheviks attempted to revolutionise authoritatively the socio-economic bases of the Old Regime. Thus, a polity was instituted which, while dedicated to the modernisation and change of the society, was extremely centralised, elitist and authoritarian. The Soviet Union professed the Marxist–Leninist ideology, according to which the State – which was once an instrument of the oppression of one class by another – would 'wither away' in the Communist period. The Soviets, hence, did not invest formal institutions of government with great power. Instead, the Communist party of the Soviet Union (C.P.S.U.) remained the main focus of decision-making and power and was supposed to be the ideological vanguard expressing the needs of the people. It was thus able to formulate policies which derived legitimacy from Communist doctrine and the commitment of party leaders. There were elective structures, and their functions were in principle mobilisatory, aimed at raising the spirit of the public and encouraging its involvement.

Notwithstanding the efforts of the regime in planning for and, since the 1950s, providing a regular flow of resources and services to the population, there are still acute problems in these fields. The erratic supply of basic resources and services – owing to delays in distribution, to shortages, to the poor quality of the products – is conducive to the emergence of 'a frantic search after commodities'. This situation has, accordingly, led to instances of private profiteering from the delivery of state resources, petty bribery and black marketing, which have become a widespread built-in feature of the Soviet economy.

In a parallel way, there have developed in these societies many personal, informal and, at most, only quasi-legal relations with the persons who have access to the goods and services unobtainable at the shops and offices.

Similarly, instances of favouritism, interpersonal obligations and sponsorship occur in the context of bureaucratic contacts, in ways that closely resemble and, to some degree, probably even go beyond what may be found in other advanced industrial societies.

The relatively closed nature of the elite and the overwhelming social uncertainty which exists in Communist society and which tends, as Z. Bauman stresses, to undermine any attempt at rational planning, reinforce such tendencies, induce behavioural patterns, and shape, along lines of patronage, a type of rational adjustment to the predominant situations. Thus, indeed, it may seem that clientelism and patronage are, as Bauman puts it, 'a systematic regulating feature of the Communist society, a functional equivalent of law and/or the impersonal market place'.[91]

Paradoxically enough, such clientelistic arrangements seem to be more pervasive and continuous, in the Soviet bloc, among the cliques of powerful personalities than between them and those persons lower in the social hierarchy. But the picture is rather mixed, even among the powerful, as can be seen in the structure of access to the centres of power.

As is well known, such access to power is monopolised in Communist societies by the representatives and interpreters of the dominant political ideology. This fact induces patterns of promotion within the political sphere on the basis of demonstrated loyalty to the C.P.S.U., which, today, is the principal *apparat* (institutional framework) in the U.S.S.R. and which penetrates such other agencies as the trade unions, the army, the political police and the administration. This demand for loyalty may be articulated and is, indeed, usually interpreted as a client-like allegiance to some of the members, cadres and contending internal factions of the C.P.S.U.

Nevertheless, there are some institutional factors in the U.S.S.R. that impose limits upon the operation of these relations. We will return, later, to the analysis of the dynamics of these factors in relation to patron–client ties existing there.

Modern Japan[92]

In modern Japan, clientelistic relations developed around community leaders and political brokers known as *yuryokusha*, literally 'influential men'. In the postwar period, these social actors stood between the formal government and political machines on the one hand and the voters on the other.

The *yuryokusha* attempted to achieve their own election to local or supralocal administrative positions or used their system of recommendation (*suisensei*) for supporting the election to these positions of candidates of their choice. They may also have gained prestige and public recognition and have been rewarded by elected politicians with positions in either the administration, private enterprises – which were interested in maintaining 'good' relations with political spheres – or public works, such as irrigation projects, etc. On their part, the *yuryokusha* provided instrumental resources and services to the residents of the community as a whole, these resources being mainly derived from their contacts with administrators at a higher level. For the clients, relational symbolic resources played a secondary role, except where interaction was limited to the locality. On the other hand, some degree of diffuse attachment has been found in the *jiban* (one's political area) and in the relations existing among high-level politicians, where the attitudes were more akin to those informing *oyabun–kobun* relationships.

The *yuryokusha* are described by Ike in the following terms:

In every community, whether rural or urban, there are a few individuals who are known as *yuryokusha*. These individuals may range in type from men of integrity to those on the criminal fringe, but in any case they are looked upon as the leaders of the community. The *yuryokusha* may or may not hold office; quite often their power is independent of office holding. If they happen to be officials, it is because they are influential in their own right. Traditionally in rural Japan, the *yuryokusha* almost always sprang from the larger landholding families, because landownership and power were related. This is to some extent still the case; but it is also true that new sources of influence have appeared in recent decades as a result of economic and social changes.[93]

Economic wealth and its transference to the political realm seem to be a primary source of power. By controlling political information and contacts, *yuryokusha* attain formal administrative or political command of local affairs, and thereby control other avenues of flow of resources in the periphery. In more urban settings, the relevance of economic resources to the acquisition of political positions is reduced and politicians occupy full-time political and administrative jobs.[94] Today, the *yuryokusha* are mainly drawn from former upper and middle strata, comprising farmers, retailers, small manufacturers and self-employed professionals, and do not operate categorial networks to advance their common interests.

Connections are considered essential for building up power domains. The political centre does not seek generalised support for actual political incumbents and, hence, the market positions of *yuryokusha* are affected only when there is an increase in living standards and security at the local level, or when the centre becomes interested in the mobilisation of the periphery. The backing of high officials and the command of local votes contribute to the privileged position enjoyed by *yuryokusha*. In fishing and agricultural communities, the threat of social and economic ostracism of dissenters increases the control that *yuryokusha* may hold. In urban settings, personality characteristics grow in importance in commanding floating votes.

Attitudes towards the *yuryokusha* are ambivalent. People look upon them with fear and dislike, because of their aggressiveness and selfishness, although they may aknowledge that they are the most intelligent, influential and capable persons in their localities. In other settings, the broker combines authoritarian and paternalistic characteristics, as what White calls a 'carte blanche leader' with whom rank and file may identify and upon whom they may rely as he embodies the highest social values and acts as spokesman for the local unit (*buraku*).[95]

Accordingly, the degree of ideological elaboration of the pattern is variable. In general, it is assumed that the relationship will adopt diffuse overtones (in spite of its instrumental focus), as the social actors incur many kinds of *on* and *giri* obligations. When a politician is building a *jiban* – that is, his constituency – he is expected to reciprocate by bringing benefits to the district. Indeed, a boss has to render some of the services expected if he wishes to retain his position of power. The degree to which he conforms to this expectation may be inversely related to the strength of his market position.

Basic characteristics of patron–client relations

As has already been indicated, however, these relations in the political realm are less reinforced by cultural conceptions and more instrumentally biased than *oyabun–kobun* relations. Accordingly, *yuryokusha* are likely to base their power domains on such strategies as obtaining the backing of officials and political machines and blocking access to information,* rather than on the commitment and support of their constituencies.

In this relation, when political forces placed at the centre attempt to penetrate the periphery through administrative and political frameworks, they are looked upon with distrust. In other words, some indistinctness seems to be exhibited in Japanese society regarding the means through which the commitment of the broader strata is to be transferred to the political sphere. This trait is of particular importance in the dynamics adopted by political clientelism, especially in urban settings where territorial and kinship ties are weak. In order to understand how these dynamics operate, we will analyse here the conditions under which the *yuryokusha* emerged as political brokers in the period following the Second World War.

This was a period of socio-economic changes which influenced the balance of power at the periphery. Thus, on the local level, the upper classes (mainly former rich farmers known as *osa-byakushō*) had been in control of the administration since the 1889 reform turned the communities into *buraku* units. These units were part of a highly centralised government, as sub-units of the administrative villages or town centres (*son* or *chō*). Along with changes in landownership (land reform was adopted in 1945), technical advances, rising standards of living and new sources of livelihood, the economic and social bondage of the farmers to the *buraku* leaders underwent transformations. The mayor, once elected by the assemblymen, was now nominated by direct votes of the population. Around 1953 *buraku* were included in wider administrative units. The familistic control of votes was now not enough to elect candidates, even when the election could be arranged without question at a village level. The distance between loci of decision and the villagers widened. In a parallel way, there was a growing consciousness of the importance of high-level politics in local affairs as well as of the lack of appropriate channels to influence it. On the other hand, attitudes of submissiveness and of regarding politics as 'other people's job' remained dominant in peripheral circles.

Similarly, with the American occupation of Japan, doubts emerged

---

* *Yuryokusha* adopt strategies of reduction of flow of information or block the development of the ability to understand mass media. To this end, the broker relies on the existence of different kinds of writing and on the natural ambiguity of Japanese syntax. Kuroda states that ambiguous expressions, which often confuse persons of lower status, are widely used by Japanese politicians. [96]

regarding the once-unquestioned character of the social order – doubts prompted by the conflictive evaluations of the character of interpersonal and institutional relations and exchanges as well as by new concepts of political participation. These influences were, however, mainly confined to the national level, and the Japanese as a whole continued to show indifference to politics, in congruence with the traditional view of this realm as marginal to the basic societal and cosmic order.

People accepted that the course of events and policy decisions were beyond their will and control. As mentioned by Ike, Japanese voters are divided into two main types: those who have a negative attitude towards politics (especially as regards the national level) and look upon it with little concern, and those who vote as they are told, out of fear.[97]

Under these conditions, *yuryokusha* played a central role in controlling and gathering votes in the postwar electoral period in Japan. They constituted, as indicated above, a main link between formal government and political machines on the one hand, and voters on the other, and, through their position, established ties of mutual services with peripheral strata. At the same time, however, the attitude towards them was ambivalent, containing strong elements of distrust, and the relations were more short term oriented. Even if they could use their contacts and influence without being challenged by attempts at mass participation, this could be explained by the tendency of the Japanese not to become involved in politics, rather than by a strong interpersonal commitment.

These conditions were conducive to the emergence of *oyabun–kobun* relations among broad sectors in industry and business more frequently than in politics, where relations were more unstable and factional splits appeared, especially at high level.

APPROACHING THE SYSTEMATIC STUDY OF VARIATIONS IN PATRON–CLIENT RELATIONS

I

The material presented above provided abundant illustrations of the fact that patron–client relations do indeed develop in many different concrete forms and play different roles within the institutional contexts of their respective societies. The distinctions and differences, to which we have only alluded above, can be analysed in a more systematic way.

The first such distinction is between different concrete forms, different types of organisation, of such relations. The most simple and obvious such distinction, which is very often stressed in the literature, is the one existing between the local dyadic interpersonal form of patron–client relations, that can be found in many traditional agrarian settings, and the more dispersed complex networks of patrons, brokers and clients, that can be found in complex or developed societies or sectors thereof.

Our material has indicated, however, that the differences in the organisational structure of patron–client relations are, in fact, much more variegated. In a systematic way, the variations can be distinguished along the following lines:

1. The scope, institutional placement and organisational character of clientelistic networks. The major distinctions here are found in the concrete organisation of such networks, in their placement, and in the linkages to wider institutional frameworks and, above all, to various formal organisations.
2. The characteristics of the occupancy of patron–client roles, and especially (a) the degree of openness of access to patron–client roles, where the main distinction is the existence or absence of normative barriers to the assumption of patrons' and clients' roles by the different social actors; (b) the criteria of incumbency, whether individuals or groups are incumbent to the patrons' and clients' roles.
3. The modes of instalment into such roles, especially whether they are assumed informally, through agreement or through some formal ceremonial or contractual sanction.
4. The contents of the clientelistic exchanges, which can be distinguished according to (a) the relative durability of the specific relationships; (b) the different packages of resources exchanged in the patron–client relations, and especially the relative emphasis on a solidarity or power differentials within such relations; (c) the relative importance of discretion, 'subversive submissiveness' (half-hearted obedience) and socio-moral restraints in such relations.
5. The degree of continuity or instability of the clientelistic patterns in general and of specific organisational structures in particular.

The second distinction, to which we have already alluded and on the basis of which we have organised the case studies presented above – and the one best illustrated here by the difference between the Russian, American, Chinese, Japanese, Israeli (see chapter 5) and Indian cases, on the one hand, and the Italian, Spanish or Latin American, Middle Eastern and southeast Asian cases on the other – is of a different order. As briefly indicated above, this is the distinction between patron–client relations as what C.H. Landé has called an 'addendum' – legitimated or non-legitimated – to the central institutional nexus of a society, when patron–client relations develop in the interstices of such nexus, and, on the other hand, their constituting a distinct mode of regulation of some of the most crucial aspects of institutional order, of construction of trust (and of generalised exchange within it), of the structuring of the flow of resources, of exchange and power relations and of their legitimation in society.

This distinction implies that, while many of the concrete organisational aspects of patron–client relations – such as the dyadic or tryadic personal relations or broader networks of brokers, the exchange of favours between the partners and the like – can be found in many different societies, yet their full institutional implications and repercussions only develop when they become part or 'manifestations' of the central mode or regulation of the flow of resources, and processes of interpersonal and institutional exchange and interaction in a society or a sector thereof.

Thus, as against most previous comparisons – which, with the partial exception of those of E. Gellner, J. Waterbury and E. Wolf, have defined some of the major differences between patron–client relations and other types of social organisation in rather concrete, organisational terms[98] – in our own comparison emphasis is placed on viewing them mainly, not as distinct types of social organisation, but as different models of the structuring of the flow of resources and of interpersonal interaction and exchanges in society: as different modes of generalised exchange.

II

The preceding analysis points out several problems to which we have to address ourselves. The first problem is to specify what is meant by patron–client relations constituting a distinct mode of regulation of some of the central aspects of the institutional order and, especially, the construction of generalised exchange within it. What are the implications of this fact as regards the structure and working of such relations, and in what way do such patron–client relations differ from those which constitute 'only' a recognised but limited part of such regulation, or from those which are only an informal addendum to the central institutional nexus?

The second problem is the nature of the social and cultural conditions which give rise to the different forms of patron–client relations or within the context of which they develop. Here, we have to analyse, first, the societal conditions which explain the development of the clientelistic mode of regulation of institutional relations, as distinct from other conditions in which patron–client relations constitute only an addendum to the central mode. Second, we have to explain systematically the great variety of organisational forms of patron–client relations and the conditions which give rise to such variety.

The investigation of these two sets of variations bears closely, as we shall see later, upon the problem of the distinction between different levels of continuity and discontinuity in the institutional order, a problem to which we have already referred above.

Let us now proceed with the analysis of these problems.

5

The clientelistic mode of generalised exchange and patron–client relations as addenda to the central institutional nexus

THE CLIENTELISTIC MODE OF GENERALISED EXCHANGE IN COMPARATIVE PERSPECTIVE

I

What is meant by clientelistic relations constituting the core of a central mode of societal institutional structure, of regulation of the flow of resources in society, of construction of trust and generalised exchange within it, or, in other words, of institutional integration? And how can such a clientelistic mode be distinguished from other modes of regulation of the institutional structure?

In any concrete social setting – a society or a sector thereof – diverse modes of construction of trust are usually operative in relation to the division of labour in society, and to the regulation of power manifest in the structuring of generalised exchange and in its institutional implications. In a concrete society, such modes assume differing importance and, although one of them usually predominates, conflicts may quite often develop between it and the others.* But, in principle, such modes can be differentiated, as they entail specific modes of construction of basic aspects of the social structure – particularly the structure of the social hierarchies and the flow and conversion of resources in relation to the construction of trust and meaning of generalised exchange in society.

One such crucial aspect of any social structure is the relation of the institutional links between generalised and specific exchange and especially the degree of linkage, first, between membership in major ascriptive categories and sectors of a society, on the one hand, and

---

* Accordingly, as we have implied above, relatively similar models may exist in a great variety of societal frameworks, at different levels of economic development and in different political regimes.

access to the centres of power, to positions of control of production, and to the major markets, on the other; second, between such access and the relative standing of different groups or categories in the major institutional markets, that is, between ownership of resources and the ability to control their use in broader settings. Such linkages generate relations between inequalities in the different aspects of social order enumerated above: between inequalities in ascriptive aspects, in access to the major centres of power and institutional markets, and inequalities within these markets. In this way is the structure of crucial aspects of social hierarchies in a society shaped.

It is from the point of view of the relations between generalised and specific exchange that some of the major characteristics of patron–client relationships stand out and can be distinguished from other kinds of social relations and organisations. It is the analytic features and dynamic propensities of what, for lack of a better word, we shall call the 'clientelistic' mode of structuring the relations between generalised and specific exchange that can best explain the crucial analytical characteristics of patron–client relations.

II

The presence of this mode of exchange is predicated on the existence of some tension between, on the one hand, potentially broad, sometimes even latent universalistic or semi-universalistic, premises and the concomitant free flow of resources and relatively broad scope of markets, and, on the other, the continuous attempts to limit such free flow.

These latent broad, even semi-universalistic, premises are evident in such societies, or sectors thereof, in the fact that, in principle here – as against societies in which the hereditary ascriptive model is predominant and which we shall discuss shortly – the members of various strata may be able to obtain some direct access to the means of production, to the major markets and to the centres of power. These members may, in principle, organise themselves towards such access and ensure their own control of the use of their resources in broader settings. Concomitantly, the centres of these societies may develop some autonomous relations to the broader strata from which the clients and brokers are recruited.[1]

At the same time, however, for reasons which we shall analyse in greater detail later, continuous attempts to circumvent these potentialities develop within these societies. Their aim is to limit, first, the free access of broader strata to the markets and centres, by the potential patrons' and brokers' monopolisation of the positions

167

controlling such access, and, second, the use and conversion of resources. It is, indeed, this combination of the potential openness of access to the markets with the continuous, semi-institutionalised attempts to limit such free access that constitutes the crux of the clientelistic model.

Thus, the structuring of relations between generalised and specific exchange, implied in the clientelistic model, is characterised, above all, by a very special type of linkage between some crucial aspects of the institutional structure of society. The first linkage is the one between, on the one hand, the respective standing of the potential patrons and clients in the semi-ascriptive hierarchical sub-communities or sub-sectors of the society and, on the other, the control of access to the centre or centres of the society, to the bases of production, to the major institutional markets, to the setting up of most public goods (i.e. goods provided by a collectivity and such that, if one member of the collectivity receives them, they cannot normally be denied to other members) and to the public distribution of private goods. The second linkage is between access to the markets and centres and the use and conversion of potentially free resources in these markets.

The crucial aspect of these two linkages in the clientelistic model is that they are very pervasive, yet not fully legitimised. They are based on the abdication by the clients of their potential autonomous access to the centre, to some of the major markets or to positions of control over the use of resources and to the setting up of public goods and services; instead, clients gain access to these spheres through the mediation of some patron, whether a person or an organisation (i.e. party or trade union), within which the clients do not obtain autonomous access to major loci of power.

Such mediation is contingent on the clients entering into a relation of exchange with the patron, which contains many aspects of routine exchange of goods or services within the various institutional markets, and which necessarily limits the scope and convertibility of the resources thus freely exchanged.

III

This 'ideal' model of the clientelistic mode of structuring generalised exchange differs from several other such models, in the context of which patron–client relations develop as addenda to the major institutional nexus.

Some of the most important such models (which, indeed, have often been compared, albeit only in organisational terms, with the clientelistic ones) are: the kinship one, found in many tribal societies; the ascriptive–hierarchical one, which is predominant in caste or feudal societies; and the different universalistic ones – pluralistic (democratic), monolithic (totalitarian), and consociational (especially found in several small European democracies).[2]

The ideal model of corporate kinship relations found, above all, in various tribal societies assumes that the access to almost all the major markets as well as to public goods is acquired through membership in such (often corporate) kinship groups. It also assumes that a large part of the exchange of resources is effected through the corporate activities of these groups or within them and that, in fact, most major markets as well as public goods are dependent upon the relations between them. Similar 'ideal' premises can be found in ascriptively (mainly kinship) based hierarchical systems. The fullest expression can be found in the Indian caste system, but many elements exist also in other primitive, or archaic, or feudal societies.

In common with the kinship model, there is also the assumption that most (even if not all) significant specific exchanges are made through ascriptive groups. Thus they combine to a great degree generalised and specific exchanges, even if the former are more fully elaborated in special ritual occasions. Whenever specific exchanges are made more openly, they are structured so as not to impinge on the dominant hierarchical–ascriptive model. The principal difference between the hierarchical and the pure corporate kinship model is, of course, in the basic premises of inequality in the relations between the ascriptive groups and, hence, usually in a sharper stress on the hierarchical relations between them.

This linkage between generalised and specific exchange generates a certain pattern of linkages between the inequalities found in the various major dimensions of the institutional order. In the ideal premises of such models, there is a very close relation, ideally almost a complete linkage, between the relative standing of any group or social category in the ascriptive hierarchical sphere, on the one hand, and its access to the centres of society, to the setting up of public goods and especially to public distribution of private goods, and to the major institutional markets, on the other. Thus, in a sense, either the virtual non-existence, or relative lack of importance, of open markets, or of any significant autonomous activities within them, is assumed.

The 'official' model of universalistic open-market or bureaucratic societies assumes that access to major markets, centres of power and the setting up of public goods (as well as, in principle, the public distribution of private goods) is vested in all the members of the wider community, without regard to their membership in any other ascriptive hierarchical sub-units (even if some of the criteria for setting up public goods and publicly distributing private goods discriminate in favour of certain social categories such as the 'poor' or the 'deprived'). It also assumes that all members may participate in the struggle to set up the criteria of distribution and that specific exchange in open markets will not be legally conditioned by membership in any sub-group.

This broad model can be subdivided into several sub-models of which three – the open–pluralistic, the monolithic–totalitarian and the consociational – are the most important. In the pluralistic model predominant in most Western European societies, in the U.S.A. and in the first Dominions, the major groups have free autonomous access to the centres of power, to the setting up of public goods and to basic units of production and markets. In the monolithic system, predominant especially in modern totalitarian societies with antecedents in monolithic imperial systems, major groups have access to the markets and public goods, but their access to the centres of power and to publicly distributed private goods is severely controlled by the centre, although not, officially at least, by any single especially ascriptive sub-group within the society.

In the consociational model, lately also designated 'Proporzdemokratie', prevalent above all in small European democracies like the Netherlands, Switzerland and Austria, the relations between generalised and specific exchange are much more complicated than in the universalistic one. Basic titles (such as citizenship and all the duties and rights entailed) are vested, according to universalistic criteria, in all the members of the broader collectivity (nation). As against this, access to the major centres of power, as well as to many public goods and publicly distributed private goods, is to a large degree mediated by the major consociational segments (or their representatives), be these religious groups, political parties, local units, etc. Within such segments, however, access to power is open to everybody. Beyond this, within most consociational systems, relatively wide markets develop, especially in the economic field. Access to them is in principle open to all members of the society, and the specific exchanges undertaken within them are not bound to membership of any of the ascriptive relationships.

The major difference between such consociational and corporatist systems, as found for instance in Latin America, is that, within the latter system, the access to the centres of power is not vested autonomously in membership in the corporative units. Access, not only to public goods and to public distribution of private goods, but also to large parts of the seemingly open markets, is mediated by the corporative units.[3]

IV

These different modes of structuring generalised exchange organise in different ways the major dimensions or aspects of the institutional order, analysed in chapter 3, as particularly important from the point of view of the possibility of breakdown in the extension of trust. These dimensions are: first, the different degrees of structural and symbolic differentiation of major institutional spheres; second, the degree to which different institutional spheres of a society are structured according to dissimilar principles, especially universalistic as against particularistic, and egalitarian as against hierarchical, principles.

The third dimension is the degree of clarity of such principles and of their application to different institutional spheres, especially to the more central institutional spheres and markets. The fourth is the clarity in specifying the degree of autonomous – as against mediated (i.e. vested in different mediators) – access of different groups to the major societal centres in general and to the centres of political and cultural (usually religious) power, in which the relations between trust, power and meaning are particularly defined.

Here, the clientelistic mode of generalised exchange is characterised by a distinction between the criteria which regulate different institutional spheres and by the relative blurring of the clarity of such principles.

As regards degrees of structural and symbolic differentiation, the clientelistic model can be distinguished on several additional levels from such models as corporate kinship groups or ascriptively based hierarchical ones, in that it requires the existence of central (not just marginal) markets and of the organisation of means of production not embedded in such ascriptive units or in the relations between them. It is based on a situation where there is already a difference between ownership of resources and control of their use in broader settings, as well as on a certain segregation between the resources dealt with in generalised and in specific exchange.

At the same time, however, as against the more 'open' universalistic models (whether pluralistic, monolithic or consociational), which tend to countervail any attempts to limit the access of different groups to the bases of production and to positions of control of the use of resources in centres and markets, it is the very essence of the clientelistic model that it establishes and maintains such limitations, even if they are not derived, as in the kinship or ascriptive hierarchical models, from the basic premises of the society. Of all the models, the clientelistic one is, as indicated above, the closest to the corporatist one. Indeed, patron–client relations tend to develop also in societies with strong corporatist elements, even if corporatism does not develop as a necessary factor of clientelism. The major difference between them is that the purely corporatist model does not necessarily include so many package-deals in the concrete relations between the major (corporate) units and their membership.

V

These differences between the clientelistic and other models are most evident in the linkages between the inequalities found in the various aspects or dimensions of institutional life and specifically in the forms of structuring of social hierarchies connected to them. These aspects are shaped in clientelism in markedly different forms from the ones that develop in either the universalistic or the ascriptive–kinship hierarchical societies. As in latter societies, a very close linkage develops in the patron–client nexus (yet not always one so precisely and normatively defined) between ascriptive hierarchical standing, on the one hand, and access to power, to public goods and to major institutional markets on the other.

That is, such linkage seems to be characterised by a certain totality or continuity that cannot easily be changed in the context of these relations. It is this totality or continuity of such inequality that distinguishes patron–client relations from the 'chance' inequalities that may develop within the markets and in the access to them in universalistic societies.

And yet, despite the seeming comprehensiveness of this inequality, in fact the concrete linkage between the inequalities in the major dimensions of institutional order that develop in the clientelistic model is rather fragile. This fragility is evident in several closely connected aspects. First, by contrast to what obtains in the ascriptive–hierarchical societies, such inequalities, and above all the linkages between them, are not in clientelistic societies or sectors thereof, fully prescribed, legitimised or assured. Indeed, as has already been implied, they are set up, in most of these societies, against some of the latter's basic formal, more open, universalistic premises.

Second, and closely related thereto, is the fact that the relative hierarchical standing of different actors – patrons, brokers and clients – is not always fully prescribed, and frequent disputes may arise in the connection.[4]

Third, the fact remains that the clients are sometimes, potentially or actually, able to accumulate resources in the various markets (especially, but not solely, in the political one) which are not commensurate with their relatively low ascriptive standing and, when combined with

172

the latent broader premises of these systems, may threaten the patrons' monopoly of access to markets and to the centre or centres of the society.[5]

It is within the context of these features, therefore, that the fully fledged types of patron–client relations analysed above develop.

PATRON–CLIENT RELATIONS AS ADDENDA TO ASCRIPTIVE HIERARCHICAL MODELS OF GENERALISED EXCHANGE

Introduction

As we have seen, patron–client relations do develop also in societies in which other, non-clientelistic, modes of structuring of generalised exchange are predominant, especially in two types of such societies.

First, they develop in societies – such as India, Rwanda, Cyrenaica or Japan – based on ascriptive hierarchical premises, and in some others – like Imperial China – which combine such hierarchical premises with universalistic criteria of macrosocietal organisation.

Second, patron–client relations also develop in various modern universalistic – in principle egalitarian – societies based on relatively open markets in which pluralistic, consociational, totalitarian models, or some mixtures thereof, are predominant.

In all these societies, there do develop various patterns of dyadic or network vertical relations which in many ways are similar to patron–client relations, and have indeed been identified as such in the societies in which they emerged, as well as in the sociological literature.

Unlike the patron–client relations which develop in societies in which the clientelistic model is predominant, however, these types of patron–client relations are, as we have seen above, of two, sometimes overlapping, types: namely, those which are relatively recognised and legitimate but limited parts of the institutional nexus, and those which constitute mostly addendum types. These two types evince several characteristics which differ from the fully fledged patron–client relations in clientelistic societies.

Let us consider, first, the restricted but relatively recognised patron–client relations which develop – as we shall see – above all in hierarchical, especially ascriptive, but to some degree also in universalistic, societies (such as Imperial China). In these relations, first of all – as against the patron–client relations existing in clientelistic societies – the roles of 'patron' and 'client' are usually correlated to ascribed statuses, and clientelistic relations seem to be subsumed within the dominant model of these societies. These relations emerge mainly as the result of

173

some openness of access to, and possibilities of personal advancement in, institutional markets and through the lack of prescription of the concrete market positions of members of status (caste) categories.

Second, such relations are usually more segmented than in clientelistic societies, and the exchange of resources they regulate does not affect the central controlling positions within institutional markets.

Third, such relations are, accordingly, also usually restricted to the concrete dyadic or tryadic setting and only rarely extend formally into chains of brokers, although sometimes they may, informally, and rather illegitimately, develop to some degree in such directions.

The differences between such unfolding and the nature of patron–client relations in clientelistic societies stand out when discussing in detail these relations both in Japan and in such ascriptive hierarchical societies as India, Bedouin Cyrenaica and pre-independence Rwanda.

Patron–client relations in Japan

The material presented for Japan indicates that there are some features common to the Japanese and to other instances of clientelism, while, at the same time, the institutional implications and format of the Japanese ties seem to differ, in some important respects, from those of the patron–client relations in the more fully fledged clientelistic settings.

We have already indicated that, in all cases, these clientelistic relations emphasise to an even greater degree than those found in other settings the combination of voluntary undertaking of such links with strong elements of inequality in hierarchical standing of the partners, and the recognition by the clients of the patrons' right to control the avenues and terms of exchange and flow of resources. In the case of Japanese *oyabun–kobun* links, this even occurs in spite of actual changes in the market positions of the partners. In addition, through such relations, and as in other clientelistic ties, clients gain some measure of protection against the uncertainties of markets and of nature, and against the arbitrariness and demands of centre, groups, organisations or individuals.

In spite of these similarities, however – and as against clientelistic relations found in Latin America, southeast Asia or in the Mediterranean – by being involved in *oyabun–kobun* relations, Japanese 'clients' are not only granted a certain degree of security, of control over sources of uncertainty, of protection or of delegation of power, but also have certain obligations that are not typical of other patron–client relations.

While in other clientelistic societies the reflection of the patron's 'social visibility' and power is sometimes used to enlarge the degree of recognition of authority, commitment to it, and to the norms upheld by it, a strong emphasis on seniority, on harmony and on *giri* obligations, and the high value placed on filial piety and paternalism.[7] It is therefore the *oyakata* who seem to invest time and resources in maintaining the *kokata's* long-term commitment. This is done by renouncing in the short term the use of the differential ranking advantages they have, and by stressing the highly expressive content of the relationship, shaped around values of long-term recognition of paternalistic authority. This phrasing of the relations confers expressive gratification upon clients and an egalitarian aura, despite their hierarchical inequality.

This translation of momentary advantages into long-lasting power domains in institutional markets is, indeed, not peculiar to *oyabun-kobun* relations but is shared with other types of clientelism in other societies. What is peculiar to Japan is the enforcement of these links – of the submission to a superior, as prescribed within the framework of a strong social consensus by the cultural outlook of this society. These links have been closely related to the wider framework of Japanese society in such other characteristics as the high commitment to the imperial centre and its symbols, the emphasis on rank differences, on resolution of dissent through consensual agreement, on solidarity, unity and particularistic trust.

We will describe at some length below some of the features of Japanese society, in order to understand how they are related to the specific unfolding of Japanese clientelistic relations.

The Japanese family system (*kozoku-zeido*) is characterised by a nuclear structure, patriarchality, seniority and birth rights, a greater emphasis on child–parent relations than on wife–husband ties, ancestor worship, and the exercise of a wide control by the head of the family over its members. Within the family unit, attitudes of integration and communal outlook are encouraged. Individual autonomy is minimised and high levels of personal involvement are demanded, while rank and exclusiveness ('departmentalism') are valued. In modern Japan, many of the features of the traditional family system (*ie*) have been modified through the processes of urbanisation and industrialisation. Nonetheless, the concept of *ie* persists in the conceptualisation, in diffuse terms, of specific settings – in a company, for instance, as if it were an *ie*. Accordingly, employees of industrial firms are treated as household members, while the *ie* encompasses the workers, even in their personal and family lives, as well as in spheres largely removed from economic activity (such as housing, recreation, gifts, etc.). Consequently, emphasis is placed on integration and a high degree of personal involvement is fostered by this system.[8]

freedom enjoyed in social markets by the client vis-à-vis other people of low standing, Japanese clients are required to adhere to certain standards in performance of duties in wider frames. Not only are *kokata* requested, like their Latin American or southeast Asian peers, to deliver resources and services, according to their patrons' wishes and priorities, but they are also accountable to the *oyabun* for responsible social behaviour in broader institutional spheres. The *oyabun* is expected to guide them as to the proper forms of behaviour in these areas, as institutions and people will address complaints to him on inadequate performance by his *kokata*. In other words, people attached to an *oyabun* feel less free to indulge in individualistic behaviour and are expected to be more committed to the proper performance of duties, in which they will have a greater emotional involvement. In E. Goffman's formulations,[6] they will be expected to be more tightly related to social situations and interactions. In addition, the *oyabun*, is, in some sense, seen as responsible before people higher in the social hierarchy for the behaviour of his dependants, since he is supposed to guide and control them in responsible conduct, and their irresponsible acts may therefore endanger his own market position.

Another difference is found in the place these relations occupy in the institutional framework. As already indicated, and in contrast to clientelistic settings, the occupational realm in Japan has been the focus for contracting *oyabun–kobun* ties. The bureaucratic realm, on the other hand, was modelled more along lines of competitive bureaucratic rules, and the political sphere was the arena for the undertaking of *yuryokusha* intercessions, which seem to have an 'addendum' character.

In addition, the *oyabun–kobun* links do not constitute a central organising principle in articulating different levels of interaction and exchange in Japanese society, despite their strong binding hold on the individuals involved in these links. Accordingly, these Japanese relations have lacked the pyramidal tendency of Latin American or southern European clientelism, and the networks have remained dispersed and, as a rule, not integrated into wider chains. In relation thereto, the gaining of access to the centre and to the resources it commands does not appear to be a main motive for undertaking such relations in Japan, nor do these relations ensure such access.

How can these singularities of Japanese clientelistic relations be explained?

In the first place, and unlike that of clientelism in the other areas referred to previously, the emergence of Japanese hierarchical links has been fostered and reinforced, to a great extent, by the widespread acceptance of certain cultural orientations, among which stand out the activities of the markets. This, in turn, might undermine some of the 'ideal' hierarchical arrangements, or, at least, induce their phrasing according to the market position of social actors.

Thus, for example, already in traditional India and even more since the expansion of the market economy, the ideal model of *jajmani* exchange was not, as a rule, operative in the relations established between members of landowning castes and *kamin* craftsmen. In these relations, such artisans as blacksmiths, carpenters, barbers, potters, weavers, basket-weavers, shoe-makers, etc., who performed the daily tasks needed in farms and houses, were paid in kind, according to seasonal arrangements rather than on a piece-work rate basis, and were expected, in return, to provide prompt and efficient service, especially during the agricultural season. Such relations resemble, more closely than do the pure *jajmani* ties, the nature of patron–client relations in clientelistic societies. Indeed, the links were less stable than in *jajmani* relations, people frequently changing partners. The details of exchange and payment were not prescribed but subject to bargaining, being partly determined by the results of the harvests, whereby the risks of producing were transferred, to a large extent, to the *kamins*. Accordingly, disputes between artisans and patrons were not uncommon, and this trend was accentuated as market forces penetrated traditional Indian society, especially during the English rule. In the long term, nevertheless, factory-made commodities flowed to local markets and reduced the bargaining positions of members of the artisan castes which produced such resources traditionally.

In addition, the changes in the occupational structure of modern India have limited the extent to which *jajmani* relations are operative and have increased 'caste-free' occupations and wage relations, especially in the urban areas.

In most ascriptively based hierarchical societies, in fact, some open markets do develop. Even in the 'primitive' societies based on equal corporate kinship groups, many 'marginal' or external markets develop. Access to them and the exchanges within them are not regulated through the relations based on the ascriptive kinship groups. This situation is more acute, as we have seen, in more complex, hierarchically organised societies, such as some African ones, or in the Indian caste system. The development of such markets may easily upset the institutional derivatives of the basic ascriptive hierarchical premises of such models.

Several ways of coping with this problem tend to develop in these societies in which either the kinship or the ascriptive hierarchical model is predominant.

One way is to keep a close connection or linkage between the relations that develop within these markets and the basic hierarchical ascriptive premises of the societies, by making certain that strong parallelisms exist between the positions, both in the ascriptive hierarchy and in the markets. Patron–client relations that develop in such societies provide at least one means for the establishment of such linkages.

Patron–client relations have thus arisen in contexts in which life chances and socio-political roles were closely related to membership in ascriptively defined sub-units, while there was yet some openness in markets and in the concrete possibilities of advancement within each social category. Sometimes, therefore, the inherited hierarchical standing of the partners neither assured nor legitimated a long-standing dependence on transactions in those more open markets. In such a social framework, there have been relations in which control of resources and access to centres were assumed to be correlated features of ascribed status. But, even in such cases, because of the absence of specifying of the concrete patrons, and even more then these relations emerged under conditions of greater openness of markets, social actors of the 'patron' category might have to legitimate and reinforce actual mediation and conversion of resources (into power, for instance) through the establishment of 'patron–client' relations.

Thus, in pre-independence Rwanda,[14] for instance, there was some openness in the access to exchange, within and between markets, for Tutsi aristocrats as well as for Hutu peasants. In fact power (derived from conquest) and enforcement stood at the base of social relations. However, the ritual ceremonial establishment of *ubuhake*, for instance, sanctioned the closeness between ascriptive membership in hierarchically standing collectivities and market positions. As already indicated, a Tutsi *shebuja* could grant usufruct of cattle and support to a Hutu *garagu* in exchange for an undertaking to render services and supply goods. More important, the personalised relations contracted were the ones which ensured that clients would not have a legitimate claim to convert resources into socio-political power.

Another way of coping with the development of such open markets in societies primarily organised according to hierarchical ascriptive models has been to segregate, as far as possible, the arrangements and the control of resources flowing in these markets from the major institutional linkages. Attempts were made to prevent the inequalities developing within these markets from impinging on the flow of resources between the ascriptive collectivities.

Such efforts were undertaken in India through adherence to the caste system, which remains conceptually central and socially and politically significant and creates, as it were, a disjunction between the social realm regulated by hierarchical ascriptive principles and the positions in the more open institutional markets.

The consequences of these dynamics for social actors were already evident in traditional India, where low castes who pursued polluting occupations could always have access to economic advantages derived from the performance of their caste specialisations and still retain a low position in the status hierarchical scheme. They could, however, renounce the profits gained through their traditional occupations and enhance their status through Sanskritisation. This dilemma, in fact, was obviated when the move towards Sanskritisation occurred among the castes of Untouchables, who had already discarded a polluting occupation and were on the way to holding alternative vocations.

The openness of economic, educational and political markets is greater in modern India and exacerbates this dilemma. This has especially been the case since educational opportunities were opened, under British rule (particularly in north India) and since, later, the introduction by the Indian government of the policy of 'protective discrimination' towards the 'backward classes'. Such developments allowed many such upwardly mobile castes and tribes who were, on the one hand, anxious to move out of their 'backward class' classification to free themselves from the derogatory social connotations associated with it, while, on the other, they were reluctant to give up their status together with their special privileges. The benefits involved included, for instance, a fixed quota of reserved political positions, administrative vacancies and promotions, educational facilities, and of services and resources to be dispensed within the caste by social actors who came to assume the role of patrons towards the rank-and-file members.

II

As the preceding analysis indicates, the patron–client ties that develop in such ascriptive hierarchical settings differ in several important respects from similar relations found in such clientelistic societies as part of Latin America, southern Europe, southeast Asia or the Middle East.

In the first place, these patron–client relations are either a relatively legitimised, but secondary, aspect of the main institutional matrix, which serves to sanction the close linkage between ascriptive social standing and access to markets and to centres of power in society, or these relations are – especially as the hierarchical model of social organisation is constrained by the development of market processes – an informal and unstable restricted arrangement established between partners not fully dissociated from the hierarchical (caste-like) scheme and not fully incorporated in modern market processes.

Second, such relations are accessory to the basic institutional model of societal organisation, remaining conceptually meaningful mainly in the context of such a model. Accordingly, such relations and exchanges are maintained – especially as open markets tend to develop – in those areas that are more closely associated with the ritual sphere, as in the relations existing to this day between *jajmans* and ritual performers such as Brahman or funeral priests, etc.

Third, while these relations are conceptually central for social actors, this centrality is not reflected in the concrete institutional structure. Indeed, such relations are mostly segmented, reduced to dyadic networks and not extended to articulate the whole matrix of exchanges and interactions in society by aggregation into pyramidal networks like those found, for instance, in Latin America or southern Europe.

Fourth, in all these cases, the different primordial identities of the partners preclude the possibility that the patron's social 'visibility' is any way reflected on clients when they act outside the clientelistic link. Thus are usually obviated some of the consequences that actual changes in the market positions of the partners induce in patron–client relations in clientelistic societies. If symbolic restraints on the exploitative features of the link do exist, they do not derive from moral primordial shared conceptions but from the terms of trade anchored in the market positions of the social actors.

Also, such patron–client relations show little tendency to change into other varieties of clientelism. If pressures do exist and changes do occur, they are more radical and do not merely affect the relative standing and character of the partners. This was the case with the East African multi-ethnic societies, where formal contracts with institutionalised rights and obligations remained unchanged until their total disappearance, when radical changes occurred in the structure of power – as in Rwanda with independence.

It is interesting to note that such normatively-based ascriptive limitation on the assumption of patron–client roles does not appear in the patron–client relations typical of clientelistic settings, in which there may arise strong inequalities in the access to markets and socio-political spheres and roles. In such settings, people may also praise primordial-type models as moral archetypes for organising social ties, even if they appear to be useless for dealing with difficulties in life, or for improving one's chances. But here social interaction is ideally based on criteria which, in principle, are unrelated to membership of ascriptive sub-collectivities. And there usually is a stress on the universalistic or quasi-universalistic openness of the social system and sometimes even on mobility opportunities.

Clientelistic mode of generalised exchange

According to these premises, people in clientelistic settings have recourse to patron-client relations in order to obtain access to social and political markets, or to improve their positions in them. In such a case, on one side the roles of patron and of client tend to be ideally open to social actors irrespective of primordial identities and on the other the roles are assumed according to structural and market positions, either achieved or ascribed. Hence, patron–client relations are here, as we have seen above, based on the clients' renouncing their potentially autonomous access to major markets or to positions of control over the use of resources and the setting up of public goods and services, except if the mediation of some patron can be secured. This mediation is contingent on the client's entering into an exchange relationship with the patron. Indeed, this can be seen as the essential character of clientelism. While there are limits to the access of different groups to the bases of production and to the use of resources in centres and markets, these limits are not derived from the basic premises of society. Different social and political standing and forms of access to markets and centres are established and reinforced through actual patron–client arrangements. These dynamics differ substantially from the patron–client relations analysed in this section, in ascriptive hierarchical societies. Here, they constitute a relatively recognised and legitimate, but limited, component of the institutional nexus.

III

The above-detailed characteristics of patron–client relations in ascriptive hierarchical societies create particular situations when attempts are made to monopolise the access to markets and power by non-legitimised individuals (for instance, by members of lower castes in India). Such attempts are usually countered by coalitions led by members of higher groups, even when the society is undergoing change towards a greater openness of markets.

Thus, in India, until the first half of the twentieth century, castes with low positions in the *varna* hierarchy (and lacking a tradition of literacy) were weakly represented in the government and in white-collar jobs. They were also precluded by high-caste politicians and by government officials – if these were wealthy and strong enough locally – from converting their strength into status and political power; this was, for instance, the case with Kolis in Punjab, north India, in the 1930s.

Since independence, the proliferation of positions of formal authority (such as village *panchayats, panchayat samitie, zila parishads,* trade unions, political parties, state legislature, etc.) and their availability, in principle, to social actors, irrespective of their caste or class, enabled members of the once non-dominant castes and sub-castes to accede to power at the local level. However, when these localised or regional power domains appeared to be militant and opposed to the more central elites, the latter often proceeded to weaken them by allying themselves to various secondary political entrepreneurs of other low-rank castes and sub-castes of the population. These strategies, based on the local government's reliance on projects and budgets derived from the state government and controlled by members of higher-ranking castes, were therefore usually successful. In this manner, more acquiescent members of other dominant castes, as well as newcomers from subordinate castes and sub-castes, were elevated by powerful leaders into the elite, as dependent and, it was hoped, reliable allies. Such trends were exemplified in the electoral alliances maintained with the Congress Party by parts of the Republican Party in the late sixties. Thus, up to the present time, and in the face of changes in the structuring of hierarchies in different parts of India, the elites have been strong enough to counter the attempts made by disadvantaged peripheral groups to convert localised power domains into non-mediated access to the centre and to the resources derived through its organs of government. As already indicated, this has been effected, first, through the recognition of reserved seats in elective councils and other administrative organs, in return for renouncing more radical demands regarding the conversion of resources at the centre; and, second, through the grant of sources of patronage to village, local or regional leaders in return for their support. This situation was conducive to a style of political campaign in which politicians rarely made appeals directly to the electorate but rather addressed them to the village leaders. Under such conditions, members of minority castes were not successful in challenging the hold of members to dominant castes, but may have attempted to join the elite as dependent elements of ruling coalitions. Especially in the more traditional areas, such control was further reinforced by rank-defining transactions which, while of decisive importance in their social significance, were left out of the regulations of the 'secular' State. These transactions involved the exchange of food, greetings, tobacco, as well as control over access to wells, to temples and to the services of ritual specialists.

PATRON–CLIENT RELATIONS AS ADDENDA TO UNIVERSALISTIC MODES OF GENERALISED EXCHANGE

The addendum type of patron–client relations, which tends to develop above all in different modern universalistic societies (whether of the pluralistic, monolithic or consociational type), is characterised by several additional features.

First of all, such addendum-like clientelistic relations are much less stable. They do not have the degree of legitimation of semi-normative prescription that the types of fully fledged patron–client relations have. Also, a greater variability develops here in the resources exchanged.

Second, in most cases the symbolism of interpersonal relations connected either to solidarity or to reciprocity and interpersonal obligations is much weaker than in the fully fledged patron–client relations. As we shall see later, in so far as symbols and concepts of mutual obligation develop in such situations, they are more often couched in terms of 'subversive friendship' (on which the reader may consult Leyton's *The Compact*, cited in note 1 to the Preface of the present work) than of honour or merit-making.

Third, many of these arrangements involve 'outright' bargains between actors, with relatively little unconditionality built into them.

The last and probably the most important characteristic is that such relations, especially in so far as they become distinctly visible, are usually perceived, by the people participating in them – above all by those on the outside, and especially by those in the more central positions – as not being legitimate and as counter to the premises, either of equality or of ascriptive hierarchy, prevailing in these societies.

Viewing these relations as non-legitimate is not a purely moralistic exercise. In contrast to what happens in clientelistic societies, the premises of either equality or ascriptive hierarchy prevailing in such societies tend to give rise to countervailing forces. These aim at undermining the emerging or existing patron–client arrangements and the linkages between the inequalities in different dimensions of the institutional order that they attempt to establish.

Such countervailing forces emerge from the mobilisation of clients' rights of access to the centre, as well as from the attempts of more central elites or of people in positions of power outside the immediate clientelistic situation. These social forces often work to undermine the legal or actual status of clientelistic monopolies, and especially the attempts of the monopolists – the would-be 'patrons' – to control access to markets and to regulate the flow as well as the conversion of resources in the society.

COUNTERVAILING FORCES TO THE DEVELOPMENT OF PATRON–CLIENT RELATIONS IN UNIVERSALISTIC SOCIETIES: THE U.S.S.R., THE U.S.A. AND ISRAEL

Let us analyse the dynamics of such relations in societies in which modern universalistic models of social exchange are predominant and find out how the attempts referred to above are made to minimise the impact and spread of clientelistic activities and, above all, to prevent their becoming transformed from 'addenda' to the central institutional nexus into the nexus itself.

The U.S.S.R.

I

In the U.S.S.R. clientelistic practices continuously develop with a view to obtaining access to the centre of society as well as to public or semi-public goods. Instances of favouritism, interpersonal obligation and sponsorship are present within and outside the context of bureaucratic contacts, especially in order to obtain resources and services not openly available in shops and offices. In many of these settings, indeed, when favours are done, obligations to repay them are contracted.

The pervasiveness of informal interactions and exchanges helps naturally to strengthen a close relationship between the stronger partners' hierarchical standing and the control of access to the major institutional markets – a relationship which those people who benefit therefrom, i.e. those in higher positions, normally try to consolidate. Accordingly, it is not unusual for influential people to have recourse to 'petitions' and to extra-legal practices in order to get preferential access to publicly distributed private goods.

However – and this is very important from the point of view of our discussion – these practices are not only essentially illegal but, from time to time, they meet with reversal or punishment (as will become clearer below), the more so as they are used closer to the central areas.

In addition, however widespread such patterns of behaviour are, informal contacts within many modern bureaucratic settings in general, and in Communist societies in particular, influence and moderate the formality of rule application. These contacts are effected without creating or cementing a continuing patron–client relation between broad categories of people or groups of different hierarchical standing. In many cases, scarce resources are offered as favours to be repaid in some other way. But, even then, the personal involvement and significance for the individual using such contacts in the short term, as well as the possibility which may exist in such relations, of a reversal of roles, confer upon them an egalitarian flavour that can hardly be described in terms of clientelism.

Such clientelistic arrangements seem to be more pervasive and continuous, in the Soviet bloc, among the powerful cliques than between them and those lower in the social hierarchy. We have seen that, within the political sphere, there are clientelistic-like patterns of promotion on the basis of demonstrated loyalty to the C.P.S.U. or to some of the members, cadres and contending internal factions of the C.P.S.U.

Studies conducted on the elites and the bureaucratic networks in the U.S.S.R. have, nevertheless, shown that, besides loyalty to some political actor, there also exist other criteria for promotion and access to loci of power.[15] Among these, education and performance are central within the sphere of the administrative and managerial–productive activities and organs of the State. Efficiency and contribution to industrialisation have become important criteria for the evaluation of officials. The drive for efficiency sometimes compels *apparats*, as well as party factions, to vie for competent men for their cadres; and, from time to time, some top officials may attempt to mobilise support for the holding of such criteria.

In order to understand the nature of the clientelistic relations and of the countervailing forces that develop in these societies, it might be worthwhile to analyse, as an illustrative case, the policy of housing – one of the most persistently scarce resources – in the U.S.S.R.[16]

In spite of the increase of per capita 'living space' in urban areas in the U.S.S.R., the scarcity of housing is felt even today. Official construction of accommodation does not keep pace with the actual rates of rural–urban migration, with the needs of those newly married or divorced, or with the rising expectations of the population. As a result, unrelated households are forced to reside in co-tenancy, and extended families to reside communally.

The housing market is controlled mainly either by the municipalities' housing authorities (as in old towns) or by enterprises and organisations. The process of housing allocation is regulated according to some general criteria governing registration on the waiting-lists and to priorities within these. These criteria include, first, such universalistic requirements as residence in the district for some period of time, or the possession of less than normal 'living space'. Second, members of some sectors of society are favoured by law and given priority access to housing; such exceptions are made for some classes of bearers of high awards, for war invalids or very sick individuals, as also for certain categories such as war heroes or occupational groups of 'responsive workers' (high officers, industrial efficiency experts, members of the armed forces or of the K.G.B.), and cultural and scientific personnel, who are granted special rights to additional 'living space' *by law* over and above the established norm.

Thus, housing becomes part of the reward system prevailing in the country, reflecting and reproducing at the same time its patterns of stratification. But most of the special arrangements with regard to the criteria of stratification are official, legal or administrative, and vested in the centre. Thus, it is the centre that exercises strict control over the criteria for the allocation of *propiska* permits (i.e. permits for residence in the more densely populated cities of the U.S.S.R.) and of flats, and over the exchange of accommodation, the approbation of the Bureaux of Housing Exchanges being required to seal a privately arranged exchange of flats.

Nevertheless, influential people make use of extra-legal practices to obtain preferential conditions of housing, and bureaucrats dealing in housing may become the focus of bribery attempts. Personal connections are as important here as in any other social setting.

These practices seem to be more prevalent, moving away from the political centre, say in Georgia or Armenia. The members of the top elite who use such practices are seldom reproved there, probably because such a measure would have serious consequences for the stability of the regime. On the other hand, the conspicuous consumption of these officials may generate such widespread delegitimatising pressures on the political centre that some of them will be dismissed, particularly – and this is very significant – if they live conspicuously. At the same time, such dismissal is often carried on without 'advertising' it too publicly, probably in order not to undermine officialdom.

The preceding illustrations – even if partial – do provide some indications as to the place that patron–client relations hold in the overall institutional setting of Communist regimes. They indicate that the basic model of regulation of the flow of resources in the U.S.S.R. is based on the assumption that all Soviet citizens have access to the major societal markets and to public goods such as education or health services, by virtue of their membership in the community.

In so far as access to public markets and goods is indeed allocated on the basis of different hierarchical or semi-hierarchical criteria – and these are more prevalent in Communist regimes than in other industrial societies – these criteria are set up by law or by administrative edicts, as in the case of housing.

In the U.S.S.R., as in other bureaucratic monolithic societies, there are clear rules of access to public goods and to the public distribution of private goods. These rules are widely known; and, on this basis an individual's chances of being included in the preferential list for allocation according to the established rules can be roughly assessed. The centre attempts to control the setting up of these rules and their application.

People do not, of course, always abide by these procedures, but attempt to ignore and bypass them. Indeed, powerful social actors may and do try to develop a close linkage between these specific positions, on the one hand, and, on the other, access to markets and to centres of power and inequalities within the markets themselves.

These practices are particularly anchored in the social manipulation of titles and the symbolic social visibility borne by the bearers of titles in bureaucratic societies in general, and in the bureaucratic monolithic societies in particular. Besides, even if the criteria for the attaining of such titles are defined in legal terms in the U.S.S.R., many instances have occurred when access to such honorific titles has been granted, together with the privileged access to resources that their award carries, on the basis of influence or manipulation of contacts.

In other cases, these practices are buttressed by the intercession of people through a *zvanok* (literally a 'call') designed to obtain bureaucratic grants on a particularistic basis. The favour is either granted or not overtly denied, depending on whether the request is supported by the implicit attribution of influence to the seeking party.

But, for various reasons (including relative openness of the criteria of access to many markets and public goods and the aim of the centre to control such criteria and access), the attempts of those highly placed officials to monopolise and to block, continually and systematically, the access of other groups to all such commodities are, in contrast to what obtains in the pure clientelistic societies, relatively weakened. Even if these attempts are certainly not negligible here, and are probably, as indicated above, more pervasive than in other industrial regimes, countervailing forces tend to develop here – as against clientelistic societies – which aim at undermining emerging or existing patron–client arrangements.

In Communist societies, such attempts to countervail the efforts of different sub-groups to monopolise access to the major markets are usually made by more central elites who try to open up and control the flow of resources within the markets. Thus, the centres of these societies take periodic measures such as launching campaigns against corruption and executing purges, in order to minimise the power of other sectors of society and their preferential access to the major markets or to the centre. Such attempts are viewed as a contravention of the basic universalistic premises of the system, or of the centre's own legitimation, which is partially couched in such universalistic terms, as well as of its positions of control. It is these orientations and policies of centres in bureaucratic monolithic societies that have been most important in precluding the emergence of enduring patron–client relations within them and their crystallisation as the major mode of regulation of the flow of resources. It is only in areas and activities without long-term significance, especially political, for the centre that these relations can be widely maintained and become more enduring.

II

Thus the pattern of patron–client relations that develops in Communist societies evinces several specific characteristics. In common with other industrial or industrialising societies, these relations are mostly of an addendum type, i.e. except in parts of the upper echelons, in personal or organisational terms, they are not continuous and enduring and do not crystallise into the major mode of regulation of the flow of resources.

At the same time, however, they are probably more widespread and pervasive in Communist than in other industrial societies and, paradoxically enough, are more enduring in some of the top echelons, among the political elites and sub-elites.

The preceding analysis indicates that the Soviet political system generates rather contradictory tendencies with respect to the development of clientelistic patterns, these tendencies differing both from other industrial societies and from pure clientelistic ones. Beyond the common tendencies of all industrial societies analysed by K. Legg, and from which the 'addendum' type of clientelism emerges, the monolithic political system of government gives rise to areas of uncertainty which, as Z. Bauman has indicated,[17] create conditions under which patron–client relations thrive. Such conditions are also fostered by the monopolistic character of the ruling groups, which seemingly reinforces the possibility of control by various 'stronger' groups over access to markets and to public goods. The combination of these factors allows a very far-reaching spread of patron–client relations, their continuous reappearance, and their concentration into somewhat more enduring patterns among the central elites.

At the same time, however, the very premises and legitimation of this regime – especially the tendencies of the central political elite to minimise the autonomous political power of any other sector (even, or perhaps especially, of its upper sectors) – and the necessity to maintain its legitimation in terms of some universalistic values, provide very strong countervailing tendencies to such attempts at monopolisation of access. These countervailing tendencies may become here, in their more extreme form, more stringent and dramatic than those in other industrial societies.

It may thus seem that, in these societies, the emergence of fully fledged clientelistic patterns would be contingent, above all, on the weakening of the political centre and on changes in the patterns of its legitimation, without the development of more autonomous social strata.

The U.S.A.

Political patronage, in the form of machine bossism, developed in the U.S.A. from the mid-nineteenth century. In a political system where, especially after the Jacksonian era, electoral success was essential for obtaining control of offices and of the resources commanded by the centre, numerous instances of short-term bargaining arrangements and relations emerged within – and in relation to the functioning of – American political organisations, usually through the efforts made by bosses to mobilise votes.

This trend was, first of all, connected, as we have seen above, to the process of accelerated urbanisation and to the economic inequalities existing in the cities. Second, it was particularly reinforced during the massive foreign immigration to the U.S.A. from the 1840s to the 1920s. It was then that the phenomenon of political bosses (i.e. of political entrepreneurs running political machines to gain votes in elections) developed more extensively, especially among people culturally distant from the ruling Protestant social groups and their ethics. The development of such political machines became manifest, in the urban settings, through the activities of full-time professional bosses. They provided immigrants with such resources as unskilled public jobs, and awarded public contracts on particularistic grounds to contractors or businessmen in return for votes or material support and gains.

For the most part, these relations were limited to political and economic considerations and often had relatively little uncondi-tionality built into them. In addition, the supply of a resource by the political bosses, apart from increasing the standard of living, could reduce rather than reinforce the original dependence on them of the immigrant or the businessman. The bosses, of course, tried to make their dependants see the grant of a favour as generating a personal commitment that had to be maintained in the face of changed market positions. But such a commitment was only effective in the short or medium term, and eventual structural changes in the economic posi-tions of the beneficiaries undermined the possibility of building long-term links of dependence among them.

In addition, these arrangements were confronted with diverse countervailing forces and developments in American society that severely curtailed their viability in the U.S.A. First among these were the attacks levelled against them by active sectors of 'public opinion' such as social reformers, civic associations or even professional and political circles, who advocated the adoption of institutional frameworks more closely akin to the premises of equality and of participation in, and universalistic access to, markets and centres of power in American society. Second, such a critical attitude towards bossism was also shared by significant sections of the broader strata as well as by people who had once been assisted by bosses and who (either themselves or their children) had since, with greater economic opportunities for mobility, become integrated into the mainstream of American society and adopted the American life-style and way of thinking. Third, even if the centre was not altogether opposed to such arrangements, some of the structural developments of American society, connected with its growing ingerence in the economy and the welfare of its citizens as well as the changing patterns of political campaigning (through the mass media, etc.), contributed to the dwindling of the political machine bossism as a main mode of political aggregation. These factors will now be analysed in greater detail.

Attacks on political machine bossism were already occurring in the late nineteenth century, launched by social reformers who expressed the unwillingness of the upper strata to accept the far-reaching modifications then affecting the composition of the population, and the advent of political elites and entrepreneurs less committed to the crystallised ethics of the country. Thus, for instance, R. Josiah Strong spoke of the serious menace to American civilisation constituted by the 'rabble-ruled' cities, controlled by people of humble origins who lacked the purity and integrity of the former (Protestant) politicians and traded in votes and buy-and-sell offices and official regulations.[18]

These criticisms were not based on a realistic appreciation of the roles fulfilled by political bosses in relation to the non-integrated parts of the population. In fact, during the years of massive immigration and until the 1920s, many of the bosses did help the newcomers on arrival to find lodgings or relatives, to prepare for citizenship examinations and to obtain nationalisation cards, as well as to solve some immediate problems of food, employment, protection, etc. Their brokerage was very much valued and sought by the immigrants and the members of the business community, as well as by the political parties to which the bosses were affiliated.

Only later, in the mid-1930s, did structural changes allow countervailing forces working towards the undermining of clientelistic arrangements to gather new momentum. Among such changes stood out the expansion of markets, increased economic prosperity, a higher level of employment and rising wages in the private sector, and, especially after the 1921 and 1924 immigration laws were passed, a decline in the number of unassimilated strata.

Clientelistic mode of generalised exchange

These socio-economic changes reduced the appeal of unskilled jobs available to be given as a patronage grant. Patronage jobs such as those, for instance, in federal censuses, in street repair or in custodial work in municipal buildings were increasingly considered as a short-term, last-resort alternative.

These changes were also accompanied by the centre's introduction of policies aimed at regulating the market forces, to some degree at least, mainly in an effort to eliminate the dangers of a capitalistic crisis, such as occurred in the late 1920s and early 1930s. At the same time, the institutional implications of universalism, equality and free autonomous access to power and to markets were more extensively realised. Public programmes of social security, sickness benefits, etc., were introduced, causing an increase in organised labour and in collective bargaining. In the public agencies, the bulk of jobs was increasingly filled by adhering to civil service procedures. With the existence of more complex technical requirements for job performance, it became inexpedient to admit unqualified personnel to these positions. The most a politician could request was that preferential treatment on a minor scale be given to his otherwise suitably qualified protégé. Simultaneously, new governmental technical requirements, such as knowledge of accounting, auditing or purchasing procedures, were introduced, rendering engagement in extra-legal 'boss' mechanisms less easy and less attractive than previously, especially when most private organisations doing business with municipalities had already, by that time, been granted franchises and concessions.[19]

These changes were relatively effective when they became intermingled with the political attitudes of broad sectors of society and of the central elites in the U.S.A. True enough, the centre did not seek directly to undermine the big city bosses. Indeed, some of the central political forces even valued the latters' disciplined vote-gathering services and, in return, granted some of them wider control over social security services and other sources of patronage. Some political machines have even managed thereby to adapt themselves to the changing conditions up to the present day. But, at the same time, and even in such cases, the bosses' modes of performance changed, as the traditional forms of machine politics came under growing attack on the grounds of their incompatibility with public interests and their lack of efficiency, honesty and civic virtue. These changes were voiced and spread, especially by urban movements and organisations such as civic or private reform associations – acting mainly outside the major parties – or by local independent parties which advocated abiding by universalistic democratic rules of public performance. In the 1950s and 1960s, new viewpoints focusing on reform emerged within the political parties, especially in the Democratic Party.

Among broader sectors, machine politics and machine politicians were also charged with being ineffective in dealing with the great urban social issues of the day (school integration and race relations, etc.), with having failed to integrate the demands of lower-class blacks and Puerto Ricans, and with being able to bargain and negotiate but not to plan and to define priorities.

Thus, public opinion became increasingly critical of inefficiency in the name of party loyalty. Patronage was seen as outright political pay-off and, as such, was discredited. In addition, political activists and supporters themselves were less motivated by the search for a resource critical to their livelihood (a job or food) or for preferential treatment by a government agency, and were more prompted by a desire to act in broader issues or in support of able and well-known politicians, or by their interest in establishing contacts with influential members of the political elite. Accordingly, political obligations could not be widely promoted by particularistic inducements, and campaigning was mainly conducted through the mass media and advertising agencies rather than on a door-to-door canvassing basis or on the control of blocks of votes.

The efforts of the reform movements were also directed towards the introduction of new electoral and administrative procedures and mechanisms. Among these changes, tested in different cities especially from the 1950s onwards, were the introduction, at the local level, of such procedural rules as non-partisan practices at large elections, commission systems and council-manager forms of municipal government (in which experts played a central role), as well as reforms in the civil service system.

The preceding analysis indicates that, even if opposed to the basic universalistic, egalitarian and participative premises of the American polity, clientelistic relations did emerge in the United States. They were found especially in those areas in which economic inequality was more marked, and particularly – from the 1850s onwards, in the period of accelerated urban growth, and until the late 1920s – among such social groups as immigrants not fully integrated into the mainstream of American society. At the same time, however, the very premises, and the bases of legitimacy, of the regime generated the emergence of very pervasive countervailing forces that tried to curtail such attempts to mediation in the access to markets and centres of power in American society. The practice of political bossism was often perceived as being non-legitimate, not only by the most active reformist movements but even by the people who benefited from them, as soon as they became integrated into society. We have seen that, under such structural conditions, the very particularistic provision of favours was hardly sufficient to create a long-term dependency within the markets or to mediate access to the centres of power. The expansion of economic markets severely hindered such attempts by political bosses.

Another aspect of the countervailing forces should be emphasised here. In contrast to what was typical in the U.S.S.R., these forces were not primarily found, in the U.S.A., at the political centre, even though it was sometimes particularly receptive to them. They mostly occurred among intermediate levels such as intellectual circles, reform and civic movements and broader sectors of the population, both inside and outside political parties.

Israel

I

We shall briefly compare the development of clientelism, and of reactions to it, in the Communist countries and in the U.S.A. to the situation obtaining in a different setting – namely, Israel – where far-ranging clientelistic phenomena developed for a period of time, despite their being contrary to the basic premises of that society.

The origins of Israeli polity were rooted, in the Mandatory period, in several social–ideological movements and sectors, each of which developed a certain autonomy, but all of which participated in the constitutional–federative framework of the Jewish National Institutions.[20]

This structure can best be characterised as an approximation to a consociational model. In such a model – prevalent in small European democracies, like the Netherlands, Switzerland, Austria, and lately also designated 'Proporzdemokratie', as well as in the Jewish community under the Mandate (the Yishuv) – some basic entitlements, such as citizenship and all the duties and rights entailed therein, are, according to universalistic criteria, vested in all members of the broader collectivity (nation). Conversely, access to the major centres of power, as well as to many public goods and to publicly distributed private goods, is mediated to a large degree by representatives of the major 'consociational' segments – be they religious groups, political parties, local units or whatever. Within such segments, however, access to power is open to everyone on a universalistic basis. Moreover, in the case of Mandatory Palestine, the segments themselves were brought together within a common universalistic framework or frameworks – for instance, the World Zionist Organisation, the Jewish Agency and the National Council (Vaad Leumi) of the Jews in Palestine – through which most of the resources were allocated to the different segments. They also served as the representative body of the Yishuv vis-à-vis the Jewish communities of the Diaspora and other sectors (Arabs, Mandate authorities) of the local society.

In the period preceding the establishment of the State of Israel, the different social–ideological movements created, from the 1920s to the 1940s, separate organisations for agricultural settlement, as well as their own credit, financing and marketing institutions.

They controlled a wide range of resources, such as housing and health services, which they provided for the sectors of the Jewish population related to them by establishing their own organisations, especially through the use of resources collected among the Jewish communities in the Diaspora and channelled by the Jewish National Institutions. In addition, these institutions constituted, at that period, a very important source of employment. Jobs were often allocated on the basis of political allegiance, proportionally to the relative strength of the different movements. In turn, the control of such administrative positions allowed the manipulation of the resources commanded in order to respond to the diverse demands of the population sector related to the specific movement.

In return, the different segments expected a far-reaching commitment on the part of their constituencies. In principle, people were motivated, as well as expected, not only to take part in political work in electoral periods, but also to engage in organisational and educational activities and even to undertake volunteer duties such as clandestine or legalised military service (as during the Second World War), or to join a collective settlement (kibbutz). Some of these expectations were more comprehensive and totalistic in the Labour-related movements than in the right-wing circles. In both, however, there was a strong mobilisatory emphasis, which cannot merely be explained as a function of the political manipulation of material resources.

Beyond this, and as in most consociational systems, relatively wide markets developed, especially in the economic field. Access to them was, in principle, open to all members of the society, and the specific exchanges undertaken within their scope were not limited to membership in any of the sectorial 'ascriptive' relationships.

Similarly, access to the major political frameworks and the basic legitimation of these frameworks were, in principle, couched in universalistic terms.

The establishment of the State of Israel and the great influx of new immigrants – particularly, but not solely, from so-called oriental countries – gave rise to several far-reaching transformations in this political structure, of great interest from the point of view of our analysis.

A double tendency emerged. On the one hand, the development of strong universalistically organised frameworks of services took place and, on the other, the earlier consociational arrangements were transformed into more blatant clientelistic ones.

Thus, first of all, there occurred a weakening of the pluralism that existed among the different sectors of the Jewish pre-State Yishuv and a growing unification and centralisation of services under the aegis of the state organisation. Second, as a result of these processes, the whole format of the relations between the State and the different sectors of society changed greatly from what they had been during the period of the Yishuv. The crux of this change was the transformation of many groups – particularly the new immigrants and the younger generations, but also the older members of various sectors – from members of relatively independent movements organised in sectors, with autonomous access to the major centres of power and resources, into individuals who were more dependent on clientelistic networks and frameworks. This gave rise to the emergence, for the first time in the history of the Jewish settlement, of a sharp and marked distinction between centre and periphery and shaped, at least initially, the relations between the two on a clientelistic model.

True enough, in some sense, the federative relationships between the different sectors of the society – the private sector, the Histadrut, the various political parties – and, with the establishment of the State, the newly emerging government sector (especially the various government corporations) were even strengthened. The many resources of the State – and of the Jewish Agency through which a large part of the funds was channelled – and often the new immigrants themselves, were allocated on a federative basis among the major political groups and parties. In a parallel manner the different ministries and their administrative services were initially divided on a coalition basis between the different parties, according to an electoral system of proportional representation. The ministries were thus assigned to the different contesting parties in accordance with their electoral strength and came to be identified as the traditional 'fief' of a given party. Accordingly the distribution of resources was initially manipulated in a way that often took on political connotations. In addition, the pool of jobs used as pay-offs to political activists was enlarged under ther aegis of the state machinery.

By controlling certain ministries, therefore, each party acquired specific zones of influence and tried to utilise the authority and the resources vested in it to widen its political influence, especially with the recently incorporated and politically inexperienced elements among the Jewish immigrants who had entered the country during the late 1940s and early 1950s. Potentialities existed to develop far-reaching clientelistic networks, above all within the coalition parties (especially the Labour and the religious ones), but also, to some degree, within the sectors of the political opposition (those of the 'bourgeois' parties and the Herut party). These clientelistic networks could allocate many resources – particularly housing and work and, in a smaller degree, education – in return for political loyalty.

All these processes seemed, indeed, to contribute to the far-reaching, though only partial, transformation of the former consociational model into a clientelistic one. Rather, they, allowed a very strong clientelistic dimension to be added to the working of the political system. The full institutional implications of such a trend were not realised, as they were countervailed by strong constraints and reactions against it, due in part to the more universalistic features of the institutional premises and format of the State, which were briefly analysed above.

The setting up of such a universalistic framework enabled the central leaderships of the different parties ruling the State, and in particular that of the Labour Party, to weaken the various sectarian tendencies and inner components of their parties, and the autonomous access of these sectors to the centres of power and of control of resources.

Thus, through the mediation of the different parties, the clientelistic features of distribution of resources from the centre, which survived from the paternalistic distributive orientations and particularistic norms of the pre-State period, were now constrained by the partial tendency of most of these movements towards a more independent access to the centres of political power as well as to 'outside' resources, be they money or manpower.

In addition, the relative partiality of the clientelistic dimension, as well as the strong reactions against it, were both due to the crucial fact that the developments went against the basic democratic, universalistic premises of this system – premises which had far-reaching institutional effects. One such effect was the establishment of widespread administrative services of the State, access to which was based on universalistic premises. While clientelistic intercessions also necessarily developed, they could very quickly become dissociated from the activities of the parties. The very multiplicity of relations weakened not only any single network, but also the whole clientelistic model.

Various clientelistic practices thus progressively lost their legitimation. In a parallel manner, the state organs increasingly gained professional autonomy, developing more universalistic rules and orientations. In housing, for instance, detailed criteria were introduced in relation to the right to obtain housing or to obtain government loans to purchase housing on the free market. In the civil service sphere, a regulation was introduced to advertise vacant positions. Similarly, in 1954 a new administrative organ, the Bureau of National Insurance, was created, and was responsible for disbursing most of the state welfare allocations (such as child allowances, birth grants, old age pensions, etc.) to the citizens according to universalistic criteria, in complete dissociation from political manipulation and partisan gains.

This process of institutionalisation of universalistic criteria was first applied in the field of welfare services, and only later in the institutions dealing with economic development, such as the Ministry of Commerce and Industry, where particularistic considerations remained paramount until the late 1960s or early 1970s.

In addition, clientelistic trends were further weakened by the widening of the labour market and of the government's 'full employment' policies, as well as by the successful absorption of many of the new groups, and by their growing access to political life – first of all on the local, but later also on the central, level.

This process became evident in the central political sphere itself – in the weakening of the hold of the older coalition forces and in the continuous strengthening of the opposition. Ultimately, the latter won the 1977 elections, ousting the Labour-controlled coalition which, from the pre-State period, had dominated the scene for about forty years, and repeating its victory in 1981. In the meantime, however, it also reinforced its own clientelistic networks.

These developments were precipitated, since the dominant (Labour) parties could no longer exert a strong ideological or clientelistic appeal among broad, especially urban and oriental Jewish, sectors of the population. Accordingly, the electorate's susceptibility to such issues as 'corruption', incompetence and the leadership's conduct during the first stage of the 1973 war translated itself in the polls into votes for the opposition parties (organised in the *Likud* coalition) and resulted in their rise to power.

These events did not, of course, nullify the emergence of many old and new *ad hoc* clientelistic networks and relations, mainly fostered now by the *Likud*, whose political activists were nominated to managerial positions in governmental and municipal organisations. But these arrangements were also continually challenged by such social forces and institutions as the opposition parties, the press and the legal system, which insisted on upholding the universalistic premises. This gave rise to continuous oscillations between the different tendencies.

Thus, here also, as in the Communist societies, we find a continuous tension between the basic premises of the system – which are against the development of clientelistic arrangements – and the many structural conditions that allow the emergence not only of such arrangements, but also, because of the very basic premises, of counter-arrangements and counter-tendencies.

While some of the structural conditions – such as scarcity of resources, which gives rise to the development of clientelistic arrangements – were similar to those identified in the Communist countries, the counteracting forces, so strongly rooted in the respective basic premises of these systems, were necessarily totally different.

II

We thus see that, in more analytical terms, such attempts to counter the power of the monopolists–patrons, in the more pluralistic societies, are usually effected through the combined activities of various elites in the centre and in the broader groups to which the clients belong. In the more monolithic systems, attempts at thwarting the efforts of different sub-groups to monopolise access to markets are usually initiated by the rulers. These try to open up and control the positions from which they can regulate the relations between generalised and specific exchange as well as the flow of resources within the more specialised markets.

True enough, all the countervailing tendencies developing in the different types of societies analysed here can never entirely negate the continuous emergence, in all these societies, of some types of patron–client relations at different levels of the social structure. Such relations tend to develop repeatedly in all these societies, even if in different social areas and with different scope.

But what these counter-attempts succeed, on the whole, in doing is preventing the transformation of such relations from addendum-types into a central mode of institutional integration.

Hence, any such long-term failure of these attempts as seemed to occur in Israel in the 1950s, or appeared in the more peripheral Republics of the U.S.S.R., or in Poland in the 1970s,[21] might indeed signal the beginning of a transformation of the social system.

THE FAILURE OF COUNTERVAILING FORCES IN CLIENTELISTIC SOCIETIES

Contrasting with the above social situations, none – or very few – countervailing forces emerge in societies in which the clientelistic model of social exchange is predominant. Such forces as do develop are either ineffective or are successful in changing only some of the personal or organisational aspects of the relations between patrons and clients or the terms of trade between them, not the pattern itself.

This can best be seen in the various movements of protest or rebellion that develop within such societies or sectors thereof.

One such type of rebellion, which has been abundantly described and analysed, was banditry, the basic characteristics of which, as well as the conditions under which it arose, have been studied by E. Hobsbawm.[22]

From the point of view of patron–client relationship, the major characteristic of rebellion is that it 'segregates' a certain portion of the population – the leader and his followers or the people whom he protects – from the concrete network of existing patron–client relationships and from the exchange that occurs within them. But, however destructive this may prove for some of the existing patrons – since it may even change some of the terms of trade between them and their clients – basically it does not change the nature of access to markets and to centres of power, or of the relations between generalised and specific exchange inherent in them. The rebel leader may become a 'rebel' patron who 'serves' the more downtrodden clients in a given population. But the basic relations between the patron and his clients do not greatly differ from those of the 'usual' patron–client relationships – although, at least in the initial phases of the struggle, a stronger emphasis tends to be put on 'purer' interpersonal relationships, as well as on some more general communal solidarity. But, in time, even this may become diluted or a matter of routine. The rebel or bandit leader may disappear, killed off by the authorities or by the patrons he has threatened. He may, on the other hand, become in some sort an accepted feature of the existing system, with which he has, *de facto*, come to terms; or, in extreme cases, he may become a semi-'legitimised' patron.

A second possible outcome of such rebellions, which constitutes a very important variation of the first, and which has been documented in the case of Brazil for instance, is the emergence of the 'rebel' as a religious leader who carries an 'old–new' message of salvation to the downtrodden. In addition, he restructures or organises his 'clients' into a new solidary community – without, however, changing its relations to the broader setting – and, on the whole, does not allow them autonomous access to power within that community.[23]

In so far as such communities are successful, they tend to develop special enclaves within an overall nexus of clientelistic politics, although they sometimes create islands of potential rebellion against them.

Rebellions, protests or movements of change within the patron–client nexus assume, of course, a great variety of forms, such as movements of clients from one patron to another, or the organisation of new networks and programmes by enterprising would-be patrons or brokers. Such movements are usually connected with change either in the volume of flow of resources that are being exchanged in a given nexus of patron–client relations or in the organisation of various institutional markets.

But in all these situations the major change is in the personal or organisational structuring of patron–client relations, which may affect the stability of some such aspects of patron–client relations. Usually, however, it does not affect the basic features of the relation between generalised and specific exchange and the premises of inequality that characterise the pattern.

The movements of rebellion will become more extreme only when situations develop in which either potential patrons or potential clients enjoy such a monopolistic position that they are not interested in entering into concrete patron–client relations which might impose limitations on their activities. But even then, as Scott's analysis of the situation in southeast Asia indicates,[24] movements of rebellion will not always give rise to a change in the pattern, unless they are able to change the criteria controlling the flow of resources.

6

The social conditions generating
patron–client relations

I

In the preceding chapter we have analysed the basic characteristics of
the clientelistic mode of structuring generalised exchange in society
and have distinguished it from the forms of patron–client relations
which develop as institutional addenda to other modes of generalised
exchange. Each of these modes entails a specific way of structuring
trust in society, and hence tends to generate a tendency to crystallisation of the formal and informal interpersonal relations in specific
manners, as is the case with the patron–client relations we have
already analysed.

We have also indicated there that the clientelistic mode of generalised exchange organises in specific ways the major dimensions of
the institutional order which are most important from the point of view
of the possibility of breakdown of extension of trust. From this perspective, the clientelistic mode of generalised exchange was characterised by a distinction between the criteria which regulate different
institutional spheres, together with the relative blurring of the clarity
of these principles; by a relative gap between the levels of structural
and of symbolic differentiation of the major institutional spheres, and
by a far-reaching *de facto* limitation in the access of broader strata to the
centres of power.

In order to understand better these characteristics of the institutional
order and the nature of the structuring of trust which is inherent in the
clientelistic mode of generalised exchange, it is necessary to study the
conditions which give rise to it, or are related to its development and
continuity.

As mentioned above, and as will be discussed in greater detail later
on, it was often assumed in the earlier literature on patron–client
relations that it is, above all, economic and political underdevelopment

or a low level of political modernisation that accounts for the evolvement and persistence of such relations. With advances in research, however, it became clearer that this was not the case. Indeed, the illustrations presented above attest the fact that in many societies – above all, Mediterranean, Latin American and southeast Asian – in which such clientelistic relations constituted part of the central mode of institutional arrangements, they persisted despite changes in levels of economic development, in the structure of political organisation and in their own concrete organisational form. For instance, the major institutional frameworks of Brazil or the Andean countries in Latin America, Thailand and the Philippines in southeast Asia, and southern Italy, western Sicily, Spain, Turkey and Lebanon in the Mediterranean basin retained some very strong clientelistic dimensions, despite the growing incorporation of local settings within the sphere of influence of national and supranational market economies and of central political administrative forces in these societies. Hence, we have indeed to isolate other social features in order to explain the development, maintenance and persistence of the clientelistic mode of structuring generalised exchange.

If such different modes or models are indeed closely related to the interweaving of trust with the social division of labour and regulation of power in society, we have to search among those components of institutional order which are most important from this point of view and which have been pointed out above in chapter 2. These are the internal cohesion of the major groups of society, the predominant structure of the elites and of their coalitions in society, the cultural orientations which these elites carry or articulate and the modes of control they exercise.

The analysis of those societies, or sectors thereof, within which the clientelistic model is predominant – above all, of most historical and contemporary Mediterranean (Catholic, Orthodox Christian and, to a smaller degree Muslim), Latin American and southeast Asian societies like Thailand, Burma, Malaysia or Indonesia – indicates indeed that, as regards these components of institutional order, they are characterised by several special features.

II

Most of these societies have been characterised by the co-existence within them of relatively broad collectivities and markets, as well as by certain traits of their major social groups and of their respective centres.

The most important of these traits, and one which has often been stressed, is the internal weakness, as evident in the relatively low degree of internal solidarity and of symbolic, and sometimes also of organisational, autonomy, especially of the lower groups in the society.[1]

A closer look at the evidence indicates, however, that such characteristics are shared by such other major societal actors as the centre or centres, the broader periphery and the major elites. In other words, in these societies in which the clientelistic mode is predominant, all these social actors evince a relatively low degree of autonomous access to the major resources which they need to implement their goals or, in broader settings, to the control of their own resources.

Such a relatively low level of autonomy is evident, in the centres of the societies in which the clientelistic mode of structuring the relations between generalised and specific exchange is predominant, not necessarily in the amount of resources at their disposal or even in their ability to penetrate the periphery administratively – although in many of these societies, such as early modern Italy or Greece, or in many African societies, the centres were, even in these respects, very weak.

But, even when the centres were much more compact and able to establish relatively wide administrative frameworks, their structural weakness was manifest in their lack of ability to act autonomously, as distinct from the mode of use of resources found in the periphery, or to penetrate the periphery independently.

Rather, they acted through channels which were either embedded in the power domains of the periphery or structured according to principles very similar to those of the periphery. In a parallel way, in most of these societies, the distinctiveness of the centre was not usually connected with attempts to effect a structural and ideological transformation of the periphery or far-reaching changes in the periphery's basic concept of social order. Accordingly, rather weak autonomous linkages developed in these societies between the centre and the periphery, creating few basic structural changes within the sectors or strata of the periphery or within the centre itself.[2]

Parallel manifestations of relatively low levels of broader corporate symbolic or organisational autonomy can be identified in these societies in the different units of the periphery at all levels of the social hierarchy.[3] The major societal units do not usually exhibit a strong collective consciousness and broader self-identity based on symbols of kinship, territoriality, class or status, or on other principles of social organisation which are community-, country- or sector-wide. Similarly, the peripheral units possess few mechanisms through which they control corporate access to outside resources and loci of decisions which affect them and little autonomous control over the conversion of their own resources. Accordingly, the peripheral units in these societies exhibit a relative lack of ability to influence the centre with respect to the principles of policy-making and allocation of resources, or to the construction of the centre's own symbols.

At the local level, most of these units – especially the villages, homesteads and, in the urban settings (especially the more modern ones), the neighbourhoods or vocational or occupational groups – display a very low level of community cohesion and solidarity, or of solidary corporate organisation.[4] Closely related to these characteristics is the structure of kinship prevalent in these societies in all – but especially in the lower (or at least more fully documented) – 'local' echelons of social hierarchy among the peasants. Most important are the relative (although, of course, varying in different societies) weakness of corporate kinship units in general, and of unilineal kinship groups in particular; a rather strong tendency to bilateral kinship, sometimes even with a strong emphasis on matrilineal descent; a relatively high predilection for narrow and unstable, cross-cutting kinship networks and alliances – showing a marked lack, beyond some minimal demarcation of exogamous units, of clear boundaries to the kinship unit or network.[5]

III

These societies were also characterised by the prevalence of symbolic idioms or images within them; among these maternal religious ones, a strong emphasis on mediators, and various conceptions of honour have been singled out as most clearly related to patron–client relations. In order, however, to understand the full importance of these specific cultural idioms and their ties with patron–client relations, it is important to realise that they are related to the basic conceptions of cosmic and social order which are prevalent in these societies.[6]

The most important of such orientations as can be found in varying degrees and combinations in all these societies were, first, the combination of a conception of tension between a 'higher' transcendental order and the mundane order (especially in the 'religious' sphere proper) with the absence or relative weakness of any sense of necessity to overcome these tensions through some 'this-worldly' activity (political, economic or 'scientific') oriented to the shaping of the social and political order or its transformation. Conversely, a strong emphasis on other-worldly orientations tended to develop in these societies.

Second, in most of these societies a strong emphasis on the givenness of the cultural and social order was prevalent, as well as a weak perception of the active autonomous participation of any of the social groups in the shaping of the contours of these orders. The major groups and elites of these societies rarely considered themselves as actively responsible for the shaping of these contours.

Third, and closely related to this, was the relatively low level of commitment to a broader social or cultural order. Among the social groups this order was mostly perceived as having to be attained or adapted to, but not – except in some extreme sectarian ideological pronunciations – as commanding a high level of commitment from those who participated in it, or who were encompassed by it.

Fourth, and bound up with the former orientation, was the relatively weak emphasis on the autonomous access of the major groups or strata to the major attributes of such orders. Such access was usually conceived as being mediated by various actors, mostly ascriptive groups or ritual experts who represented the 'given' order, with a concomitant stress on mediating symbols and supernatural powers.

These orientations have been most fully articulated in the realm of Buddhist civilisations, and to a smaller degree in that of Catholic and Muslim societies. Especially in Islamic countries, there existed ideally a strong emphasis on commitment to the social and cosmic order and on direct autonomous access to it. But even there and in Catholic countries such ideal orientations became, through complex historical processes, weakened, and the other ones, indicated above, relatively predominant.[7]

IV

Closely related to the preceding characteristics, there was also a certain structure of the major elites and coalitions that tended to develop, and to persist in these societies despite the impact of processes of development and concomitant organisational changes.

Autonomous elites tended to develop here, both in the political and in the functional (professional) and cultural spheres. Most such elites were inclined to become, symbolically at least, very strongly embedded in broader ascriptive groups, having but little autonomous self-definition and orientation, even when they were already very specialised – as in the case of professors or holders of administrative positions in the more modern societies. Such elites were usually closely connected with the articulators of solidarity in the major ascriptive groups.

Such lack of symbolic autonomy was, of course, characteristic of the activities of such elites in 'mundane' spheres. With respect to purely religious activities, some of these elites – especially the ones dealing with the cultural sphere, such as the Catholic clergy or the Buddhist

Sangha – were visibly more autonomous in their orientations and activities.

It was such comparatively embedded elites that constituted the basic coalitions in these societies. On the one hand, they were the carriers of the basic cultural orientations institutionalised there, while on the other they were the ones who maintained in these societies the basic patterns of control over the flow of resources.

The central characteristics of these patterns of control were the attempts to limit, against the official premises of the society, the access of many groups to relatively broad institutional markets; to minimise the free conversion of resources between different institutional markets in general and between the centre and periphery in particular; and to vest control in the hands of the respective coalitions of elites at different levels of the social structure.

V

These patterns of control had important repercussions on the structuring of the major institutional spheres in these societies – above all, of their economies and social hierarchies.

Most of these societies were chiefly characterised by extensive and extractive (i.e. plundering rather than developing) economies, with a relatively low level of internal specialisation among the different internal economic units, and a consequent weak propensity for the development or incorporation of technological innovations oriented towards transforming their bases of production. Trade was oriented outwards, mostly regulated by the rulers or by external groups, impinging only weakly on relatively narrow internal markets and only indirectly increasing the internal flow of resources.

Within these economies, certain types of policies and systems tended to develop. The most important among these policies were, to use B.F. Hoselitz's terms,[8] mostly of expansive character – i.e. they were aimed at expansion of control of large territories, rather than being inward looking and characterised by intensive exploitation of a fixed resource basis. These policies were mostly extractive and redistributive.

Parallel to these policies, in many of these societies – and especially in the more centralised ones, in the 'traditional' periods of their history – the rulers attempted to control the ownership of land by vesting it either in their own hands entirely or in those of fellow aristocrats, and by turning most of the peasant families into tenants. These rulers also tried to supervise and control the extent to which the various plots of land which were owned by different kinship units could be freely transferred. Such policies were in sharp contrast to those of the Emperors in many centralised imperial systems who often attempted to weaken the position of the aristocracy by promoting a free peasantry.[9]

In the more modern settings, a certain continuation of such dispersed modes of land ownership developed, as well as a strong tendency towards the development of urban service, under the control of the State.

These types of economies were often connected with absentee ownership, with a great chasm existing between urban and rural sectors, and with oligarchic landowning groups which were mostly oriented towards external, outside markets.[10]

In close relation to these policies, there developed, within these societies, specific patterns of absorption of highly active, more clearly differentiated economic groups (especially merchants or manufacturers), which could contribute to the accumulation and extraction of resources. Both the traditional and the modern rulers of these societies were indeed very often interested in coopting such units, but only so long as these were 'external' to the central structural core of society; so long too as such units did not impinge on their internal structural arrangements, and especially on the basic conception of the relations between the centre and the periphery. They were hence incorporated in special, segregated enclaves. This tendency also explains the strong predisposition in many such societies to allow ethnically alien groups, which could be segregated to a greater degree than indigenous elements, to engage in structurally more differentiated activities.[11] Thus, in most societies, some type of dual, bi-sectoral economy tended to develop, composed of one underdeveloped, internal sector, and of another externally oriented sector, the two being connected by the extractive and regulatory policies of the central elites.

These were the types of economic structures and policies that were often inclined to become dependent on external forces and, when new openings became available in the international framework, to develop in the direction of growing dependency.[12]

These patterns of economic control also had repercussions for the structuring of social hierarchies in the societies studied here.[13]

Organisationally, the patterns of stratification in these societies were in general characterised by the relative weakness of independent (especially middle) sectors, and by the preponderance within such middle sectors of service, bureaucratic elements, and within the higher strata of oligarchic groups.

Structurally, the social hierarchies of these societies were, on the one hand, characterised by many highly elaborated hierarchies of rank and position, often related to the differential access of various groups to the centre. On the other hand, however elaborate the system of rank-hierarchy in the centre or subcentre was, and despite some embryonic tendencies, strata with countrywide status consciousness did not usually develop in these societies. Instead, smaller territorial, semi-occupational or local sectors tended to become major status units, all of them developing rather strong tendencies to status segregation with little autonomous political orientation.

Concomitantly, narrow status consciousness tended to develop in these societies, together with a low level of society-wide strata organisation or consciousness, a very strong tendency to segregation between small family, territorial, ethnic and political groups, as well as a preponderance of vertical (either corporate or less fully organised) networks of narrow status segments linked together by continuously shifting, vertical ties of allegiance and contact.

These ties that developed in these societies or in sectors thereof were, however (unlike the more institutionalised vertical links existing between different status groups predominant in ascriptive, hierarchically organised societies), more shifting and not based on ascriptive corporate units. Unlike the vertical ties developing between the centre and various status sectors in the more universalistic monolithic (imperial or totalitarian) societies, the ties within the context of the patron–client nexus are characterised by complex criss-crossing lines.

VI

The social conditions which give rise to the non-clientelistic models of generalised exchange differ of course from those connected with the clientelistic model. Without going in this case into as detailed an analysis as that of the clientelistic mode of generalised exchange, we shall point out some of their most salient features.

The modes of structuring of these non-clientelistic models of generalised exchange are connected with the predominance of solidary elites which, as in historical societies, may have been either autonomous or embedded (as in India) in relatively broad autonomous ascriptive units such as the various caste units, or (as in tribal units) embedded in solidary ascriptive units. They are also characterised by the existence of relatively solidary and autonomous social strata, by comparatively autonomous centres and by the development of somewhat cohesive social strata with articulated status consciousness.[14]

VII

The configuration of different conditions within which the different models of generalised exchange developed also generated, as we have indicated above, different modes of structuring of trust in society. We shall now proceed to indicate how the social conditions within the framework of which the clientelistic mode of generalized exchange develops generate some of the basic characteristics of the structuring of trust in these societies, and how these characteristics are related to the development and basic features of patron–client relations.

The preceding analysis indicates that the social structure of 'clientelistic' societies is characterised by a relatively low level of trust within the major ascriptive groups, by the relative fragility of the expansion of such trust beyond the basic primordial units to broader institutional complexes, and by the combination of such extension with the structuring of meaning and the regulation of power in society.

This fragility is evident in the fact that the application of the (usually universalistic) criteria of allocation of resources and of access to power that are officially predominant in the respective macrosocietal settings of these societies is very uncertain – hence in the lack of trust among the various social actors, who behave according to these criteria and are not confident of their own and others' ability to shape their respective environments.

Closely related to these characteristics, and in close connection with the cultural orientations specified above, a particular definition of personal and collective identity tends to develop in these societies. This emphasises the relatively passive stance of persons and collectivities with regard to their social, natural and cosmic environments.

Some of the basic aspects of such identity can best be understood in relation to the various personalised concepts – of obligation, of honour, of personal 'sentiment' and even, in some cases, of ritual attachment – that have been prevalent in many such clientelistic societies and that often symbolise and legitimise the patron–client relations which develop within them.

Thus, for instance, in Mediterranean areas, the concept of honour is attached to personal pre-eminence and precedence and, while also related to virtue, especially in the case of women's shameful or pure behaviour, is in fact not built around actual behaviour. It is rather established around the public recognition of the ability to 'settle' affairs, to defend a coveted rank against challenges which attempt to establish superiority over the person wronged. This implies that here honour depends upon the ability of social actors to lay claim to it; and – as has been shown by, among others, Pitt-Rivers – it is in countries such as Spain that a powerful position places social actors beyond the loss of reputation as a result of moral misbehaviour. Such a reputation may, however, be denied to low-standing individuals and families, even if the pure behaviour of their women would make them deserve the accordance of honour within the community.

In such a setting, the establishment of claims of domination over other social actors seems to be more salient than virtue and conduct, according to the code of honour. Thus, while social actors may relate honour to the obligation to abide by their undertakings and by their given 'word' (*palabra*), a greater stress is placed on their ability to pay for others, to grant hospitality to strangers, to bestow protection, or to show beneficence as a means of enhancing their reputation and the degree to which they are socially recognised. Similarly, while a man's honour is epitomised in, and may be endangered by, his women's (his mother's, sister's, wife's, daughter's) sexual behaviour, he may enhance his reputation vis-à-vis other individuals by demonstrating his aggressive manliness, which can be evidenced in (among other ways) his overcoming other women's shame and moral 'fortitude'.[15]

These concepts of honour or of prestige and reputation that develop within the context of the clientelistic model are characterised by some very specific features. They are distinct both from relatively similar conceptions – such as those of different types of ritual kinship, or of the *giri* system in Japan, which are usually defined either as part of, or as being rooted in, the identity of broader kinship units or strata – and from purely interpersonal identities and relations like 'pure' friendship, which attempt to transcend any organised group or fully structured relations.[16]

As against the first type of conception, the concept of honour that develops in connection with patron–client relations is usually defined as not being fully prescribed within the limits of any ascriptive collectivity or framework of institutional relations, but as appearing purely personal. However, it is characterised by certain emphases on the upholding of specific, institutional relations between different ascriptive groups or categories, as can be seen in that placed on maintaining women's honour.

Similarly, as against such conceptions as ritual friendship, *giri* or the like, the concept of honour discussed here usually involves a tension between asymmetrical hierarchical relations and the purely interpersonal, potentially egalitarian components inherent in it.

In all these ways, these conceptions of honour, and their symbolic expression, involve a strong ambivalence between the unconditionality implied by the solidary relations and the relatively strong, yet not clearly specified, power and instrumental elements inherent in these relations.

In this context, it is interesting to note that the importance of the conception of honour, and of its function in patron–client relations, is best illustrated by the fact that in those situations in which such a conception is, or becomes, weakened or diluted, it is usually the

212

potentially injured party – the patron or the client – that attempts to develop and uphold them. This indicates that it is important, from this party's point of view, to uphold these conceptions as guarantees of the goodwill and honourable conduct of his partner.

VIII

The very strong stress on the conception of interpersonal honour that is central to many patron–client relations emphasises the low level of trust that tends to prevail in the societies in which they arise. This low level of trust is closely related to the relative lack of clarity in the specification of the criteria that regulate different institutional spheres and of the criteria of access to the political and cultural centres, characteristic of a clientelistic model of generalised exchange. It is also manifest in the fact that in these societies there develops a situation in which no category of social actors enjoys a 'corporate' legitimation of its attempts to assure positions and resources for itself, either through direct relations with other actors or through autonomous access to the major controlling agencies that regulate the flow of resources and the allocation of positions.

In each category of major social actors prevalent in these societies – but, paradoxically enough, above all among the higher groups as well as among the occupants of the centre – these conditions generate potential competition between different members of each social category with respect to their possible access to basic resources and to the positions which control these resources.

All these characteristics tend in turn to generate a certain pattern of interaction and struggle among members of the same social categories or classes – a pattern characterised by continuous contest, manipulation and perpetual imbalance.

This contest or struggle entails a strategy, according to which actors belonging to different social categories or strata approach one another in order to gain resources which are not easily accessible to them in the framework of their respective social spheres or categories. It is out of this strategy that tendencies develop to create patron–client relations. In this framework, it is appropriate to speak, as R. Paine did, in terms of a generative transactional model of patronage.[17]

These conditions give rise to the likelihood that, in order to get access to the resources which they seek, and which are controlled by their prospective partners, people will enter into a relationship in which dependence is involved from the start. Such dependence is constructed by such means as the patron's allowing access to his hitherto unknown or 'closed' resources, by the creation of a following and of obligations, at the same time as the need for instrumental or power resources is announced. Thus, resources are translated into influence and clients accept the right of the patron to determine the basic rules of the relationship. Clients are expected to embrace those values and are rewarded by the patron for their loyalty and dependence. In such a manner, the relationship goes beyond mere instrumental exchange, hindering – as Paine has pointed out – the possible short-term interests of social actors in 'economising' in presentations to their role-partners.

Accordingly, through the construction of such interpersonal relations, they attempt to construct a new area of trust in the very central institutional nexus of their respective societies, and to become institutionalised. But such institutionalisation of these relations, notwithstanding the trust which is formulated within them, is never fully assured, and many of the ambivalences in relation to the basic premises of the society are transposed, in the patron–client relations themselves, to a new plane.

IX

It is this type of structuring of trust – together with the above characteristics of the social actors and of interaction between them in general, and of the struggle over power and resources in particular, as tend to develop in these societies – that can explain some of the most important aspects of the patron–client relations evolving there.

First of all, these combined factors explain the crucial fact that the exchange inherent in these patron–client relations in clientelistic societies takes place simultaneously on two distinct yet interconnected levels.

One such level is related to the exchange of various concrete services, goods or resources. As a result of the variable positions of patrons and clients in the respective markets of specific exchange, a high degree of diversity and change may occur in the concrete contents and terms of such exchange.

But in all such relations another level of exchange exists, connected to some crucial aspects of generalised exchange. The client 'buys', as it were, protection, first, against the exigencies of markets or nature; second, against the arbitrariness or weakness of the centre, or against the demands of other strong people or groups. The price the client pays is not just the rendering of a specific service but his acceptance of the patron's control over his (the client's) access to markets and to public goods, as well as over his ability fully to convert some of his own resources. As against the restraint found in societies in which the hierarchical–ascriptive model is prevalent, this limitation cannot be derived from the full institutional premises of the society, and its acceptance is always potentially precarious.

Hence these relations of generalised exchange are not, here as in the ascriptive models, fully prescribed or subject to special, ritual and power negotiations which differ from those undertaken in relation to specific market exchange. In the clientelistic model they themselves constitute a focus of the continuous power struggle connected with negotiations about specific exchange.

It is also due to these features that the patrons are willing to accept, in principle at least, some of the limitations that patronage may entail, even though they always attempt, of course, to get the best possible terms for themselves.

Thus, by combining contractual and precontractual elements, the exchange that develops seemingly tries to overcome the precariousness of the linkage between generalised and specific exchange and the relative fragility of trust that is prevalent. At the same time a strong ambivalence with respect to the basic premises of the society itself and of the structuring of trust in it is entailed in the symbolism or ideology of this exchange.

The ambivalence is manifest in the tendency to construct the clientelistic exchange in package deals combining symbols of solidarity, expressed above all in terms of personal bonds and attributes, with concrete, specific, unequal exchanges.

It is these combinations between contractual and precontractual elements, between solidary package deals and inequality, that constitute the mechanism through which the precariousness of the linkage between generalised and specific exchange inherent in patron–client relations appears to be overcome. But this very combination is fraught with contradictions. First of all, it does not allow a clear distinction between contractual and precontractual elements or a clear and unequivocal specification, such as exists in principle in the ascriptive models of the relations between the two.

Second, and closely connected to the first contradiction, these relations are characterised by a combination of inequality and asymmetry of power with apparent solidarity, and of exploitation and potential coercion with voluntary relations.

Third, these patron–client relations are based on a lack of distinction between the public and the private spheres. It is indeed of their essence that these two systems should be continuously interwoven and interpenetrated, as is especially evident in the concepts typical of godparenthood (of *compadrazgo*, etc.) or in the similar notions which are often connected with patron–client relations.

X

For all these reasons the institutionalisation of patron–client relations evinces some special characteristics. It is, first of all, characterised by a combination of a strong continuity in the clientelistic mode – being the major institutional mode of structuring generalised exchange – with a high degree of fragility in its concrete organisational features. In the earliest anthropological studies of patronage, as we have seen, a picture emerged of very stable and continuous personal patron–client relations – a stability and continuity accounted for in no small degree by the strong interpersonal relations and moral bonds which 'overcome', as it were, the considerable inequality in positions and power. With the proliferation of studies, a recognition emerged that most patron–client relationships – certainly those existing in the more complex societal settings, but even those found in more restricted rural areas – can be characterised by different combinations of continuity in the general pattern of patron–client relations, along with variable forms of instability and change in the concrete character of relations and of organisational structure, and in the positions and fortunes of individual patrons, as well as by continuous competition between these patrons for clients.

A second aspect of the institutionalisation of patron–client relations is that the broader societal and cultural conditions analysed above are not in themselves sufficient to assure the development of various concrete types of patron–client relations and interactions. The different forms of these relations only develop when these broader factors are connected with several complementary conditions which, in a sense, activate the potential for entering into such relations.

Among such activating conditions are, first, a certain ecologico-social organisational matrix that does not render difficult or altogether preclude contacts between members of different social strata and, hence, the contracting of patron–client links. Otherwise, despite the presence of cultural and societal factors pressing, as it were, for their establishment, such relations could not have emerged at all, or only very rarely. For instance, the huge rural migration to the Brazilian cities of the centre–east and southeast regions, and the high rates of unemployment and underemployment there, produced a great distance between the *favela* dwellers of such cities as Rio de Janeiro and São Paulo and other urban sectors. Contacts between the two sectors of the population were sporadic at best and reduced the possibility of establishing patron–client relations and hence the proneness of broad strata to seek such relations anywhere save in domestic and auxiliary services. These contacts often generated social disorganisation in the poor areas and serious explosions of urban violence. These processes took place in spite of the persistence of cultural conceptions which, ideally, were conducive to the establishment of clientelistic ties whenever possible.[18]

Second, in order that patron–client relations should be contracted, the broader societal and cultural conditions had to be connected to a certain balance of power between the various social strata and categories such as would not alter their corporate weakness and the interest of social actors in becoming engaged in clientelistic arrangements. It was especially important that market conditions should not emerge which allowed even individual patrons to command such a monopoly of resources that it made them totally independent of any client. This situation occurred sometimes under conditions of colonisation, where local powerholders were backed by the colonial authorities, or where potential clients were unable to convert, independently of any patron or broker, the resources they controlled. This may sometimes be the case under conditions of modernisation and widened markets, and such seems to have been the trend in central Italy in the last decades.

When such complementary conditions are absent, the patrons – or, in obverse conditions, the potential clients – are not interested in entering into patron–client relations, and simple power or market relations tend to develop, often giving rise to extreme coercive attitudes on the part of the patrons or to the 'class-like' reorganisation or withdrawal of the clients.

Similarly, within societies where the broader societal and cultural conditions conducive to the emergence of patron–client relations are predominant, such relations are not uniformly present among various sectors and strata, and there are settings in which such ties are absent or marginal – as, for instance, in the case of the Castilian village of Valdemora or that of San Miguel de Serna in Colombia.

Thus, in the case of Valdemora, studied by Freeman,[19] the corporative body of neighbours (the *común de vecinos*) fulfils the functions that patron–client relations perform in other settlements, obviating their emergence and fostering a strong egalitarian ethos. It is the *común* that delivers resources and facilities and ensures mutual aid for its members. The egalitarian ethos is reinforced first by the difficulty, in the long term, of concentrating property under conditions of scattered and fragmented landholdings and a low level of technical mechanisation and productivity, and, second, by exogamous patterns of marriage.

In the village of San Miguel de Serna, described by W.T. Stuart,[20] the emphasis is likewise egalitarian, and political identity and sponsorship

217

are rooted in an ideology of kinship, while prestige is derived from involvement in communal activities, such as membership in *cofradías* and associated drinking in *tiendas*. There, patron–clientelism remained unattractive, for example, for people standing high in the stratification scale, such as big landowners (*hacendados*) and stewards. These social actors were as a rule not involved in politics, and were motivated in their holdings by instrumental drives, replacing a large work-force by mechanisation. Outsiders such as politicians were not motivated to invest energies and material resources in the village, because the small size of the local population provided no incentives to campaign there.

These cases demonstrate that in some circumstances the search for a patron as a personalised form of 'insurance' against the threats and demands of the environment, and in order to obtain access to institutional markets and the centres of society, is not considered to be the appropriate mechanism for social actors to overcome such conditions as insecurity, institutionalised scarcity of resources or social uncertainty. The tendency to seek actively such personalised patron–client relations develops mainly in those cases where certain patterns of societal organisation combined with ecological contacts prevail, and where such conditions as the cultural orientations and the weakness of the major social actors are complemented by certain microsocietal balances of power that do not obviate the full consequences of such conditions. When such broader and microsocietal conditions complement one another clients do evince some degree of compliance with a patron's requests and decisions, even when their short-term interests push them in the opposite direction. Similarly, under such conditions patrons are responsive to some degree to their actual and potential clients' approaches and claims and it is, in principle, in their interests to 'play the clientelistic game' – that is to derive prestige and socio-political pre-eminence at the price of accepting the limitations that the link imposes on their use of force and on the instrumental gains that could be obtained by their having recourse to such use.

XI

Given the various characteristics of patron–client relations in general, and the various ambivalences built into them in particular, and also given their tendency to become institutionalised and to reinforce in a way the very patterns towards which their attitude is ambivalent, it is no surprise that, in the societies in which these relations are predominant, other types of highly symbolic interpersonal relations tend to develop, partly in conjunction with and partly in opposition to them. These relations attempt, as it were, to overcome the ambivalences inherent in the institutionalised patron–client nexus and to go beyond them into the realm of pure, undiluted meaning and trust, uncontaminated by exigencies of power or instrumental considerations.

Thus we proceed naturally to the analysis of the other types of interpersonal relations, already mentioned, that develop in all societies – namely ritual friendship, blood brotherhood, ritual kinship and different types of more informal friendship. These various types of personal relations develop both in clientelistic and in non-clientelistic societies – i.e. in societies in which different crystallisations of patron–client relations develop – constituting there a central institutional nexus or some formal or informal addendum to such a nexus. In all these societies the patterns of those relationships and the connections between them are closely related to the overall pattern of construction of trust that is prevalent.

We shall attempt to analyse these different patterns in detail in chapter 8.

Before doing so, however, we have yet another problem to tackle – namely, the analysis of the organisational variations in patron–client relations beyond the variations already analysed in conjunction with the institutionalisation of different models of generalised exchange.

vvvo

Variations in patron–client relations

I

Patron–client relations can be found, as we have seen, in a great variety of societies at diverse levels of development or modernisation. Hence, beyond the features shared by all these types of relations and beyond the differences between full clientelistic networks and addendum-like patron–client relations, a great diversity also develops in their concrete organisation in the different settings.

To give but a few preliminary illustrations derived from the preceding analysis, the patron–client relations which develop mostly in agricultural estates are structured around the access to land and other basic means of livelihood of the peasants, herdsmen and labourers. Such relations also exist between debtors and creditors, who carry them, at least partially, beyond the economic sphere. These links also emerge between, on the one hand, peasants and, on the other, merchants, businessmen and professionals, who have control over access to avenues of commerce and specialised knowledge about national institutions and their procedural requirements. They may also arise in urban settings around politicians proffering help to marginal sectors of the population – such as rural–urban migrants – in settling down, by legalising squatter dwellings, or in dealing with the authorities, in securing a job or in filling in technical forms to gain access to certain public goods or to obtain a loan. Patron–client relations are also built up within political machines, through the provision of diverse inducements to brokers engaged in maintaining control over electorates; within the administration, between bureaucrats and citizens who seek preferential treatment for their applications and requests for grants, licences or contract leases; and through the use of material rewards available to office holders interested in coopting local men commanding wide powers in various peripheral sectors of society.

Variations in patron–client relations

We have already pointed out that the material analysed indicates that the following dimensions are among the most important ones:

1. *The scope, institutional placement and organisational character of clientelistic networks*

   We may distinguish here variations in these relations according to their scope, their concrete organisation, their placement, and their linkages to wider institutional frameworks – above all, to various formal organisations. The major distinctions are: first, whether the patron–client relations are characterised by a localised personal structure, or whether the networks of patrons, brokers and clients are linked in different ways to wider institutional frameworks such as organs of central administration, and different formal organisations such as political parties, trade unions, etc.; and, second, the exact institutional location of such networks.

2. *The nature of the assumption of patron–client roles which are related, above all, to*:

   (a) The existence or absence of normative barriers to the free assumption of roles by different social actors.

   (b) The criteria of such incumbency and, especially, whether it is collectivities or individuals that can assume the roles either of patron or of client.

3. *The styles of instalment into the relationship*, i.e. whether the patron–client ties are set up through a tacit assumption of 'patron' and 'client' roles, or whether such relations are constructed through some formal, ceremonially or contractually sanctioned installation.

4. *The contents of the clientelistic exchanges*, which can be distinguished according to:

   (a) Long- and short-term ties.

   (b) The different packages of resources exchanged in the patron–client relations and, especially, the relative emphasis placed on solidarity or power differentials.

   (c) The degree of discretion, subversive submissiveness and socio-moral restraints prevalent in these relations.

5. *The degree of continuity or instability of clientelistic patterns* in general, and of specific networks in particular.

Variations along these lines can be found in the patron–client relations described above, in different societies. These variations are summarised here, as they relate to the most clear-cut instances already reported.

With respect to the organisational character and institutional placement of patron–client relations, networks with a localised, personal structure were found in the following cases: among the rural *aghas* in eastern Turkey; in the links of some Peruvian and Bolivian *hacendados* with *colonos*; in the bonds emerging in indirectly ruled villages of continental southeast Asia; among the clusters of Mexican *caudillos*, *caciques* and their followings in the first two decades of the twentieth century; in the links of the pariah entrepreneurs with Thai bureaucrats in Thailand; in the ties that administrators and merchants maintained with peasants and shepherds in Greece in the 1950s and 1960s; and in the relations between professionals and rural populations in modern Brazil.

Different patterns were found among the networks linked to wider institutional frameworks. Clientelistic clusters remained dispersed in the networks of the southern Italian *notabili* and the southern Spanish *caciques* during the greater part of the nineteenth century, among the politicians in the Philippines during the period of American rule and electoral contests, among the Brazilian *coronéis* during the Old Republic (1899–1930) and in the Lebanese *muqata'ji*, in the 1860–1920 period; also in the networks which existed in Colombia, in the nineteenth and early twentieth centuries, as well as in western Sicily, modern eastern Turkey and pre-Protectorate Morocco.

In other cases, the linked networks were integrated in chain-to-centre structures, as occurred in southern Italy in the postwar period, in the P.R.I. machine politics in Mexico, from the 1930s, in urban Brazil around the *pelegos* and *cabos eleitorais* from the late 1930s, in Spain, during the Franco regime, in some Latin American societies under military rule from the 1960s, in the Philippines since the 1940s or 1950s and in the developed areas of Turkey, from the late 1940s.

With respect to the character of occupation of roles, the client role, as we have seen, has been assumed in a collective manner in Iraq and in other Middle Eastern areas, in eastern Turkey, in some central American Indian villages and among the Greek Sarakatsani *tselingas*. In modern settings, such collective incumbency is found among the peasants' and workers' unions and organisations, promoted by politicians and other nationally oriented elites, in Italy, Venezuela, Mexico, Brazil, the Philippines and Indonesia. Cases of individual occupation of the role of client are found elsewhere in southern Europe, southeast Asia and Latin America.

With respect to the patron role, instances of collective occupation were found in the relations of the Republican Roman State vis-à-vis *civitas liberae*, as well as in those cases – such as occurred in Rwanda and southwestern Cyrenaica – where the patron–client links were addenda to the ascriptive hierarchical systems which were described in chapter 4 and discussed in chapter 5. In modern settings, such cases appear where trade unions and other formal organisations act as collective patrons towards their members. As a rule, however, most reported cases in modern societies are those of individual occupation of the role of patron.

With respect to the dimension of the styles of installation, some clientelistic relations are assumed informally and tacitly, as occurred in most of the networks in Christian southern Europe and Buddhist southeast Asia. Conversely, cases of installation through some formal ceremonial or contractual sanction are found among the Catholic *compadrazgo* and in the Japanese *oyabun–kobun* relationship.

With respect to the character of clientelistic exchange, some relations are built with a short-term reciprocity within them, such as those intercessions with the bureaucrats and other powerholders on behalf of clients, which were found in Italy, Spain, Sardinia and other Mediterranean societies as well as in urban Latin America and southeast Asian settings and in the Middle East. Long-term reciprocity characterises both the ties found in western Sicily or the Bolivian and other Latin American *hacienda* settings, in which the balance of power strongly favours patrons and brokers, and the Thai *nāi–phrai* bonds, as well as the networks of *gauchos* and *patrones* in the ranch complex of the southern Latin American lowlands (pampas), in which the balance of power is less lopsided.

Regarding the relative importance of elements in exchange, instrumental considerations dominate the ties maintained by merchants having a monopsonic hold on access to retail markets with peasants, as described for Mexico, Bolivia and Greece. Considerations relating to the power of solidarity are more predominant in the networks of *al-tabaʿiyya* in northern Iraq, of the *futuwwat* in Egypt and the *zuʿama* and *muqataʿji* in Lebanon; in the Brazilian, Colombian and Mexican networks, among the western Sicilian *mafiosi*, in the ties emerging in the Spanish *pueblos* and the central Italian *mezzadria* areas, and in the Thai and Indonesian networks. In some of these, power differentials and the use or threat of application of force are most prominent as constitutive factors of exchange, while in others, the emphasis is placed on interpersonal commitment to reciprocate, and on mutual solidary relations between the patrons and the clients.

Socio-moral restraints on the discretionary use of power by the patrons were found in the networks of the western Sicilian *mafiosi*, the Lebanese bosses (*qabadayat*), the Burmese networks, the *aliran* patrons in Indonesia and the links existing in the central Italian *mezzadrian* areas. The absence of such restraints, however, characterised the links of the Lebanese *zuʿama* and the networks of *caciquismo* in Spain during the late nineteenth and early twentieth centuries. The lack of self-restraint on the part of the clients from adopting attitudes of half-hearted obedience towards patrons, and from attempting to undermine patron–client relations as soon as their market positions allowed it, was typically exhibited in Thai clientelism. The existence of such socio-moral restraints has characterised Catholic South American and Mediterranean patron–client relations.

Finally, various combinations of continuity, discontinuity and instability characterise the patron–client relationships described in chapter 4.

II

How can the variations found in the organisational patterns of patron–client relations in different societies, or sectors thereof, be explained?

As most of the variations occur within the framework of the clientelistic mode of structuring generalised exchange and evince much less continuity, it is clear that they cannot be explained by the circumstances which were singled out above as conducive to the emergence of this mode – namely by the general societal and cultural conditions; the low level of autonomy of the centres, the elites and the major social strata; the cultural orientations which these elites articulate and which emphasise passive and mediating orientations of the social order; the modes of control the elites exercise, as well as the low internal cohesion of the major social strata.

The explanation of these variations seems to be most closely related to other aspects of the institutional order which may develop in different configurations within the clientelistic (as well probably as other) modes of structuring generalised exchange and which affect the structure of the major resources in a society and the standing of the different groups and the potential patrons and clients with respect to the major resources and positions – namely, the structure of the division of labour and the distribution of power, and the interrelations between these two.

Among the most important of those aspects of the social division of labour and of the structure of power to have potentially such influence are, first, the levels of economic and political development or modernisation; and, second, the structure of the centre – above all of the coalitions within it and the profile of the centre. (Such a profile is mostly manifest in the major policies undertaken by the centre, especially those which structure access to the major institutional markets and resources, and in the mode of permeation of the periphery by the centre. A supplementary factor of importance in this context is the structure of the central administration.) Third are the character and configurations of the major social actors, the different groups and strata from which the potential patrons and clients are recruited, and the degree of their internal cohesion, as well as their solidary relations and the extent to which they share common moral conceptions; and, fourth, the differential access of these major groups to the major resources in which they are interested.

All these aspects of the social division of labour and of the structure of power in society show variations in different clientelistic (as well as other) societies, in different sectors of the same society, or at different periods. It is by means of these variations that the differences (indicated above) existing in the diverse organisational dimensions of patron–client relations can be explained.

The fact that these variant structures change more frequently than the clientelistic mode of structuring generalised exchange, and that they occur in different configurations, leads us to one of the theoretical problems mentioned in our review of the study of such relations in the social sciences. We refer to the possibility that different aspects of the institutional order – especially those related to the construction of trust and meaning as against the regulation of power and the social division of labour –can be relatively autonomous. Hence, they can be combined in different configurations in societies, and in sectors thereof, and can evince different levels of continuity.

III

On the basis of the material already presented, we shall now proceed to analyse these variations in greater detail.

Several organisational aspects of patron–client relations are indeed, as has often been indicated in the past, linked to different 'stages' of their national or sectoral development which, to some degree, can also exist simultaneously side by side in different sectors of such societies, according to the respective levels of modernisation and development in these sectors.

Such levels of economic and political development influence the scope of the patron–client relations that occur in the respective societies or sectors. The more 'traditional' and less developed the social setting is, in either economic or political terms, the narrower and more localised will be the scope of patron–client relations. This scope is extended, and various forms of linkage between local patron–client relations, as well as between them and more central organisations, tend to develop, hand-in-hand with processes of growing economic and political differentiation induced by the crystallisation of modern political centres and the penetration of market forces and processes into peripheral, especially agrarian, areas.

Thus, in the nineteenth and early twentieth centuries, many of the agrarian areas of Latin America, southern Europe, the Middle East and southeast Asia were characterised, first, by a 'seigneurial' appropriation of the basic resources, of the means of livelihood and, above all, of the lands, which, in the form of fragmented small strips, were leased to peasants in return for labour, cash or rent in kind. These areas were characterised, second, by the development, in the framework of rent capitalism, of pre-capitalistic forms of organisation of work; and, third, by landowners' and merchants' monopsonic control over positions of access to peasant labour and to a large share of their production.

These economic conditions, in turn, were usually associated with a low level of mechanisation and of capital investment, a lack of credit facilities and a low degree of development of communications. In all these situations, the low ability of the landless workers and of the minifundist peasants to ensure their livelihood in a relatively independent way, the precariousness of agricultural contracts and the multiplicity and criss-crossing effects of part-time occupations among the peasants led to the emergence of 'captive' clienteles characteristic of such localised clientelistic networks. At the same time, the differential distribution, among the rural population, of contracts with big landowners, together with the minimal free movement and alternatives for livelihood open to the peasants, seem to have induced an interest on the part of privileged (permanent, resident) workers in maintaining the prevailing power relations.

In the majority of such cases, the political centres barely penetrated their hinterland, and mostly with exacting demands. These elements were considered alien and oppressive, did not inspire trust or commitment among the peripheral sectors and even lacked a monopoly over the use of force and violence.

The clientelistic relations that developed under these conditions were mostly limited to one patron with a few clients, and were focused around persons and their abilities and actions, rather than around offices and their incumbents. In principle, they were not organised around supralocal contacts of the patrons. Even when, as may often have been the case, the patrons participated in broader coalitions with those sectors and peripheral sectors were affected by their decisions, the clients were usually relatively isolated from such links.

The forms of organisation of clientelistic relations became transformed with the commercialisation of the economy, with the development of processes of accelerated urbanisation and with expansion in the extractive capacity and the sporadic mobilisatory activities of the central administration. These processes and their sequences have affected in various degrees the settings of clientelism analysed in our previous chapter – as for instance in Mexico, Indonesia, the Philippines or Italy, since the late nineteenth century, or in Bolivia and eastern Turkey, since the 1940s.

All these developments had far-reaching consequences for the structuring of clientelistic networks.

In the first place, with the occurrence of such changes, the landowners and local potentates started to emphasise more diversified entrepreneurial activities, in relation to processes of work and marketing, and in their domains, they implemented instrumental arrangements in respect of tenants and labourers, such as cash rents or debt-peonage.

Second, the development of greater socio-geographic mobility gave rise to diversification in the sources of livelihood among the broader strata of the population. The economic role of the urban private sector and of the centre, as dispensers of public and private goods and as employers, grew in importance.

Third, these developments were often paralleled by the penetration of the political and administrative organs of the State into the periphery.

These trends naturally tended to curtail the role of traditional patrons, both as controllers of access to sources of livelihood and as political controllers of peripheral social forces, within the framework of broader coalitions. At the same time, the various political developments and the expansion of administrative forces which accompanied the extension of electoral franchise seemingly increased the political power of the periphery.

Accordingly, these developments weakened the monopolistic power domains of the patrons, gave rise to a greater variety of alternative avenues for clients and created new sources of bargaining for the clients, such as votes and organising skills.

Yet, despite all these developments, the clientelistic arrangements, even if organised in new ways, tended to persist, as shown in chapter 4, not only in the margins of these societies but in the very central cores of their institutional structures. The major resources distributed by the central agencies or market forces (often scarce employment, public services, access to administration and to public goods) were still regulated by clientelistic criteria and relations. They were dispensed by the various patrons, be they individual politicians, administrators or organised bodies (like parties, trade unions or their representatives). In return, the patrons received, or hoped to receive, votes or some kind of loyalty, and even some personal services, although those assumed a smaller importance here than in traditional patronage.

Such patrons, whether individuals or party or union activists, often manipulated their positions in order to build a personal following and gain access to official positions, for instance in the administration, and used the resources controlled by these positions to build a wider clientelistic network.

Such clientelistic relations, however, greatly differed in their structure from those occurring in the more traditional settings. Instead of the limited, directly personal relations to one patron, more complicated networks of patrons, brokers and clients emerged. These were often organised pyramidally, consisting in chains that may have run right through the administration and political organisations, thus linking the clientelistic networks to the centre or centres of society.

The level of economic and political development is thus very important for explaining the general differences existing in the scope of patron–client relations in traditional and modern types of settings. Contrary to what has often been assumed, however, this factor is not sufficient to explain many other differences in the organisational structure of patron–client relations in the new, more complex types of network mentioned above. The most important of such differences are to be found in the institutional placement of such networks, in their concrete structure, in the character of the link and in the forms of installation in and occupation of patron and client roles, in the scope of the exchanges, in the balance of effective instrumental and power elements prevalent at the base of the resources, and in the forms of their control.

In the following sections, we shall analyse systematically the structural conditions which are related to these dimensions of patron–client networks.

ORGANISATIONAL ASPECTS OF CLIENTELISM: INSTITUTIONAL PLACEMENT AND STRUCTURE OF NETWORKS

I

Let us start by analysing the institutional placement of patron–client relations and the forms that clientelistic networks assume in societies. From this perspective, even in the more developed or modern societies, the first general distinction is the one existing between localised types of clientelism, as against different forms of clientelistic linkages to wider institutional frames effected through different types of formal or semi-formal organisations.

The purest form of such localised networks can be found in the various traditional sectors characterised by a low level of economic or political development – such, for instance, as the networks of rural *aghas* in eastern Turkey, the ties that Peruvian or Bolivian *hacendados* established with *colonos* and labourers in the nineteenth and twentieth centuries in, respectively, the Peruvian sierras area and in the Bolivian *yungas*, or in the patron–client relations that existed in the villages of indirectly ruled, continental southeast Asian areas.[1] In such localised patron–client relations, the networks exhibited a dispersed structure, the clusters of patron–client relations, placed outside the more formal channels of societal organisation, being unrelated to one another and, seemingly, self-sufficient.

Such localised networks, however, are not only confined to traditional sectors but can also be identified in cases where the forces of market and political centralisation operate more effectively, although such networks exhibit here different characteristics. Such, for instance, were the clusters of Mexican *caudillos* and *caciques*, in the 1910s and 1920s; or, in Thailand, the links that tied 'pariah' entrepreneurs to bureaucrats; or the networks maintained by patrons with peripheral strata as in Greece, in the 1950s and 1960s, in the case of the administrators' and merchants' relations with peasants and shepherds; or, in Brazil, until the present time, the ties linking professionals (lawyers and physicians) with the rural population.

The localised networks which developed in some such cases, as distinct from the purely traditional ones, tended to be characterised, by a greater instability and transiency. These features were generated either by competition among the potential and actual patrons under conditions of high mobility (geographic, occupational, etc.) or by market forces and political actors who attempted to break the clientelistic power domains and to incorporate potential clients within the framework of market expansion. In so far as these networks were political, the clients would be incorporated within wider political frameworks – as was evident, for instance, in the Mexican developments after the 1930s and 1940s. In other cases, especially where the patron–client relations were focused on the economic sphere – in some Greek and Bolivian settings (after the early 1950s) and probably in other developing countries in situations of mediated access to avenues of commercialisation of agricultural products – these networks continued to be found by the side of more complex ones built on organisational linkages to wider institutional frameworks, such as bureaucracies, political parties or trade unions.

By contrast with this localised type of patron–client relations, which also emerged in the more developed or modern societies, were clientelistic networks which maintained some form of organisational linkage to wider institutional frameworks. Two major patterns of 'linked'

Patrons, clients and friends

clientelistic networks can be distinguished here: 'organisational brokerage' and what, following P.A. Allum,[2] can be called 'patron-brokerage'.

'Patron-brokerage' is characterised by a dispersed structure of networks, formally unrelated to one another except through the activities of the brokerage heads. The networks remain dispersed, despite their being separately related to the same institutional frameworks, such as bureaucracies, political parties or trade unions. Among the best illustrations of such 'patron-brokerage' networks are those of the *caciques* of southern Spain in the first half of the nineteenth century; the *notabili* of southern Italy, the Thai *nāis* and the Colombian rural patrons, in the nineteenth and early twentieth centuries; the networks in pre-Protectorate Morocco and modern eastern Turkey; the western Sicilian *mafiosi*; the Philippine politicians, until the end of the American rule in 1941; the Brazilian *coronéis*, at the regional state level, during the period of the Old Republic (1889–1930), and the Lebanese *muqata'ji* in the period from 1860 to 1920.

In all these cases, politicians or administrators at the national or regional levels sought the support of local elites in their political contest for access to the centre and attempted, accordingly, to coopt local notables. These notables, whose supremacy was initially based on such assets as local economic and traditional professional power, obtained these initiatives and, in return, were allowed the grant of a control over state and municipal resources, which were now more significant at the local level and could further their patronage leverage. The coopting of these notables did not, however, lead to a centralised restructuring of the networks; instead these remained dispersed and formally untouched – except through the mobilisation of their patrons – by direct impingement of the national forces already operative in these societies.

The patterns of 'organisational brokerage' shared with those of patron-brokerage the tendency to become linked to, and even to merge with, formal organisations. At the same time, however, in the case of organisational brokerage, the different networks tended to be integrated in related chain-to-centre structures. Some of the clearest of the cases already analysed of such clientelistic organisational brokerage were the following: the networks created by P.R.I. machine politics, in Mexico from the 1930s; and in southern Italy in the postwar period; the ones found in urban Brazil, from the late 1930s, around the activities of the *pelegos*, during the populistic corporative organisation of workers and later of the *cabos eleitorais*, who gathered electoral support in the period 1945–64; the relations existing in Spain during the Franco period; in the Philippines from the 1940s or 1950s; in the more

230

developed areas of Turkey from the late 1940s; in some Latin American countries under military rule from the 1960s; and in Lebanon, in the networks of the *zuʿama*, during the period of independence.

In all these cases, the search for mass support as a source of legitimacy, whether under conditions of mass suffrage and enduring political competition or under authoritarian polities, made it necessary for the political actors to obtain votes or to mobilise masses in some way.

Almost all these potential patrons retained control of the administration or of political or bureaucratic–administrative offices, and they all tended to engage in a redistributive activity to secure wide support through the grant of actual favours or through the promise of help proffered by party- and faction-directed brokers. The effectiveness of such brokerage depended, of course, on the brokers' access to the organs of the State and to the channels of delivery of its resources, as well as on their ability to use them in a particularistic way to gather political support. Whatever the degree of their success, the networks developed by them were structured in a 'linked' form, and dispersed separate clientelistic power domains tended to become less central in these settings.

II

As already indicated, neither the difference between the localised clientelistic pattern in the traditional and semi-traditional sectors and the various forms of complex 'linked' networks, nor the difference between patron-brokerage and organisational brokerage, can be fully understood if explained – as has been suggestively done by J.C. Scott and A. Weingrod and widely pursued in case studies[3] – only in terms of the different levels of economic or political development; especially if explained by the degree of incorporation of local settings within the sphere of influence of the national and supranational market economies and of penetration of these peripheral and semi-peripheral clientelistic-prone areas by political forces and by the administrative organs of the centres. As shown above, these factors affect, in general, the scope of patron–client networks in clientelistic societies. But the whole range of differences mentioned in respect of the institutional organisation of patron–client networks can hardly be explained solely by this factor. Rather, it is the other aspects of the social division of labour and of the structure of power – i.e. the structure of the centre, its major policies and the nature of the major coalitions existing within the centre – that are of special importance for understanding the differences in the structure and institutional placement of patron–client networks.

We shall start by inquiring into those aspects of the centre which are of special importance in generating localised, as against more centrally linked, networks of patron–client relations in the more 'developed' societies.

From this point of view, it seems worthwhile to compare, for instance rural Greece, as illustrated by the case of the Sarakatsani, with southern Italy. These are social settings which shared almost identical levels of economic and political development and in which the major peripheral forces were relatively demobilised and lacked access to the major institutional markets and to valued resources except through patron–client links.

In the case of the Greek Sarakatsani, the clientelistic relations they maintained were localised, placed outside the scope of bureaucracies, political parties and trade unions. Conversely, in the period following the Second World War, in southern Italy as well as in countries such as Brazil, Mexico, Venezuela and Colombia in Latin America, Thailand and the Philippines in southeast Asia, and the Lebanon and Turkey in the Middle East, patron–client relations were built on linkages to those wider institutional frameworks.

These two types of social settings differ, above all, in what we should term the 'profile' of their respective centres: that is, in the significance of the resources controlled by the administrative organs of the centre for the major social actors potentially involved in patron–client relations; and, second, in the importance attached by potential patrons, and in particular brokers, to the political leverage obtainable, vis-à-vis potential opponents, by keeping on good terms with and being supported by political forces at the centre, and the perils and losses entailed by being detached from that centre.

The impingement of the Greek centre on the periphery was rather weak, as illustrated in the case of such peripheral groups as the Sarakatsani, and was manifest in the tax drives and the general administrative regulations. In the period following the Second World War, the centre in Italy presented a high 'profile' in society. This was evident in the growing relevance of resource allocation by municipal bodies and by state agencies, such as the Cassa per il Mezzogiorno. A few other examples, already analysed, are given here. In the post-Revolutionary regime in Mexico, nomination to candidature, within the framework of a single-party system, and access to office in the machinery of the State, became highly attractive and important, involving as they did a high degree of discretionary use of formal power for personal benefit. In Lebanon, in the period of independence, the

Variations in patron–client relations

resources commanded by the administration acquired significance for broader social strata which was manifest in the importance of governmental concessions, public works contracts, employment in governmental and private sectors through the recommendation of politicians and administrators, developmental projects, such as electrification of villages, expansion of telephone and postal services, better public health and educational services, and special treatment in the implementation of the laws.

In these and in other settings, mentioned above, there were few opportunities to attain wealth, prestige and power apart from the administrative political or other bureaucratic (labour, peasant union, etc.) offices which were open to wide sectors of the society. In other situations, the hold over positions in the machinery of the State had far-reaching consequences, outside the formal bureaucracy, especially as regarded the resources available for particularistic disbursement by the people having the right contacts there.

These profiles of the centre greatly influenced those basic strategies of the major social actors, of the would-be patrons especially, that were explicit in cases where the patrons had to rely on resources controlled by the organs of the centre or by sectors of the elite in order to build their power domains, or, conversely, where they were in direct control of resources at the local level.

Concomitantly, the scope and structure of patron–client links varied in these societies. Thus, in Greece, the low profile of the centre increased, for the broader strata, the importance of informal channels for obtaining access to crucial social resources, even to those controlled, in principle, by the centre or related to it. In this situation, the would-be patrons were encouraged to develop clientelistic relations by using resources at the local level, and networks of patronage emerged which were almost entirely unrelated to the central administration.

By contrast, in southern Italy as well as in Mexico and Lebanon, would-be patrons had to manipulate, beyond the local setting, the contacts with and avenues of access to more central organisations and to frameworks of exchange. Accordingly, parallel clientelistic networks emerged here, linked to formal channels of societal organisation, in which party-directed bosses, or other brokers related to those channels, gained both ascendancy and significance in the framework of electoral contests or of partial mobilisatory devices in authoritarian polities.

As already indicated in the case studies, the strength of these brokers depended, on the one hand, on successful political connections and on the subsequent control they attained over the organs of the State and the resources derived through them, and, on the other, on their ability to manipulate them to gather electoral support and/or wide followings. Accordingly, the control of access to administrative offices and civil service appointments, and influence over the allocation of public funds, often became the main aim of clientelistic attachments, for patrons and brokers as well as for clients. These clientelistic ties assumed that the patrons should command influence at administrative and political levels in order to be able to cope with bureaucratic requirements and to obtain valuable resources commanded by the centre. Consequently, clientelistic networks became linked to these more formal and central channels of societal organisation.

It can thus be said that it is the nature of the profile of the centre, in general, and its permeation of the periphery, in particular – especially as these affect the opportunities commanded by the administrative organs or derived from them – that are of crucial importance in determining whether localised or linked clientelistic networks can develop in any given society or sector thereof.

III

However, as already mentioned, there developed in various societies different modes of linkages, different types of linked forms of clientelistic networks (the major patterns being those of patron-brokerage and organisational brokerage), as well as significant variations within each of these forms.

We shall start by analysing the conditions conducive to the development of patron-brokerage as against organisational clientelistic brokerage. The first pattern comprises dispersed clusters of patron–client networks while, in the second, such networks tend to become interrelated in a chain-to-centre structure, in which the clusters at the periphery are linked, across local, regional and other levels, to the networks found close to the centre.

These differences can largely be explained by the different configurations of coalitions of elites and entrepreneurs which develop within the framework of a relatively high profile of the centres and a concomitant capability on their part to permeate peripheral sectors and strata. Of special importance here is the character of the central coalitions in society and, particularly, the degree of relative autonomy of the central political elites, in relation to the various – above all local and traditional – social strata, elites and entrepreneurs.

Several typical configurations of such coalitions can be identified in the cases presented above. One such configuration, which was identified in the southern Italian Mezzogiorno, under the rule of a coalition of northern bourgeoisie and southern landed rent-capitalistic forces, was characterised by the predominance of a relatively non-autonomous central elite embedded in the upper – central and local – social strata.

Such elites tended to adopt what may be called 'encapsulative policies', i.e. policies which encapsulate lower power domains either through alliance (not always, of course, established on a formal level) with local landowners and powerful local and regional entrepreneurs, or by coopting local powerful figures as part of the administration in these peripheral areas.

These policies were usually implemented without direct interference in local affairs and, accordingly, tended to reinforce the existence of relatively narrow markets with a somewhat limited flow of resources between them. Also, the control of access to those markets was mainly maintained in the hands of the local upper strata. The central and local social forces adjusted to each other and tried not to encroach on each other's power domains.

Accordingly, different types of patron-brokerage, i.e. relatively dispersed clusters of patron–client networks linked to wider institutional frameworks but only related through their 'heads', tended to develop in all these cases. Social relations in local traditional power domains were not substantially changed but had new resources and sources of influence added to them through the brokering activities of patrons, in contact with social forces placed at the supralocal levels of political activity and administrative regulation, closer to the centre of society.

Differences may, of course, have developed, even under such policies, in the forms of incorporation of local settings and of the consequent structure of the patron-brokerage networks. Thus, when the coalitions of the more central forces with local notables and entrepreneurs were tacit – as when western Sicilian *mafiosi* were contacted by regional politicians – or when the central forces were no more than the representatives of the local powerful magnates of the countryside – as in the nineteenth-century Brazil – networks of patron–client relations remained traditional, and localised ties tended to retain a fragmented dyadic character. In such cases, while tactical power was gained by such patrons and brokers at the local level, through their contacts with the more central political forces, the links with wider administrative and political frameworks remained unstable. Accordingly, the specific networks may have been affected by the changes in the attitudes and policies of the central forces – as can be seen, for instance, in the impermanent character of the western Sicilian *mafiosi's* power domains and, in Brazil, in the processes of dislocation of the old order and the advent of the first republic in the late 1880s.

As against this, when there was some degree of coopting of local potentates into some wider regional or national organisation – as occurred in modern eastern Turkey, pre-Protectorate Morocco, Brazil in the period 1889–1930, Lebanon in 1860–1920, the Philippines in 1907–41, or Colombia in the nineteenth and early twentieth centuries – the character of the networks was modified. In such cases, even if the ties of these clientelistic networks to more central frames of interaction remained sparse and were mostly established through the coopting of leaders' contacts within wider institutional frameworks of societal organisation, the networks were still related to central formal policies or social channels. The patrons became part of the political and administrative municipal, regional, etc., machinery of the State. Formal powers were often, then, delegated to them and, thereby, as representatives of the centre, they gained greater leverage than previously vis-à-vis social forces at the local level, placed in a position of dependence in relation to them. The following cases illustrate this tendency. In eastern Turkey, from the 1940s to at least the 1970s, local patrons who, due to their vote-gathering, were important to national party leaders were given office as mayors and members of municipal councils. In Colombia, powerful regional *caudillos*, and local *gamonales* related to them, were given formal governmental positions and control over bureaucratic jobs and budgets in return for electoral support for politicians of the national 'cadre' parties. In republican Brazil, *coronéis* bargained with political forces, at the state and national levels, over the delivery of electoral support in exchange for office holding and attached benefits, as well as for the centre's agreement not to interfere in regional and local settings.

Similar patterns can be found in the twentieth-century Philippines, where village factions and leaders were coopted by national politicians and wangled favours for their clients from the administration; also in pre-Protectorate Morocco, where patrons, recognised by important leaders of the *makhzan* or by the Sultan himself, were appointed *cuwwad* (tribal chiefs) and invested with administrative functions as military chiefs, civil governors, tax collectors or criminal judges.

Even in such situations, however, the particular form of encapsulative incorporation of the power domains of these social groups – which assumed that the patrons retained many of their traditional functions with the addition of new ones connected to brokerage – precluded the possibility of the dispersed structure of clientelistic ties being restructured in a chain-to-centre form.

In such cases – especially in the more traditional societies analysed here, such as pre-Protectorate Morocco or nineteenth-century Thailand, but also under conditions of greater development of communications and wider impingement of local settings, as typically

exemplified in southern Italy – the inherent instability and impermanence of specific networks of patron-brokerage is only tempered,
but not eliminated, by the recognition of those patrons as local representatives and agents of the national and political forces. Thus, local
contestants, ambitious pretenders and rival factions often attempted,
in many such situations, to undermine established power domains
with the explicit or tacit support, at the higher levels of organisation,
of the actual or potential holders of power. These central forces may
have been interested in weakening what they considered excessively
strong, stable or influential independent local or regional power
domains, consequently changing or reformulating previous lines of
coalition with social forces at the local level. This was particularly likely
to occur in the more modern societies, where internal stresses in the
older clientelistic relationship were operative. In southern Italy, for
example, such internal stresses appeared with the undermining of
traditional economic sources of control and a growing uncertainty as to
the outcome of electoral acts, conducted along more democratic idioms
and involving wider sections of the population. In some cases, this
induced politicians to rely on party organisational support. In others,
the inability of political machines to dominate local notables with their
own sources of patronage was one of the main motives leading to the
establishment of party-directed bosses at the local and regional levels.
Thus, new methods of party-directed clientelism flourished there,
characterised by a pyramidal clustering of linked networks of clientelism, which were related to formal organisations within the context of
Italian political competition over control of the organs and resources of
the State.

IV

By contrast to the cases, analysed above, of coalitions of relatively
embedded central elites and strong local ones, other configurations
may develop within the framework of clientelistic societies with relatively high profile of centres. In these configurations the central elite is
more autonomous and attempts to minimise the power of the higher
ascriptive social strata in general, and of the local magnates in particular, and to undermine their direct relations of control of broader
strata. The policies of such coalitions tend to allow the development of
what we have called 'organisational brokerage', i.e. a pattern of
clientelistic brokerage characterised by networks organised around
linkages to the broader societal organisations, being integrated in
related chain-to-centre structures.

Several typical configurations of such coalitions can be identified in the material already presented. The most important were, first, those led by political elites, backed by party machines in the framework of competitive electoral polities, and, second, the coalitions led by elites with populistic and authoritarian non-coercive orientations.

Common to all of them is the fact that these coalitions led by the central elites, working within the framework of a high 'profile' of the centre, attempt to extend the scope of the institutional markets, mainly of the political market, through extended franchise, and break down to some degree the established power domains and the access to these markets open within those domains. The policies adopted by such elites often lead to the reconstruction of clientelistic networks around the formal central channels of political parties, central administration, trade unions, the police, etc. In these cases, patrons and brokers base their power on their positions within those central organisations and on their contacts with holders of positions of the latter sort, such as high-standing politicians, administrators and other bureaucrats. Accordingly, clientelistic networks are based on linkages to those central organisations, being characterised by chains extended across local, regional or state levels, often reaching to the very centre of society.

Despite such common characteristics, however, it is possible to indicate differences in the nature of these coalitions and in the policies they implement – differences which affect the placement of the networks of patron–client relations in their respective societies.

In some of these settings, under conditions of expanding mass suffrage and a competitive electoral system, such coalitions strove to accede to positions of power with the backing of political machines. This was evident, most of all, in Latin American twentieth-century 'façade-democracies',[4] which developed intermittently until the 1960s and 1970s, particularly in Brazil, Chile, Uruguay, Venezuela, Colombia and Peru; in Turkey, after 1945, and in independent Lebanon; and, during most of the twentieth century, in Italy and the Philippines. Votes were gathered through distributive activities such as the grant or promise of resources and services commanded by the centre and its administrative organs. Such activities were often related to the undermining of localised networks of patron-brokerage and to the heightened relevance of the brokering activities of party- and faction-directed entrepreneurs. The effectiveness of these would-be patrons depended on their contacts with political and administrative forces or on their effective or probable access to the organs of the State and to the channels of delivery of its funds, resources and services, as well as on their ability to use such resources in a particularistic way to gather support.

Variations in patron–client relations

The other types of coalitions referred to above, namely the populistic and the authoritarian ones, in their attempts to reformulate the criteria of access to the institutional markets, developed policies that broadened the access of the different strata to those markets. Such policies naturally constituted a potential threat to the clientelistic arrangements existing in these societies.

We will now analyse the dynamics of such processes and their effects on the moulding of the clientelistic organisational networks discussed here, in settings in which coalitions, of either the populistic or the authoritarian type, were predominant.

Populistic coalitions – typically illustrated by the Latin American instances, such as Brazil during Vargas' rule and Argentina under Perón[5] – emphasised, at an ideological level, the revolutionary character of the regime and the deliberate opening of institutional markets. This was done in order to establish (from above) a universalistic and more 'just' access to resources for all social actors without, in principle, using traditional intermediaries between the masses and the leadership at the centre of society. This emphasis on direct access to the centre of society by the broader strata and on the redistributive aspect of the centre affected 'older' forms of clientelism, such as localised traditional patron–client relations and networks of patron-brokerage unrelated to the present administration and to the political forces allied to it. But clientelism, here, is transformed rather than altogether undermined. On the one hand, the stress put on the State and its regulative and distributive activities by the ruling coalitions increased *de facto* the importance of mediators in shaping and especially in implementing redistributive policies, therefore leading to the remodelling of mediation within the framework of the central societal organisations. Networks became related to these broader channels of organisation and mostly linked to the very locus of power at the centre, as illustrated in the activities of the unions' *pelegos* in Brazil. On the other hand, the policies of populistic coalitions did not radically affect the uneven command of assets of different sectors of the population, and, in the long term, other forms of patron–client relations tended to emerge there, especially when the pool of resources for redistribution at the centre became reduced.

As against the populistic configurations, authoritarian non-coercive coalitions (typically represented in the case studies by Mexico, under P.R.I. rule, and by Franco's Spain, as well as by, among others, Tunisia under the rule of the Destour Socialist Party (generally called Neo-Destour) and military regimes which have ascended to power in Third World countries since the mid-twentieth century, such as Paraguay under Stroessner, Argentina, Bolivia, Peru, Brazil, Greece, Nigeria and Indonesia) tended to implement the following policies: first, ones that attempted to open access to the centre to those wide sectors of the population that were ready to recognise its pre-eminence and to become incorporated in the social and professional organisations controlled by the power-holders; and, second, policies designed to deny their former secure control of such access to the various 'local' traditional forces. Thus, many of these polities, while they based themselves on either regimentation, manipulation or persuasion of the broader strata and restricted some of the formal freedoms maintained by the liberal democracies, attempted at the same time to introduce an ideological opening of the regime.

'Clientelism' and related phenomena of favouritism were condemned and used as arguments to discredit previous power-holders (often civilians), who were shown as corrupt and as having led the country into economic stagnation and underdevelopment.[6] In the Latin American countries mentioned here, for instance, these coalitions ascended to power mostly through the use of force, justifying their coups as being in the name of the common good. These coalitions were supposedly the soundest 'interpreters' of this common good, which could be attained through economic growth and by reorganising the foundations of the corrupt civilian administration. Some of these regimes – such as the Brazilian one for instance – tried to replace it with improved, rational and honest patterns of administrative performance and with tighter control on the bureaucracy. At the same time, they banned free party politics and reduced the autonomy of the parliamentary sphere. All these measures, of course, affected the patterns of clientelism found in these societies. In the first place – and mainly during the initial stage of such regimes, when the ideological factors were strongly emphasised – the clientelistic networks, while still present, had mostly a 'discrete' character and were formally unrelated to wider organisational structures connected with the State. Linkage between the administration and extra-bureaucratic forces were discouraged and, if present, involved 'unrecognised' contacts rather than more complex ties. Even then, the undermining of such clientelistic networks, found across the boundaries of the administration, was not general. As has been shown in detail in a study made by L. Guasti on Peru,[7] such particularistic attachments are still widely used, even if they assume a more class-demarcated character. According thereto, middle-class individuals relate to people of similar social standing in the administration and peasants approach migrants to the cities when looking for help and intercessors.

In the long run, these links often tend to resume the connections with wider frames of societal organisation. Several factors conduce to this transformation. In the first place, in such polities, the proximity of people to the loci of political–administrative power is a major asset which can be used by ambitious power-holders to build clientelistic power domains as soon as the centre gives up, *de facto*, its pretence to retain tight control over the performance of the bureaucracy. Second, the full consequences of such policies on clientelistic networks are often only fully realised during the initial phases of establishment of the regime, when the ruling coalition attempts to concentrate power and decisions within the administration, trying to cut off any contacts with local-level patrons and brokers. Such attempts are usually ephemeral, and the subsequent isolation of the centre from the masses at the periphery constrains the at least partial reversal of these policies.

This reversal or reformulation of policies was mostly effected in the direction of a mediated mobilisation of support for the regime among the broader strata, or in the guise of renewed electoral contests and parliamentary political activities. These activities were often conducted by political parties through networks of organisational brokerage which assumed clientelistic features in situations where the broad conditions of clientelism were still operative.

Thus, in all these instances occurring in societies where conditions conducive to clientelism were present and where, both under mass suffrage and enduring political competition and under populistic or authoritarian polities, the search for mass support as a source of legitimacy for the regime was prevalent, special types of clientelistic networks, sooner or later, emerged. Although the concrete contours and institutional location of these networks varied greatly, as will be seen in the following analysis, they assumed organisational brokerage forms.

V

Despite their common characteristics, different types of 'linked' clientelism varied with respect to the concrete arena in which the linkage was effected between the informal power domains and the formal (bureaucratic, etc.) organisations. One indication of such variability is that in some cases, as in Colombia for instance, peasant clientelistic organisations may be created by urban-based political elites in order to gain power, or, as mentioned by J.D. Powell in the case of Venezuela,[8] to break the power holding of traditional elites at the national level.

In other instances, the trade unions became the main frameworks within which networks of organisational clientelistic brokerage, linked to holders and contesters of formal office, emerged – as already described for Brazil after 1930 and, elsewhere, by R. Sandbrook for Kenya in the 1950s and 1960s.[9]

Such variations are related to the structure of stratification of the different societies analysed here and to the concrete organisation of the social forces in different historical situations. But, in addition to the differences in such concrete terms, variations also exist with respect to the level of the formal organisations most liable to be affected by clientelistic considerations and informal power domains.

In many cases, such as Italy, Colombia and the Philippines until the 1970s, those are the higher levels of the political and socio-economic spheres in general, and, in particular, of such organisations as become the main arenas for the patron–client networks which penetrate the administration and the governmental bureaucracy. In other instances – well illustrated by the Egyptian *shillal*, the Brazilian *panelinhas*, the Mexican and Thai cliques and the Philippine setting since the 1970s – while the making of high-level decisions remains open to clientelistic considerations, intra-bureaucratic networks seem to be more important at the medium or lower level of such organisations.

Such differences in the concrete placement of clientelistic networks within a 'linked' structure are influenced by additional aspects of the centre which have not yet been analysed: namely by the structure of the administration and, especially, by the difference between what S. Tarrow[10] called 'diffuse' and the more integrated administrations, as well as by the ways in which they influence the capacity of the centre to implement its articulated policies. Diffuse administrations are characterised by a fragmentation of jurisdiction and by relatively ineffective control over bureaucratic performance – due either to overlapping control or to the blurring and over-formalisation of policies. An integrated administration is characterised by greater cohesiveness and by greater bureaucratic control over the implementation of policies.

In diffuse territorial administrations – such as can be found, for instance, in Italy, Colombia or the Philippines – there tends to develop a blurring of distinction between the administration and the political allegiances that influence it. Accordingly, in such a situation, political clienteles, which arise out of internal competition between party and other political factors, pervade the central areas of administration and the control over high positions in the formal organisations, as well as the implementation of the policies.

As against the clientelistic settings regulated by diffuse administrations, there are other cases – as in modern Thailand and Egypt, Brazil, Peru since the late 1960s, and the Philippines in the 1970s – in which the administration has a more integrated character. Such administrations are characterised by a greater compactness in decision making and tighter controls over bureaucrats in charge of implementation of policies, even while decision making remains open to clientelistic pressures. In such situations, the relevance of political allegiances to lower-level patrons seeking to influence administrative decisions is, to a certain degree, diminished. Conversely, intra-bureaucratic personal relationships tend to develop. In some respects, these ties are similar to the patron–client relations, in the personal character of the links, their informality, their mixture of instrumentality and solidarity; at the same time, they are more influential. As indicated above, such intra-bureaucratic networks are best illustrated by the Egyptian *shillal*, the Brazilian *panelinhas*, the Thai cliques that cut across formal departmental bureaucratic lines, and the networks established within the Philippine administration as a result of the banning of electoral politics in the 1970s. We shall discuss the development of one of these cases here in somewhat greater detail – namely, the Egyptian *shillal*. C.H. Moore[11] found that within the bureaucratic–authoritarian regime of Egypt in the sixties and the seventies, older vertical clientelistic networks were replaced by more 'horizontal' *shillal*, while 'clientelism' was used as a label to discredit opponents rather than as an indication of its presence. Vertical clientelistic relations throughout the administration were precluded by the fact that potential clients in the bureaucracy gained a secure hold over bureaucratic positions, following the initial grant of access to office accorded by some 'patron'. At the same time, temporary circles of 'friends' emerged, employed in different ministries and public companies, which provided their members and dependants with bureaucratic support, information and economic gains, from the public funds, at the expense of more universalistic forms of access to the resources commanded by the centre.

VI

We are now able to summarise the features and social conditions that characterise some of the main organisational patterns of clientelism developing in the relatively modern or modernising settings already identified. Schematically, these patterns can be described as follows:

A. 'Localised', patron–client relations of a traditional kind. These are characterised by the following features:

>   Power domains are built locally; patrons are interested in keeping governmental agencies away from the established power domains. There is dispersed structure and non-merger of clientelistic networks with formal channels of societal administration.

The societal conditions which gave rise to this pattern are: low profile of centre for social actors; mutual adaptation of central, local, higher and lower groups, and avoidance of penetration into the hinterland by central forces, which are considered alien and which do not inspire trust and commitment among peripheral sectors involved in localised power domains.

B. Forms of clientelistic networks linked to wider institutional frames ('linked' clientelism):

1   Patron-brokerage. This is characterised by the following features and societal conditions:

(a) Supralocal strategy of patrons for establishing power domains; dispersed structure of networks, but tendency to become linked to formal and informal channels of administration.

(b) A relatively high profile of the centre for social actors; policies of adaptive relations with the periphery, accompanied by an interest on the part of the central elites in coopting local notables as part of the coalition ruling in those peripheral areas; structure of coalitions: non-autonomous central elites embedded in upper, central and local, strong social strata.

2   Organisational clientelistic brokerage. This is characterised by the following features and societal conditions:

(a) Supralocal orientations of patrons; tendency to merge with broader formal channels of articulation and chain-to-chain networks.

(b) A high profile of centre for social actors; policies of expansion of institutional markets and attempts to reformulate established power domains; partial impingement and mobilisation of broader strata by the centre and formal organisations; structure of coalitions: central elites relatively autonomous, attempting to minimise the power of higher ascriptive social strata and their direct relations to the latter. Different liberal electoral, populist and authoritarian coalitional strategies.

In social settings, where patron-brokerage and organisational clientelistic brokerage appear, there are variations in the forms of linkage between formal and informal power domains and the institutional loci of patron–client relations. In diffuse administrations, political and socio-economic clienteles pervade the administration, blurring the distinction between administrative decisions and political particularistic allegiances. In more integrated administrations of clientelistic settings, intra-bureaucratic networks were found to be more influential than extra-bureaucratic attachments in attaining particularistic influence on policy implementation and redistributive measures.

MODES OF PATRON–CLIENT ROLE TAKING

I

As has been indicated above, the variations in this aspect of the structure of patron–client relations are twofold: first, there are clientelistic relations in which the roles of patron and client are prescriptively assigned to different social strata according to various particularistic–primordial, non-market criteria, i.e. in which there are ethnic, cultural and other barriers to the assumption of clientelistic roles, while there are other relations in which these roles are open in principle to any social actor according to his market positions, irrespective of his primordial identities. These variations have been analysed above, in the context of patron–client relations emerging in ascriptive hierarchical societies such as India, Rwanda or Cyrenaica, in which such relations constitute a relatively legitimised addendum to the institutional matrix of the societies. The reader is referred to chapter 5 for the detailed discussion of such variations and their institutional consequences.

Second, variations in this aspect of the structure of patron–client relations are found with respect to the criteria of occupation of the roles of both patron and client, i.e. whether it is collectivities or individuals that can assume such roles. The relative importance of these criteria is conditioned by the composition of the major social units and their standing in relation to strategic resources and centres of power in society. In what follows, we analyse the forms of occupation of the client role and, subsequently, to the role of patron.

II

Collective occupation of the role of client is found in Middle Eastern areas such as Iraq and eastern Turkey, where it arises within or involving supralocal groups of unilineal descent and including extended kinship ties, or in tribal areas, where the coopting of sheikhs by authorities and politicians sometimes leads to the emergence of clientelistic relations involving a whole tribal group. The same situation occurred in central America in connection with the relations of Indian villages to *hacendados*. We have also described how the Greek Sarakatsani *tselingas* are related to patrons through the heads of their groups, and in western Sicily how the *mafiosi* networks include a

245

mixture of kith and kin that may adopt a corporate – even if loose – character. Finally, there are numerous instances of clientelistic corporate mobilisation of peasant and workers' organisations by politicians and nationally oriented elites in modern Italy, Venezuela, Mexico, Brazil, the Philippines, Indonesia, etc., in return for particularistic collective rewards granted through mass manipulators and organisers.

Such cases of collective occupation of the client role appear in situations in which, on the one hand, the major social strata are either organised in corporate or categorial cooperative units such as descent groups and corporate villages, or participate in modern settings within categorial formal frameworks such as trade unions and peasant organisations; while, on the other hand, the units involved are relatively weak and are unable to provide autonomously the social actors with the 'critical' resources needed. Under such conditions, potential or actual patrons and brokers who are interested in mobilising those units or categories of people for particularistic gains often activate them within wider frames of interaction. Sometimes it is also the potential clients that promote the emergence of such clientelistic ties among collective social units and organisations around powerful figures, in order to gain security and even as a locus of identity in a clientelistic setting.

Contrasting with such instances of collective occupation of the role of client, there are many cases, indeed the majority, in which this role is vested in individuals as such. This seems to be characteristic of two main types of situations. In the first – as above all in southern European, southeast Asian and Latin American instances of clientelism, especially under conditions of modernisation and capitalistic development – social actors are, to use E.R. Wolf's term, 'freed' from corporate kinship, territorial or other primordial links.[12] Strategic resources are then not bonded to corporate units and are converted into legally free floating resources; individuals are drawn into individual-centred coalitions in order to advance their positions in society.

An individual occupation of the role of client can, however, also occur in a somewhat different situation, less typical of the social settings analysed here but well exemplified in the relationships found among pastoralist age groups in East Africa, and analysed in detail by U. Almagor among others.[13] There, strategic resources are bonded within discrete corporate units such as kinship groups, or are at the disposal of prominent family leaders such as elders in age-group systems. Under such circumstances, clientelistic attachments are used as an alternative means of overcoming the harsh terms and the excessively limited opportunities of access to markets available within the framework of corporate groups.

III

Variations are found as well in the criteria of occupation of the role of patron. In most of the cases analysed above, the occupants are individuals. This is probably due to the personalistic character of patron–client relations which arise in a context of narrow strata identities and of contest and struggle among members of the same stratum.

True enough, patrons can usually count on wide networks of social contacts and relations, based on friendship, affinity and other ties outside the local sphere of establishment of clientelistic attachments. They maintain those connections, however, as personal assets outside these links, withholding them from their clients. Thus, when some favour is granted to a client by one of his patron's friends or by an organisation in which the patron has interceded on the client's behalf, thus creating new ties, these can either remain mediated by the original patron or constitute additional ties between the client and a new patron, without involving the emergence of collective patronage.

However, instances of collective occupation of the role of patron can be identified in the case studies presented above under different sets of conditions. Thus, corporate occupation of the role of patron characterises the link of foreign *clientelae* of the late Republican Roman State to *civitas liberae*, the *dozoku* patterns in rural Japan, and in modern settings cases of organisations such as trade unions or parties acting as collective patrons to their members, as occurs in the Mexican P.R.I. and the Tunisian Neo-Destour organisation.

There is no one common denominator beneath all these cases of collective occupation, except for the obvious fact that, in such situations, it is collective social actors that either monopolise access to the centres of power and to institutional markets or for whom access to these is mediated.

Thus, on the one hand, the analyses of the Ancient Roman foreign *clientelae* and of the Japanese *dozoku* relationship indicate that, in some historical and traditional settings, collective patronage may occur when there is a stress on the basic, almost primordial, different standing of the major collective social units involved in such relations – be they Romans and non-Romans or *oya* and non-*oya* houses in the Japanese case. It was because of such lack of any common shared premises that the statuses of the collective social actors were defined by means of legal, quasi-legal and ritual idioms, which prescribed the limits of the social actors' ability to assume either patron or client roles. Under such circumstances, it was the would-be patron who proposed – motivated by different interests – the establishment of a clientelistic link with some of the collective social actors who stood in low, unadvantageous positions in relations to centres of power and strategic resources.

Collective patronage may also arise under different conditions, above all in modern settings where there are formal universalistic premises for access to markets and centres of power. Such development may take place with organisations – such as the Mexican P.R.I., the Tunisian Neo-Destour, the Colombian Conservative and Liberal parties, etc. – which are either close to those centres of power or dominate them, and act as collective and 'surrogate' patrons to their members, blocking the free access to resources the latter could have had by virtue of their membership in the organisation. The emergence of such forms of collective occupation of the patron role is connected above all with attempts made by the established centres of power to control, or to foster controlled forms of, mass mobilisation, in order both to gain wide support for the regimes or the organisations that sustain them and to avoid the emergence of alternative and less supple means of interest aggregation.

It is, however, rather difficult to assess, in any such case, whether emphasis should be put on the organisational–structural aspects of the working of the trade union or other formal organisation as a collective patron, or whether in the transactional sequence the leaders and brokers acting as gatekeepers between the members of the organisation and outside agencies and social forces may be considered individual patrons manipulating organisational power and advancing their own interests. Such assessment of the character of the relationship must indeed be related to the emic perception which both leaders and followers have of their organisation and of the rewards they obtain through their participation in it. From the observer's point of view, both these characterisations usually depend on the focus of the research.

STYLES OF INSTALLATION: THE FORMS OF CONSTRUCTION OF PATRON–CLIENT RELATIONS

The variations in this dimension relate, as we have seen, to whether the patron–client roles are assumed informally, through some tacit understanding, or whether such relations are established through some arrangements sanctioned ceremonially or contractually. These variations affect several basic aspects of the interaction between patrons and clients, which we shall point out later.

An informal, tacit, 'open' assumption of roles can be found in the patron–client relations occurring in north Mediterranean Christian societies, as well as in Buddhist settings with hierarchical ranked statuses even if not as fixed as in Brahminism.

A formal, 'closed', style of arrangement is found in such ritualised patterns as the hierarchical frameworks of Christian *compadrazgo*, or of the Japanese *oyabun–kobun* link in a less clientelistic setting.

In both patterns, the entrance into a clientelistic network and the position assumed by people in such a network are not defined ascriptively *a priori* – by birth for example – but evolve in a series of tentative approaches, of trial and error, by the social actors seeking, in social and political competitive clientelistic frameworks, to improve their life perspectives. However, once the relationship is set up, the character of the installation in the clientelistic bond, be it ritualised or non-ritualised (i.e. 'close' or 'open'), shapes, as indicated, the emergence of different forms of interaction between patrons and clients. First, it affects above all the degree to which the relationship is prone to instabilities and changes connected with the partners' positions within institutional markets. Thus, when patrons or clients are approached for the purpose of establishing clientelistic relations in an informal, tacit manner, the client accepts the patron's right to determine ever anew the form and content of the actual exchange. At the same time, the relation remains potentially unstable and changes are often induced by actual transactional modifications in the positions of the partners within the institutional markets.

As against such a form of construction of patron–client relations, a 'closed' style of installation guarantees the fixing of the terms of trade formulated when the relationship is contracted. This formalisation renders the link less vulnerable to the actual transactional positions of the partners.

Second, these variations in the style of installation to patron–client roles affect the forms of articulation of personal involvement of the partners in their relationship, and in particular whether such an involvement is active or passive and how often the partners can make use of the relationship without leading to the severance of a strong or active mutual personal commitment. In other words, the character of the installation in the relationship strongly affects the profile of implementation of the ties by the partners.

On the one hand, non-ritualised links are actually used by clients or by patrons according to their market positions. On the other hand, in ritualised patterns, and notwithstanding the high reverence and social significance involved in these links an improper or excessive use of such clientelistic relations is precluded by the fact that the partners avoid approaching each other 'too much'. It is widely assumed that a request from a ritual partner cannot be refused and that to ask for a large number of services would lead to the severance of an active commitment between the partners and indeed to the complete 'cooling' of the relationship. It is therefore considered that the use of such a link depends on the goodwill of each of the partners. In such cases, there should be neither an open emphasis on the issue of self-interest nor a need to refresh the partner's memory concerning previous favours. Requests which either are too trivial or may endanger a ritual partner's position should not be made, and the partner should not be forced to grant the needed service. In doubtful cases, requests for favours may be presented in the guise of pleas for advice. The partner – the godparent or co-parent, etc. – must decide freely if he will propose his good offices and on what terms.

VARIATIONS IN CLIENTELISTIC EXCHANGES

I

As indicated above, clientelistic exchanges involve many aspects of routine exchange of goods and services, through which the client renounces the free use of many resources which (potentially at least) were at his disposal, and the patron achieves the maintenance or expansion of his position of power and of preferential access to markets. In the fully fledged clientelistic settings, however, this instrumental or power-based routine exchange is always combined with elements of symbolic significance, including solidarity or reciprocity, 'merit-making', unconditionality and long-range credit and obligations between patrons and followers.

Thus, as we have seen, exchange in patron–client relations is constructed in different societies in such a way as to combine access to crucial resources – whether to land, water, manpower or employment opportunities, to scarce skills or favours and services in such spheres as education, public health, social security, or to official certificates, licences or loans – with promised reciprocity, signs of goodwill, elements of force and respect, solidarity and interpersonal obligations. The fulfilment of these obligations is regarded as being closely related to the evaluation of personal identity or face-saving, according to such symbolic codes as *honor, omerta, bun*, loyalty, moral preeminence, etc.

Despite this characteristic, shared by all types of patron–client relations, there is however a great diversity of patterns of exchange, as regards both concrete services, goods and resources exchanged and the terms of trade and the forms under which elements of routine exchange are combined to constitute the kind of package deal contracted for by patrons, brokers and clients.

Many variations occur in these respects, the most important among which are, first, the short-term or long-term character of reciprocity which mutually binds patrons and brokers to clients. Second, long-term ties differ with respect to the balance in the terms of trade, which in some cases strongly favours the patrons, while in others it is more equitable.

Third, there are variations with regard to the relative importance of instrumental considerations and of elements of power and solidarity as constitutive elements of exchange. Here we distinguish, in the first place, between those patron–client relations in which the personal involvement of patrons and clients in political 'games' or in solidary bonds is minor, and those relations in which such a factor is significant. Second, we can further distinguish between those relations in which power elements are particularly emphasised and those in which the emphasis is laid on the personal involvement in solidary links between patrons and clients as constitutive elements of exchange.

Third, and independently of the relative stress on elements of power and solidarity, patron–client relations also differ in the degree to which it is recognised that the partners are accountable to one another, in terms of a shared socio-moral model of interaction which is acknowledged by the partners.

II

Before we go into the detailed analysis of these variations and of the structural and symbolic conditions that explain their emergence, it should be pointed out that the basic combination of routine and generalised exchange which characterises all patron–client relations has important implications for the study of such variations.

In the first place, the lack of a clear distinction between the elements of routine and of generalised exchange lead to the fact that not only the concrete resources exchanged, but also the perception of the relationship and its contents, may be and often are changed, manipulated and reformulated ever anew by the partners over time or as they change frameworks of interaction. This renders the task of the observer particularly difficult in respect to the assessment and distinction of these elements on – to use the term of the social anthropologists – etic and emic levels respectively. Discrepancies often crop up between, on the one hand, the definition of the roles according to cultural criteria and vernacular symbolic idioms (such as honour, friendship, etc.), through which patrons and clients express their mutual rights and

251

obligations, and, on the other, their actual behaviour within those relations. These difficulties are particularly prominent in the comparative study of the variations in clientelistic exchanges.

Bearing these difficulties in mind, we now turn to the analysis, in a systematic way, of the detailed variations existing in the patterns of exchange in different patron–client relations.

Institutional markets, resources and the time perspective of reciprocity in patron–client relations

I

The first main dimension of differentiation in clientelistic exchanges is related to the relative durability of arrangements of mediated access (to resources and to avenues for their conversion) effected. As indicated above, we shall distinguish here between clientelistic links established along a lasting, long-term dependency and others built with an expectation of short duration.

Short-term attachments are found, in the Mediterranean area in Italy, Spain and Sardinia; in urban settings of Latin America and southeast Asia; in the Middle East, where officials are often requested to intercede with higher governmental administrators, as illustrated by the Jordanian *wastah*. On the other hand, many of the cases of patron–client relations included in the case studies are built on a more long-range reciprocity, as illustrated by patterns as diverse as the western Sicilian networks, the Thai *nāi–phrai* links, the ties found in the Bolivian and other Latin American *haciendas*, and the patron–client relations of the ranch complex of the Uruguayan and Argentinian *pampas* and the Brazilian region of Rio Grande do Sul, as well as in Japan.

Under what conditions are these different patterns liable to emerge? The central clue to the understanding of these conditions lies in the nature of the resources sought by the partners and of the access to them, i.e. in the positions within markets of potential and effective patrons and of the clients needing these resources.

In the case of short-term clientelistic attachments, clients and patrons get mediated access to resources – mostly, second-order resources – which, in principle, are free-floating and are not 'critical' either to the basic livelihood of clients or to the socio-political standing of patrons. Such attachments usually assume the form of grant of sponsorship and intercessions by the patron or broker, to allow the client to obtain access to such resources as bureaucratic contacts, licences, scholarships, administrative exemptions, civil service appointments, decisions on jurisdictive competence, specific public goods according to particularistic criteria, army transfers, etc.

In cases of long-term attachments, the clients, and sometimes the patrons, have sought to obtain through these relations resources which they have deemed 'critical' and basic to their livelihood and social standing, and access to which has been blocked. In such cases there have been few alternative avenues open to them apart from the established clientelistic forms of monopolistic mediation. Such resources may have been basic resources needed for subsistence (like lands, water sources or work) or some educational or craft expertise of clients or, under conditions of severe unemployment, the grant of employment.

Such different types of resources involved in short- or long-range patron–client relations are thus above all connected to the structure of markets in different societies or sectors thereof.

Thus, long-term attachments have been found – as has been the case in western Sicily, the Andean countries, Thailand or Indonesia in the nineteenth and a great part of the twentieth century – where markets were of a narrow scope, where there existed relatively few free-floating second-order resources and a very marked institutionalised scarcity of basic resources for livelihood or for production, and their grant was often presented and perceived as a favour, as a particularistic sign of personal concern. In such circumstances, either the members of the clientelistic strata or the would-be patrons had to enter into a relationship in which dependency was comprehensive and the people involved stressed long-term interpersonal attachments and obligations, as well as personal credit and involvement. This long-term character of reciprocity was often expressed in such symbolic terms as honour, personal significance, or particularistic commitment.

As against these situations, short-term attachments are found where market structures are characterised by a high flow of resources, a wide scope of activities, open access to goods, services and information, and the greater personal mobility which follows capitalistic development or rural–urban migration. Such market structures, while they do not by themselves obliterate the emergence of clientelistic attachments, are however conducive to their phrasing according to a short-term reciprocity in patron–client exchanges.

Under such conditions, a widening scope of free-floating resources strains clientelistic limitations to free market exchange. Patrons then have to strive more in order to maintain their control over avenues of information and flow of resources. However, their ability to achieve success in this respect is limited as the scope of markets widens, and the centre may become interested in or constrained into implementing policies of active societal permeation and organisation, and class or related categorial loyalties may press and even try to replace clientelistic attachments.

Under such circumstances, potential patrons and brokers usually attempt to limit access to resources; but, if they succeed, the avenues of control remain as a rule multiple and specific. Thus, even if the basic institutional matrix of a society remains clientelistic, a structure of institutional markets characterised by the existence of alternative avenues of access to resources which, to a great extent, are of a second-order nature hampers the establishment of long-term obligations towards a single patron. Loyalty becomes tenuous and apart from the goodwill of the partners, which eventually may preclude their being cheated by one another, no assurances or sanctions are available to enforce reciprocation of help in the future. In these instances, great emphasis is placed on conditional obligations, and the duration perspective of the reciprocity which mutually binds people participating in the patron–client relations is, accordingly, a short-term one.

II

Among patron–client relations characterised by a long-term prospect of reciprocity, there develop differences with respect to the balance in the terms of trade epitomised in the exchange maintained by patrons and clients. Such balance is above all influenced by the relative importance – the 'need' – of the resources controlled by each of the potential partners.

In some cases – western Sicily, the Andean countries and parts of Mexico, the regions once under direct colonial rule in southeast Asia, the Philippines – the balance in the terms of trade strongly favoured patrons and brokers vis-à-vis clients, the patrons being, through their dominant control of basic sources of livelihood, the sole prescribers of the nature of exchanges with their followers. In these settings, access to lands and other basic resources necessary for livelihood was 'critical'; population pressures on them were high and access to them was mediated. Such blocking of free access to basic resources was facilitated by various factors, among which were such ecological ones as tenuous patterns of communication and transport, political ones such as the isolation of a certain area, or cultural ones such as the crystallisation of wide social acceptance of mediated forms of access to resources.

An extreme example of these conditions was found in western Sicily where there existed and still exists an extreme discrepancy between the population pressures and the possibilities of access to basic sources of livelihood such as strips of land, work opportunities, herdsmanship or sharecropping arrangements, this giving rise to a high measure of conflict and violence in society. Similarly, pressures and struggles over resources existed in many of the Latin American countries, particularly in the Andean ones and in Mexico, and in parts of Indonesia and the Philippines. In all these settings, the terms of trade in patron–client relations strongly favoured patrons and brokers vis-à-vis clients. As against these clientelistic settings, this kind of conflict was to some degree obviated in Japan, under relatively similar conditions, through the symbolic emphasis given to commitment and mediated access to resources, as well as through the stress, inherent in this culture, put on harmonic social intercourse and a strong sense of communal interdependence.

In other of the cases analysed here – such as the *nāi–phrai* links in the Siamese kingdom and the patron–client relations in the ranch complex of the southern corner of Latin America – the balance of dependence does not favour the patrons or brokers altogether. Such patron–client relations emerged in settings in which there was a need for manpower, which was in short supply, and for its control and mobilisation. Vague territorial boundaries, warfare, and ecological difficulties in monopolising the basic resources necessary to livelihood, have usually been associated with such a lack of manpower.

Under such conditions, there develops – especially insofar as there is no institutional backing of patrons by the centres of power – a tendency in patron–client relations to emphasise the personal virtues of both clients and patrons, together with an emphasis on the long-term perspective of reciprocity which binds both partners.

In the South American pampas ranch complex, a great emphasis was placed under such conditions on the dependants' – the *gauchos'* – personal pride, expertise and independence, as well as on their commitment to their *patrón*. In the Thai cases, such an emphasis was decreased by the support given by the Siamese kingdom to *nāi–phrai* links, which constituted from its point of view a way of controlling and regulating manpower. Hence, clientelistic bonds were highly formalised and exclusive there, and the tendency of clients to assume attitudes of subversive submission, typical of the Thai situation, was weakened to a great extent. Nevertheless, away from the central areas and in the more peripheral regions, the relations between patrons and clients assumed a more informal and a milder character, even when established by patrons with indebted peasants, defined as slaves, who entered voluntarily into bondage ties. In such cases, as has been indicated in chapter 4, slaves retained many of their former rights, such as creating a family and inheriting or passing on property, even if these rights were, in principle, exercised through the patron's mediation. In addition, these 'slaves' carried little stigma or none at all when freed, and smoothly reentered society.

The relative importance of instrumental considerations, solidarity and power differentials in exchange

Another major dimension of differentiation in clientelistic exchanges is that which relates to the respective degrees of importance attached to instrumental considerations and elements of power, solidarity, personal trust and symbolic meaning, as constitutive elements of exchange.

In some patron–client relations, considerations relative to personal involvement in political 'power games' or in solidary bonds between patrons and clients are of relatively minor importance – although to some degree they exist, by their very nature, in all clientelistic exchanges. Such situations develop – as shown in the cases of Mexico, Bolivia and Greece detailed in chapter 4 – mainly in the area of ties contracted in the economic sphere, such as those linking peasants producing for the retail markets. In these cases, the relations of clientelism established by patrons are aimed at ensuring the continued dependency of clients within the major institutional markets and hence the provision of material resources and gains designed to allow patrons to maintain life-styles and standards of consumption typical of the upper, local, regional or national stratum. Accordingly, the overt expression of support of clients is marginal to the 'power games' in which some of these patrons may be engaged outside local settings. In addition, little personal involvement is found on the part of either 'patrons' or 'clients' in such relations.

By contrast, in most patron–client relations considerations relative to power, solidarity, personal trust and symbolic meaning are more important as constitutive elements of exchange. They were, as we have seen, to be found in the Middle East, in *al-taba'iyya* in northern Iraq, *futuwwat* in Egypt and the Lebanese networks of *zu'ama* and *muqata'ji*; in Latin America, in the patterns found in Brazil, Mexico and Colombia; in southern Europe, in the western Sicilian *mafiosi* and the links emerging both in the Spanish *pueblos* and in the central Italian mezzadrian zone; and, in southeast Asia, in the Thai and Indonesian networks. In all these relations, the respective importance of the considerations involving power and solidarity is reflected in certain behavioural emphases, such as the display of force, the endeavour to construct personal solidarity, the ritualistic expression of support of a patron by his clients or the reflection of the patron's social distinction and political influence on clients.

Variations in patron–client relations

In these cases, especially in the Latin American and Middle Eastern networks mentioned here, there has developed a strong stress on the 'social visibility' – i.e. on the social standing and prestige – of the patron as well as on the manipulation of its reflection on the clients as a means for the latter to attain influence in the socio-political arena, in interactions vis-à-vis peers and in institutional contacts. In such cases, clients are often identified socially and politically with the status of the patron. Sometimes, such identification leads to the crystallisation of idiomatic expressions, such as the Brazilian 'você sabe com quem está falando?' (literally, 'do you know with whom you are talking?') recently analysed by the anthropologist Roberto da Matta, [14] and aimed at creating a hierarchical distance between persons of otherwise equal standing or at elevating the comparatively low status of a person by emphasising his close relationship to a prominent social actor. It is interesting to note that such expressions are often also employed beyond the realm of patron–client relations proper.

The relative significance of some combinations of elements of power, solidarity, trust and meaning was also manifest in other instances (such as the Indonesian 'entourages', the Lebanese networks, and the links of Ancient Republican Rome) in the ritualistic behaviour of clients towards patrons. In these cases, clients were expected and even required to show overt reverence and respect to their patrons, both as proof of their lasting personal obligations and as a means of advertising power and the patron's magnificence. Such emphasis on the demonstration of the patron's power, prestige and strength and on their reflection on the clients is less marked in patterns having an instrumental bias, but even there it is not altogether absent.

In all these cases, people conceive the clientelistic link as a means for delayed or reflected – rather than merely direct, instrumental – benefit in fields related to the macrosocietal order, above all in the political and socio-relational spheres.[15] Accordingly, such elements of exchange as the overt expression of support of a patron by his clients, the reflection of the positions of patrons on clients, or the construction of personal solidary obligations, become more noticeable within patron–client relations.

The set of patterns analysed in the last part of the preceding section – i.e. those in which there is a stress on the personal involvement in political 'games' or on the solidary bonds of patrons and clients – is, however, very variegated.

In some of the cases, such as those of the western Sicilian *mafiosi*, the Thai *cao nāi*, the Mexican *caciques drásticos* and the Egyptian *futuwwat as baltagi*, power elements are particularly emphasised. In other patron–client relations – the central Italian mezzadrian traditional links, the Andalusian *pueblos'* relations between elites and followings, the

Patrons, clients and friends

Egyptian *futuwwat as ibn el-balad*, the networks found in some of the Brazilian *fazendas* in the nineteenth century and those emerging around professionals in rural modern Brazil – the emphasis is laid, when constructing exchanges, on the elements of personal involvement and mutual solidarity relating patrons and clients to each other.

What are the conditions that bring about the emergence of such different emphases? Here, the patrons' solidary association with or dissociation from peripheral strata is particularly important. This is evident when comparing the central Italian mezzadrian links with the western Sicilian *mafiosi's* brokerage and the Spanish *caciquismo*, all drawn from the same cultural area, and therefore keeping constant the cultural variability found in clientelistic settings.

Thus, in the central Italian mezzadrian networks, the patrons were clearly associated with peripheral strata: they maintained close and regular contacts and solidary relations with their peasant partners. Accordingly, themes of personal commitment, long-range credit and solidarity were emphasised in patron–client relations as constitutive factors of a diffuse and multiplex exchange, not limited to a single institutional sphere.

In western Sicilian and in Spanish clientelistic relations, patrons and brokers had – whether in contexts permeated by violence and only partially incorporated within a national State (as in western Sicily), or in an authoritarian polity (as in Spain) – rather weak broader strata. Under such conditions, when there was no mobilisation of popular support through local leaders maintaining solidary association with the population, would-be clients had little bargaining power, and clientelistic exchanges exhibited more coercive content and were more restricted than in the foregoing cases.

Such configurations of factors are found as well in the other cases of patron–client relations mentioned at the beginning of this section. Thus, in Egypt, *futuwwat as ibn el-balad* lived in the quarters they protected and 'ruled', and their interests were identified by the broader strata as being complementary to the needs of their followers. Similarly, in the Spanish *pueblos*, diffuse patron–client relations were established between members of the local and regional leadership and other residents associated in a solidary manner to them, giving a 'lopsided-friendship' character to the ties, to use the expression of Pitt-Rivers.[16] In the relatively isolated *fazendas* of northeast Brazil in the nineteenth century, paternalism was emphasised in the links of clientelism that arose around the landowners in the countryside. In all these cases, patrons maintained close solidary contacts with the peripheral strata from which clients were drawn and, accordingly, personal involvement and mutual solidarity were relatively prominent as constitutive factors of exchange between patrons and clients.

By contrast, in northeast Brazil and other Latin American areas which were fully integrated into the economic world markets, the absenteeism of landowners (*fazendeiros, hacendados*) was accompanied by the lack of any strong association of would-be patrons and clients, and hence by the emergence of dependence ties having a more instrumental and coercive character. In the Middle East, as we have seen above, there are numerous instances of patrons and brokers who, dissociated from broader patronymic groups, stress accordingly elements of force and backing from beyond the local communities. In such cases, as in the patron–client ties in Mexican squatter areas, or among the urban migrants in Indonesia, although external signs of deference might be required, power elements – along with instrumental considerations – were more significant in the context of such relationships.

Discretion, subversive attitudes and socio-moral restraints

I

We shall now proceed to discuss an additional aspect important in the emergence of differences in the contents of clientelistic exchanges – namely, the recognition or lack of recognition of some mutual accountability and indebtedness of the partners in terms of a shared socio-moral model of interaction.

The major distinction to be drawn here is between those relations having such socio-moral restraints, and others in which such restraint on the patrons' discretionary use of power or on the assumption by clients of rather subversive attitudes – albeit couched in submissive terms – towards patrons, is either altogether lacking or very weak.

The existence of such socio-moral restraints on the patrons' discretionary use of power – as foreseen from their favourable market positions – is well illustrated by the western Sicilian *mafiosi*, by the Lebanese *qabadayat*, by the Burmese networks, by the Indonesian *aliran* patrons and by the links existing in the central Italian mezzadrian area. Their absence characterises among others the links of Lebanese political entrepreneurs (*zu'ama*) and the networks of *caciquismo* in Spain.

The existence of socio-moral restraints on the adoption by clients of subversive attitudes towards patrons beneath the submissive terms of the relationship, and on their launching attempts to undermine patron–client bonds as soon as their market positions allow it, is typically to be found in southern European and Latin American patron–client relations. A lack of such socio-moral restraints is typical of Thai clientelism. Less clear-cut examples are found in the other patterns described in chapter 4.

The most important factor influencing the recognition or lack of any recognition of mutual accountability and indebtedness of partners, beyond what might be expected from the vantage point of their market positions, seems to be the real or pretended (but publicly affirmed) acknowledgment by patrons and clients of the sharing of a common moral order, from which models are derived for structuring personal and institutional interactions as well as the nature and the contents of such socio-moral models.

It is important to stress that this factor varies in patron–client relations independently of the patrons' solidary association with or dissociation from those peripheral strata from which their clients are drawn. We shall illustrate this distinction by further examining the data on the networks of the western Sicilian *mafiosi* – a case of clear dissociation of brokers from peripheral strata with which they never-theless shared certain socio-moral models of behaviour.

As was pointed out in the analysis of western Sicilian clientelism, the *mafiosi* were connected with absentee landlords and offered politicians dominance over rural political support and, in return, were granted special opportunities for livelihood as well as immunity from judicial actions, influence over governmental decisions and access to informa-tion sought by the common peasants. *Mafiosi* had no solidary ties of association with the grassroots, with which they maintained clientelis-tic exchanges in which instrumental and power elements were of paramount importance. At the same time, however, both these brokers and the people who were the victims of their violent actions or their threats embraced the same behavioural codes, according to which the *mafiosi's* actions received legitimation among broader strata, as they were deemed to evince a behaviour above reproach. *Mafiosi* were supposed to honour personal trust and affection, to help the poor on totally unselfish terms, to be brave and to repel any affronts to their honour. Probably because of his peasant origins, the *uomo d'onore* (the *mafioso*) was considered to be the ideal and prototypical simple man who spoke on behalf of everyone and especially of the weak. There-fore, the broader strata's and the brokers' acknowledgment of sharing a common socio-moral order allowed 'Robin Hood expectancies' to emerge regarding the behaviour of the *mafiosi*, in spite of the latter's clear dissociation from these peripheral sectors. Their ideals and expectations were not disregarded by the *mafiosi* as a whole and in part moulded their behaviour in the western Sicilian countryside.

Similarly, the bosses of the urban quarters of Lebanese cities, the *qabadayat*, acted as political brokers for *zuʿama* politicians and, being involved in activities including protection, racketeering or hashish smuggling, themselves relied on force and coercion in their contacts and relations with the broader strata. Despite this, however, the local population was inclined to idealise the *qabadayat's* role and considered them as the protectors of the local residents, as the upholders and guardians of the moral codes of honour and proper behaviour and as the defenders of the weak and poor. Such projected images were not rejected by the *qabadayat*; rather, they were adopted by them as conferring prestige, conditioning in part, as they did, the contents of the patron–client relations emerging around them, in a somewhat paternalistic manner, responsive to clients' demands and expectations.

Acceptance of the moral checks that clients attempt to impose on the patron's use of power can also be found in patterns where patrons are associated with peripheral forces. In such cases, as shown typically by the traditional patron–client relations existing around the *signori* in central Italy and in many instances of Japanese *oyabun–kobun* links, the patrons' sharing in the models of proper behaviour maintained by the broader strata may serve to legitimate fully the protective solidarian and/or paternalistic content of the relationship.

As against the preceding cases of patrons' and brokers' sharing of social interaction models common to the broader strata, there are other patron–client relations in which the partners do not acknowledge such sharing of a common moral order. In such cases, typically represented by the Spanish 'linked' networks of *caciquismo* and the Lebanese *zuʿama*, patrons are quite autonomous in relation to those 'Little' traditions and peripheral models of social organisation and proper interaction. In the cases mentioned, the discretionary use of resources by patrons was not counterbalanced by any capacity on the part of the clients to demand a degree of accountability from their patron. There existed there greater scope for the patrons to manoeuvre resources without being in any degree accountable to their clients in terms of a shared socio-moral conception.

II

As indicated above, differences in patron–client relations also existed with regard to the presence or absence of clients' self-restraint in adopting subversive attitudes towards patrons – albeit couched in submissive terms – and in attempting to undermine patron–client relations (seen as oppressive) as soon as their positions within markets allowed it. These differences can be explained by taking into account the contents of the socio-moral models sustained by the broader strata.

Patrons, clients and friends

In some settings – such as the Catholic Latin American and Mediterranean ones – the existence of socio-moral considerations constituted a major factor in ensuring submissiveness on the part of clients and in minimising the emergence in them of subversive submission towards patrons, even in clientelistic bonds in which there was a strong element of power. In these settings, such attitudes have been rather scarce in spite of attempts made by ideological movements to foster their spread among sectors of the peasantry and the working classes. Under changing market conditions and forms of access to centres of power, people have, of course, tried to advance their social standing. At the same time, however, there are numerous indications that they have continued to attach a high symbolic significance to their connection with powerful figures, and have enjoyed the reflection on them of their patron's social 'visibility' in their interactions on both an interpersonal and an institutional level. It has been pointed out in the literature on clientelism that in patron–client relations this personal involvement focused on the mundane spheres resembles the devotion to saints and the particularistic approach to them within a religious context that is characteristic of these settings.[17]

By contrast, Thai clientelism seems to be characterised by the clients' lack of self-restraint in assuming subversive attitudes along with submission towards patrons, in attempting to undermine patron–client relations or to change patrons (for 'better' ones) as soon as their positions in the institutional markets allowed it. In spite of the strong emphasis laid in Thai society on hierarchical relations and in spite of the strong Buddhist tendency towards passive acceptance of authoritarian rule in the national realm, the relations established between patrons and followers needed continuous validation and were characterised by shifting allegiances. As soon as they could, people sought to improve their social rank and facilities – even by revolting, as happened in the early 1970s in northern Thailand. This contributed to giving Thai society its pronounced – but only partial – fluidity and 'looseness'.

As already indicated, the contents of the socio-moral models sustained by the broader strata in these societies seem decisive in influencing whether clients tend or not, as a rule, to adopt subversive attitudes towards patrons.

In the first set of instances, especially in the Catholic settings of Latin America and the Mediterranean basin, an ethic of loyalty developed in association with concepts of honour and personal significance. This ethic controlled the inclination of people to assume subversive attitudes in patron–client relations. This does not mean that clients did not change patrons and did not attempt to improve their terms of trade

262

with patrons or even to undermine these relations. The changes of clientelistic affiliation manifest in these societies, however, involved highly emotional shifts of allegiance and personal commitment and obligations, and were often justified – especially in the traditional settings, but also in modern sectors – in terms of the supposed infringement by the patron of some assumed moral obligations he was supposed to have undertaken in the past.

In Thai society, by contrast, such ethics of loyalty, personal significance and honour have not crystallised. Patrons and clients, of course, assumed interpersonal obligations, but they were rather based on conceptions of mutuality and reciprocity, of merit-making and 'face-saving'. Accordingly, clients were reported to have retreated from certain attachments rather 'suddenly' in a covert manner and without any deep emotional feelings of anger.

CONTINUITIES, DISCONTINUITIES AND INSTABILITY OF PATRON–CLIENT RELATIONS

I

The preceding analysis of variations in patron–client relations has shown that the major organisational aspects of such relationships, being affected by different aspects of the social structure, may vary within the generalised model of exchange of the societies we have analysed above. The fact that these variations in patron–client relations are found within the clientelistic mode of generalised exchange indicates that different levels of continuity and discontinuity may be found in such relations.

Indeed, most patron–client relations – certainly those in the more complex and differentiated settings, but also those in the simple or more isolated rural areas – present a picture of variable combinations of continuity and discontinuity of the different patterns of clientelism along with various forms of instability and change in the concrete character and structure of specific networks, in their fortunes and in the relations between the various clientelistic clusters found in social settings. Thus our analysis does indeed indicate that it is necessary to study the dynamics of continuity and change peculiar to these relations on several distinct – although to some degree interconnected – levels, rather than to search for persistence and change in a unidimensional pattern, as has usually been done in previous studies.

As already evident, the most basic level is that of the extent of continuity and change in the very clientelistic structuring of access to

resources and loci of power found in certain societies. Such a clientelistic mode of generalised exchange may indeed, as we have seen, remain
central despite variegated transformations in different aspects of the
division of labour and the structure of power in society, if the structural
and symbolic conditions – the expansive, extractive and plurisectoral
character of the economy, the low level of autonomy of the centres and
major social strata and the passive and mediating cultural orientations
and symbols of these societies, which have been analysed in detail in
chapter 6 – are still operative.

While there may be a far-reaching persistence in the predominance
of such a mode of generalised exchange in different social settings,
discontinuities may arise within each such setting at other levels of the
structuring of patron–client relations.

While we cannot always find exact data on the various degrees of
instability and discontinuity found at the various levels of construction
of patron–client relations in different societies, yet it is possible to
present here at least some conjectures regarding the basic nature of
these levels of possible discontinuity in such relations.

One such level is related to the changing importance in any social
setting of the various patterns of clientelism described above. Over
time, some of these patterns may become more salient while others are
relegated to the margins of the institutional matrix or may altogether
disappear. To offer but one example, while the establishment in
Thailand of a constitutional monarchy and a formal electoral system in
1932 did not alter the basic clientelistic patterns of that society, the new
forms of political organisation added new arenas for clientelistic
arrangements. These became ultimately oriented to the control of
resources at the disposal of the administrative organs of the State.
Consequently, and especially during periods of military influence and
rule, those clientelistic circles with bureaucratic incumbents were
assured of a relatively long-lasting existence, while those not having
such a hold were more ephemeral and marginal.

Such discontinuities in the relative importance of various clientelistic
patterns in any basically clientelistic setting are influenced by the
various aspects of the division of labour and the structure of power that
were analysed in the preceding sections of this chapter.

As we saw there, it is the levels of economic and political development that affects the scope of patron–client relations; the centre's
profile in general, and the centre's penetration of periphery in particular – especially as they affect the opportunities commanded by the
administrative organs or derived from them – are of crucial importance
in determining whether localised or linked clientelistic networks are
liable to develop in any society or sector thereof; the configurations of

coalitions of elites and entrepreneurs which develop within the framework of a relatively high profile of the centres, and a concomitant capability on their part to permeate peripheral sectors and strata, influence the emergence of different modes of linkage of clientelistic networks to the formal institutional matrix of society; the structure of the central administration conditions which level of the formal organisational matrix is most liable to be affected by clientelistic considerations and informal power domains, and influences therefore the concrete placement of clientelistic networks within a linked structure. Similarly, we have seen that it is the identity of the major social actors and their standing in relation to strategic resources and centres of power that influences the forms of incumbency to patron–client roles. The differential access of these major social units to the resources sought by them, as well as the nature of the resources within the framework of different forms of structure of institutional markets, is particularly important in influencing the emergence of short-term clientelistic attachments and various forms of long-term patron–client relations. The patrons' association with or dissociation from peripheral strata is important in connection with the relative significance of power and solidarity as constitutive elements of clientelistic exchanges; and the contents of moral–behavioural conceptions found in societies, and the extent to which the major social actors share common moral conceptions, were found to be important factors in influencing variations with regard to the existence of some mutual accountability among patrons and clients and some degree of restraint on the part of clients from adopting subversive attitudes, or in the discretionary use of power by patrons in their relations with clients.

Accordingly, changes in these basic aspects of the division of labour and of the structure of power in society – changes which may indeed take place in any society – carry with them parallel modifications in the relative significance of different clientelistic patterns that develop there.

Thus we have seen, for instance, that under conditions of expanded social and political participation and a greater geographical and occupational mobility, patron–client networks of a limited scope tend to undergo increasing pressures, as manifest in the networks of a patron-brokerage structure, where 'patrons–brokers' attempt to retain localised power domains though there are socio-economic and political pressures for an 'opening' of such domains and for the direct inclusion of people within the framework of the State and of expanded markets. Where more autonomous central elites take power and launch policies intended to minimise the power of the higher ascriptive social strata, especially of the local magnates and in those power domains which they consider too entrenched, then (in turn) these instabilities are exacerbated. Under such conditions, the reformulation by the central elites of lines of coalition with political and social local forces leads, as we have seen above, first of all to the emergence at the local level of rival clusters and factions attempting to weaken each other with the tacit or explicit support of powerful figures and forces at higher levels of the institutional structure. Second, the policies of such coalitions tend to replace networks of a patron-brokerage nature by clusters of 'organisational brokerage' as a main form of clientelistic linkage between political centres and their peripheries.

To adduce another example, the weakening of the patrons' solidary association with the broader strata leads – as we have seen in the cases of the Egyptian *futuwwat*, the Brazilian *fazendeiros* in the nineteenth century and the Spanish *caciques* – to a diminishing emphasis in clientelistic exchanges on the mutuality that binds patrons and clients and to a greater emphasis on coercive elements as constitutive factors of clientelistic package deals.

Another illustration of such dynamics of instability and change is found in respect of the very perception of the content of the relationship, which – related as it is to the terms of trade set up between patrons and clients, as subjectively evaluated according to their respective market positions – remains problematic, especially when changes occur in the institutional environment. It is particularly problematic during processes of political and economic modernisation, because of the non-ritual and informal character of most patron–client relations. Under such conditions, when there is a widening gap between the expectations of access to resources through alternative channels and their 'preempted' allocation through established channels of patronage, the networks come to be perceived as oppressive, even when maintaining their previous scope of exchange.

II

Another level of instability in patron–client relations is connected with the permanency or impermanency of specific networks, i.e. with the degree of fragility of such networks, as manifest in the extent of replacement and recombination of personal allegiances and interactions. The analyses of the case studies in chapter 4 indicate that shifts and instabilities at this level are not necessarily correlated with instabilities and discontinuities in the character of the networks or in the predominance of the clientelistic mode of generalised exchange: thus, for instance, the western Sicilian, Thai or Burmese networks, which – while they were a relatively long-term feature of the institutional matrix of their societies – were still characterised by the impermanence of specific arrangements. Similarly, but in a somewhat inverse pattern, the composition of the Egyptian networks of *futuwwat* was of relatively high stability, while the pattern itself was relatively short-term in that society.

The relative fragility of personal allegiances and interactions is rooted in some of the core characteristics of the clientelistic mode of generalised exchange, which – as we have seen above – gives rise to instabilities at this level of construction of patron–client relations.

Among these data stands out, first, the fact that the limitations placed on the ability of the social actors to convert their resources fully are, in these relations, not derived from the institutional premises of clientelistic societies. Consequently, the acceptance of such limitations is precarious and any concrete attempt to monopolise resources and the avenues for their conversion may be and often is contested by other patrons, brokers, and clients, as well as by people not included in the networks of clientelism.

Second, because they are not fully prescribed, normatively, the forms of generalised exchange structured by patron–client relations constitute a focus of struggle continuously connected to negotiations on specific exchanges. Under conditions of modernisation and widening of institutional markets, but also in the more traditional settings, a propensity arises to engage in continuous negotiations over such exchanges, especially within those patterns lacking a formal ceremonial setting-up of links.

Thus, it seems that the instabilities and the propensities to change associated with concrete patron–client relations are in fact inherent in the basic structuring of social exchange occurring in clientelism. They are, however, expressed in different forms and degrees in the frameworks of the various patterns analysed above. Thus, to adduce a few examples from the preceding sections of this chapter, the existence of some mutual accountability of patrons and clients in terms of participation in a common socio-moral order (and specifically, in the case of the clients, the crystallisation of ethics of loyalty in a certain social setting) tends to enhance the stability of personal allegiances and interactions. Similarly, a ritual style of installation in the clientelistic relationship renders it less vulnerable to transactional demands originating in changes in the positions of the partners within institutional markets. Changes in these and other aspects of construction of patron–client relations are influenced, as we have already indicated, by continuities and discontinuities in the different dimensions of the division of labour and the structure of power within the framework of clientelistic societies.

III

The preceding examination of the different degrees of continuity and discontinuity in various aspects or dimensions of patron–client relations brings together some of the major lines of our analysis, some of the major analytical considerations which have guided our study.

At the end of chapter 2 we indicated that the analysis of patron–client relations suggests the possibility that different aspects of the institutional order evince different levels of continuity or discontinuity. Above all, they suggest that the tempo and direction of change in some crucial aspects of social division of labour – as manifest above all in levels of technological and economic development – may differ from those that develop in the construction of trust and meaning, and in the regulation of power.

Our analysis throughout the former chapters has enabled us to go beyond these general indications. This analysis has first of all confirmed in detail the fact that there indeed occur differences in tempo of continuity between, on the one hand, patterns of construction of trust and institutionalisation of general exchange and, on the other hand, aspects of the institutional order closely related to changes of social division of labour and to different aspects of power relations.

Second, this analysis has indicated in greater detail some of the specific conditions and mechanisms which shape these different aspects of the institutional order and their different levels or rates of continuity or discontinuity. It has indicated that it is the basic cultural orientations and characteristics of the structure of elites, and of their control over access to markets and centres and over conversion of resources, that influence the crystallisation of the basic modes of generalised exchange; while levels and organisation of resources, and occupation, by different groups, of positions of power and control within different markets, influence the organisational aspects of the social division of labour and the actual power relations within markets and in the relations between centres and peripheries.

We have shown how the different combinations of these social forces shape the structuring of different dimensions of patron–client relations and how they explain the differences between the pure clientelistic mode of generalised exchange and patron–client relations as addenda to the major institutional nexus, as well as the variations between the different organisational aspects of such patron–client relations.

All these variables do, however, explain not only the structure of patron–client relations but also, as we have indicated in chapters 1 and 3, other types of interpersonal relations; we shall now turn to the analysis of these relations.

8

Ritualised interpersonal relations; privacy and friendship

In the preceding chapters we have indicated how the development of different types of patron–client relations – of the fully fledged clientelistic relations and of those patron–client relations which constitute addenda to the major institutional nexus – is very closely related to different modes of structuring of trust in the respective societies in which these relations develop. In chapter 7 we have also pointed out that, on the whole, these forms of structuring of trust tend to persist beyond manifold changes in the structure of the division of labour and beyond various, if not all, modifications in the structure of power relations in societies.

These modes of structuring of trust are, however, manifest not only in patron–client relations but also in other types of interpersonal relations to which we have referred at the beginning of this book – as in blood brotherhood, pseudo-kinship and the like, and in the great variety of bonds which have been classed in different societies as friendship. Indeed the analysis of the nature of the construction of trust in patron–client relations, presented at the end of chapter 6, pointed out the necessity of considering how these other types of interpersonal relations are connected to such a construction in clientelistic and non-clientelistic societies. It is only when we take into consideration all these different types of interpersonal relations, as they develop in the various societies, that we can assess the problems and vicissitudes of the construction of trust in such settings. Accordingly in this chapter we shall attempt such an analysis.

We face here a difficulty inherent in the fact, already mentioned, that all these interpersonal relations have been studied much less systematically and thoroughly than the different types of patron–client relations. Yet, despite this quite significant difficulty, we shall attempt to present here a systematic – even if by its very nature tentative and preliminary – analysis of such different types of interpersonal relations and to relate them to several basic societal conditions – especially to the different modes of structuring of trust, of generalised exchange, that are prevalent in the societies within which these relationships develop.

It is not difficult to present a preliminary and superficial outline of the spread of such relations in different societies – at least as it has been portrayed in the relevant sociological, anthropological and psychosociological literature. According to the findings of this literature, the more formalised and institutionalised relationships, such as blood brotherhood and different types of ritual kinship or of semi-formal friendships, are to be found above all in tribal societies; various types of ritual kinship and of pseudo-kinship, such as above all the *compadrazgo*, as well as of the Japanese *oyabun–kobun* bond, are to be found in sectors of so-called traditional societies in particular; while more complex, especially modern societies, are characterised by a great variety of informal types of friendship.

But such an outline, which basically explains these differences in terms of one aspect of the social division of labour – namely of the level of structural differentiation – while correct in its broad contours, does not tell us much about the more dynamic aspects of these relations. Above all, it does not tell us, first, how different patterns of such relations, involving distinct configurations of the major aspects of interpersonal relations, are related in different societies to the structuring, within them, of symbolic orientations which are supportive, ambivalent in relation or opposed to the prevailing institutional order. Second, they do not tell us about the relation of these different patterns of interpersonal links to different modes of structuring of trust, of generalised exchange, in the societies in which they develop.

This outline does not tell us how such different patterns of relations structure the basic ambivalences which are inherent in them – i.e. that between the emphases on purely solidary or spiritual relations, as against concrete (power and instrumental) obligations; that between the tendency to institutionalise such relations, as against seemingly taking them out of the institutional order; and that between the tendency to uphold the pristine values which are at the basis of social order, as against a 'subversive orientation', an attitude of covert defiance, towards this order. Nor does this outline tell us how these different types of interpersonal relations are organised according to the various structural dimensions we have outlined above – namely their formalisation or institutionalisation, the nature of obligations they entail, and their institutional location.

True enough, whatever the difference between these various relations, they all tend, as we have indicated above, to construct a realm of trust and of participation in spiritual, pristine values and trust beyond the major institutionalised sectors of a society. But the way in which such a realm is constructed, the way in which it is connected on the one hand with intimacy in personal relations, and on the other hand with the broader institutional setting and its premises, differs greatly in societies according to the dimensions outlined above, and these vary – as we have seen already in our analysis of patron–client relations – according to the nature of the construction of trust within the institutional matrix of society.

Thus we have to go beyond this bare outline. Accordingly, in the following pages, we shall attempt to analyse – with all the reservations due to the relatively scanty and unsystematic nature of the material – the relations between the patterns and images of various interpersonal relations and the societal conditions which shape them in different societies, as well as the character and prevalent forms of construction of trust and meaning within those societies.

In this endeavour we shall go beyond the explanation in terms of the social division of labour in general, and of the structural differentiation in particular, and shall deal with those other conditions which we have identified in chapter 3 as most important in influencing the construction of trust, of generalised exchange. These were, first, the extent of symbolic differentiation between the various institutional spheres – i.e. the extent of recognition of such a distinction in the symbolic realm of a society; second, the degree to which different institutional spheres of a society are structured according to relatively similar or dissimilar principles, especially universalistic versus particularistic and egalitarian as against hierarchical ones; and, third, the degree of clarity of such principles and of their application to different institutional spheres in general, and to the specification of the degree of autonomous (as against mediated) access of different groups to societal, political and cultural (usually religious) power in particular.

It is the various combinations of these dimensions – which are, as we have indicated above, closely related to the structure of control over the flow of resources as exercised by the major coalitions of elites and to the major cultural orientations carried by such elites – that generates in different societies various modes of extension of trust between institutional spheres, as well as certain areas of breakdown of such extension. As it is above all in such areas that the tendency to the development of different patterns of interpersonal relations develops, it is also the different combinations of these factors that generate various forms of combination of the formalisation or absence of formalisation of such interpersonal relations, and that condition the nature of obligations and the degree of personal involvement they entail, the institutional location of the trust generated by them and the strength and mode of

271

their ambivalent relations and oppositionary tendencies to the premises of the institutional order of their respective societies.

The analysis that follows will be focused on these aspects of interpersonal relations in general and of friendship in particular, aspects which are indeed central to the lines of investigation of this book. We shall not deal specifically with other aspects of such relations, such as their multiplexity or uniplexity, or the various patterns of friendship formation in different societies or among different occupational and residential social strata within any single society which have been also recently explored in the literature:[1] the material on them, while very suggestive, is still too sparse to allow a systematic comparative analysis.

Following these considerations, we shall now present a survey of some of the best-documented patterns of interpersonal relations and shall elaborate later, on the basis of the survey, on what in a sense has been the central concern of our analysis in this book – namely the relation between, on the one hand, the construction of trust in society and, on the other hand, the development of such interpersonal relations as an attempt to construct new areas of trust; or, in other words, on the ambivalence of trust in the social order.

This presentation will start with the simple distinction, based on levels of structural differentiation, between the so-called tribal, 'intermediate' or historical traditional societies and modern ones; but we shall then go beyond this distinction, taking into account the other aspects of social structure referred to above.

RITUALISED INTERPERSONAL RELATIONS IN 'TRIBAL' SOCIETIES

I

Many of the tribal societies in which interpersonal relations have been described – such, for instance, as the Tikopia or the Didinga and Zande in Africa – have also been portrayed in sociological literature as characterised by relative clarity in the demarcation of the principles structuring the different institutional spheres; i.e. they have been portrayed as exhibiting relatively clear combinations and demarcations of universalistic or particularistic, and of egalitarian or hierarchical, criteria of membership and allocation of roles.[2]

Some of these societies (such as the African ones), as well as the more complex traditional ascriptive hierarchical societies, have been characterised by a fair degree of similarity in the basic principles according to which the different institutional spheres have been structured. Such principles have been mostly particularistic and either relatively egalitarian or hierarchical. But, in spite of this similarity, these particularistic principles have entailed – when applied to such institutional spheres as the economic or political and broader cultural ones in these societies (especially the more complex among them – no longer 'tribal' ones) – some broader definition than in the realm of kinship and family, and hence there have developed some discontinuities between the respective institutional spheres.

In other societies – such as those tribal societies like the Zulu, Yoruba or Yako in Africa, and some American Indian societies, in which primordial universalistic criteria were more central than kinship ones – there existed stronger differences in the principles according to which the different institutional spheres were structured, and hence discontinuities arose between such spheres.

The most important of such differences were, of course, those between the realm of family, kinship and local ritual settings on the one hand, and the broader universalistic economic and political settings on the other. These differences became even more far-reaching, as is well known, and as will be discussed below, in different modern societies.

Such relative clarity of institutional principles entailed in most of these societies a relative smoothness in the extension of trust between the major institutional sectors and in its interweaving with the regulation of power and social division of labour.

And yet, even in these societies, there have developed some areas or sectors of breakdown of trust or of extension of trust, above all in those sectors in which the discontinuities between different institutional sectors were most fully articulated. There were three main areas of potential breakdown of trust in these societies.

The first such areas developed in what can be designated the 'open spaces' in the interrelations between the different ascriptive units, such as families or strata, as well as between them and the more differentiated occupational groups. The potential for breakdown of trust increased where any clear specification of the relations between these units and groups, or of the obligations they entailed for individual members, was lacking. The analysis of these conditions has been undertaken already by S.N. Eisenstadt in his early work on ritualised personal relations (see chapter 1, above).

The second such area is that of transition between different institutional spheres which are structured according to different principles or criteria. The best illustration of the former such situation is that of transition between the family and kinship and the more universalistic political or economic spheres which can be found in many tribal societies, as well as in most of the bureaucratic historical–imperial societies, and almost by definition in all modern societies.

Third, and closely related to the former ones, are areas of transition between different institutional spheres and organisations regulated by universalistic principles (the number and diversity of these increase, of course, with growing structural differentiation, particularly in modern universalistic societies).

II

It is above all in these various types of situations, and not in the more central institutional areas, that an abundance of interpersonal relations, characterised by relatively little structural and symbolic differentiation, tends to develop in tribal societies.

Most of the interpersonal relations that develop within such so-called tribal societies and within some sectors of traditional societies – or at least those which have been reported by ethnographers – tend to be highly formalised and institutionalised, and hence are clearly circumscribed and distinct from other relations, especially from kinship. They are also characterised by a relatively high level of ideologisation or symbolisation. Such relations usually also contain relatively clear definitions of the obligations they entail, obligations which tend to encompass both instrumental and solidary elements.

Such types of interpersonal relations as blood brotherhood or semi-institutionalised friendship and different kinds of pseudo-kinship – which in an earlier publication were identified by the global term of ritualised personal relations,[3] and which resemble very closely what Y. Cohen termed inalienable friendship[4] – tend to develop in these institutional interstices between different ascriptive groups, above all in those areas in which the details of the interrelations between such groups are not clearly specified.

In the areas of transition between institutional sectors with different regulative principles – above all in those between the family and the universalistic sectors of society in the tribal and peasant societies – more organised groups, such as age-groups, tend to develop.

These formalised relations which occur in societies or sectors thereof, and which are characterised by a low level of structural and symbolic differentiation and hierarchism seem to be open to all members of the society, although we do not have exact data about their real distribution. At the same time, however, it seems that in fact such relations are limited, through different, not clearly specified, mechanisms of social control, lest they become too widespread and predominant at the expense of kinship relations.

274

Privacy and friendship

Common to all these relations is the almost total lack of recognition or even semi-legitimation of a realm of privacy which can also serve as a repository of trust beyond what is fully embedded in the institutional matrix and closely related to its basic ideological premises.

True enough, the more recent ethnographic evidence brought together in the Newfoundland Symposium indicates that in such societies many interpersonal relations develop, with different undertones of friendship, but mostly seeming to share a rather strong tendency towards formalisation.[5]

This does not mean, of course, that some private, intimate relations do not develop in such societies. Although the ethnographic evidence is here rather sparse, it seems that such less formal private relations are here on the whole semi-clandestine, barely visible, and lack both clear institutional boundaries and the specification of clear obligations.

The formalised relations that develop in most such tribal societies seem also to be closely related in concepts of personal identity predominant in these societies, concepts which are rooted within relatively solidary, closed groups; their presumptive models of cultural order do not envisage wide-ranging alternative conceptions of social or cultural order, or any open social space which will not be regulated in terms of some of the prevalent formative principles and groups.

The idiom and symbolism of such relations and of the trust they attempt to construct is couched in these societies in quite highly ideologised ways, in terms very close to the kinship idioms prevalent within them – although, in fact, such relations are often oriented away from the concrete kinship groups and commitments. Indeed most of the relations stress that such obligations cannot be fully realised within the 'natural' kinship settings. And yet the opposition to the basic institutional premises of these societies is neither total nor strong. At most, they are oriented away from the concretisation of these premises in the kinship settings, and they tend to stress to some degree the upholding of the more pristine values underlying the existing primordial kinship system, as was also the case in the Homeric *plutores* or in the medieval *fidei*, which stressed that the participants in such relations had to be willing to commit to one another the most important resources – personal help, wealth or participation in the common endeavour – underlying the basic institutional setting of the society.

Hence any opposition to the basic institutional premises that might develop in these societies in terms of such pristine values is rather muted. Such opposition seems not to be overtly expressed in these formalised relations, but rather possibly (we say possibly because the

275

evidence here is very scanty indeed) in the more informal and probably more fleeting – although perhaps often significant emotionally – interpersonal relations that may develop in these societies.

Further, more detailed, research on interpersonal relations in different tribal and archaic societies will, it is to be hoped, bring out a greater range of variations in such interpersonal relations and in the societal conditions to which they are related. It would be of special interest, in this context, to investigate the cases of those societies in which the clarity of institutional principles is relatively weak and of those which are characterised by a relatively low level of solidarity in their major ascriptive kinship and territorial groups. But such research has as yet to be done.

INTERPERSONAL RELATIONS IN TRADITIONAL OR HISTORICAL SOCIETIES

I

Societies of greater ranges of complexity, of higher degrees of structural and symbolic differentiation – so-called 'intermediate', historical or traditional societies – evince a more mixed picture of the types of interpersonal relations that develop within them.

Here we may already distinguish between, on the one hand, historical societies of the imperial type like China, feudal–imperial ones like Japan or hierarchical ascriptive ones, and, on the other hand, the various clientelistic societies analysed above. The first set of societies is characterised by a relative clarity of the principles regulating different institutional spheres, with strong universalistic elements in the imperial ones and a greater emphasis on particularistic hierarchical elements in the latter. Contrasting with these, the various clientelistic societies are characterised, as we have indicated, by a relative lack of clarity of such principles.

On the whole, the interpersonal relations that develop in all these societies are less formalised, their boundaries are less fixed, and they entail less clearly prescribed obligations and stronger orientations to diffuse emotional obligations than are found in the less differentiated societies. There tends also to develop within these societies some recognition of a realm of privacy, especially when there is a high level of structural and symbolic differentiation.

We have seen that in the less differentiated and 'traditional' clientelistic societies, there tend to develop more fully ritualised and formalised clientelistic and semi-clientelistic godparent relations, with comparatively clearly specified sets of obligations, while the more private and informal types of interpersonal relations that develop in such societies tend to be less visible. This is probably related to the fact that, given the very strong tendency within them towards the development of a cultural idiom which stresses the fusion of different social spheres, and especially that of family and economic and class relations, the recognition of private spheres is usually very weak within these clientelistic societies.

Yet, as in the more differentiated clientelistic societies, there does also develop *de facto* a growing privatisation of many such areas of interpersonal relations, together with a smaller degree of formalisation, a less clear specification of the obligations entailed and a greater ubiquity in society.

Similarly, in ancient Greece, it was with the decomposition of the Homeric band-organisations and the crystallisation of the city-state, based already on more differentiated social and economic relations, that the clear institutional image of the *plutores* gave way to a wider range of interpersonal relations, many of them more informal and private – and to Aristotle's distinction between different types of friendships.[6]

II

But beyond these characteristics which seem common to all such societies in the 'middle' range of structural differentiation, several far-reaching differences develop between the clientelistic and non-clientelistic societies regarding other aspects of structuring of interpersonal relations.

Within the non-clientelistic 'historical' or traditional societies characterised by a relatively high clarity in the specification of the principles regulating different institutional spheres, most of the semi-formalised interpersonal relations (like the Chinese *kan-ch'ing* or the traditional Japanese relations based on *giri* obligations) develop in the interstices between the familial realms and the broader institutional, especially economic or political, spheres.[7]

These interpersonal relations are couched in terms of some of the general moral virtues upheld within these societies, which presumably are also predominant in the sphere of kinship and are somehow diluted in the broader settings. As far as we know, they do not evince any strong oppositionary tendencies to the basic premises of the social order, nor do they tend to become connected with strong sectarian tendencies, although it might be interesting to investigate to what extent they are interwoven into such frameworks as the Chinese secret societies.

277

They seem also to be connected to a concept of personal identity which is rooted in relatively solidary and autonomous groups.

Many of these interpersonal relations are also connected with some addendum semi-clientelistic or clique relationships. Thus, for instance, in China, as has been shown in a recent study by Lucian W. Pye,[8] there develops an ambiguity of such personal bonds among the elite, along lines already evident in traditional China. According to his findings,

the prime bases of factions are power constellations of clusters of officials who for some reason or other feel comfortable with each other, who believe that they can share mutual trust and loyalties, and who may recognize common foes. More often than not, the real motivation is that of career security and enhancement, whether it be at the lowest county or provincial committee level or among those on the Politburo and the State Council jockeying for greater influence. The glue that holds factions together can thus be either mutual career self-interest or the highly particular sentiments associated with personal ties in Chinese culture, i.e. the spirit of *guanxi (kan-ch'ing)* ... Leaders do not necessarily strive consciously to build up networks of followers – in fact, there is a taboo in the ethics of the CCP against precisely such endeavours, a taboo so strong that senior officials are not supposed to engage in explicit talent searches among the younger cadres. What happens instead is that the networks tend to take a hierarchical shape and eventually strive to attach themselves to particular leaders. Consequently, any leader who has had a successful career in the Party will inevitably find that he has developed a chain of potential supporters. Unless he acts to satisfy their needs, they will, in time, abandon him for another, more supportive leader. As a result he will be alone, and as his peers discover his vulnerability, competitors will arise to seek his downfall in order to use his position to satisfy their own networks of supporters.

In the more ascriptive hierarchical societies, these interpersonal relations are above all manifest in some special types of patron–client relations such as the Indian *jajmani* networks or the Rwandan *buhake*. As we have indicated above (in chapter 4), such relations are a limited but institutionalised addendum to the ascriptive hierarchical mode of societal articulation there. Such interpersonal relations are usually segmented, and the exchange of resources they regulate does not affect the central positions within markets; they are restricted to the dyadic or tryadic setting and only rarely – mostly in the context of modern polities – develop formally into wider chains of brokers, although extranormatively there are pressures in such directions.

III

The structuring of interpersonal relations is quite different in clientelistic societies which are characterised by a relative blurring in the specification of the realms of application of the different criteria that regulate the basic institutional spheres, entailing in consequence numerous discontinuities in the transitions between such spheres and a potential breakdown of transmission of trust in many, including the central, institutional sectors. Accordingly, different interpersonal relations are usually widespread in such clientelistic societies, especially in those with a growing structural differentiation.

The relations range from the relatively fully institutionalised patron–client relations analysed above, through various relations of pseudo-kinship (of which the *compadrazgo* is the best known), and which are to different degrees connected, but not identical, with the fully institutionalised patron–client relations, to a very wide range of different semi-formalised relations of friendship, many of which are imbued with strong clientelistic orientations.[9]

The various interpersonal relations are, in these societies, spread through different institutional spheres, occupying not only the interstices between such spheres, but even the central institutional matrix of the social settings. They are often structured in such a way as to maximise the overlap between such different institutional spheres – accordingly also minimising the recognition within them of any realm of privacy.

Most of these relations are characterised by some features which we have noted already above in our analysis of patron–client relations – a certain fragility, as well as a rather weak construction of trust within and between them, and a strong ambivalence in relation to the basic premises of the society.

As we have seen, all these relations are characterised by attempts to construct areas of trust in the central and peripheral institutional areas of the societies; yet such construction is never fully attained, and many of these ambivalences are continuously transposed in all these interpersonal ties to a new place or level, and accordingly rather ambivalent relations tend also to develop between such different bonds.

Similarly, many of these relations are characterised by an ambivalent attitude to the major institutional premises of the societies in which they develop in general, and to the relatively weak structuring of trust within them in particular.

These various ambivalences are manifest in the idioms of these relations, which do not specify clear rules with regard to the emphases to be placed on purely solidary or spiritual bonds as against concrete obligations, or in respect of the tendency to uphold the pristine values of the social order as against that towards subversion and replacement of this 'polluted' order. Indeed, these potentially opposing tendencies, and the mutual ambivalences that are inherent in the different interpersonal relations which develop in these societies, can be best seen in

279

the contrast between kinship and spiritual kinship, and between kinship and friendship, often stressed in many of these societies.

The crux of the paradoxical and ambivalent relations between friendship or pseudo-kinship on the one hand and kinship on the other lies in the many characteristics of friendship and of spiritual kinship that ideally are similar to those of kinship; while at the same time friendship appears both symbolically and organisationally distinct from kinship and even potentially opposed to it.

This paradoxical relation between kinship and friendship comes out very forcefully in ritual kinship, blood brotherhood and similar phenomena, above all in different aspects of pseudo-kinship, where kinship-like obligations are undertaken by a voluntary act but where this voluntary act, unlike marriage, does not really recreate the existing pattern and organisation of kinship and descent relation. Rather this act specifies some areas of life which are, as it were, taken out of the sphere of kinship relations, even standing to some degree in opposition to it, although seemingly governed by rules similar to those of kinship.

This ambivalent – and yet seemingly complementary – relation between friendship and kinship can already be discerned, as Erik Schwimmer's analysis of the Papuan Orokaiva systems attests,[10] in tribal societies. It becomes, however, most fully articulated in the already more differentiated clientelistic societies, in the relations between kinship proper and pseudo-kinship that develop within them. There, spiritual kinship is rather sharply contrasted with real kinship and is defined as being based on a kind of trust informed by spiritual values different from those which are prevalent in the realm of kinship proper.

Stephen Gudeman's study of the *compadrazgo* relations brings out this ambivalent and yet in a way complementary relationship between one type of friendship-like behaviour and kinship.

Parent and godparent are united in contrast to the child by a generational difference. They in turn are linked by choice, as are the parents. The model for both is the same. The contrast of these two structures is reflected on different levels.

In the family a birth normally follows formation of the conjugal tie. In the *compadrazgo* a baptism precedes or is the reason for founding the *compadre–compadre* bond. The parents initiate the child into the physical world and household; the godparents initiate him into the spiritual world and community. One is ritually unmarked, the other marked.

In the family the mother–child bond is thought to be unbreakable; a mother is rarely renounced. However an individual may have several fathers or the pater may not be the genitor. The family presents a system of one mother but possibly several fathers. In the *compadrazgo* by baptism, by contrast, there is only one godfather but two godmothers, and the godfather is more important. In the family the parent–child bond is more important than the conjugal tie, but in the *compadrazgo* the *compadre–compadre* tie is more important than the godparent–godchild one; that is, in one the 'vertical' bond takes precedence over the 'horizontal' tie, whereas in the other the reverse is true. Moreover in the family a child is like his sibling in that he shares the same set of parents. In the *compadrazgo* each child in a given family is individuated by having a different set of godparents.

Kinship originates in birth, it is founded on blood. The *compadrazgo* begins in baptism (or confirmation or marriage) – the counterpart to birth – and is founded on spiritual affinity. But where the household enterprise itself and material goods provide the 'glue' for kinship, respect, that is immaterial actions, provides the 'glue' for the *compadrazgo*. Both are forms of property in the broadest sense, but they are opposed as the concrete is to the abstract . . .

The godparent–godchild and *compadre–compadre* bonds are spiritual. They are marked by respect and lie at the sacred end of the continuum. The ties amount principally to positive assurances of mutual esteem and prohibitions on profane elements entering. *Compadres* do not contract debts or have sexual relations. The taboos of respect separate off the bonds of the *compadrazgo* and assure their sacredness.

In this sense it is through the *compadrazgo* that the peasants come closest to reaching God during life on earth. The complex is an expression of discipline and good. The *compadrazgo* is formed upon church rites and through it the people carry into their lives something of the church.

The *compadrazgo* also provides a means of placing all individuals in the 'ideal order', and it gives them an enduring position in society. In parallel to Pitt-Rivers I would note that the godparent–godchild tie is complementary to that of parent and child. Godparents are explicitly linked to the moral aspect of their godchild's personality. Through the mediation of his godparents an infant enters the spiritual world. Godparents should counsel and teach their godchildren, and through this process children are individuated from their siblings. *Compadres* themselves have a mutual moral bond. A *compadre*, whether father or godfather, is always assured of being respected and respecting thereby lifting him to a spiritual level. *Compadres* are eternal: they greet one in heaven and intercede with God on one's behalf. The *compadrazgo* implants a perpetual sacred obligation between persons.

In contrast relations of kinship and marriage fall towards the other end of the continuum. The family is primarily a material and sexual organisation. Coition is said to be polluting. Through his parents a child enters the natural world: and his parents are the guardians of his material and physical life. The family is man's expression, then, of his more 'earthy' character. Kinship ties are in one sense immutable, in another they have a lack of permanence. Sexual freedom on the part of men is valued; paternity may be denied. When an individual enters a household he nearly always assumes the role of a nuclear kinsman with the existing members, regardless of his original link. Thus kinship bonds are somewhat optative; they can be broken, utilised and to some degree formed as persons desire.[11]

IV

But the oppositionary tendencies or orientations which tend to develop in the interpersonal relations prevalent in these societies with respect to their basic institutional premises are of a rather special nature. They are characterised by organisational weakness and weak connections with any outspoken sectarian tendencies or groups; by a striving to be near to the exemplary (usually religious) figures which represent their cultural ideas and values in the most pristine way and at the same time by a rather ambivalent attitude to such figures; and by the consequent tendency towards the diffusion and defusion of the oppositionary tendencies and activities. These characteristics are related not only to the lack of clarity in the specification of the major criteria regulating the major institutional spheres in general and the access to the centres of these societies in particular, but also to the major characteristics of their elites and major groups which were analysed above – namely their relatively low level of autonomy and solidarity, the relative weakness of their centres and of the commitment accorded to them, and the specific types of cultural orientations that are articulated by these elites. These characteristics explain the most important features of the oppositionary tendencies that develop in the clientelistic and semi-clientelistic interpersonal relations.

The most organised way in which these oppositionary orientations become manifest is paradoxically in the rebellions which, as we have seen above, tend to develop in these societies, and in which the rebel leader undertakes the role of the patron and/or of a spiritual leader. In more modern settings, the more extreme of these oppositionary tendencies will typically be organised around terrorist groups, which often exhibit many of the same organisational features mentioned above, such as fragility and ideological orientations characterised by a certain totalistic and extreme opposition to the prevailing social order.

INTERPERSONAL RELATIONS AND PRIVACY IN MODERN SOCIETIES

I

The numerous interpersonal relations that develop within societies with a high level of structural and symbolic differentiation – i.e. above all within modern societies – are on the whole characterised by relatively little formalisation and institutionalisation, and by a lack of clear specification in the obligations which they entail and in their institutional location and boundaries. At the same time, in these societies, there tends to develop a more open and less clandestine definition of private realms in which interpersonal relations flourish. This is connected to the proliferation of a wide scope and variety of such – at least partially recognised – realms of privacy in modern societies. The attitudes to such realms vary from condemnation, typical in some ideological movements that develop in modern societies in general and in totalitarian ones in particular, to the – even if sometimes rather ambivalent – acceptance that characterises especially 'open market', universalistic societies. Particularly in the latter, the private spheres come to be considered as an essential part of social life – spheres that lessen tensions derived from instrumental pressures and allow 'for backstage areas and remissive spaces where it is not always incumbent upon individuals to maintain their proper roles ... In private one can relax, blow off steam, recoup after encounters with difficult and unbearable people.'[12]

In modern societies in general, various types of informal relations – ranging from friendship to mere acquaintanceship – tend to develop in the different areas of institutional discontinuity found in these societies. First, they tend to develop, as perhaps best illustrated by youth encounters and gangs, in the areas of transition between institutional spheres structured according to different principles, and especially between the family and kinship spheres and the more universalistic political and economic ones. Second, these relations also develop – as shown in the sometimes problematic transitions and conversion of resources between the political and the economic spheres – in the areas of transition between different institutional realms and organisations regulated by universalistic principles – the number and diversity of which increase with growing structural differentiation, especially in modern societies. Third, these informal relations tend to develop in many social spaces which are seemingly 'open' – i.e. unregulated, and continuously multiplied in modern societies – between the different ascriptive units such as families and strata as well as between the more differentiated occupational groups. By the very nature of the institutional structure of modern societies, such relations are highly dispersed and diversified, in principle open to all members of society and yet undertaken in various degrees and modes by different social actors.

In the clientelistic pre-modern societies such relations tend not only to develop, as we have seen above, within these institutional realms, but also to penetrate the central institutional areas themselves.

These various – usually informal – interpersonal relations in general, and friendship in particular, that develop above all in the non-clientelistic modern societies may differ greatly as to the degree to which they are defined in ideological terms. On the one hand, there are those relations like the romantic German student friendships and fraternities, membership in various youth movements or the various cases of friendship depicted in classical Russian literature, in which such relatively informal friendships – albeit in the first case already with a high tendency towards some formalisation – are conceived in highly ideological terms which stress the spiritual values of trust, of possible participation in common activities and of a very high degree of emotional involvement.[13] On the other hand, there are numerous, less well documented, informal friendships, which may range from those defined in some sort of ideological terms to 'mere' acquaintanceship. The more ideological types of such friendships stress high emotional involvement, and also place a strong emphasis on both the 'moral' and the purely 'spiritual', even semi-charismatic, qualities of the partnership. The more intensive types of such interpersonal relations of friendship or comradeship, are often seen as 'totally' unconditional, overriding even the most powerful institutional obligations.[14]

But in most cases these personal relationships involve rather circumscribed and limited patterns of obligations, even if they are sometimes connected with deeper emotional commitments. These specific characteristics of friendship are closely related to its voluntary aspects, to the seemingly greater emphasis within it on both the 'moral' and the purely psychological and 'spiritual' virtues, irrespective of, but not necessarily unrelated to, the more concrete institutionalised role-obligations that such relations entail.

Relations of this kind are very often based on the apparently paradoxical, semi-institutional, public recognition of the legitimacy of the search through them for privacy, for something beyond the glare of public life.[15] The theme of privacy may indeed become a central focus of the ideological definition of such relations.

Even such denial of a legitimate realm of privacy as is found in many of the social movements that develop in modern societies in general and in totalitarian societies in particular – sometimes coupled with a tendency to official institutionalisation of some such relations – already attests a very widespread prevalence of such a realm of privacy. Similarly, the tendency of some of these relations to be phrased in highly ideological terms attests the fact that they mostly lack institutionalisation or formalisation in modern societies.

II

These various interpersonal relations found in modern societies differ not only with respect to the degree of their ideologisation, but also –

though in close connection with this – with respect to the mode of their relations to the basic institutional premises of the respective societies in which they develop.

They differ especially with respect to the strength and mode of their ambivalent and oppositionary orientations to these premises, as well as in the degree of their connection with various sectarian and oppositionary movements that develop in their respective societies.

We have indicated already that some of these oppositionary or subversive orientations are often inherent in such relations, especially in those that are more intensive and embracing, and that demand a high degree of personal involvement from people engaged in them. Almost all such relations entail at least potentially some competitive – but to some extent complementary – orientations towards family life, although the intensity of such elements depends to no small degree on the structure of interpersonal relations within the family.They tend also to contain some (latently strong) oppositionary tendencies to the basic institutional premises of their respective societies, but the intensity and concrete ideological and organisational expressions of these tendencies may vary greatly between different cases, ranging from some type of segregation from the fully organised oppositionary tendencies and frameworks to a close connection with them – with all the tensions involved therein.

First there are the various informal, often clandestine, friendships which are perceived and defined, both by the participants in such relations and by others, as being – because of their emphasis on pristine, purer trust, meaning and intimacy – opposed, to some degree at least, to the more formalised institutional settings or as subversive of them. According to these perceptions, these formalised settings in general, and the centres of the society in particular, seem often to dilute or defile such trust or meaning. Accordingly, these relations seek to instal a purer type of *communitas* unrestricted by the exigencies of the social division of labour and of power, and seen as in principle opposed to them and transcending them.[16]

Yet with all these oppositionary orientations, such informal relations tend, particularly in the more open, pluralistic types of societies, only rarely to evolve into fully fledged organisational opposition to the existing institutional order, or to merge with it. Rather, they tend to stress a view of the realm of pure trust and meaning as being not directly opposed in institutional terms to the existing order, but rather as being beyond it, above it. Hence they often seek to go beyond the glare of public life into the realm of privacy and to segregate themselves from the institutional complexes and centres.

As against this, there are other situations, in complex modern and historical societies, in which some interpersonal relations become imbued with articulated ideological oppositionary premises and connected or even merged with different subversive movements or sects. Such has been the case, for instance, in the many youth movements (in the German ones in particular) and in many of the semi-revolutionary student upheavals of the sixties and in Russian 'intelligentsia' circles, involving ties of friendship and comradeship, throughout the nineteenth century and possibly even today.

Here, however, we encounter a fact to which we have already alluded above, and which is of great importance to our analysis – namely that there often tends to develop some very acute tension or contradiction between the realm of pristine truth or values built into these interpersonal relations and the propensity to reconstruct the institutional order expressed by the oppositionary movements and sects.

In order to understand the nature of these tensions, it might be worthwhile to refer to some material about interpersonal relations in different closed societies – be they ships and underground movements as studied by V. Aubert, or age groups in sects and social movements, or monastic orders.[17]

Common to all of them is the relatively strong opposition voiced by the 'official' leaders of such groups to the development within them of close interpersonal friendships. Thus, to quote Ramsøy summarising Aubert:

In a study of the merchant marine in a society where it is a significant element economically and culturally, Aubert and Arner (1959) found that the culture and the social structure of the Norwegian merchant marine include a near taboo on personal friendships. This trait is probably a consequence of (as well as a contribution to) other structural elements: the ship is a 'total institution' (Goffman 1958); top positions can only be reached from the bottom; there is an extraordinarily high rate of turnover; work roles dominate (to the extent that terms of address and reference are largely job titles, the alternative being home region); there is a cultural and realistic emphasis on crises requiring disciplines; and, finally, there is a peculiar combination of equality and inequality (in a number of respects the crew are sailors 'in the same boat,' yet each man and his position is unique through pay and shift arrangements). In outline, the occurrence and forms of friendship among the crew are reinforcing consequences of the nature of the ship as a place of work, in particular through its arrangements for interaction, physical closeness, and recruitment. In a significant contrast, friendship is a standard occurrence among the crew in the Hull distant-water fishing (Tunstall 1962); the distant-water trawler lacks the character of the total institution that is inherent in the Norwegian merchant vessel.[18]

Similar attitudes are often found in religious and political sects or in monastic orders. In all these cases, such opposition to the development of intimate private relations is based on fear on the part of the respective authorities that such relationships may undermine the structure of authority and the monopoly of trust and meaning on which it is based in such closed communities, bringing individuals to concentrate themselves in 'selfish', restricted communion with people close to them instead of assuming communal obligations and collective endeavours.[19]

But the structure of such authority does differ greatly between close communities on the one hand and sects, monasteries and sectarian political movements on the other hand. Closed communities such as ships or monasteries are based on a very tenuous or brittle balance inherent in the very minute technical division of labour undertaken within a very close spatial area, and the development of close interpersonal relations is sometimes considered to be a threat to such balance; hence the denial of realms of privacy within their framework. The authority structure of such communities is not, however, based on any regulation of attitudes towards the broader, macro-societal, trust and meaning or on demands of total commitment to its premises on the part of the participants. Hence there develops in all such organisations the tendency to accept or even to encourage the development of more meaningful interpersonal relations in the wider world, beyond their own confines.

The situation is different in sects or sect-like socio-political movements, as well as in organisations like monasteries which usually originate from sects or movements. In these frameworks, opposition to the development of close interpersonal relations and of realms of privacy is rooted not only, not even mainly, in the problems of maintaining an existing division of labour within limited spatial frameworks – although in monasteries such an element obtains. Rather, such opposition is based on the demands made on all the participants for total commitment, couched in terms almost identical to those pervading interpersonal relations, i.e. in terms of trust, solidarity and pristine values. Hence in these types of communities there is little willingness to allow members to develop 'outside' interpersonal relationships, and at the same time little tolerance is shown towards the emergence of such relationships within the boundaries of the organisation – though relationships of this latter kind are in fact more difficult to curtail and often do develop there.

In more general terms, all these materials indicate that there is a kind of contradiction or tension between interpersonal relations and oppositionary movements and organisations, and that these tensions derive from the fact that, on the one hand, these interpersonal relations share with various sects and groupings concerned with the nature of the sacred – as well as with religious heterodoxies or movements of political protest – the stress on liminality, on *communitas*, on charismatic dimensions; and that, on the other hand, these liminal tendencies are worked out through different orientations in the two types of settings. The interpersonal relations focus, as we have seen, on those symbols which, by virtue of their reference to the most general spiritual qualities of human nature – however differently conceived in specific cultures – transcend any such organisation and in some ultimate sense contradict it.

As against this, the imagery of trust and pristine values tends in the oppositionary sects and groups to be focused around the reconstruction of the societal centres and the establishment of a new institutional order in terms of such pristine values.

Hence, there may easily develop some basic tensions between these orientations and those of the interpersonal relations which attempt to embody the pure essence of human relationships seemingly beyond any institutional order. Accordingly, whenever such connections between interpersonal relations and oppositionary movements and sects are established, there develops within them a tendency to an intensive ideologisation and formalisation of such relations.

The imagery of trust and pristine values – focused as it is around the reconstruction of the social order – tends in the oppositionary groups also to deny the possibility of its wider spread in more informal and private relations.

Hence, the intensive ideologisation of interpersonal relations in such frameworks is very strongly connected, first, with attempts at deprivatisation of such relations and with the denial of legitimacy to a private sphere; and, second, with attempts at symbolic de-differentiation of some of the institutional spheres, manifest above all in some highly symbolic, idealistic tendencies to conceive the merging of the peripheral spheres with the more central ones.

It is these tendencies to deprivatisation of such relations, to the concomitant de-differentiation of some of the institutional spheres, and to the concentration of the imagery of trust and pristine values around the reconstruction of the centre, that attest this very basic tension – which can be also found in many closed societies – between the 'liminary' or subversive spirit of various interpersonal relations and the attempts at construction and reconstruction of trust in the framework of religious or political sects or in movements of change.

For short periods of time, the two such types of orientation may become interwoven in various sectarian groups through the combination of participation in such groups with interpersonal comradeship.

But with the first stirring of the sectarian groups towards institu-tionalisation – especially insofar as they become transformed into centres of power, into continuous political oppositions, or even into semi-institutionalised sects on the margins of society – there tend to arise strong tensions and conflicts between, on the one hand, the obligations of membership of such groups, of party comradeship, of the upholding of collective values and loyalties, and, on the other, the virtues and interpersonal relations embedded in friendship. The com-petition and conflict between the two may well become very intense and the focus of many a personal tragedy.

A parallel tension tends to develop between the exemplary uphol-ders of the predominant cultural values – be they monks, ascetics or saints – who emphasise total commitment to such cultural values and orientations, and the exponents of those relations that emphasise the interpersonal aspect, that of trust and empathy. Here again, in some cases, these two types of relations may merge, but usually only temporarily. Each of these emphases generates different types of interpersonal relationships – and there may easily develop tension between the demands of the saint for followers and those of comrade-ship and interpersonal loyalty.

III

There do not exist enough systematic data on the exact distribution of the different types of such interpersonal relations in different sectors of modern societies – the necessary research has yet to be done. An impressionistic view seems to indicate that in principle most types of such relations can be found in almost all modern societies – but there exist great differences in their relative importance in different societies or sectors thereof.

One important difference which seems to cut across most modern societies is the relative structural and symbolic differentiation of differ-ent sectors within them. Thus, in most modern societies there exist different ecological or occupational sectors or groups (like the closed societies analysed above) which are characterised by relatively low levels of structural and symbolic differentiation. In most such sectors there tends indeed to develop, as we have seen, a relatively strong opposition to the development of fully recognised private personal interrelations, and a concomitant tendency to control whatever such relations may develop.

Thus it is above all in the more differentiated sectors of modern societies that there develop the more diversified types of informal interpersonal relations.

The distribution of such types of interpersonal relations varies as between modern societies – above all (and beyond varying levels of differentiation) according to the models of generalised exchange predominant within these societies or sectors thereof, and according to the nature of the breakdown of extension of trust within them.

In the pluralistic – and to some degree also in the consociational– modern societies based on open institutional markets, on an ideology of universalistic citizenship and on broad and open access to the major societal centres – a relatively wide spread of semi-informal relations develops, ranging from various modes of friendship and comradeship in common associations and clubs to different types of acquaintanceship.

Most of these relations evince a high degree of informality, of non-institutionalisation; they lack any clear definition of the obligations they entail. At the same time, however, most of these relations are based on the recognition of the legitimate ubiquity in society of realms of privacy, with different degrees of intensity in emotional and spiritual involvement, loyalty and commitment, and of ideological elaboration.

They are closely related to a concept of personal identity which is deeply rooted in relatively solidary groups and in a high degree of consonance between such groups and the orientations to the centre prevalent within them, these in turn being connected with highly autonomous and solidary elites and strata and with (as has been indicated above) open access to the centre and some degree of commitment to it.

These relations usually evince some diffuse oppositionary orientations towards the institutional order. These oppositionary orientations are, however, couched in terms of the upholding of pure interpersonal relations and values which necessarily go beyond any existing institutional order, but which on the whole accept such orders within their own realms. Hence these relations evince little emphasis either on the reconstruction of centres or on the involvement in highly institutionalised political activities of different movements, parties and sectors. Rather, they are characterised by a tendency, in different degrees, to isolate themselves in their private realms from such activities.[20]

Accordingly, there develop here also – except in periods of upheaval, to be discussed shortly – rather tenuous connections with sectarian groups or movements or with carriers of exemplary pristine models of culture.

These types of interpersonal relations are also connected with addendum-like patron–client relations which involve relatively little deep personal involvement, and the spread of which, into the central institutional spheres, is curtailed (as we have seen) by various social forces and mechanisms.

The structuring and symbolism of trust within these addendum-like patron–client relations do indeed differ greatly from those that we have identified in clientelistic societies. First, the trust they engender is either much more purely personal or more conditional, and the terms of exchange between the partners are somewhat more fully formulated – although never, of course, officially.

Second, they are usually not based on conceptions of honour similar to those of some clientelistic societies. True enough, in such settings, some elements of unconditionality do also develop between the patron and clients, but they are but rarely upheld by such conceptions of honour, except when these conceptions are brought over (as in the case of various immigrant groups) from other settings.

Third, ambivalence in relation to the basic premises of the institutional structure or even negation of social order does not constitute such an essential component of these relations and is certainly not highly articulated, as it is in those relations which develop in clientelistic societies.

Insofar as such ambivalence or negation develops in these societies, it is not usually articulated through these or in other interpersonal relations (such as different types of friendship or comradeship) with which the patron–client relations may overlap.

It is only in periods of upheaval or in various marginal sectors of these societies that these interpersonal relations and addendum-like patron–client relations tend to become connected with sectarian or oppositionary movements which attempt to impinge on the centre. In such situations, the tensions between interpersonal loyalties and the demands of the sectarian movements may develop early. These tensions, however, tend on the whole to become diffused with the growing institutionalisation of such movements in a relatively pluralistic framework.

In consociational societies, or in such sectors of pluralistic societies, the various interpersonal relations analysed here seem, as far as we can ascertain, to be circumscribed by the respective consociational sectors. Similarly, the addendum-like patron–client relations that develop in these societies seem also to be circumscribed by these different sectors, which mediate access to the centres of power.

IV

Yet, as indicated above, other interpersonal relations with strong articulated oppositionary orientations develop also within universalistic – especially modern – societies. Such relations exhibit strong tendencies to become combined or to merge with oppositionary movements or sects. Among the most important illustrations of such tendencies stand out, as already indicated, the European student and youth movements in general (and the German ones in particular), the groupings found among the Russian intelligentsia, and similar tendencies that have developed in different periods in various modern universalistic societies.

Such oppositionary orientations and tendencies tend particularly to develop, in the modern universalistic societies, in historical situations in which there emerge clearly defined and striking contradictions between the universalistic premises of these societies and the actual access to the centre, or in situations in which there is very marked discord between different groups aspiring to the reconstruction of the centre, especially the secondary elite groups, and the actual holders of positions at the centre.

While such potential is to some degree inherent in all modern societies, it becomes fully realised under those specific historical circumstances in which blockage of access to the political and cultural centres tend to intensify the uncertainties and difficulties inherent in the transition between institutional spheres structured according to different institutional principles and gives rise to oppositionary tendencies focused ideologically around the denial of legitimacy to the existing centre and around the envisaged reconstruction of those centres in terms of the trust and meaning denied to the actual centre.

In such cases, there develops a tendency to a very intensive ideologisation and formalisation of interpersonal relations, with concomitant attempts at their deprivatisation; these in their turn are very closely connected with attempts at symbolic de-differentiation of some of the institutional spheres, above all with the merging of the peripheral spheres with the more central ones in some highly symbolic idealistic ways. The imagery of trust and of pristine values tends to become here very much concentrated around the reconstruction of the centre, the possibility of its spread into more peripheral and private spheres being denied.

The conceptions of personal identity which develop in such situations are very strongly rooted in the opposition between the solidary and autonomous groups and elites, and their orientation towards the centre, and the actual symbolism and organisation of the centre.

It is in such situations that the tensions and contradictions between the pure interpersonal relations and the totalistic tendencies of sects or of the exemplary upholders of pristine values become most fully articulated and visible.

Such tendencies also become manifest in various sectors of modern universalistic societies or in specific groups or organisations in which the structural and symbolic tendencies specified above – especially relatively high differentiation combined with blockage of access – tend to develop. Such developments occur in various 'closed societies', such as monasteries, ships or marginal sects, as well as in periods of great upheaval.

Contrasting with these, the patterns of interpersonal relations that develop in modern totalitarian societies are shaped by the combination of the widespread existence of realms of privacy, the potential sectarian and oppositionary tendencies rooted in limitations of access to the centre inherent in these regimes, and the attempt of the regime to control the areas of privacy and to formalise and institutionalise many of the interpersonal relations in different official forums such as official youth movements and the like.[21]

9

vvvvvvvvvvvvvvvvvvvvvvvvvvvvvvvvvvvvvvvvvvvvvvvvvvvvvvvvvvvvvvvvvvvvvvvvvvvvvv

Concluding remarks: the dialectics of trust and the social order

I

The foregoing summary description of the different patterns of inter-personal relations that develop in various societies of sectors thereof – together with the more detailed analysis of different patterns of patron–client relations presented above – enables us to draw some (even if preliminary) conclusions, not only as we have done in the preceding chapters about the social conditions which generate different patterns of such interpersonal relations, but also about the central analytical focus of our discussion – namely about the ambivalence and dialectics of trust in the social order. These are above all manifest in the relations between the modes of construction of trust in the institutional order and the attempts at the construction of new areas of trust – and of participation in the realm of some pristine, common meaning – in the various types of interpersonal relations, seemingly beyond this order or in opposition to it.

We have seen that, whatever the differences between various types of such interpersonal relations, they all tend to construct realms of trust and of participation in a spiritual realm beyond the major institutionalised sectors of a society – specifically, but not exclusively, beyond that of kinship – in which trust and participation in the realm of meaning are seemingly most fully institutionalised.

The attempt to construct such areas of trust and to imbue the search for personal attachment with special meaning or meta-meaning, and with the search for pure trust, is implicit in the construction of social order because of the tendencies inherent in the structure of socialisation and of institutionalisation, towards potential breakdown of the extension of trust between different fields of social relations and institutional spheres.

It is for the same reason that attempts to construct interpersonal

294

relations as areas of such trust entail, as we have seen above, several basic tensions – namely those between the emphases on purely solidary or spiritual relations as against concrete (power and instrumental) obligations; between the tendency to institutionalise such relations, and their apparent removal from the institutional order into the realm of privacy; and between the tendency to uphold the pristine values which are at the basis of any social order and subversive and oppositionary orientations to this order.

But the ways in which such realm of trust and of participation in pure pristine values is constructed, and in which these various tensions are worked out – i.e. in which the dialectics and ambivalence of trust in the social order become manifest – vary, as we have seen, greatly in different societies. They vary in close relation to the discontinuities in the extension of trust over different institutional spheres, in accordance with configurations of the dimensions of social structure (specified above) which shape the institutionalisation of trust within it – i.e. with the degree of structural and symbolic institutionalisation of the major institutional spheres; with the degree to which different institutional spheres of a society are structured according to relatively similar or dissimilar principles, especially universalistic versus particularistic and egalitarian as against hierarchical ones; and with the degree of clarity of such principles and of their application to different institutional spheres in general, and in the specification of the degree of autonomous – as against mediated – access of different groups to societal, political and cultural (usually religious) power in particular.

II

The working out of the tension between the formalisation and institutionalisation of these areas of trust, of interpersonal relations and the search for a realm of trust and privacy beyond the nexus of formal institutional structure is influenced above all by one central aspect of the social division of labour – i.e. the degree of social and symbolic differentiation of institutional spheres which is prevalent in a society.

Thus, we have seen that a relatively small degree of structural and symbolic differentiation has been correlated in many of the tribal societies – as well as (although to a much smaller degree) in some sectors of more complex societies – with the tendency to the development of such institutionalised and formalised relations, and to relatively clear definitions of their institutional placement and boundaries. Such relations are often couched in such societies in highly crystallised – often ritualised – ideological terms and a weak, often totally non-existent, recognition and public visibility of a private realm, of a realm of private intimacy.

As against this, we have seen that when the degree of structural and symbolic differentiation is greater – as already evident in various 'traditional' societies such as China, and more fully developed modern societies – such interpersonal relations are less formalised and institutionalised, their boundaries are less clearly defined, and the legitimacy of the existence of a realm of privacy is more broadly recognised. Accordingly, the scope and variety of manifestations of such realm of privacy are greater, and private relations range in such settings from deeper and 'close' friendships to mere acquaintanceships and 'fair-weather' friendships.

Such varying degrees of institutionalisation of interpersonal relations and the concomitant, and somehow inversely correlated, degrees of recognition of a realm of privacy, entail far-reaching consequences for the structuring of trust in different societies, especially in regard to the dialectics between the institutionalisation of trust and attempts to take such trust beyond the institutional order.

Thus, in the less differentiated societies and especially in those which are characterised not only by a low level of structural differentiation but also (and perhaps above all) by a low level of symbolic differentiation, the search for the construction of areas of trust and the search for pristine trust and values beyond the fully institutionalised ones tends in itself to become defined in terms of clear institutional obligations.

Such institutionalisation and formalisation of trust entail the almost total lack of public recognition or semi-legitimation of any realm of privacy which can serve as an area or repository of any trust beyond that which is fully embedded in the institutional matrix of society and in its basic ideological premises. In such situations, the very attempts at the reconstruction of areas of trust beyond the fully institutionalised ones tend to become to a considerable degree embedded within the formal institutional matrix of these societies – even if, in intention, they go beyond it; and in such situations there develop almost no areas in which pristine trust can be embedded without becoming fully formalised and institutionally sanctioned.

The situation is different in the more differentiated societies and especially in most modern universalistic societies (with the partial, but only partial, exception of the totalitarian ones). Growing structural and symbolic differentiation usually entails a very great degree of recognition of a private realm within which it is possible to construct some trust beyond the fully institutionalised nexus of a society. But this recognition is accompanied by a far-reaching transformation of the nature and expression of such trust – namely by its almost total de-institutionalisation and by a greater blurring in the specification of instrumental or power obligations within such areas.

Such development enables at least some of these relations to become the embodiment of the fullest pristine expression of trust and of the moral or spiritual dimensions of the personal realm; but just because of this, such relations may seemingly lose any organisational efficacy, and may seemingly lack significant direct relations to the institutional order. This is evident in the fact, already mentioned above, that very often people assume that specific claims made in the name of such relations may undermine those relations altogether or at least affect their moral or emotional binding force.

At the same time, such de-institutionalisation may itself, because of its tendency to segregate the realm of private trust from areas of institutionalised trust, enlarge both the scope for trust in society and the capacity of any society for absorbing new developments and tensions – thus in a sense becoming, at least indirectly, supportive of that society's institutional order. But any such absorption tends to generate anew a tension between the institutionalisation and the privatisation of trust, and to bring it close to the tension between the oppositionary or liminal tendencies inherent in such interpersonal relations and the more organised oppositionary tendencies embodied in the different conceptions of alternative social order and in anti-systems such as emerge within the structure of any social order.

III

The root of this tension lies, as we have seen, in the fact that the attempts to construct new areas of trust through interpersonal relations, as well as the more oppositionary organisations, movements and ideologies, do on the one hand share some common characteristics or tendencies, while on the other hand they tend to work out these common characteristics or tendencies in rather different, and even opposite, ways. They share the stress on the inadequacy of the institutionalised order to represent pure trust and values, the tendencies to express liminality, and to stand in a relation of opposition and subversion to the institutional order. In interpersonal relations these tendencies are worked out in attempts to construct a realm of pristine trust or values beyond any institutional order, thus indirectly perhaps giving support to the existing institutional order; while in the oppositionary movements and sects these tendencies are oriented to the institutional reconstruction of the societal structure.

It is therefore but natural that the liminal or subversive orientations inherent in the attempts to construct areas of pristine trust tend to become opposed to their 'contamination' by attempts at any concrete institutional changes in general, and at changes of the societal centre in particular. At the same time, however, the two types of such oppositionary and subversive activities and orientations tend also to become closely interwoven.

Both these tendencies – to the interweaving as well as to the opposition between these different types of liminal and oppositionary orientations – are inherent in the very construction of such relations. The extent to which one of them becomes predominant in any society or sector thereof, in any period of its history, and the degree to which it becomes connected with the formalisation or privatisation of inter-personal relations, as well as the institutional spheres in which these relations become most prominent, depends on the areas of breakdown of extension of trust as they are shaped in different societies according to the configurations of the different dimensions of social structure mentioned above. It is also such configurations that influence the degree and modes in which such relations become supportive or subversive of the given institutional order. Of special importance here are the degrees to which different institutional spheres of a society are structured according to relatively similar or different principles – especially universalistic versus particularistic and egalitarian as against hierarchical ones; the degree of clarity of such principles and of their application to different institutional spheres in general and in the specification of the degree of autonomous as against mediated (i.e. vested in different mediators) access of different groups to the major societal centres in particular; and the relative strength of the centres, above all the commitment to them, prevalent in different societies.

IV

The clarity of the principles regulating different institutional spheres in general and the access to centres of power in particular first of all influences the institutional location of the areas of breakdown of trust. Here the crucial difference is that between the location of such areas in the intersection between the major institutional spheres, or at the margins of the major social groups, and the development of such breakdown of trust in the very central institutional spheres of a society.

When such clarity is present, the breakdown of trust tends to be located in the more marginal or interstitial institutional sectors, while when such clarity is less, such areas of breakdown tend to become spread out in marginal sectors of society and in the areas between different institutional spheres, as well as within the more central, institutional spheres.

The degree of autonomous – as against mediated – access of different groups to the major social centres, the degrees of clarity in the specification of such access and the strength of commitment to societal centres and their symbols influence the strength and nature of the ambivalent and oppositionary orientations that develop in such different interpersonal relations and the mode of their connection with organised oppositionary movements and sects.

Thus, where there is a strong emphasis on mediated access – or, and especially, insofar as there develops *de facto* a blockage of what in principle is perceived as legitimate access – the trustful perception of the societal centres tends to be very feeble. In such cases there tends to develop a sharp breakdown of the extension of trust towards such centres and concomitantly also very strong ambivalent, potentially even oppositionary, tendencies towards the basic premises of the institutional order.

The relative symbolic and organisational strength of such oppositionary tendencies depends to a great extent on the degree of strength and cohesion in the centres to which they are opposed and on the structure of the ruling elites in the centre, as well as on the internal strength and solidarity of the major strata. The stronger all these tendencies – i.e. the more trust is institutionalised according to what has been designated above the totalitarian or semi-totalitarian models of generalised exchange – the more symbolically articulate and organised such oppositionary tendencies are.

At the same time, within such societies there tends to develop a continuous oscillation between on the one hand the tendency to the interweaving of the liminal and subversive tendencies inherent in the construction of the interpersonal relations and the fully organised sects and oppositionary movements, and on the other a continuous tension between them. The tendencies towards interweaving of these two modes of liminal and oppositionary orientations are strongest in periods of attempts to reconstruct societal centres, while the tensions between them become very strong especially during periods of the institutionalisation of new centres.

When, by contrast to these situations, the major societal centres are weak, when the dominant elites in a society are embedded in ascriptive units and when societal trust tends to be institutionalised according to the clientelistic mode of generalised exchange, such oppositionary tendencies are less symbolically articulate and organisationally strong. In such settings, these oppositionary tendencies tend to become diffused in different institutional spheres, but at the same time both the interweaving of and the tensions between the liminal potentialities of interpersonal relations and sectarian organisation are less sharply articulated.

In societies or situations characterised by more or less strong centres in which fairly autonomous elites are predominant, and to which access is relatively open (i.e. when trust is institutionalised according to kinship, clear hierarchical, or pluralistic models of generalised exchange) the oppositionary tendencies inherent in interpersonal relations mostly take the form – whether highly ritualised, as in the less differentiated societies, or more private, as in the more differentiated settings – of going beyond the existing institutional order without necessarily challenging it directly, even giving it some indirect support, by enlarging the scope of trust in society.

These various conditions which generate different patterns of interpersonal relations, different modes of attempts to construct new areas of trust, may continuously change within any society – giving rise to new patterns of such relations; but the search for them, for the construction of such trust, never subsides.

V

The different ways in which the major dimensions of the structuring of interpersonal relations in general, and of construction of areas of trust within them in particular, are organised are very closely related to conceptions of personal identity prevalent in the various societies or sectors thereof. The dimension of personal identity that is central here is that of the relation of personal significance to collective values and collective identity, and to the attributes of membership in the major social frameworks and collectivities.

Here the paradoxical fact is that the weaker such roots are, or the weaker the solidarity of such groups, the stronger is the tendency – as is the case in the concept of honour prevalent in clientelistic societies – to sever personal identity from any collective boundaries, stressing opposition to them and independence of them. This is, however, a brittle and weak autonomy, being hampered by its lack of solidary roots, and hence is in fact bound to a very strict and limited range of activities. Identity under these conditions is also characterised by relatively weak commitment to the centre, as well as by mild but pervasive oppositionary tendencies to it, giving rise to the continuous (but ineffective) search for the construction, within the very central areas of society, of new areas of trust.

The modes of personal identity that develop in those societies in which non-clientelistic models of generalised exchange are institutionalised are rooted – albeit in different ways – in the solidary collectivities. Such rootedness makes possible an active association with a very wide range of different, including innovative, activities which may spread out in different directions. Such activities are usually connected to the development of active, autonomous orientations to the societal centres; they either formulate attempts to construct areas of private trust beyond these centres, are indirectly supportive of them, or become combined with attempts at their reconstruction. In this manner, the concrete directions of these activities and the modes of their interweaving within public and private spheres vary greatly in such societies according to the cultural orientations predominant in them.

VI

We see thus that the construction of areas of trust through different interpersonal relations and the working out of the major tensions inherent in them is indeed very closely connected – in a dialectic fashion – with the modes of institutionalisation of trust within the social order.

In all societies these attempts to construct areas of trust, by going beyond the institutional order and/or by attempts to change it, are greatly influenced by those very forces which shape the institutionalisation of trust in society, and their concrete modes change according to continuously changing configurations of these forces; but they are always there, never attaining their full goals, always attempting to construct new areas of trust which go beyond the institutional order and which yet become a basic dimension or aspect of this order.

Thus, although these attempts at the construction of areas of trust beyond the given institutional order develop in all societies, they can never be fully successful – they can never indeed go thoroughly beyond that order. They thus attest some of the inherent constrictions of the human condition in general and of the manifestation of such constrictions in the construction of social order in particular.

Notes

vvvvvvvvvvvvvvvvvvvvvvvvvvvvvvvvvvvvvvvvvvvvvvvvvvvvvvvvvvvvvvvvvvvvvvvvvvv

Preface

1 S.N. Eisenstadt, *From Generation to Generation*, New York, Free Press, 1956; *idem*, 'Friendship and the Structure of Trust and Solidarity in Society', in E. Leyton, ed., *The Compact: Selected Dimensions of Friendship*, Newfoundland Social and Economic Papers No. 3, Memorial University of Newfoundland, 1974, pp. 138–45.

2 S.N. Eisenstadt and L. Roniger, 'Patron–Client Relations as a Model of Structuring Social Exchange', *Comparative Studies in Society and History*, 22:1 (1980), 42–77; *idem*, 'The Study of Patron–Client Relations and Recent Developments in Sociological Theory', in S.N. Eisenstadt and R. Lemarchand, eds., *Political Clientelism: Patronage and Development*, London, Sage Publications, 1981, pp. 271–95; *idem*, 'Clientelism in Communist Systems: A Comparative Perspective', *Studies in Comparative Communism*, 14:2-3 (1981), 233–45; *idem*, 'Cultural and Structural Continuities and Development – Transformation and Persistence of Patron–Client Relations', *Schweizerische Zeitschrift für Sociologie*, 8 (1982), 29–52.

Chapter 1

1 See J. Pitt-Rivers, *The Fate of Schechem or the Politics of Sex*, Cambridge, Cambridge University Press, 1977, chapter 1 ('The Anthropology of Honour') and chapter 2 ('Honour and Social Status in Andalusia'), pp. 1–47; also *idem*, 'Honour and Social Status', in J.G. Peristiany, ed., *Honour and Shame: The Values of Mediterranean Society*, London, Weidenfeld and Nicolson, 1965, pp. 19–77.

2 On the work of Georg Simmel, see K.H. Wolff, ed., *The Sociology of Georg Simmel*, New York, Free Press, 1950, especially pp. 118–169 and 307–78; and D. Levine, ed., *Georg Simmel on Individuality and Social Forms*, Chicago, Ill., University of Chicago Press, 1971. On such studies of interpersonal relations in social psychology, see J. Klein, *The Study of Groups*, London, Routledge and Kegan Paul, 1956; J.E. McGrath and I. Altman, *Small Group Research*, New York, Holt, Rinehart and Winston, 1966; and R.D. Mann,

Interpersonal Styles and Group Development: An Analysis of the Member–Leader Relationship, New York, John Wiley and Sons, 1967. For sociological studies at this stage see F.J. Roethlisberger and W.J. Dickson, *Management and the Worker: An Account of a Research Program, conducted by the Western Electric Co. Hawthorne Works*, Cambridge, Mass., Harvard University Press, 1970 (c.1939); L.W. Warner and D.S. Lunt, *The Social Life of a Modern Community*, New Haven, Conn., Yale University Press, 1941; W.F. Whyte, *Street Corner Society: The Social Structure of an Italian Slum*, Chicago, Ill., University of Chicago Press, 1958; E. Shils, 'Primary Groups in the American Army', in *idem, Center and Periphery: Essays in Macrosociology*, Chicago, Ill., University of Chicago Press, 1975, pp. 384–405; *idem*, 'Primordial, Personal, Sacred, and Civil Ties', *ibid.*, pp. 111–26; and E. Katz and P.F. Lazarfeld, *Personal Influence*, New York, Free Press, 1955.

3 In anthropology they were connected with the study of such phenomena as ritual kinship or friendship, and anthropologists tended to concentrate on the institutionalised types of friendship and on personal patron–client relationships, to be found in tribal settings and rural communities. Among the best-known studies are S.W. Mintz and E.R. Wolf, 'An Analysis of Ritual Coparenthood (Compadrazgo)', *Southwestern Journal of Anthropology*, 6:4 (Winter 1950), 341–68; G.M. Foster, 'Cofradia and Compadrazgo in Spain', *ibid.*, 9:1 (Spring 1953), 1–28; H. Tegaeus, *Blood Brothers*, New York, Philosophical Library, 1952; I. Ishino, 'The Oyabun–Kobun: A Japanese Ritual Kinship Institution', *American Anthropologist*, 55:1 (1953), 695–707; J. Pitt-Rivers, *The People of the Sierra*, London, Weidenfeld and Nicolson, 1954; *idem*, 'Ritual and Kinship in Spain', *Transactions of the New York Academy of Sciences*, Series 2,20 (1958), 424–31; M. Kenny, *A Spanish Tapestry: Town and Country in Castile*, New York, Harper and Row, 1966 (c. 1961); H.W. Hutchinson, *Village and Plantation Life in Northeastern Brazil*, Seattle, Wash., University of Washington Press, 1957; S.H. Freed, 'Fictive Kinship in a North Indian Village', *Ethnology*, 2 (1963), 86–104; T.M. Kiefer, 'Institutionalized Friendship and Warfare among the Tausug of Jolo', *Ethnology*, 7:3 (1968), 225–44; H. Eidheim, 'Lappish Guest Relationships under Conditions of Cultural Change', *American Anthropologist*, 68 (1966), 426–37; G.M. Foster, 'The Dyadic Contract: A Model for the Social Structure of a Mexican Peasant Village', *American Anthropologist*, 63:6 (1961), 1173–92; and *idem*, 'The Dyadic Contract in Tzintzuntzan, II: Patron–Client Relationship', *ibid.*, 65:6 (1963), 1280–94. In sociology, as indicated, it was closely related to the study of 'primary' groups and relations as emerging in more formalised settings such as bureaucracies. In political science the study of these phenomena was initially concentrated on political machines and 'bossism' in more developed countries. See for instance H.J. Carmen and R.J. Luthin, *Lincoln and the Patronage*, New York, 1943; F.J. Sorauf, 'Patronage and Party', *Midwest Journal of Political Science*, 3 (1959), 115–26; J.Q. Wilson, 'The Economy of Patronage', *Journal of Political Economy*, 69:4 (1961), 369–80; S. Mandelbaum, *Boss Tweed's New York*, New York, John Wiley and Sons, 1965; E. Banfield and J.Q. Wilson, *City Politics*, Cambridge, Mass., Harvard University Press and M.I.T. Press, 1965. In the literature on those pheno-

mena in developing countries at this stage of enquiry see R. Wraith and E. Simkins, *Corruption in Developing Countries*, London, George Allen and Unwin, 1963; M.G. Smith, 'Historical and Cultural Conditions of Political Corruption among the Hausa', *Comparative Studies in Society and History*, 6:1 (1964), 164–94; J.D. Greenstone, 'Corruption and Self-Interest in Kampala and Nairobi', *ibid.*, 8:1 (1966), 199–210; M. Nash, 'Party Building in Upper Burma', *Asian Survey*, 3:4 (1963), 197–202; *idem*, *The Golden Road to Modernity*, New York, John Wiley and Sons, 1965; C.H. Landé, *Leaders, Factions and Parties: The Structure of Philippine Politics*, Southeast Asian Studies, New Haven, Conn., Yale University Press, 1965.

4 For illustrations of these developments in the conceptualisation of patron–client relationships since the late 1960s, see, for instance, E. Wolf, 'Kinship, Friendship and Patron–Client Relationships in Complex Societies', in M. Banton, ed., *The Social Anthropology of Complex Societies*, A.S.A. Monographs, London, Tavistock Press, 1966, pp. 1–22; A. Weingrod, 'Patrons, Patronage, and Political Parties', *Comparative Studies in Society and History*, 7:4 (1968), 377–400; the issue of *Sociologische Gids* that deals with patron–client relations, 16:6 (1969); R. Lemarchand and K. Legg, 'Political Clientelism and Development: A Preliminary Analysis', *Comparative Politics*, 4:2 (1972), 149–78; W.T. Stuart, 'The Explanation of Patron–Client Systems: Some Structural and Ecological Perspectives', in A. Strickon and S. Greenfield, eds., *Structure and Process in Latin America: Patronage, Clientage and Power Systems*, Albuquerque, New Mexico University Press, 1972, pp. 19–42: R. Kaufman, 'The Patron–Client Concept and Macropolitics: Prospects and Problems', *Comparative Studies in Society and History*, 16:3 (1974), 284–308; L. Graziano, *A Conceptual Framework for the Study of Clientelism*, Cornell University Western Societies Program Occasional Papers, No. 4, New York, 1975; J.S. La Fontaine, 'Unstructured Social Relations', *The West African Journal of Sociology and Political Science*, 1:1 (1975), 51–81; E. Gellner and J. Waterbury, eds., *Patrons and Clients in Mediterranean Societies*, London, Duckworth, 1977, especially the following papers: E. Gellner, 'Patrons and Clients', 1–6; J. Scott, 'Patronage or Exploitation?', 21–40; A. Weingrod, 'Patronage and Power', 41–52; and J. Waterbury, 'An Attempt to Put Patrons and Clients in Their Place', 329–42; J. Davis, *People of the Mediterranean: An Essay in Comparative Social Anthropology*, London, Routledge and Kegan Paul, 1977, chapter 4; S.W. Schmidt, L. Guasti, C.H. Landé and J.C. Scott, eds., *Friends, Followers and Factions*, Berkeley, University of California Press, 1976; and R. Lemarchand, 'Comparative Political Clientelism: Structure, Process and Optic', in S.N. Eisenstadt and R. Lemarchand, eds., *Political Clientelism, Patronage and Development*, London, Sage Publications, 1981, pp. 7–32.

5 See L. Roniger, 'Clientelism and Patron–Client Relations: A Bibliography', in S.N. Eisenstadt and R. Lemarchand, eds., *Political Clientelism, Patronage and Development*, pp. 297–330. The wide geographical and cultural occurrence of patron–client relationships encompassed a great variety of links, as will be detailed below.

6 See, for instance, N. Ike, *Japanese Politics: Patron–Client Democracy*, New

York, Knopf, 1957; B. Galjart, 'Old Patrons and New: Some Notes on the Consequences of Patronage for Local Development Projects', *Sociologia Ruralis*, 7 (1967), 335–46; A. Weingrod and E. Morin, 'Post Peasants: The Character of Contemporary Sardinian Society', *Comparative Studies in Society and History*, 13:3 (1971), 301–24; A. Blok, 'Peasants, Patrons and Brokers in Western Sicily', *Anthropological Quarterly*, 42:3 (1969), 155–70; P.A. Allum, *Politics and Society in Postwar Naples*, Cambridge, Cambridge University Press, 1973; M. Bax, 'Patronage Irish Style: Irish Politicians as Brokers', *Sociologische Gids*, 17 (1970), 179–91; S. Khalaf, 'Changing Forms of Political Patronage in Lebanon', in E. Gellner and J. Waterbury, eds., *Patrons and Clients*, pp. 185–206. For a broad treatment of the adaptability of patron–client relations, see S.N. Eisenstadt and L. Roniger, 'Cultural and Structural Continuities and Development–Transformation and Persistence of Patron–Client Relations'; as well as J.D. Powell, 'Peasant Society and Clientelistic Politics', *American Political Science Review*, 64:2 (1970), 411–25; J.C. Scott, 'Corruption, Machine Politics, and Political Change', *ibid.*, 63:4 (1969), 1142–58; R. Lemarchand and K. Legg, 'Political Clientelism and Development: A Preliminary Analysis', *Comparative Politics*, 4:2 (1972), 149–78; J.C. Scott, 'Patron–Client Politics and Political Change in Southeast Asia', *American Political Science Review*, 66:1 (1972), 91–113; C.H. Landé, 'Networks and Groups in Southeast Asia: Some Observations on the Group Theory of Politics', *ibid.*, 67:1 (1973), 103–27; P. Schneider, J. Schneider and E. Hansen, 'Modernization and Development: The Role of Regional Elites and Noncorporated Groups in the European Mediterranean', *Comparative Studies in Society and History*, 14:3 (1972), 328–50; K.R. Legg, *Patrons, Clients and Politicians: New Perspectives on Political Clientelism*, Institute of International Studies, Working Papers on Development, No. 3, Beverley Hills, Calif. (1975).

7 See among others S. Gudeman, 'The Compadrazgo as a Reflection of the Natural and Spiritual Person', The Curl Prize Essay 1971, *Proceedings of the Royal Anthropological Institute for 1971*, pp. 45–7; *idem*, 'Spiritual Relationships and Selecting a Godparent', *Man* (N.S.), 10:2 (1973), 221–37; M. Bloch and S. Guggenheim, 'Compadrazgo, Baptism, and the Symbolism of a Second Birth', *Man* (N.S.), 16 (1981), 376–86; and J. Pitt-Rivers, *The Fate of Schechem*.

8 Among the psychosociological analyses, see K.D. Naegele, 'Friendship and Acquaintances: An Exploration of Some Social Distinctions', *Harvard Educational Review*, 28:3 (1958), 232–52; S. Duck, *Personal Relationships and Personal Constructs: A Study of Friendship Formation*, London, John Wiley and Sons, 1973; see also below. On anthropological works, see R. Paine, 'Anthropological Approaches to Friendship', in E. Leyton, ed., *The Compact: Selected Dimensions of Friendship*, pp. 1–44. For socio-metric studies of friendship, see among others W.W. Hartup, 'The Origins of Friendships', in W. Lewis and L.A. Rosenblum, eds., *Friendship and Peer Relations*, New York, John Wiley and Sons, 1975, pp. 11–26; and some of the other articles included in this volume. See also G.V. Coelho, 'A Guide to Literature on Friendship: A Selectively Annotated Bibliography', *Psychological Newsletter*,

10 (1959), 365–94; and Z. Rubin, *Children's Friendships*, Cambridge, Mass., Harvard University Press, 1980.

9 See also P. Stringer and D. Bannister, eds., *Constructs of Sociality and Individuality*, New York, Academic Press, 1979; and R.L. Burgess and T.L. Huston, eds., *Social Exchange in Developing Relationships*, New York, Academic Press, 1979.

10 See L.C. Lee, 'Toward a Cognitive Theory of Interpersonal Development: Importance of Peers', in W. Lewis and L.A. Rosenblum, eds., *Friendship and Peer Relations*, pp. 207–21; E. Mueller and T. Lucas, 'A Developmental Analysis of Peer Interaction Among Toddlers', *ibid.*, 223–57; E. Bates, 'Peer Relations and the Acquisition of Language', *ibid.*, 259–92; J. Youniss, 'Socialization and Social Knowledge', in R. Silberstein, ed., *Soziale Kognition*, Berlin, Technische Universität Berlin, 1977, pp. 3–22; *idem*, 'Dialectical Theory and Piaget on Social Knowledge', *Human Development*, 21 (1978), 234–47; and *idem*, *Parents and Peers in Social Development*, Chicago, Ill., University of Chicago Press, 1980.

11 See for instance K.D. Naegele, 'Youth and Society: Some Observations', in E.H. Erikson, ed., *Youth: Change and Challenge*, New York, Basic Books, 1963, pp. 43–63; T. Parsons and W. White, 'The Link Between Character and Society', in S.M. Lipset and L. Lowenthal, eds., *Culture and Social Character: The Work of David Riesman Reviewed*, New York, Free Press, 1961, pp. 89–135; and J. Coleman, *The Adolescent Society*, New York, Free Press, 1961.

12 S.N. Eisenstadt, *From Generation to Generation*, New York, Free Press, 1956.

13 S.N. Eisenstadt, 'Ritualized Personal Relations: Blood Brotherhood, Best Friends, Compadre, etc. Some Comparative Hypotheses and Suggestions', *Man*, 96 (1956), 90–5.

14 See C. Du Bois, 'The Gratuitous Act: An Introduction to the Comparative Study of Friendship Patterns', in E. Leyton, ed., *The Compact*, pp. 15–32; S.N. Eisenstadt, 'Ritualized Personal Relations'; and Y.A. Cohen, 'Patterns of Friendship', in Y.A. Cohen, ed., *Social Structure and Personality*, New York, Holt, Rinehart and Winston, 1961, pp. 351–86.

15 E. Wolf, 'Kinship, Friendship, and Patron–Client Relationships'; E. Leyton, ed., *The Compact*.

16 J. Pitt-Rivers, 'Ritual Kinship in Spain', *Transactions of the New York Academy of Sciences*, Series 2, 20 (1958), 424–31; *idem*, 'Kinship, III: Pseudo-Kinship', *International Encyclopaedia of the Social Sciences*, New York, Macmillan and Free Press, 1968, volume 8, pp. 408–13; *idem*, 'Ritual Kinship in the Mediterranean; Spain and the Balkans', in J.G. Peristiany, ed., *Mediterranean Family Structures*, Cambridge, Cambridge University Press, 1976, pp. 317–34; O. Ramsøy, 'Friendship', in *International Encyclopaedia of the Social Sciences*, New York, volume 6, pp. 12–17; R. Paine, 'Anthropological Approaches to Friendship'; and C. Du Bois, 'The Gratuitous Act'.

17 S.N. Eisenstadt, 'Ritualized Personal Relations', p. 90.

18 Y. Cohen, 'Patterns of Friendship'; E. Wolf, 'Kinship, Friendship, and Patron–Client Relationships'; C. Du Bois, 'The Gratuitous Act'.

19 C. Du Bois, 'The Gratuitous Act', p. 20.

20 K.D. Naegele, 'Friendship and Acquaintances',
21 S.N. Eisenstadt, 'Ritualized Personal Relations', pp. 91–4.
22 K.O.L. Burridge, 'Friendship in Tangu', *Oceania*, 27 (1957), 177–89. Quotation from pp. 187–9.
23 S. Gudeman, 'The Compadrazgo as a Reflection'; and *idem*, 'Spiritual Relationships and Selecting a Godparent'; E.N. Goody, 'Forms of Pro-Parenthood: The Sharing and Substitution of Parental Roles', in J. Goody, ed., *Kinship*, Penguin Modern Sociology Series, Harmondsworth, 1971, pp. 331–45; P.G. Rivière, 'The Couvade: A Problem Reborn', *Man* (N.S.), 9:3 (1974), 423–35; and P. Pease Chock, 'Time, Nature and Spirit: A Symbolic Analysis of Greek–American Spiritual Kinship', *American Ethnologist*, 1:1 (1974), 33–47.
24 M. Bloch and S. Guggenheim, 'Compadrazgo, Baptism, and the Symbolism of a Second Birth', pp. 378–9 and 384–5.
25 E. Shils, 'Primordial, Personal, Sacred, and Civil Ties'.
26 See, for instance, V.W. Turner, *The Ritual Process: Structure and Anti-Structure*, Chicago, Ill., Aldine Press, 1969.

Chapter 2

1 See S.N. Eisenstadt, 'The Schools of Sociology', *American Behavioral Scientist*, 24:3 (1981), 329–44; *idem*, 'The Sociological Tradition: Origins, Boundaries, Patterns of Innovation, and Crises', in J.Ben-David and T.N. Clark, eds., *Culture and its Creators: Essays in Honor of Edward Shils*, Chicago, Ill., and London, University of Chicago Press, 1977, pp. 43–71.
2 These themes are analysed in detail in S.N. Eisenstadt and M. Curelaru, *The Form of Sociology: Paradigms and Crisis*, New York, John Wiley and Sons, 1976; and *idem*, 'Macrosociology: Theory Analysis and Comparative Studies', *Current Sociology*, 25:2 (1977).
3 E. Durkheim, *The Division of Labor in Society*, New York, Free Press, 1964; *idem*, *The Rules of Sociological Method*, New York, Free Press, 1964; *idem*, *On Morality and Society*, ed. and with an introd. by R.N. Bellah, Chicago, Ill., University of Chicago Press, 1973; and *idem*, *Selected Writings*, ed. and with an introd. by A. Giddens, Cambridge, Cambridge University Press, 1972; M. Weber, *The Religion of China*, New York, Free Press, 1951; *idem*, *Ancient Judaism*, New York, Free Press, 1952; *idem*, *The Religion of India*, New York, Free Press, 1958; *idem*, *The Protestant Ethic and the Spirit of Capitalism*, New York, Scribner, 1958; K. Marx, *Early Writings*, ed. by T.B. Bottomore, New York, McGraw-Hill, 1963; and *idem*, *Selected Writings in Sociology and Social Philosophy*, ed. by T.B. Bottomore and M. Rubel, Harmondsworth, Penguin Books, 1965.
4 See E. Durkheim, *The Division of Labor*; F. Tönnies, *Community and Society*, East Lansing, Michigan State University Press, 1957; and *idem*, *On Sociology, Pure, Applied and Empirical: Selected Writings*, Chicago, Ill., and London, University of Chicago Press, 1971.
5 On this approach, see among others A.R. Radcliffe-Brown, *Structure and Function in Primitive Society*, London, Cohen and West, 1952; A.R.

Radcliffe-Brown and D. Forde, eds., *African Systems of Kinship and Marriage*, London, Oxford University Press, 1950; B. Malinowski, 'Culture', in *Encyclopaedia of the Social Sciences*, New York, Macmillan, 1931, volume 4, pp. 621–45; E.E. Evans-Pritchard, *Social Anthropology*, London, Cohen and West, 1951; *idem*, ed., *Institutions of Primitive Society*, Oxford, Basil Blackwell, 1954; M. Fortes and E.E. Evans-Pritchard, eds., *African Political Systems*, London, Oxford University Press, 1940. See also A. Kuper, *Anthropologists and Anthropology, 1922–1972*, London, Allen Lane, 1972, chapters 2–6.

6 T. Parsons and E. Shils, eds., *Toward a General Theory of Action*, Cambridge, Mass., Harvard University Press, 1951; T. Parsons, *The Social System*, New York, Free Press, 1964 (c. 1951); T. Parsons and N.J. Smelser, *Economy and Society*, New York, Free Press, 1965 (c. 1956); R.K. Merton, *Social Theory and Social Structure*, rev. edn, New York, Free Press, 1963; K. Davis and W.E. Moore, 'Some Principles of Stratification', *American Sociological Review*, 10 (1945), 242–7; K. Davis, *Human Society*, New York, Macmillan, 1949; and T. Parsons, *Essays in Sociological Theory*, rev. edn., New York, Free Press, 1963 (c.1949). See E. Shils' contribution to the analysis of the symbolic and charismatic dimensions of society in his *Center and Periphery: Essays in Macrosociology*, Chicago, Ill., University of Chicago Press, 1975.

7 See in detail S.N. Eisenstadt and M. Curelaru, *The Form of Sociology*; and *idem*, 'Macrosociology'.

8 R.K. Merton, *Social Theory and Social Structure*; N. Gross, W. Mason and A. McEachern, *Explorations in Role Analysis*, New York, John Wiley and Sons, 1958; S.A. Stouffer and J. Toby, 'Role Conflict and Personality', *American Journal of Sociology*, 56:5 (1951), 395–406; B.J. Biddle and E.J. Thomas, eds., *Role Theory*, New York, John Wiley and Sons, 1966.

9 See S.N. Eisenstadt and M. Curelaru, *The Form of Sociology*, especially chaps. 7 and 8.

10 See among others E. Shils and M. Janovitz, 'Cohesion and Disintegration in the Wehrmacht in World War II', in E. Shils, ed., *Center and Periphery; Essays in Macrosociology*, pp. 345–83; S.N. Eisenstadt, *The Absorption of Immigrants*, London, Routledge and Kegan Paul, 1978 (1954); E. Katz and P.F. Lazarfeld, *Personal Influence*, New York, Free Press, 1955; and E. Shils, 'Primordial, Personal, Sacred, and Civil Ties', in *Center and Periphery*, pp. 111–26, originally published in the *British Journal of Sociology*, 8 (1957), 37–52.

11 Criticisms of the structural–functional model were connected with the development of new theoretical approaches and with attempts to revive alternative ones. The most important of these approaches have been: (1) the 'conflict' school or model as developed by R. Dahrendorf and closely related to the structural–functional school by L. Coser and Max Gluckman. See R. Dahrendorf, *Class and Class Conflict in Industrial Society*, Stanford, Calif., Stanford University Press, 1959; J. Rex, *Key Problems in Sociological Theory*, London, Routledge and Kegan Paul, 1961; L. Coser, *The Functions of Social Conflict*, London, Collier–Macmillan, 1964 (c. 1956), M. Gluckman, *Order and Rebellion in Tribal Africa*, New York, Free Press, 1963; (2) the exchange school, as developed by G.C. Homans, P.M. Blau and J.

Coleman. See G.C. Homans, *Social Behaviour: Its Elementary Forms*, New York, Harcourt, Brace and World, 1961; P. Blau, 'Justice in Social Exchange', *Sociological Inquiry*, 34:1–2 (1964), 193–206; *idem, Exchange and Power in Social Life*, New York, John Wiley and Sons, 1964; J. Coleman, 'Foundations for a Theory of Collective Decisions', *American Journal of Sociology*, 71:6 (1966), 615–27; and *idem*, 'Political Money', *American Political Science Review*, 64:4 (1970), 1074–87; (3) the 'group interest' model as developed by R. Bendix and R. Collins. See R. Bendix, *State and Society*, Boston, Mass., Little, Brown, 1968; and R. Collins, *Conflict Sociology: Towards an Explanatory Science*, New York, Academic Press, 1975; (4) the 'symbolic interactionist' and ethnomethodology models with their stress on the social construction of reality and the development of meaning, of the basic but often hidden premises of social life, through the social interaction in daily life and in microsocietal situations. See H. Blumer, *Symbolic Interactionism*, Englewood Cliffs, N.J., Prentice-Hall, 1969; E. Goffman, *The Presentation of Self in Everyday Life*, Garden City, N.Y., Doubleday Anchor Books, 1959; *idem, Encounters*, Indianapolis, Bobbs-Merrill, 1961; G.P. Stone and H.A. Farberman, eds., *Social Psychology through Symbolic Interaction*, Waltham, Mass., Xerox College Publishing, 1970; H. Garfunkel, *Studies in Ethnomethodology*, Englewood Cliffs, N.J., Prentice-Hall, 1967; and A. Cicourel, *Cognitive Sociology*, Harmondsworth, Penguin, 1973; (5) the 'symbolic–structuralist' model, as developed by Claude Lévi-Strauss. See C. Lévi-Strauss, *Structural Anthropology*, New York, Basic Books, 1963; *idem, The Savage Mind*, London, Weidenfeld and Nicolson, 1966; *idem, Totemism*, Boston, Mass., Beacon, 1969; *idem, The Elementary Structures of Kinship*, Boston, Mass., Beacon, 1969 (c. 1949); and *idem, Mythologuiques*, 3 vols., Paris, Plon, 1968–71; (6) the Marxist models which were revived in the late 1960s. See M. Godelier, *Rationality and Irrationality in Economics*, New York, Monthly Review, 1972; *idem, Horizons: Trajets marxistes en anthropologie*, Paris, Maspero, 1973; A. Touraine, *Pour la sociologie*, Paris, Seuil, 1974; L. Sebag, *Marxisme et Structuralisme*, Paris, Payot, 1964; M. Bloch, ed., *Marxist Analysis in Social Anthropology*, London, Malaby Press, 1975; and N. Poulantzas, *Les Classes sociales dans le capitalisme d'aujourd'hui*, Paris, Seuil, 1974; (7) the 'systems' or 'secondary cybernetics' approach to the analysis of social systems, developed especially by Walter Buckley, M. Maruyama and K. Deutsch. See W. Buckley, *Sociology and Modern System Theory*, Englewood Cliffs, N.J., Prentice-Hall, 1967; M. Maruyama, 'The Second Cybernetics: Deviation-Amplifying Mutual Casual Processes', in W. Buckley, ed., *Modern Systems Research for the Behavioral Scientist*, Chicago, Ill., Aldine Press, 1968, pp. 304–13; and K. Deutsch, *The Nerves of Government*, New York, Free Press, 1963. For a detailed analysis of these approaches, see S.N. Eisenstadt and M. Curelaru, *The Form of Sociology*, especially chapters 8–9.

12 See, for instance, A. Gouldner, *The Coming Crisis of Western Sociology*, New York, Basic Books, 1970; and the works by E. Shils mentioned above. It should be remarked, however, that the autonomy of individuals in their role behaviour was already recognised by scholars of the functional school

of anthropology. See among others R. Firth, 'Some Principles of Social Organization', in *idem, Essays on Social Organization and Values*, London, Athlone Press, 1964, pp. 59–87.

13 See the bibliography in note 11 above; also E. Goffman, *Interaction Ritual: Essays on Face-to-Face Behaviour*, Garden City, N.Y., Doubleday–Anchor, 1967; *idem, Behavior in Public Places: Notes on the Social Organization of Gatherings*, New York and London, Free Press and Collier–Macmillan, 1963; and *idem, Relations in Public: Microstudies of the Public Order*, New York, Harper and Row, 1971.

14 See S.N. Eisenstadt and M. Curelaru, *The Form of Sociology*, chapter 10: 'Major Analytic Developments and Openings', pp. 245–95.

15 For the emphasis put on interpersonal relations and exchange by scholars who dealt with patron–client relations, see E. Wolf, 'Kinship, Friendship, and Patron–Client Relationships', in M. Banton, ed., *The Social Anthropology of Complex Societies*, A.S.A. Monographs, London and Tavistock, pp. 1–22; J. Boissevain, *Friends of Friends: Networks, Manipulators, and Coalitions*, Oxford, Basil Blackwell, 1974; A.C. Mayer, 'The Significance of Quasi-Groups in the Study of Complex Societies', in M. Banton, ed., *The Social Anthropology of Complex Societies*, pp. 97–122; M.J. Swartz, *Local-Level Politics: Social and Cultural Perspectives*, Chicago, Aldine Press, 1966, especially pp. 53–68, 199–204, 227–41 and 243–69; J. Boissevain, 'The Place of Non-Groups in Social Sciences', *Man* (N.S.), 3:4 (1968), 542–6; J. Pitt-Rivers, 'The Kith and the Kin', in J. Goody, ed., *Character of Kinship*, Cambridge, Cambridge University Press, 1973, pp. 89–105; J. Boissevain and J.C. Mitchell, eds., *Network Analysis: Studies in Social Interaction*, Paris and The Hague, Mouton, 1973; C.H. Landé, 'Networks and Groups in Southeast Asia: Some Observations on the Group Theory of Politics', *American Political Science Review*, 67:1 (1973), 103–27; *idem*, 'Group Politics and Dyadic Politics: Notes for a Theory', in S. Schmidt *et al.*, eds., *Friends, Followers and Factions*, Berkeley, Calif., University of California Press, 1976, pp. 506–10; A. Weingrod, 'Patronage and Power', in E. Gellner and J. Waterbury, eds., *Patrons and Clients in Mediterranean Societies*, London, Duckworth, 1977, pp. 41–52; and J.C. Scott, 'Political Clientelism: A Bibliographical Essay', in Schmidt *et al.*, eds., *Friends, Followers and Factions*, pp. 488–9.

16 On the concept of honour in societies in which patron–client relations can also be found, see J.G. Peristiany, ed., *Honour and Shame: The Values of Mediterranean Society*, London, Weidenfeld and Nicolson, 1965; P. Schneider, 'Honour and Conflict in a Sicilian Town', *Anthropological Quarterly*, 42:3 (1969), 130–54; J.K. Campbell, *Honour, Family, and Patronage: A Study of Institutions and Moral Values in a Greek Mountain Community*, Oxford, Clarendon Press, 1964; J. Pitt-Rivers, 'Honour and Social Status', in J.G. Peristiany, ed., *Honour and Shame*, pp. 19–78; *idem*, 'Honor', in *International Encyclopaedia of the Social Sciences*, volume 6, pp. 503–10; J. Davis, 'Honour and Politics in Picticci', *Proceedings of the Royal Anthropological Institute, 1969*, pp. 64–81; J. Schneider, 'Of Vigilance and Virgins: Honour, Shame and the Access to Resources in Mediterranean Societies', *Ethnology*, 10:1 (1971), 1–24. On the image of limited good, see G. Foster, 'Peasant

Society and the Image of Limited Good', *American Anthropologist*, 67:2 (1965), 293–315. For controversies about the concept, see, for instance, D. Kaplan and B. Saler, 'Foster's Image of the Limited Good: An Example of Anthropological Explanation', *American Anthropologist*, 68:1 (1966), 202–5; J.W. Bennett, 'Further Remarks on Foster's Image of Limited Good', *ibid.*, 206–9; and Foster's reply, *ibid.*, 210–14. See also S. Piker, 'The Image of Limited Good: Comments on an Exercise in Description and Interpretation', *American Anthropologist*, 68:5 (1966), 1202–11; G.M. Foster, 'A Second Look at Limited Good', *Anthropological Quarterly*, 45:2 (1972), 57–64; and J.R. Gregory, 'Image of Limited Good or Expectation of Reciprocity?', *Current Anthropology*, 16:1 (1975), 73–92. On 'amoral familism' see E. Banfield, *The Moral Basis of a Backward Society*, New York, Free Press, 1958; A.J. Wichers, 'Amoral Familism Reconsidered', *Sociologia Ruralis*, 4:2 (1964), 167–81; A. Pizzorno, 'Amoral Familism and Historical Marginality', *International Review of Community Development*, 15–16 (1966), 55–66; and R.A. Miller, Jr, 'Are Familists Amoral? A Test of Banfield's Amoral Familism Hypothesis in a South Italian Village', *American Ethnologist*, 1:3 (1974), 515–35.

17 A discussion of this problem in relation to studies on modernisation can be found in S.N. Eisenstadt, ed., *Post-Traditional Societies*, New York, W.W. Norton, 1974.

18 On *compadrazgo* and parallel forms of ritual kinship, see the references in chapter 1, note 7; and H.G. Nutini and B. Bell, *Ritual Kinship: The Structure and Historical Development of the Compadrazgo System in Rural Tlaxcala*, Princeton, N.J., Princeton University Press, 1980; D.V. Hart, *Compadrinazgo: Ritual Kinship in the Philippines*, De Kalb, Ill., Northern Illinois University Press, 1977; L. Bervecos, *El compadrazgo en América Latina: análisis antropológico de 106 casos*, Mexico, Instituto Indigenista Interamericano, 1976; R.A. Miller, 'The Golden Chain: A Study of the Structure, Function, and Patterning of *Comparatio* in a South Italian Village', *American Ethnologist*, 5:1 (1978), 116–36; and also below. On Russian friendship, see V.C. Nahirny, 'The Russian Intelligentsia: from Men of Ideas to Men of Convictions', *Comparative Studies in Society and History*, 4:4 (1962), 403–35; and chapter 8 below.

Chapter 3

1 A. Aichhorn, *Wayward Youth*, London, Putnam and Co., 1944; E.H. Erikson, *Childhood and Society*, rev. edn., London, Hogarth Press, 1964: Harmondsworth, Penguin Books, 1969 (c. 1950); C. Frankenstein, *Psychodynamics of Externalization: Life from Without*, Baltimore, Md, Williams and Wilkins, 1968; *idem, Varieties of Juvenile Delinquency*, London, New York and Paris, Gordon and Breach Science Publishers, 1970; *idem, The Roots of the Ego: A Phenomenology of Dynamics and of Structure*, Baltimore, Md, Williams and Wilkins, 1966; *idem*, 'On Institutional Care: Readings' for 'Problems of Delinquency and Underprivileged Youth', Jerusalem, Hebrew University Office for Overseas Students, 1970 (this is a short version of the Hebrew original *Haadam bi-mtzukato* – 'Men in Distress' – published Tel Aviv, Am

Oved and Dvir, 1964); R.A. Spitz, *La Première Année de la vie de l'enfant. Genèse des premières relations objectales*, Paris, Presses Universitaires de France, 1958; J. Bowlby, 'Separation Anxiety', *International Journal of Psychoanalysis*, 41 (1960), 89–113; *idem, Attachment and Loss*, London, Hogarth Press and the Institute of Psychoanalysis, volume 1, 'Attachment' (1969); volume 2, 'Separation, Anxiety and Anger' (1973); *idem, Loss, Sadness and Depression*, Harmondsworth, Penguin Books, 1981, volume 3. See also A.H. Modell, *Object Love and Reality: An Introduction to a Psychoanalytic Theory of Object Relations*, New York, International University Press, 1968; and H.R. Schaffer, ed., *The Origins of Human Social Relations*, London and New York, Academic Press, 1971.

2 On the relation of trust and social complexity, see N. Luhman, *Trust and Power*, New York, John Wiley and Sons, 1979, especially chapter 3, 'Familiarity and Trust', and chapter 4, 'Trust as a Reduction of Complexity', pp. 18–31.

3 M. Fortes, *Kinship and the Social Order*, Chicago, Aldine Press, 1965. See also D.M. Schneider, *American Kinship: A Cultural Analysis*, Englewood Cliffs, N.J., Prentice-Hall, 1968; F.L. Hsu, ed., *Kinship and Culture*, Chicago, Aldine Press, 1971; J. Goody, *Comparative Studies in Kinship*, London, Routledge and Kegan Paul, 1969; and M. Bloch, 'The Long Term and the Short Term: The Economic and Political Significance of Kinship', in J. Goody, ed., *The Character of Kinship*, Cambridge, Cambridge University Press, 1973, pp. 75–89.

4 See note 11 in chapter 2. A treatment of these different orientations in social exchange theory can be found in P. Ekeh, *Social Exchange Theory: The Two Traditions*, Cambridge, Mass., Harvard University Press, 1964; and J.H. Turner, *The Structure of Sociological Theory*, Homewood, Ill., The Dorsey Press, 1974, pp. 211–320.

5 M. Mauss, *The Gift: Forms and Functions of Exchange in Archaic Societies*, London, Cohen and West, 1954. (Originally published as 'Essai sur de don', *Année Sociologique* (n.s.), 1 (1925), 30–126.)

6 C. Lévi-Strauss, *The Elementary Structures of Kinship*, Boston, Mass., Beacon Press, 1969 (c. 1949); T. Parsons, 'On the Concept of Influence', *Public Opinion Quarterly*, 27 (1963), 37–62; *idem*, 'Rejoinder to Bauer and Coleman', *ibid.*, 83–92; *idem*, 'On the Concept of Political Power', *Proceedings of the American Philosophical Society*, 103:3 (1963), 232–62; *idem*, 'A Revised Analytical Approach to One Theory of Social Stratification', in *idem*, ed., *Essays in Sociological Theory*, rev.edn., New York, Free Press, 1963, pp. 386–439; J.S. Coleman, 'Political Money', *The American Political Science Review*, 64:4 (1970), 1074–87.

7 E. Durkheim, *The Division of Labor in Society*, New York, Free Press, 1964. For further treatment of the precontractual elements of social life, see, for instance, T. Parsons, *The Structure of Social Action*, especially pp. 301–38, 460–70 and 708–14; J.A. Davis, 'Structural Balance, Mechanical Solidarity, and Interpersonal Relations', *American Journal of Sociology*, 68:4 (1963), 444–62; and H. Befu, 'Gift-Giving and Social Reciprocity in Japan', *France–Asie/Asia*, 188 (1966/7), 161–77. See also T. Parsons, 'Durkheim on Religion

Revisited: Another Look at the Elementary Forms of Religious Life', in C.Y. Glock and P.E. Hammond, eds., *Beyond the Classics: Essays in the Scientific Study of Religion*, New York, Harper and Row, 1973, pp. 156-81.

8 On unconditionalities and titles, see S.N. Eisenstadt, *Social Differentiation and Stratification*, Glenview, Ill., Scott Foresman and Co., 1971; and *idem*, 'Prestige, Participation and Strata Formation', in J.A. Jackson, ed., *Social Stratification*, Cambridge, Cambridge University Press, 1968, pp. 62–103.

9 On public goods and public distribution of private goods, see A. Kuhn, *The Study of Society: A Unified Approach*, Homewood, Ill., The Dorsey Press, 1963; M. Olson, *The Logic of Collective Action*, New York, Schocken, 1965; O.E. Williamson, 'Market and Hierarchies: Some Elementary Considerations', *American Economic Review*, 63:2 (1973), 316–25; *idem, Some Notes on the Economics of Atmosphere*, Fels Discussion Papers No.29, University of Pennsylvania, The Fels Center of Government, 1973; R.A. Hanson, 'Toward an Understanding of Politics Through Public Goods Theory: A Review Essay', in W. Loehr and T. Sandler, eds., *Public Goods and Public Policy*, Beverly Hills, Calif., Sage Publications, 1978, pp. 67–95; M. Feeley, 'Coercion and Compliance', *Law and Society Review*, 4 (1970), 505–20; and R.M. Spann, 'Collective Consumption of Private Goods', *Public Choice*, 29 (1974), 62–81.

10 On hospitality, see J. Pitt-Rivers, 'The Stranger, the Guest and the Hostile Host: Introduction to the Study of the Laws of Hospitality', in J.G. Peristiany, ec., *Contributions to Mediterranean Sociology*, pp. 13–30; and the issue of *Anthropological Quarterly* dealing with 'Visiting Patterns and Social Dynamics in Eastern Mediterranean Communities', 47:1 (1974).

11 See C. Lévi-Strauss, *The Elementary Structures of Kinship*; and M. Fortes, *Kinship and the Social Order*. See also M. Sahlins, 'On the Sociology of Primitive Exchange', in M. Banton, ed., *The Relevance of Models for Social Anthropology*, New York, Praeger, 1965, pp. 139–236; and *idem, Tribesmen*, Englewood Cliffs, N.J., Prentice-Hall, 1968, chapters 4 and 5.

12 T. Parsons *et al.* eds., *Theories of Society*, New York, Free Press, 1961; *idem*, 'On the Concept of Value Commitment', *Sociological Inquiry*, 38:2 (1968), 135–60; L. Mayhew, 'Ascription in Modern Societies', *ibid.*, 105–20; T.S. Turner, 'Parsons' Concept of "Generalized Media of Social Interaction" and its Relevance for Social Anthropology', *ibid.*, 121–34.

13 E. Mueller and T. Lucas, 'A Developmental Analysis of Peer Interaction Among Toddlers', in M. Lewis and L.A. Rosenblum, eds., *Friendship and Peer Relations*, pp. 223–57; M. Lewis *et al.*, 'The Beginning of Friendship', *ibid.*, pp. 27–66; L. Rosenblum *et al.*, 'Peer Relations in Monkeys: The Influence of Social Structure, Gender, and Familiarity', *ibid.*, pp. 67–98; and some of the other articles included there. See also M.W. Piers, ed., *Play and Development*, New York, W.W. Norton, 1972.

14 M. Buber, *I and Thou*, Edinburgh, T. and T. Clark, 1975 (c. 1970), p. 150. See also G. Bateson, *Steps to an Ecology of Mind*, London, Granada Publishing, 1978 (c. 1973).

15 See R. Paine, 'In Search of Friendship: An Exploratory Analysis in "Middle Class" Culture', *Man* (N.S.), 4:4 (1969), 505–24; S.N. Eisenstadt, *From Generation to Generation*. On youth movements see chapter 8 below.

Chapter 4

1 J. Boissevain, 'Patronage in Sicily', *Man* (N.S.), 1 (1966), 18–33.
2 S.F. Silverman, 'Patronage and Community–Nation Relationships in Central Italy', *Ethnology*, 4:2 (1965), 172–89.
3 S. El-Messiri, 'The Changing Role of the Futuwwa in the Social Structure of Cairo', in E. Gellner and J. Waterbury, eds., *Patrons and Clients in Mediterranean Societies*, London, Duckworth, 1977, pp. 239–54.
4 M. Johnson, 'Political bosses and their gangs', *ibid.*, pp. 207–4.
5 E.L. Peters, 'The Tied and the Free (Lybia)', in J.G. Peristiany, ed., *Contributions to Mediterranean Sociology*, Paris and The Hague, Mouton, 1968, pp. 167–88.
6 L.M. Hanks, 'The Thai Social Order as Entourage and Circle', in G.W. Skinner and A.T. Kirsch, eds., *Change and Persistence in Thai Society: Essays in Honor of Lauristan Sharp*, Ithaca, N.Y., and London, Cornell University Press, 1975, pp. 197–218.
7 C. Bailey, *Broker, Mediator, Patron, and Kinsman: An Historical Analysis of Key Leadership Roles in a Rural Malaysian District*, Athens, Ohio, Ohio University Center for International Studies, Southeast Asia Program, 1976.
8 A. Carter, *Elite Politics in Rural India: Political Stratification and Political Alliances in Western Maharashtra*, Cambridge, Cambridge University Press, 1974, pp. 114–15.
9 S. Schmidt, 'The Transformation of Clientelism in Rural Colombia', in S. Schmidt *et al.*, eds., *Friends, Followers, and Factions*, Berkeley, University of California Press, 1976, pp. 305–23.
10 D.C. Heath, 'New Patrons for Old: Changing Patron–Client Relationships in the Bolivian Yungas', *Ethnology*, 12:1 (1973), 75–98.
11 F. Rothstein, 'The Class Basis of Patron–Client Relations', *Latin American Perspectives*, 6:2 (1979), 25–35.
12 S. Greenfield, 'Patronage, Politics, and the Articulation of Local Community and National Society in pre-1968 Brazil', *Journal of Inter-American and World Affairs*, 19:2 (1977), 139–72.
13 Based mainly on A.B. Callow, Jr, *The Tweed Ring*, London, Oxford University Press, 1966; and S.J. Mandelbaum, *Boss Tweed's New York*, New York, John Wiley and Sons, 1965.
14 C.H. Landé, 'Introduction. The Dyadic Basis of Clientelism', in S. Schmidt *et al.*, *Friends, Followers, and Factions*, pp. xiii–xxxvii.
15 The materials on Republican Rome are based on L. Roniger, 'Modern Patron–Client Relations and Historical Clientelism: Some Clues from Ancient Republican Rome', *Archives Européennes de Sociologie*, 24 (1983), 63–95, where these relations are analysed in greater detail. See also N. Roland, *Rome, démocratie impossible? Les acteurs du pouvoir dans la cité romaine*, Paris, Actes Sud, 1981; and for a later period P. Veyne, 'Clientèle et corruption au service de l'Etat: la vénalité des offices dans le Bas-Empire romain', *Annales* (Paris), 36:3 (1981), 339–60.
16 On *fides*, see M. Gelzer, *The Roman Nobility*, Oxford, Basil Blackwell, 1969, pp. 62ff.; and P.A. Brunt, ' "Amicitia" in the Late Roman Republic', in R.

Seager, ed., *The Crisis of the Roman Republic: Studies in Political and Social History*, Cambridge, Heffer and Sons, 1969, pp. 197–218.

17 On the relationship analysed in this section, see S. Treggiari, *Roman Freedmen during the Late Republic*, Oxford, Clarendon Press, 1969; A. Watson, *The Law of Persons in the Later Roman Republic*, Oxford, Clarendon Press, 1967, pp. 226–36; P.A. Brunt, 'The Roman Mob', in M.I Finley, ed., *Studies in Ancient History*, London, Routledge and Kegan Paul, 1974, pp. 74–102; and G. Boissier, *Cicero and his Friends: A Study of Roman Society in the Time of Caesar*, New York, Cooper Square, 1970, especially, pp. 109–12.

18 T. Mommsen, *The History of Rome*, London and New York, J.M. Dent and E.P. Dutton, 1930, volume 1, p. 61. See also E. Badian, *Foreign Clientelae (246–70 B.C.)*, Oxford, Clarendon Press, 1958.

19 N.D. Fustel de Caulanges, *The Ancient City*, Garden City, N.Y., Doubleday Anchor Books, (1864), p. 227. For a rigorous treatment of the legal position of freedmen in relation to patrons, see S. Treggiari, *Roman Freedmen*, pp. 68–81.

20 On the relationship described here, see L.R. Taylor, *Party Politics in the Age of Caesar*, Berkeley, University of California Press, 1971; A.W. Lintott, *Violence in Republican Rome*, Oxford, Clarendon Press, 1968; M. Gelzer, *The Roman Nobility*; and N. Roland, *Rome, démocratie impossible?*

21 L.R. Taylor, *Party Politics*, p. 42.

22 L.R. Taylor, *Party Politics*, p. 43.

23 M. Gelzer, *The Roman Nobility*, pp. 104–6.

24 For this section, see E. Badian, *Foreign Clientelae*; A.N. Sherwin-White, *The Roman Citizenship*, Oxford, Clarendon Press, 1973, especially part i; I. Shatzman, *Senatorial Wealth and Roman Politics*, Latomus, vol. 142, Brussels, 1975, part ii; and Taylor, *Party Politics*.

25 On the forms of the establishment of *clientelae* dealt with in this paragraph see Gelzer, *The Roman Nobility*, pp. 87ff.; Taylor, *Party Politics*, chapter 2; and Badian, *Foreign Clientelae, passim*.

26 P.A. Brunt, ' "Amicitia" in the Late Roman Republic', p. 205. On the nature of unstructured social relations see E. Leyton, ed., *The Compact: Selected Dimensions of Friendship*; J.S. La Fontaine, 'Unstructured Social Relations', *West African Journal of Sociology and Political Science*, 1:1 (1975), 51–81; and J. Boissevain, *Friends of Friends: Networks, Manipulators, and Coalitions*, Oxford, Basil Blackwell, 1974.

27 See on these cases Taylor, *Party Politics*, especially chapter 1; Gelzer, *The Roman Nobility*, especially pp. 85, 103–5; and Treggiari, *Roman Freedmen*, especially pp. 177–93.

28 *Idem*.

29 E. Badian, *Foreign Clientelae*, p. 41. This section is based mainly on this work.

30 E. Badian, pp. 43 and 82.

31 On clientelism in southern Italy see L. Graziano, 'Patron–Client Relationships in Southern Italy', *European Journal of Political Research*, 1:1 (1973), 3–34; M. Rossi-Doria, 'The Land Tenure System and Class in Southern Italy', *American Historical Review*, 64 (1958), 55–66; A.H. Galt, 'Rethinking

Patron–Client Relationships: The Real System and the Official System in Southern Italy', *Anthropological Quarterly*, 47:2 (1974), 182–202; B. Caizzi, ed., *Nuova antologia della questione meridionale*, Milan, Edizioni de Comunità, 1973; J. Davis, 'Honour and Politics in Pisticci', *Proceedings of the Royal Anthropological Institute*, (1969), 68–81; idem, 'Town and Country', *Anthropological Quarterly*, 43 (1969), 171–85; idem, 'Morals and Backwardness', *Comparative Studies in Society and History*, 12 (1970), 340–53; P.A. Allum, *Politics and Society in Postwar Naples*, Cambridge, Cambridge University Press, 1973; M. Caciagli and F.P. Belloni, 'The "New" Clientelism in Southern Italy: The Christian Democratic Party in Catania', in S.N. Eisenstadt and R. Lemarchand, eds., *Political Clientelism, Patronage and Development*, London, Sage Publications, 1981, pp. 35–55; J. Chubb, 'Naples under the Left: The Limits of Social Change', *ibid.*, pp. 91–124; for further references see L. Roniger, 'Clientelism and Patron–Client Relations: A Bibliography', *ibid.*, pp. 304–8. On the Italian institutional context of such relations, see among others L. Graziano, *Clientelismo e sistema politico. Il caso dell'Italia*, Milan, Franco Angeli, 1980; G. Sartori, 'Proporzionalismo, frazionismo e crisi dei partite', *Rivista Italiana di Scienza Politica*, 1 (1971), 629–55; S. Tarrow, *From Center to Periphery: Alternative Models of National Local Policy Impact and an Application to France and Italy*, Cornell University Western Societies Program Occasional Papers No. 4, New York, Cornell University Press, 1976; idem, 'Local Constraints on Regional Reform: A Comparison of Italy and France', *Comparative Politics*, 7:1 (1976), 1–36; A. Zuckerman, *Political Clienteles in Power: Party Factions and Cabinet Coalitions in Italy*, Beverly Hills and London, Sage Publications, 1975; idem, 'Clientelist Politics in Italy', in E. Gellner and J. Waterbury, eds., *Patrons and Clients*, pp. 63–80; F. Snowden, 'On the Origins of Agrarian Fascism in Italy', *Archives Européennes de Sociologie*, 13:2 (1972), 268–95; F. Cazzola, *Carisma e democrazia nel socialismo Italiano. Strutura e funzione della direzione del P.S.I.*, Rome, V. Ferri, 1967; G. Podbielski, *Italy: Development and Crisis in the Post-War Economy*, Oxford, Clarendon Press, 1974; and C. Giordano and R. Hettlage, *Persistenz im Wandel*, Tübingen, J.C.B. Mohr, 1979.

32 L. Graziano, 'Patron–Client Relationships in Southern Italy', p. 10.

33 S. Tarrow, *Peasant Communism in Southern Italy*, New Haven, Yale University Press, 1967, p. 74.

34 In this section we analyse the networks of *mafiosi* in particular. Other aspects of western Sicilian settings, specifically the forms of its incorporation in the Italian State, are described in the preceding section. On western Sicilian clientelism, see A. Blok, 'Peasants, Patrons, and Brokers in Western Sicily', *Anthropological Quarterly*, 42:3 (1969), 155–70; idem, 'South Italian Agro-Towns', *Comparative Studies in Society and History*, 11 (1969), 121–35; idem, 'Mafia and Peasant Rebellion as Contrasting Factors in Sicilian Latifundism', *Archives Européennes de Sociologie*, 10 (1969), 95–116; R. Aya, *The Missed Revolution: The Fate of Rural Rebels in Sicily and Southern Spain, 1840–1850*, Amsterdam University Papers on European and Mediterranean Societies No. 3, 1975; A. Blok, *The Mafia of a Sicilian Village, 1860–1960: A Study of Violent Peasant Entrepreneurs*, Oxford, Basil Blackwell, 1974; J.

Boissevain, 'Patronage in Sicily', *Man* (N.S.), 1 (1966), 18–33; *idem*, 'Poverty and Politics in a Sicilian Agrotown', *International Archives of Ethnography*, 50 (1966), 189–236; E. D'Alessandro, *Brigantaggio e mafia in Sicilia*, Messina and Florence, G. D'Anna, 1959; E. Hobsbawm, 'Political Theory and the Mafia', *Cambridge Journal*, 7 (1974), 738–55; W.E. Mühlmann and R.J. Llaryora, *Klientschaft, Klientel und Klientel-System in einer sizilianischen Agro-Stadt*, Tübingen, J.G.B. Mohr, 1968; P. Schneider, 'Honor and Conflict in a Sicilian Town', *Anthropological Quarterly*, 42:3 (1969), 130–54; *idem*, 'Coalition Formation and Colonialism in Western Sicily', *Archives Européennes de Sociologie*, 13 (1972), 255–67; and J. Schneider and P. Schneider, *Culture and Political Economy in Western Sicily*, New York, Academic Press, 1976.

35 A. Blok, *The Mafia of a Sicilian Village*, p. 11.

36 On central Italy, see S. Silverman, 'Patronage and Community–Nation Relationships'; *idem*, 'Agricultural Organization, Social Structure and Values in Italy: Amoral Familism Reconsidered', *American Anthropologist*, 70 (1968), 1–20; *idem*, 'Exploitation in Rural Central Italy: Structure and Ideology in Stratification Study', *Comparative Studies in Society and History*, 12 (1970), 327–39; and R. Wade, 'Political Behaviour and World View in a Central Italian Village', in F.G. Bailey, ed., *Gift and Poison*, Oxford, Basil Blackwell, 1971, pp. 252–80.

37 S. Silverman, 'Patronage and Community–Nation Relationships', p. 188.

38 On Spanish patterns of clientelism, see R. Aya, *The Missed Revolution*; J. Corbin, 'Social Class and Patron–Clientage in Andalusia: Some Problems on Comparing Ethnographies', *Anthropological Quarterly*, 52:2 (1979), 99–114; M. Kenny, 'Patterns of Patronage in Spain', *Anthropological Quarterly*, 33 (1960), 14–23; *idem*, 'Parallel Power Structures in Castile: The Patron–Client Balance', in J.G. Peristiany, ed., *Contributions to Mediterranean Sociology*, Paris and The Hague, Mouton, 1968, pp. 155–62; *idem*, *A Spanish Tapestry: Town and Country in Castile*, New York, Harper and Row, 1966; and J. Pitt-Rivers, *The People of the Sierra*, New York, Criterion, 1954. On *compadrazgo* in Spain see G.M. Foster, 'Cofradía and Compadrazgo in Spain and Spanish America', *Southwestern Journal of Anthropology*, 9 (1953), 1–28; and J. Pitt-Rivers, 'Ritual Kinship in Spain', *Transactions of the New York Academy of Sciences*, Series 2, 20 (1958), 424–31. On *caciquismo*, see F.B. Pike, *Hispanismo, 1898–1936*, Notre Dame, University of Notre Dame Press, 1971, chapter 1; R. Kern, 'Spanish Caciquismo: A Classic Model', in *idem*, ed., *The Caciques: Oligarchical Politics and the System of Caciquismo in the Luso-Hispanic World*, Albuquerque, University of New Mexico Press, 1973, pp. 42–55; J. Costa, 'Oligarquía y caciquismo como la forma actual de gobierno en España', in *Oligarquía y caciquismo: Colectivismo agrario y otros escritos*, Madrid, Alianza, 1967, pp. 15–45; and J. Romero-Maura, 'Caciquismo as a Political System', in E. Gellner and J. Waterbury, eds., *Patrons and Clients*, pp. 53–62. See also J. Martínez-Alier, *Labourers and Landowners in Southern Spain*, London, George Allen and Unwin, 1971; and E. Malefakis, *Agrarian Reform and Peasant Revolution in Spain*, New Haven, Conn., Yale University Press, 1970; J.J. Linz, 'An Authoritarian Regime: Spain', in E. Allardt and Y. Lettunen, eds., *Cleavages, Ideologies and Party Systems*, Transactions of the

Westermarck Society, Helsinki, 1964, pp. 291–342; and R. Carr, *Spain, 1808–1939*, London, Oxford University Press, 1966.
39 M. Kenny, 'Patterns of Patronage in Spain', in S. Schmidt *et al.*, eds., *Friends, Followers, and Factions*, p. 356.
40 M. Kenny, 'Parallel Power Structures in Castile'.
41 On Greece, see K. Legg, *Politics in Modern Greece*, Stanford, Calif., Stanford University Press, 1969; *idem*, 'Political Change in a Clientelist Polity: The Failure of Democracy in Greece', *Journal of Political and Military Sociology*, 1:2 (1973), 231–46; *idem*, 'Retreat to the Barracks: Perspectives on the Collapse of the Military Regime in Greece', unpublished MS, n.d.; N. Mouzelis, 'Class and Clientelistic Politics: The Case of Greece', *Sociological Review* (N.S.), 26:3 (1978), 471–97; S.E. Aschenbrenner, 'Folk Model vs. Actual Practice: The Distribution of Spiritual Kin in a Greek Village', *Anthropological Quarterly*, 48:2 (1975), 65–86; S.G. McNall, *The Greek Peasant: Values in Conflict*, Washington, American Sociological Association, 1974; *idem*, 'Value Systems that Inhibit Modernization: The Case of Greece', *Studies in Comparative International Development*, 9:3 (1974), 46–63; and W.H. McNeill, *The Metamorphosis of Greece Since World War II*, Chicago and London, University of Chicago Press, 1978. On the Sarakatsani in particular, see J.K. Campbell, *Honour, Family and Patronage: A Study of Social Institutions and Values in a Greek Mountain Community*, Oxford, Clarendon Press, 1964. On clientelistic mediation focused in the economic sphere, see J.K. Campbell, 'Two Case Studies of Marketing and Patronage in Greece', in J.G. Peristiany, ed., *Contributions to Mediterranean Sociology*, pp. 143–58.
42 W.H. McNeill, *The Metamorphosis of Greece*, p. 228.
43 *Ibid.*, p. 95.
44 Before we go into the analysis of patron–client relations in another geographical area, it should be emphasised that we have analysed in detail only some of the patterns of clientelism found in southern Europe. The cases of Malta, southern France (especially the zone of Nice, Quercy and Corsica), Sardinia, Cyprus – as well as of Ireland in northern Europe – resemble most of the patterns which were presented above and hence were not discussed in particular. The reader is referred for Malta to the following works: J. Boissevain, 'Maltese Village Politics and their Relation to National Politics', *Studies*, 1:3 (1962), 211–22; *idem*, 'Factions, Parties, and Politics in a Maltese Vilage', *American Anthropologist*, 66 (1964), 1275–87; *idem*, *Saints and Fireworks: religion and Politics in Rural Malta*, London, Athlone Press, 1965; and *idem*, 'When the Saints Go Marching Out: Reflections on the Decline of Patronage in Malta', in E. Gellner and J. Waterbury, eds., *Patrons and Clients*, pp. 81–96. On France, see J.F. Médard, 'Le Clientelisme politique sous la Vème République: Persistance ou renouveau?', MS, 1978; *idem*, 'Political Clientelism in France: The Center–Periphery Nexus Reexamined', in S.N. Eisentstadt and R. Lemarchand, eds., *Political Clientelism, Patronage and Development*, pp. 125–71, and bibliographical references there; and B. Percivall, 'Truffles and Politics in Quercy', *Ethnos*, 39 (1974), 44–52. On Sardinia, see A. Weingrod, 'Patrons, Patronage, and Political Parties', *Comparative Studies in Society and History*, 10 (1968), 376–400; and A.

Weingrod and E. Morin, 'Post Peasants: The Character of Contemporary Sardinian Society', *ibid.*, 13 (1971), 301–24. On Cyprus, see P. Loizos, 'Politics and Patronage in a Cypriot Village, 1920–1970', in E. Gellner and J. Waterbury, eds., *Patrons and Clients*, pp. 115–36; and M. Attalides, 'Forms of Peasant Incorporation in Cyprus during the Last Century', *ibid.*, pp. 137–56. On Ireland, see M. Bax, 'Patronage Irish Style: Irish Politicians as Brokers', *Sociologische Gids*, 17 (1970), 179–91; *Harpstrings and Confessions: An Anthropological Study of Politics in Northern Ireland*, Amsterdam, Amsterdam University Press, 1973; *idem*, 'The Political Machine and its Importance in the Irish Republic', *Political Anthropology*, 1:1 (1975), 6–20; and J.H. Whyte, 'Landlord Influence at Elections in Ireland: 1760–1885', *English Historical Review*, 80 (1965), 740–60.

45 On clientelism in Turkey, see E. Akarli and G. Ben-Dor, eds., *Political Participation in Turkey*, Istanbul, Bogazici University Publications, 1975, especially the articles by A. Kudat, 'Patron–Client Relations: The State of the Art and Research in Eastern Turkey', pp. 61–88; by E. Özbudun, 'Political Participation in Rural Turkey', pp. 33–60; and by S. Sayari, 'Some Notes on the Beginnings of Mass Political Participation', pp. 121–33; A. Sertel, 'Ritual Kinship in Eastern Turkey', *Anthropological Quarterly*, 44:1 (1971), 37–50; P.G. Magnarella, 'Descent, Affinity and Ritual Relations in Eastern Turkey', *American Anthropologist*, 75 (1973), 1626–33; M. Meeker, 'The Great Family Aghas of Turkey: A Study of Changing Political Culture', in R. Antoun and I. Harik, eds., *Rural Politics and Social Change in the Middle East*, Bloomington, Indiana University Press, 1972, pp. 237–66; S. Sayari, 'Political Patronage in Turkey', in E. Gellner and J. Waterbury, eds., *Patrons and Clients*, pp. 103–14; and E. Özbudun, 'Turkey: The Politics of Clientelism', in S.N. Eisenstadt and R. Lemarchand, eds., *Political Clientelism, Patronage and Development*, pp. 249–68.

46 E. Özbudun, 'Turkey: The Politics of Clientelism', p. 261.

47 On Jordan, see A. Farrag, 'The Wastah among Jordanian Villagers', in E. Gellner and J. Waterbury, eds., *Patrons and Clients*, pp. 225–38; and P. Gubser, *Politics and Change in Al-Karak, Jordan: A Study of a Small Arab Town and its District*, London, Oxford University Press, 1973.

48 On northern Iraq, see A. Vinogradov, 'Ethnicity, Cultural Discontinuity and Power Brokers in Northern Iraq: The Case of the Shabak', *American Ethnologist*, 1:1 (1974), 207–18; and A. Rassam, 'Al-Taba'iyya: Power, Patronage, and Marginal Groups in Northern Iraq', in E. Gellner and J. Waterbury, eds., *Patrons and Clients*, pp. 157–66. On patron–client relations in Iraq in general, see D. Pool, 'The Politics of Patronage: Elites and Social Structure in Iraq', Princeton University Ph.D. thesis, 1972.

49 A. Rassam, 'Al-Taba'iyya', p. 158.

50 On the Ottoman period, see G. Baer, 'Patrons and Clients in Ottoman Cairo', MS, University of Jerusalem, 1979; on the *futuwwat*, see S. el-Messiri, 'The Changing Role of the Futuwwa in the Social Structure of Cairo', in E. Gellner and J. Waterbury, eds., *Patrons and Clients*, pp. 239–54. On the *shillal* analysed below, see C.H. Moore, 'Clientelist Ideology and Political Change: Fictitious Networks in Egypt and Tunisia', *ibid.*, pp. 255–74.

51 On Lebanon, see A. Hottinger, 'Zuama in Historical Perspective', in L. Binder, ed., *Politics in Lebanon*, New York, John Wiley and Sons, 1966, pp. 85–105; P. Gubser, 'The Zu'ama of Zahlah: The Current Situation in a Lebanese Town', *Middle East Journal*, 27:2 (1973), 173–89; I.F. Harik, 'The Iqta' System in Lebanon: A Comparative Political View', *ibid.*, 19:4 (1965), 405–21; J.G. Jabbra and N.W. Jabbra, 'Local Political Dynamics in Lebanon: The Case of 'Ain el-Qasis', *Anthropological Quarterly*, 51:2 (1978), 137–51; M. Johnson, 'Political Bosses and their Gangs: Zu'ama and Qabadayat in the Sunni Muslim Quarters of Beirut', in E. Gellner and J. Waterbury, eds., *Patrons and Clients*, pp. 207–24; and S. Khalaf, 'Changing Forms of Political Patronage in Beirut', *ibid.*, pp. 185–206.

52 On Moroccan clientelism, see K. Brown, *People of Salé: Tradition and Change in a Moroccan City, 1830–1930*, Manchester, Manchester University Press, 1976; *idem*, 'Changing Forms of Patronage in a Moroccan City', in E. Gellner and J. Waterbury, eds., *Patrons and Clients*, pp. 309–28; E. Gellner, *Saints of the Atlas*, Chicago, Ill., Chicago University Press, 1969; *idem*, 'The Great Patron: A Reinterpretation of Tribal Rebellions', *Archives Européennes de Sociologie*, 10 (1969), 61–9; E. Burke, 'Morocco and the Near East', *ibid.*, 70–94; J. Waterbury, *The Commander of the Faithful. The Moroccan Political Elite: A Study in Segmented Politics*, London, Weidenfeld and Nicolson, 1970; *idem*, 'Endemic and Planned Corruption in a Monarchical Regime', *World Politics*, 25:4 (1973), 533–55; E. Hagopian, 'The Status and Role of the Marabout in pre-Protectorate Morocco', *Ethnology*, 3 (1964), 42–52; L. Rosen, 'Rural Political Process and National Political Structure in Morocco', in R. Antoun and I. Harik, eds., *Rural Politics and Social Change in the Middle East*, pp. 214–36; B.G. Hoffman, *The Structure of Traditional Moroccan Rural Society*, The Hague and Paris, Mouton, 1967; E. Gellner and C. Micaud, eds., *Arabs and Berbers: From Tribe to Nation in North Africa*, London, Duckworth, 1973; and D. Seddon, *Moroccan Peasants: A Century of Change in the Eastern Rif, 1870–1970*, Folkestone, Kent, Dawson, 1981. On *elfuf* alliances and factions and the networks of interpersonal obligations in the rural society, see J. D. Seddon, *Moroccan Peasants*, especially chapter 4, 'Local Politics and the State', pp. 82–109; *idem*, 'Local Politics and State Intervention: Northeast Morocco from 1870 to 1970', in E. Gellner and C. Micaud, eds., *Arabs and Berbers*, pp. 109–39; and B.G. Hoffman, *The Structure of Traditional Moroccan Rural Society*.

53 On clientelism in Latin America, see R. Kern, ed., *The Caciques*, Albuquerque, University of New Mexico Press, 1973; J. Malloy, ed., *Authoritarianism and Corporatism in Latin America*, Pittsburgh, N.J., University of Pittsburgh Press, 1977; H.J. Wiarda, ed., *Politics and Social Change in Latin America*, Amherst, University of Massachusetts Press, 1974; P. Singelmann, 'The Closing Triangle: Critical Notes on a Model for Peasant Mobilization in Latin America', *Comparative Studies in Society and History*, 17:4 (1975), 389–409; A. Strickon and S. Greenfield, eds., *Structure and Process in Latin America: Patronage and Power Systems*, Albuquerque, University of New Mexico Press, 1972; and E. Hermitte and L. Bartolomé, eds., *Procesos de articulación social*, Buenos Aires, C.L.A.C.S.O. and Amorrortu, 1977. For

some of the patterns of patron–client relations not anlysed in detail below, see F. Hicks, 'Interpersonal Relationship and Caudillismo in Paraguay', *Journal of Inter-American Studies and World Affairs*, 13:1 (1971), 89–111; M. Crespi, 'Changing Power Relations: The Rise of Peasant Unions in Traditional Ecuadorian Haciendas', *Anthropological Quarterly*, 44:4 (1971), 223–40; S.W. Mintz, 'Pratik: Haitian Personal Economic Relationships', in J.M. Potter, M.N. Diaz and G.M. Foster, eds., *Peasant Society: A Reader*, Boston, Mass., Little, Brown, 1967, pp. 98–110; J.R. Gregory, 'Image of Limited Good, or Expectation of Reciprocity?', *Current Anthropology*, 16:1 (1975), 73–92; and E. Hermitte and L. Bartolomé, *Procesos de articulación social*.

54 See S. Schmidt, 'The Transformation of Clientelism in Rural Colombia'; *idem*, 'Bureaucrats as Modernizing Brokers: Clientelism in Colombia', *Comparative Politics*, 6:33 (1974), 425–50; *idem*, 'La Violencia Revisited: The Clientelist Bases of Political Violence in Colombia. The Case of Cali', *Journal of Latin American Studies*, 6:1 (1974), 97–111; and A. Osborn, 'Compadrazgo and Patronage: A Colombian Case', *Man* (N.S.), 3 (1968), 593–608.

55 On Brazilian clientelism see A. Brumer, 'O sistema paternalista no Brasil', *Revista do Instituto de Filosofia e Ciencias Humanas da Universidade Federal do Rio Grande do Sul*, 4 (1976), 57–79; G. Freyre, 'The Patriarchal Basis of Brazilian Society', in J. Maier and R. Weatherhead, eds., *Politics and Change in Latin America*, New York, Praeger, 1964, pp. 155–73; B. Galjart, 'Class and "Following" in Rural Brazil', *América Latina*, 7:3 (1964), 3–24; *idem*, 'A Further Note on Followings', *ibid.*, 8:3 (1965), 145–52; B. Hutchinson, 'The Patron–Dependent Relationship in Brazil: A Preliminary Examination', *Sociologia Ruralis*, 6 (1966), 3–30; and A.O. Cintra, 'A politica tradicional brasileira: uma interpretação das relações entre o centro e a periferia', *Cadernos DCP* (Belo Horizonte), 1 (1974), 59–112. On *coronelismo* in particular see V.N. Leal, *Coronelismo, enxada e voto*, São Paolo, Editora Alfa–Omega, 1978 (c. 1948); Eul-Soo Pand, *Coronelismo e oligarquias (1889–1934)*, Rio de Janeiro, Civilização Brasileira, 1979; and P. Cammack, 'O "coronelismo" e o "compromiso coronelista": Uma critica', *Cadernos DCP*, 5 (1979), 1–20. An interesting work on patron–client relations in modern peripheral areas is S. Greenfield, 'Patronage, Politics, and the Articulation of Local Community and National Society in pre-1968 Brazil', *Journal of Inter-American Studies and World Affairs*, 19:2 (1977), 139–72. See also R. Roett, *Brazil: Politics in a Patrimonial Society*, Boston, Allyn and Bacon, 1972; X. Stephen, ed., *Authoritarian Brazil*, New Haven, Conn., Yale University Press, 1973; and S. Schwartzman, *São Paolo e o Estado Nacional*, São Paulo, D.I.F.E.L., 1975.

56 On the Peruvian patterns see F. La Mond Tullis, *Lord and Peasant in Peru: A Paradigm of Political and Social Change*, Cambridge, Mass., Harvard University Press, 1970; H.L. Karno, 'Julio César Arana: Frontier Cacique in Peru', in R. Kern, ed., *The Caciques*, pp. 89–98; L. Guasti, 'Peru; Clientelism and Internal Control', in S. Schmidt *et al.*, eds., *Friends, Followers, and Factions*, pp. 422–38; D. Collier, *Squatters and Oligarchs: Authoritarian Rule and Policy Change in Peru*, Baltimore, Md, Johns Hopkins University Press, 1976; J. Cottler, 'The Mechanisms of Internal Domination and Social Change in

Peru', in I.L. Horowitz, ed., *Masses in Latin America*, New York, Oxford University Press, 1970, pp. 407–44; and L. Guasti, 'Clientelism in Decline: A Peruvian Regional Study', in S.N. Eisenstadt and R. Lemarchand, eds., *Political Clientelism: Patronage and Development*, pp. 217–48.

57 For Bolivia, see J. Dandler, *Politics of Leadership: Patronage and Brokerage in the Campesino Movements of Cochabamba, Bolivia (1935–1954)*, Michigan University Microfilms, Ann Arbor, 1971; and D.C. Heath, 'New Patrons for Old: Changing Patron–Client Relationships in the Bolivian Yungas', *Ethnology*, 12:1 (1973), 75–98.

58 On the relations analysed here, see A. Strickon, 'Estancieros y gauchos: clase, cultura y articulación social', in E. Hermitte and L.J. Bartolomé, eds., *Procesos de articulación social*, pp. 55–9; idem, 'The Euro-American Ranching Complex', in A. Leeds and A. Vayda, eds., *Man, Culture, and Animals: The Role of Animals in Human Ecological Adjustments*, Washington, American Association for the Advancement of Science, 1965; idem, 'Carlos Felipe: Kinsman, Patron, and Friend', in A. Strickon and S.M. Greenfield, eds., *Structure and Process in Latin America: Patronage, Clientage, and Power Systems*, Albuquerque, University of New Mexico Press, 1972, pp. 43–69.

59 On Mexican clientelism, see S. Kaufmann Purcell, 'Mexico: Clientelism, Corporatism and Political Stability', in S.N. Eisenstadt and R. Lemarchand, eds., *Political Clientelism, Patronage and Development*, pp. 191–216; L. Paré, 'Caciquisme et structure du pouvoir dans le Mexique rural', *Canadian Review of Sociology and Anthropology*, 10:1 (1973), 20–43; A. Ugalde, 'Contemporary Mexico: From Hacienda to PRI Political Leadership in a Zapotec Village', in R. Kern, ed., *The Caciques*, pp. 119–34; F. Rothstein, 'The Class Basis of Patron–Client Relations', *Latin American Perspectives*, 6:2 (1979), 25–35; L. Lomnitz, 'Mechanisms of Articulation between Shantytown Settlers and the Urban System', *Urban Anthropology*, 7:2 (1978), 185–205; R.F. Adie, 'Cooperation, Cooptation and Conflict in Mexican Peasant Organizations', *Inter-American Economic Affairs*, 24:3 (1970), 3–25; B. Anderson and J.D. Cockcroft, 'Control and Cooptation in Mexican Politics', *International Journal of Comparative Sociology*, 7 (1966), 11–28; R. Bartra *et al.*, *Caciquismo y poder político en el México rural*, Mexico, Siglo XXI, 1975; R.Th. Buve, 'Patronaje en las zonas rurales de México', *Boletín de Estudios Latino-americanos y del Caribe* (Amsterdam), 16 (1974), 118–56; W.A. Cornelius, Jr, 'Contemporary Mexico: A Structural Analysis of Urban Caciquismo', in R. Kern, ed., *The Caciques*, pp. 135–50; G.M. Foster, *Tzintzuntzan: Mexican Peasants in a Changing World*, Boston, Little, Brown, 1967; P. Friedrich, 'A Mexican Cacicazgo', *Ethnology*, 4:2 (1965), 190–209; idem, 'The Legitimacy of a Cacique', in M.J. Swartz, *Local-Level Politics*, pp. 243–69; idem, *Agrarian Revolt in a Mexican Village*, Englewood Cliffs, N.J., Prentice-Hall, 1970; M.S. Grindle, *Bureaucrats, Politicians, and Peasants in Mexico: A Case Study in Public Policy*, Berkeley, University of California Press, 1977; idem, 'Patrons and Clients in the Bureaucracy: Career Networks in Mexico', *Latin American Research Review*, 12:1 (1977), 37–65; G. Huizer, 'The Role of Patronage in the Peasant Political Struggle', *Sociologische Gids*, 16:6 (1969), 411–18; J.M. Ingham, 'The Asymmetrical Implications of Godparenthood in Tlayacapan,

Morelos', *Man* (N.S.), 5 (1970), 281–9; H. Nutini and G.R. White, 'Community Variations and Network Structure in the Social Functions of Compadrazgo in Rural Tlaxcala, Mexico', *Ethnology*, 16:4 (1977), 353–84; and U. Köhler, 'Patterns of Interethnic Economic Exchange in Southeastern Mexico', *Journal of Anthropological Research*, 36 (1980), 316–37.

60 S. Kaufman Purcell, 'Mexico: Clientelism, Corporatism and Political Stability', p. 203.

61 See C.F. Keyes, *The Golden Peninsula: Culture and Adaptation in Mainland Southeast Asia*, London, Macmillan; New York, Collier Macmillan, 1977; C.H. Landé, 'Networks and Groups in Southeast Asia: Some Observations on the Group Theory of Politics', *American Political Science Review*, 67:1 (1973), 103–27; J.C. Scott, 'Patron–Client Politics and Political Change in Southeast Asia', *ibid.*, 66:1 (1972), 91–113; *idem*, 'The Erosion of Patron–Client Bonds and Social Change in Rural Southeast Asia', *Journal of Asian Studies*, 32:1 (1972), 5–37; *idem*, *The Moral Economy of the Peasant: Rebellion and Subsistence in Southeast Asia*, New Haven, Conn., Yale University Press, 1976; J.C. Scott and B.J. Kerkvliet, 'How Traditional Rural Patrons Lose Legitimacy: A Theory with Special Reference to Southeast Asia', *Cultures et Développement*, 5:3 (1973), 501–40; and W.F. Wertheim, 'Sociological Aspects of Corruption in Modern Asia', in *idem*, ed., *East–West Parallels: Sociological Approaches to Modern Asia*, The Hague, Van Hoeve, 1964, pp. 103–31. See also below and the bibliographical references in chapter 5.

62 J.C. Scott, 'Corruption, Machine Politics, and Political Change', *American Political Science Review*, 63:4 (1969), 1142–58.

63 On Indonesian clientelism, see K.D. Jackson, *Urbanization and the Rise of Patron–Client Relations: The Changing Quality of Interpersonal Communications in the Neighborhoods of Bandung and the Villages of West Java*, Cambridge, Mass., Center for International Studies, M.I.T., 1974; K.D. Jackson and L.W. Pye, *Political Power and Communications in Indonesia*, Berkeley, University of California Press, 1978; W.F. Wertheim, 'From Aliran Towards Class Struggle in the Countryside of Java', *Pacific Viewpoint*, 10:2 (1969), 1–17; R. Kahane, 'Hypotheses on Patronage and Social Change: A Comparative Perspective', *Ethnology* 23:1 (1984), 13–24.

64 K.D. Jackson, *Urbanization and the Rise of Patron–Client Relations*.

65 K.D. Jackson and L.W. Pye, *Political Power and Communications*, p. 36.

66 On Philippine patterns, see C.H. Landé, *Leaders, Factions, and Parties. The Structure of Philippine Politics*, Yale University Southeast Asian Studies, Monograph No. 6, New Haven, Conn., 1965; F. Lynch, *Four Readings in Philippine Values*, Quezon, Ateneo of Manila Press, 1964; D. Wurfel, 'Elites of Wealth and Elites of Power, the Changing Dynamic: A Philippine Case Study', in *Southeast Asian Affairs, 1979*, Institute of Southeast Asian Studies, Heinemann Educational Books, 1979, pp. 233–45; J.V. Abueva and R.P. de Guzmán, eds., *Foundations and Dynamics of Filipino Government and Politics*, Manila, Bookmark, 1969; R.E. Agpalo, *The Political Elites and the People: A Study of Politics in Occidental Mindoro*, Manila, College of Public Administration, 1972; M.R. Hollensteiner, *The Dynamics of Power in a Philippine Municipality*, Quezon City, University of the Philippines Com-

munity Development Research Council, 1968 (c. 1963); K.G. Machado, 'From Traditional Faction to Machine – Changing Patterns of Political Leadership and Organization in the Rural Philippines', *Journal of Asian Studies*, 33:4 (1974), 523–47; *idem*, 'Continuity and Change in Philippine Factionalism', in F.P. Belloni and D.C. Beller, eds., *Faction Politics: Political Parties and Factionalism in Comparative Perspective*, Santa Barbara and Oxford, A.B.C.–Clio, 1978, pp. 193–217; T. Nowak and K.A. Snyder, 'Urbanization and Clientelist Systems in the Philippines', *Philippine Journal of Public Administration*, 14 (1970); and *idem*, 'Clientelist Politics in the Philippines: Integration or Instability?', *American Political Science Review*, 68:3 (1974), 1147–70.

67 B. Staufer, *The Philippine Congress: Causes of Structural Change*, Beverly Hills and London, Sage Publications, 1975, p.33.

68 Thanks are due to Professor E. Cohen of the Hebrew University of Jerusalem for his comments on the Thai material. On Thailand, see E.B. Ayal, ed., *The Study of Thailand*, Athens, Ohio, Ohio University Center for International Studies, 1978; and N. Jacobs, *Modernization Without Development: Thailand as an Asian Case Study*, New York, Praeger, 1971. On *nāi–phrai* links in the Siamese kingdom, see A. Rabidhadana, *The Organization of Thai Society in the Early Bangkok Period: 1782–1872*, Ithaca, N.Y., Cornell University Press, 1969; and *idem*, 'Clientship and Class Structure in the Early Bangkok Period', in G.W. Skinner and A.T. Kirsch, eds., *Change and Persistence in Thai Society: Essays in Honor of Lauristan Sharp*, pp. 93–124. On later patterns of clientelism in Thailand see L.M. Hanks, Jr, 'Merit and Power in the Thai Social Order', *American Anthropologist*, 64 (1962), 1247–61; *idem*, 'The Corporation and the Entourage: A Comparison of Thai and American Social Organization', *Catalyst*, Summer 1966; D.W. Millar, 'Patron–Client Relations in Thailand', *Cornell Journal of Social Relations*, 6:2 (1971), 215–25; F.W. Riggs, 'Interest and Clientele Groups', in J.L. Sutton, ed., *Problems of Politics and Administration in Thailand*, Bloomington, Indiana University Press, 1962, pp. 153–92; *idem*, *Thailand: The Modernization of a Bureaucratic Polity*, Honolulu, East–West Center Press, 1966; E. Shor, 'The Thai Bureaucracy', *Administrative Science Quarterly*, 5 (1960), 66–86; C.D. Neher, *The Dynamics of Politics and Administration in Rural Thailand*, Athens, Ohio, Ohio University Center for International Studies, Southeast Asian Series No. 30, 1974; H.P. Phillips, *The Peasant Personality: The Patterning of Interpersonal Relations in the Village of Bang Chou*, Berkeley, University of California Press, 1965; D.F. Haas, 'Clientelism and Rural Development in Thailand', *Rural Sociology*, 43:2 (1978), 280–92; also cf. J.M. Potter, *Thai Peasant Social Structure*, Chicago, Ill., University of Chicago Press, 1976.

69 L.M. Hanks, 'The Thai Social Order as Entourage and Circle', in Skinner and Kirsch, eds., *Change and Persistence*, pp. 197–218.

70 F.W. Riggs, 'The "Sala" Model', *Philippine Journal of Public Administration*, 6 (1962), 3–16.

71 F.W. Riggs, *Administration in Developing Countries: The Theory of Prismatic Society*, Boston, Houghton Mifflin, 1964.

72 See among others L.M. Hanks, Jr, 'American Aid is Damaging Thai Society', *Transaction*, 5:10 (1968), 29–34; L. Guasti, 'Peru: Clientelism and Internal Control'; and R. Lemarchand, 'Comparative Political Clientelism: Structure, Process and Optic', in S.N. Eisenstadt and R. Lemarchand, eds., *Political Clientelism, Patronage and Development*, pp. 7–32.

73 H.J. Rubin, 'Will and Awe: Illustrations of Thai Village Dependency upon Officials', *Journal of Asian Studies*, 32:3 (1973), 425–44; p. 431. See also R.L. Mole, *Thai Values and Behaviour Patterns*, Rulant, Vermont and Tokyo, Tuttpe, 1973; and H.J. Rubin, 'Rules, Regulations, and the Rural Thai Bureaucracy', *Journal of Southeast Asian Studies*, 11:1 (1980), 50–73.

74 On Burma, see M.E. Spiro, 'Factionalism and Politics in Village Burma', in M. Swartz, *Local-Level Politics*, pp. 401–21; L.M. Hanks, 'Entourage and Circle in Burma', *Bennington Review*, 2:1 (1968), 32–46; and S.M. Bekker, 'The Concept of Anade: Personal, Social and Political Implications', in J.P. Ferguson, ed., *Essays on Burma*, Volume 16 of *Contributions to Asian Studies*, Leiden, E.J. Brill, 1981, pp. 19–37.

75 S.M. Bekker, 'The Concept of Anade', p. 21.

76 On Chinese networks, see M. Fried, *Fabric of Chinese Society*, New York, Praeger, 1953; Hsia-T'ung Fei, *China's Gentry: Essays in Rural–Urban Relations*, Chicago, Ill., Chicago University Press, 1953; G.W. Skinner, 'Marketing and Social Structure in Rural China', *Journal of Asian Studies*, 24 (1964/65), 3–43, 195–228, and 363–99; L.W. Pye, *Warlord Politics: Conflict and Coalition in the Modernization of Republican China*, New York, Praeger, 1971; and *idem, The Spirit of Chinese Politics*, Cambridge, Mass., M.I.T. Press, 1968; on the *mu-fu* system, see K.E. Folsom, *Friends, Guests and Colleagues: The Mu-Fu System in the Late Ch'ing Period*, Berkeley, University of California Press, 1968; on interpersonal networks in Communist China, see A.J. Nathan, 'A Factionalism Model for CCP Politics', *China Quarterly*, 53 (1973), 34–66; and L.W. Pye, *The Dynamics of Factions and Consensus in Chinese Politics: A Model and Some Proposals*, A Project Air Force Report for the United States Air Forces, Rand Corporation, Santa Monica, Calif., 1980.

77 See, for instance, R. Mousnier, *Peasant Uprisings in Seventeenth Century France, Russia and China*, London, George Allen and Unwin, 1971.

78 K.E. Folsom, *Friends, Guests and Colleagues*, pp. 78–189.

79 See A.J. Nathan, 'An Analysis of Factionalism of Chinese Communist Party Politics', in F.P. Belloni and D.C. Beller, eds., *Faction Politics*, Santa Barbara and Oxford, A.B.C.–Clio, 1978, pp. 387–414; and L.W. Pye, *The Dynamics of Factions and Consensus*.

80 On the *oyabun–kobun* relationship and its context, see I. Ishino, 'The Oyabun–Kobun: A Japanese Ritual Kinship Institution', *American Anthropologist*, 55:1 (1953), 695–707; J.W. Bennet and I. Ishino, *Paternalism in the Japanese Economy: Anthropological Studies of Oyabun–Kobun Patterns*, Minneapolis, University of Minnesota Press, 1963; C. Nakane, *Japanese Society*, London, Weidenfeld and Nicolson, 1970; T.P. Rohlen, *For Harmony and Strength: Japanese White Collar Organization in Anthropological Perspective*, Berkeley, University of California Press, 1976; J.C. Abegglen, *The Japanese Factory*, New York, Free Press, 1958; and H. Befu, 'Power in Exchange:

Strategy of Control and Patterns of Compliance in Japan', *Asian Profile* (Hong Kong), 2:6 (1974), 601–22.

81 See R.K. Beardsley *et al.*, *Village Japan*, Chicago, Ill., Chicago University Press, 1959.

82 I. Najita, *Japan*, Englewood Cliffs, N.J., Prentice-Hall, 1974, p. 7. In modern times, *giri* obligations are interrelated with the once opposed concept of *on* which refers to the subordinate's sense of indebtedness and even love for favours bestowed by a superior, and with the concept of *onjō–shugi* (paternalism). On these concepts and their significance, see H. Befu, 'Gift Giving in a Modernizing Japan'; N. Ike, *Japanese Politics*, pp. 30ff.; C. Nakane, *Japanese Society*; and R.P. Dore, *City Life in Japan*.

83 See, for instance, the comment on clientelism in Japan by N. Ike in *Studies in Comparative Communism*, 12:2–3 (1979), 159–211.

84 On the *jajmani* relationship see J.P. Parry, *Caste and Kinship in Kangra*, London, Henley and Boston, Routledge and Kegan Paul, 1979; H. Gould, 'The Hindu Jajmani System: A Case of Economic Particularism', *Southwestern Journal of Anthropology*, 14 (1958), 428–37; P.M. Kolenda, 'Toward a Model of the Hindu Jajmani System', *Human Organization*, 22 (1963), 11–31; T.O. Beidelman, *A Comparative Analysis of the Jajmani System*, New York, Association for Asian Studies, Augustin, 1959; J. Benson, 'A South Indian Jajmani System', *Ethnology*, 16:3 (1976), 239–50; W. Wiser and C. Wiser, *Behind Mud Walls 1939–1940*, Berkeley, University of California Press, 1971; O. Lewis and V. Barnouw, 'Caste and the Jajmani System in a North Indian Village', in J.M. Potter *et al.*, eds., *Peasant Society: A Reader*, pp. 110–34; and J.Elder, 'Rajpur: Change in the Jajmani System of an Uttar Pradesh Village', in K. Ishwaran, ed., *Change and Continuity in India's Villages*, New York, Columbia University Press, 1970, pp. 105–27. See also note 13 in chapter 5.

85 L. Dumont, *Homo Hierarchicus. Essai sur le système des castes*, Paris, Gallimard, 1968.

86 See, for instance, R. Lemarchand, 'Power and Stratification in Rwanda: A Reconsideration', *Cahiers d'Etudes Africaines*, 6:24 (1966), 592–610; *idem*, 'Les Relations de clientèle comme agent de contestation: Le cas du Ruanda', *Civilisations*, 18:4 (1968), 553–78; also L. Mair, 'Clientship in East Africa', *Cahiers d'Etudes Africaines*, 6 (1961), 315–25; J.P. Maquet, *The Premise of Inequality in Rwanda*, Oxford, International African Institute, 1961; and note 14 in chapter 5.

87 The sources for the appreciation of these relations are E.L. Peters on Cyrenaican Bedouins: see 'The Tied and the Free (Lybia)', in J.G. Peristiany, *Contributions to Mediterranean Sociology*, pp. 167–88; and 'Patronage in Cyrenaica', in E. Gellner and J. Waterbury, eds., *Patrons and Clients*, pp. 275–90.

88 On machine politics and bossism in the U.S.A. see, for instance, E.C. Banfield, ed., *Urban Government: A Reader in Administration and Politics*, New York, Free Press; London, Collier Macmillan, 1969, pp. 165–236; A.B. Callow, ed., *The City Boss in America: An Interpretative Reader*, New York, Oxford University Press, 1976, parts I–IV; F.J. Sorauf, 'Patronage and Party', *Midwest Journal of Political Science*, 3:2 (1959), 114–26; J.Q. Wilson,

'The Economy of Patronage', *Journal of Political Economy*, 49 (1961), 369–80; E.C. Banfield and J.Q. Wilson, *City Politics*, Cambridge, Mass., Harvard University Press, 1965; M. Tolchin and S. Tolchin, *To the Victor: Political Patronage from the Clubhouse to the White House*, New York, Random House, 1971; and R.E. Wolfinger, 'Why Political Machines Have Not Withered Away and Other Revisionist Thoughts', *Journal of Politics*, 34 (1972), 365–98.

89 W.L. Riordon, *Plunkitt of Tammany Hall*, New York, Dutton, 1963.

90 On clientelism in the Soviet Union, see P. Fainsod, *Smolensk under Soviet Rule*, Cambridge, Mass., Harvard University Press, 1958; P. Frank, 'How to Get On in the Soviet Union', *New Society*, 5 June 1969, 867–8; H. Smith, *The Russians*, London, Sphere Books, 1976; G. Ionescu, 'Patronage under Communism', in E. Gellner and J. Waterbury, eds., *Patrons and Clients*, pp. 97–102; J.P. Willerton *et al.*, 'Clientelism in the Soviet Union', *Studies in Comparative Communism*, 12:2–3 (1979), 159–211. J. Hough, *The Soviet Prefects: The Local Party Organs in Industrial Decision-Making*, Cambridge, Mass., Harvard University Press, 1969; and T.H. Rigby, 'Crypto-Politics', *Survey* 50 (1964), 183–94.

91 Z. Bauman, 'Comment on Eastern Europe', in *Studies of Comparative Communism*, 12:2–3 (1979), 184–9.

92 On the *yuryokusha* in Japan and on clientelism in the political sphere, see among others H. Baerwald, 'Factional Politics in Japan', *Currrent History*, 60 (1964), 223–9; N. Ike, *Japanese Politics: Patron–Client Democracy*, New York, Knopf, 1972 (c. 1957); S.C. Flanagan, 'Voting Behavior in Japan: The Persistence of Traditional Patterns', *Comparative Political Studies*, 1:3 (1968), 391–412; M. Maruyama, *Thought and Behaviour in Modern Japanese Politics*, London, Oxford University Press, 1963; H. Fukui, 'Japan: Factionalism in a Dominant-Party System', in F.P. Belloni and D.C. Beller, *Faction Politics*, pp. 43–72; G.L. Curtis, *Election Campaigning, Japanese Style*, New York, Columbia University Press, 1971; R.A. Scalapino and J. Masumi, *Parties and Politics in Contemporary Japan*, Berkeley, University of California Press, 1971 (c. 1962); Y. Kuroda, *Reed Town, Japan: A Study in Community Power Structure and Political Change*, Honolulu, University Press of Hawaii, 1974; and N.B. Thayer, *How the Conservatives Rule Japan*, Princeton, N.J., Princeton University Press, 1969.

93 N. Ike, *Japanese Politics*, p. 75.

94 On this point see Kuroda, *Reed Town*. On the sources of electoral financing, see Baerwald, 'Factional Politics', p. 224. Flanagan ('Voting Behavior') indicates that *yuryokusha* must have sufficient wealth to take care of organisations, to manage festivals, weddings, etc. On the use of power for economic gains, see N. Ike, *Japanese Politics*, pp. 76ff.

95 J.W. White, 'Tradition and Politics in Studies of Contemporary Japan: Review Article', *World Politics*, 26:3 (1974), 400–27.

96 Y. Kuroda, *Reed Town*, pp. 183–4.

97 N. Ike, *Japanese Politics*, pp. 202–8. On participation in local and national electoral politics, see Kuroda, *Reed Town*; and Flanagan, 'Voting Behavior', *passim*.

98 See, for example. A. Weingrod, 'Patrons, Patronage and Political Parties';

A. Hall, 'Concepts and Terms: Patron–Client Relationship', *Journal of Peasant Studies*, 1 (1974), 506–9; L. Graziano, *A Conceptual Framework for the Study of Clientelism*; J. Boissevain, 'Patrons and Brokers'; A. Blok, 'Variations in Patronage', *Sociologische Gids*, 16:6 (1969), 365–78. For notable applications of such an approach to case studies, see P.A. Allum, *Politics and Society in Postwar Naples*; S.F. Silverman, 'Patronage and Community–Nation Relationships in Central Italy', *Ethnology*, 4:2 (1965), 172–89; J. Boissevain, 'When the Saints Go Marching Out: Reflections on the Decline of Patronage in Malta', in E. Gellner and J. Waterbury, eds., *Patrons and Clients*, pp. 81–96. Compare these definitions with E. Gellner, 'Patrons and Clients'; J. Waterbury, 'An Attempt to Put Patrons and Clients in Their Place'; and E. Wolf, 'Kinship, Friendship, and Patron–Client Relationships'.

Chapter 5

1 For examples of the limitation in scope and convertibility of the free flow of resources in these societies, see R. Aya, *The Missed Revolution: The Fate of Rural Rebels in Sicily and Southern Spain 1840–1850*; J.K. Campbell, 'Two Case-Studies of Marketing and Patronage in Greece', in J.G. Peristiany, ed., *Contributions to Mediterranean Sociology*, pp. 143–54; S. Sayari, 'Political Patronage in Turkey', in E. Gellner and J. Waterbury, eds., *Patrons and Clients*, pp. 103–14. For the pressures on clientelistic arrangements in these societies, see among others J. Boissevain, 'Poverty and Politics in a Sicilian Agrotown', *International Archives of Ethnography*, 50 (1966), 198–236; S. Tarrow, 'Economic Development and the Transformation of the Italian Party System', *Comparative Politics*, 1:2 (1969), 161–83; and *idem*, 'Local Constraints on Regional Reform: A Comparison of Italy and France', *Comparative Politics*, 7:1 (1974), 1–36. For a general treatment of this subject see S.N. Eisenstadt, 'Beyond Classical Revolution – Processes of Change and Revolution in Neo-Patrimonial Societies', in *idem*, ed., *Revolution and the Transformation of Societies: A Comparative Study of Civilizations*, New York, Free Press, 1978, pp. 272–310; see also below.
2 On the pluralistic model and open-market bureaucratic societies see S.N. Eisenstadt, ed., *Political Sociology*, pp. 488–521; and *idem*, 'Bureaucracy, Bureaucratization, Markets and Power Structure', in *idem*, ed., *Essays on Comparative Institutions*, New York, John Wiley and Sons, 1965, pp. 177–215. On the totalitarian model, see Z. Brzezinski, 'The Nature of the Soviet System', *Slavic Review*, 20:3 (1961), 354–68; R. Lowenthal, 'The Logic of One-Party Rule', in A. Brumberg, ed., *Russia under Krushchev: An Anthology for Problems of Communism*, New York, Praeger, 1962; T.H. Rigby, 'Traditional Market and Organizational Societies and the USSR', *World Politics*, 16:4 (1964), 539–57; J.J. Linz, 'Totalitarian and Authoritarian Regimes', in F.I. Greenstein and N.W. Polsby, eds., *Handbook of Political Science*, Reading, Mass., Addison-Wesley, 1975, pp 175–411; and T.H. Rigby, A. Brown, and P. Reddaway, eds., *Authority, Power and Policy in the USSR: Studies Dedicated to Leonard Shapiro*, New York, St Martin's Press, 1980. On caste systems see L. Dumont, *Homo Hierarchicus: Essai sur le*

système des castes, Paris, Gallimard, 1966; *idem*, ed., *Contributions to Indian Sociology*, Paris and The Hague, Mouton, 1966; M. Singer, 'The Social Organization of Indian Civilization', *Diogenes*, 45 (1964), 84–119; *idem*, ed., *Traditional India: Structure and Change*, Austin, American Folklore Society, University of Texas Press, 1959; K. David, 'Hierarchy and Equivalence in Jaffna: North Sri Lanka Normative Codes as Mediator', in *idem*, ed., *The New Wind: Changing Identities in South Asia*, Paris and The Hague, Mouton, 1976, pp. 179–276; and J.P. Perry, *Castle and Kinship in Kangra*, London, Henley and Boston, Routledge and Kegan Paul, 1979. On feudal models, see S.N. Eisenstadt, *Political Sociology*, chapter 7. On consociational models, see H. Daalder, 'The Consociational Democracy Theme', *World Politics*, 26:4 (1974), 604–21; A. Liphart, 'Consociational Democracy', *idem*, 21 (1969); *idem*, *The Politics of Accommodation: Pluralism and Democracy in the Netherlands*, Beverly Hills, University of California Press, 1968. See also G. Lembruch, *Proporzdemokratie. Politische System and politische Kultur in der Schweiz und Oesterreich*, Tübingen, Mohr, 1968 *idem*, 'Konkordanzdemokratie im politische System der Schweiz', *Vierteljahresschrift*, 9:3 (1968); and *idem*, 'Konkordanzdemokratie im internationalen System', *Politische Vierteljahresschrift*, vol. 10, Sonderheft.

3 On corporatism in Latin America, see J. Malloy, 'Authoritarianism and Corporatism in Latin America: The Modal Pattern', in *idem*, ed., *Authoritarianism and Corporatism in Latin America*, Pittsburgh, Pa, University of Pittsburgh Press, 1977, pp. 3–19; D.A. Chalmers, 'The Politicized State in Latin America', in *ibid.*, pp. 23–46; G.A. O'Donnell, 'Corporatism and the Question of State', in *ibid.*, pp. 47–87; S. Schwartzman, 'Back to Weber: Corporatism and Patrimonialism in the Seventies', in *ibid.*, pp. 89–106; R.R. Kaufman, 'Corporatism, Clientelism, and Partisan Conflict: A Study of Seven Latin American Countries', in *ibid.*, pp. 109–48; X. Stephen, ed., *Authoritarian Brazil*, New Haven, Yale University Press, 1973; and D. Collier, *The Authoritarianism in Latin America*, Princeton, N.J., Princeton University Press, 1979.

4 On these aspects of patron–client relations and especially on their fragility, see among others A. Blok, *The Mafia of a Sicilian Village*: E. Wolf, 'On Peasant Rebellions', *International Social Science Journal*, 21:2 (1969), 286–93; E. Gellner, 'How to Live in Anarchy', *The Listener*, 3:4 (1958), 579–83: *idem*, 'Patrons and Clients', in E. Gellner and J. Waterbury, eds., *Patrons and Clients*, pp. 1–6; F.H. Cardoso, 'Tensões sociais no campo e reforma agraria', *Revista brasileira de estudos politicos*, 12 (1961), 7–26; P. Friedrich, *Agrarian Revolt in a Mexican Village*; A. Hottinger, 'Zu'ama in Historical Perspective'; D. Pool, *The Politics of Patronage: Elites and Social Structure in Iraq*; and S. el-Messiri, 'The Changing Role of the Futuwwa'.

5 On possibilities of severing the relationship, see, for instance, A. Blok, 'Mafia and Peasant Rebellion as Contrasting Factors in Sicilian Latifundism', *Archives Européennes de Sociologie*, 10 (1969), 95–116; P. Singlemann, 'The Closing Triangle: Critical Notes on a Model for Peasant Mobilization in Latin America', *Comparative Studies in Society and History*, 17:4 (1975), 389–409. The quasi-legal or quasi-ritual fixation of modes of occupation of

roles may provide a way of avoiding the above possibility. See E.L. Peters, 'The Tied and the Free (Lybia)', in J.G. Peristiany, ed., *Contributions to Mediterranean Sociology*, pp. 167–88; and the analysis of the Japanese *oyabun–kobun* relationship in chapter 4. For a full treatment of these aspects see also chapter 7 below.

6 E. Goffman, 'Tightness and Looseness', in *Behavior in Public Places*, New York, Free Press, 1963, pp. 198–215.

7 On these cultural orientations, see C. Nakane, *Japanese Society*, London, Weidenfeld and Nicolson, 1970; R.P. Dore, *City Life in Japan: A Study of a Tokyo Ward*, London, Routledge and Kegan Paul, 1958; H. Befu, 'Gift Giving in a Modernizing Japan', *Monumenta Niponica*, 23:3–4 (n.d.), 445–56; *idem*, 'Gift-Giving and Social Reciprocity in Japan', *France–Asie/Asia*, 188 (1966/7), 161–77; I. Najita, *Japan*, Englewood Cliffs, N.J., Prentice-Hall, 1974; and also the section on Japan in chapter 4.

8 See C. Nakane, *Kinship and Economic Organization in Rural Japan*, London, Athlone Press, 1967; J.C. Abegglen, *The Japanese Factory*; T.P. Rohlen, *For Harmony and Strength*; and J.W. Bennett and I. Ishino, *Paternalism in the Japanese Industry*.

9 J.W. White, 'Tradition and Politics in Studies of Contemporary Japan: Review Article', *World Politics*, 26:3 (1974), 400–27.

10 See R.P. Dore, *City Life in Japan*, pp. 94ff.

11 C. Nakane, *Japanese Society*, p. 140.

12 See among many others Y. Kuroda, *Reed Town, Japan*; T.C. Smith, 'Japan's Aristocratic Revolution', in S.N. Eisenstadt, ed., *Political Sociology*, pp. 430–6; and M. Maruyama, 'The Ideology and Dynamics of Japanese Fascism', *ibid.*, pp. 537–41; on the feudal period, see J.W. Hall, 'Feudalism in Japan: A Reassessment', *Comparative Studies in Society and History*, 5 (1962), 15–51; and K. Asakawa, 'Some Aspects of Japanese Feudal Institutions', in S.N. Eisenstadt, ed., *Political Sociology*, pp. 239–45. On related aspects of centre–periphery relations and modernisation in Japan, see also M.B. Jansen and L. Stone, 'Education and Modernization in Japan and England', *Comparative Studies in Society and History*, 9:2 (1966/7), 208–32.

13 On these aspects of construction of exchange in the Indian settings, see the bibliographical references in chapter 4, as well as A. Béteille, *Studies in Agrarian Social Structure*, New York, Oxford University Press, 1974; J. Breman, *Patronage and Exploitation: Changing Agrarian Relations in South Gujarat, India*, Berkeley, University of California Press, 1974; and S. Epstein, 'Productive Efficiency and Customary Systems of Rewards in Rural South India', in R. Firth, ed., *Themes on Economic Anthropology*, London, Tavistock Press, 1967, pp. 229–52. On the transformations of the social structure in India and the dilemmas and problems of different strata in modern contexts which are analysed below, see among others A.T. Carter, *Elite Politics in Rural India: Political Stratification and Political Alliances in Western Maharashtra*, Cambridge, Cambridge University Press, 1974; A. Béteille, *Castes, Old and New: Essays in Social Structure and Social Stratification*, London, Asia Publishing House, 1969; and D.G. Mandelbaum, *Society in India*, 2 vols., Berkeley, University of California Press, 1970.

14 See R. Lemarchand, ed., *African Kingdoms in Perspective: Political Change and Modernization in Monarchical Settings*, London, F. Cass, 1977; the issues of *Cahiers d'Etudes Africaines*, 6 (1961), 292–325, and 9 (1969), 350–414. For references to works on similar links in East Africa, see L. Roniger, 'Clientelism and Patron–Client Relations: A Bibliography', pp. 316–18.

15 See, for instance, J.A. Armstrong, *The European Administrative Elite*, Princeton, Princeton University Press, 1973; F. Parkin, 'Class Stratification in Socialist Societies', *British Journal of Sociology*, 20:4 (1969), 355–74; and the issue of *Studies in Comparative Communism* devoted to 'Leadership and Political Succession', 9:1–2 (1976).

16 The data for the following description are drawn mainly from H.W. Morton, 'Who Gets What, When and How? Housing in the Soviet Union', *Soviet Studies*, 32:2 (1980), 235–59; and *idem*, 'Housing Problems and Policies of Eastern Europe and the Soviet Union', *Studies in Comparative Communism*, 12:4 (1979), 300–22.

17 Z. Bauman, 'Comment on Eastern Europe'.

18 J. Strong, 'Perils – the Boss, the Machine, the Immigrant: A Nineteenth Century View', in A.B. Callow, Jr, ed., *The City Boss in America*, New York, Oxford University Press, 1976, pp. 14–17.

19 On the changes analysed in these sections, see among others J.Q. Wilson, ed., *City Politics and Public Power*, New York, John Wiley and Sons, 1968; A.B. Callow, Jr, *The City Boss in America*, parts v and vi, pp. 171–327; M.S. Stedman, Jr, *Urban Politics*, Cambridge, Mass., Winthrop Publishers, 1975 (c. 1972); and M.J. Wells, 'Brokerage, Economic Opportunity, and the Growth of Ethnic Movements', *Ethnology*, 18:4 (1979), 399–414.

20 On this, see S.N. Eisenstadt, *Israeli Society*, New York, Basic Books, 1967, especially chapters 4, 5 and 9; and *idem*, *Transformations of Israeli Society*, London, Weidenfeld and Nicolson, forthcoming. A preliminary discussion of clientelism in Israel is found in S.N. Eisenstadt and L. Roniger, 'Clientelism in Communist Systems: A Comparative Perspective', *Studies in Comparative Communism*, 14:2–3 (1981), 233–45; see also Y. Azmon, 'The Changing Fortunes of the Israeli Labor Party', *Government and Opposition*, 16 (1981), 432–46; and P. Burstein, 'Political Patronage and Party Choice among Israeli Voters', *Journal of Politics*, 38 (1976), 1024–32.

21 See J. Tarkowski, 'Poland: Patrons and Clients in a Planned Economy', in S.N. Eisenstadt and R. Lemarchand, eds., *Political Clientelism, Patronage and Development*, London, Sage Publications, 1981, 173–88; and J.P. Willerton, Jr, 'Clientelism in the Soviet Union: An Initial Examination'; also the comments on Eastern Europe by Z. Bauman and the concluding comments by T.H. Rigby, *Studies in Comparative Communism*, 12:2–3 (1979), 159–211.

22 E. Hobsbawm, *Primitive Rebels: Studies in Archaic Forms of Social Movements in the 19th and 20th Centuries*, Manchester, Manchester University Press, 1971 (c. 1959); *idem*, *Bandits*, London, Weidenfeld and Nicolson, 1969; and D. Moss, 'Bandits and Boundaries in Sardinia', *Man* (N.S.), 14:3 (1979), 477–96; cf. A. Blok, 'On Brigandage, with Special Reference to Peasant Mobilization', *Sociologische Gids*, 18:2 (1971), 208–16.

23 M.I. Pereira de Queiroz, 'Brazilian Messianic Movements: A Help or a

Hindrance to "Participation"?', *Bulletin of the International Institute for Labor Studies*, 7 (1970), 93–121; *idem, La 'guerre sainte' au Brésil: le mouvement messianique du 'contestado'*, Arts and Sciences Bulletin No. 187, Sociologia I, 5, São Paulo, University of São Paulo, (1957); *idem, Messianismo e conflito social: A guerra sertaneja do contestado, 1912–1916*, Rio de Janeiro, Civilização brasileira, 1966; B.J. Siegel, 'The Contestado Rebellion, 1912–16: A Case Study in Brazilian Messianism and Regional Dynamics', *Journal of Anthropological Research*, 33 (1977), 202–13; H.J. Benda, 'Peasant Movements in Colonial Southeast Asia', *Asian Studies*, 3:3 (1965), 420–34; F. Hills, 'Millenarian Machines in South Vietnam', *Comparative Studies in Society and History*, 13:3 (1971), 325–50; B. Dahm, 'Leadership and Mass Response in Java, Burma and Vietnam', Paper presented to the International Congress of Orientalists, Canberra, Jan. 1971, on file at Kiel University; M. Osborne, *Region of Revolt: Focus on Southeast Asia*, Oxford, Pergamon Press, 1970; and J. van der Kroef, 'Javanese Messianic Expectations: Their Origin and Cultural Context', *Comparative Studies in Society and History*, 1:4 (1959), 299–323.

24 J.C. Scott, 'The Erosion of Patron–Client Bonds and Social Change in Rural Southeast Asia,' *Journal of Asian Studies*, 32:1 (1972), 5–37.

Chapter 6

1 Some of the best illustrations for this point are found in E. Banfield, *The Moral Basis of a Backward Society*, New York, Free Press, 1958; A. Blok, 'Coalitions in Sicilian Peasant Society', in J. Boissevain and C. Mitchell, eds., *Network Analysis and Studies in Human Interaction*, Paris and The Hague, Mouton, 1973, pp. 151–66; E. Wolf, *Peasants*, Englewood Cliffs, N.J., Prentice-Hall, 1966; P. Schneider, 'Honor and Conflict in a Sicilian Town', *Anthropological Quarterly*, 42:3 (1969), 130–54; J. Schneider, 'Of Vigilance and Virgins'; J. Schneider and P. Schneider, *Culture and Political Economy in Western Sicily*; O.Fals-Borda, *El reformismo por dentro en América Latina*, Mexico, Siglo XXI, 1972; E. Hermitte and L. Bartolomé, eds., *Procesos de articulación social*, Buenos Aires, C.L.A.C.S.O.–Amorrortu, 1977; M. Johnson, 'Political Bosses and their Gangs: Zu'ama and Qabadayat in the Sunni Muslim Quarters of Beirut', in E. Gellner and J. Waterbury, eds., *Patrons and Clients*, pp. 207–24; J.D. Seddon, 'Local Politics and State Intervention: Northeast Morocco from 1870 to 1970', in E. Gellner and C. Micaud, eds., *Arabs and Berbers: From Tribe to Nation in North Africa*, London, Duckworth, 1973, (c. 1972), pp. 109–39; J.D. Powell, 'Peasant Society and Clientelist Politics', *American Political Science Review*, 64:2 (1970), 411–25; H. Alavi, 'Peasant Classes and Primordial Loyalties', *Journal of Peasant Studies*, 1:1 (1973), 23–62; F. Lynch, *Four Readings in Philippine Values*, Institute of Philippine Culture Papers, No.2, Quezon City, Ateneo de Manila Press, 1964; H. Hess, *Mafia and Mafiosi: The Structure of Power*, Farnborough, Saxon House, 1973. Cf. among others W.F. Wertheim, 'From Aliran to Class Struggle in the Countryside of Java', *Pacific Viewpoint*, 10:2 (1969), 1–17; P. Singelman, 'The Closing Triangle: Critical Notes on a Model for Peasant

Mobilization in Latin America', *Comparative Studies in Society and History*, 17:4 (1975), 389–409; and G. Huizer, *El Potencial revolucionario del campesino en América Latina*, Mexico, Siglo XXI, 1973.

2 On the distinction between strong and weak centres, see S.N. Eisenstadt, *Political Sociology*, New York and London, Basic Books, 1971; *idem*, *Social Differentiation and Stratification*, Glencoe, Ill., Scott Foresman and Co., 1971, especially chapter 8; and *idem*, *Traditional Patrimonialism and Modern Neopatrimonialism*, Beverley Hills, Calif., Sage Research Papers in the Social Sciences, 1973. Further elaboration can be found in *idem*, *Revolution and the Transformation of Societies*, New York, Free Press, 1978, especially chapters 4, 5. The structurally weak character of those centres has been a recurrent theme in the sociological literature. See, for instance, S. Tarrow, *From Center to Periphery; idem*, 'Local Constraints on Regional Reform: A Comparison of Italy and France', *Comparative Politics*, 7:1 (1976), 1–36; S. Silverman, 'Patronage and Community–Nation Relationships'; C.H. Landé, 'Networks and Groups in Southeast Asia'; and J.G. Scott, 'Patron–Client Politics and Political Change'. On the symbolic institutional characteristics of centre and periphery, see G. Roth, 'Personal Rulership, Patrimonialism and Empire-Building in the New States', *World Politics*, 20:2 (1968), 194-206; A.R. Zolberg, *Creating Political Order: The Party States of West Africa 1870–1960*, Cambridge, Cambridge University Press, 1971; F.W. Riggs, *Thailand: The Modernization of a Bureaucratic Polity*, Honolulu, East–West Center Press, 1966; Thaung, 'Burmese Kinship in Theory and Practice under the Reign of King Mindon', *Journal of the Burma Research Society*, 42:2 (1959), 171–85; B. Schricke, *Indonesian Sociological Studies*, The Hague and Bandung, W. Van Hoeve, 1957; J.C. Van Lear, *Indonesian Trade and Society*, The Hague and Bandung, W. Van Hoeve, 1955, pp. 1–221; R. Heine-Geldern, 'Conception of State and Kinship in Southeast Asia', Southeast Asian Program Data paper no.18, Ithaca, N.Y., Cornell University Press, 1956, pp. 1–13; L. Hanke, ed., *History of Latin American Civilization*, 2 vols., Boston, Mass., Little, Brown, 1967; M. Sarfatti, *Spanish Bureaucratic Patrimonialism in America*, Institute of International Studies, Politics of Modernization Series No.1, Berkeley, University of California Press, 1966; C.H. Haring, *The Spanish Empire in America*, New York, Oxford University Press, 1947; S.E. Finer, *Comparative Government*, London, Allen Lane; Harmondsworth, The Penguin Press, 1970; A. Zuckerman, *Political Clienteles in Power: Party Factions and Cabinet Coalitions in Italy*, Beverley Hills, Calif., and London, Sage Publications, 1975; and D. Collier, ed., *The New Authoritarianism in Latin America*, Princeton, N.J., Princeton University Press, 1979.

3 See, for instance, C.H. Landé, 'Networks and Groups in Southeast Asia: Some Observations on the Group Theory of Politics', *American Political Science Review*, 67:1 (1973), 103–27; J. Boissevain, 'Poverty and Politics in a Sicilian Agrotown', *International Archives of Ethnography*, 50 (1966), 189–236; D. Meertens, 'South from Madrid: Regional Elites and Resistance', in J. Boissevain and J. Friedl, eds., *Beyond the Community: Social Process in Europe*, European–Mediterranean Study Group of the University of Amsterdam, 1975, pp. 65–74; Eul-Soo Pang, *Coronelismo e oligarquias (1889–1934)*, Rio de

Janeiro, Civilização Brasileira, 1979; E.D. Akarli and G. Ben-Dor, eds., *Political Participation in Turkey*, Istanbul, Bogazici University, 1975; and J. Waterbury, *The Commander of the Faithful. The Moroccan Political Elite: A Study in Segmented Politics*, London, Weidenfeld and Nicolson, 1970.

4 See, for example, R. Aya, *The Missed Revolution: The Fate of the Rural Rebels in Sicily and Southern Spain 1840–1950*, Amsterdam University Papers on European and Mediterranean Societies, No. 3, 1975; J.D. Powell, 'Peasant Society and Clientelist Politics'; K.D. Jackson, *Urbanization and the Rise of Patron–Client Relations: The Changing Quality of Interpersonal Communications in the Neighbourhoods of Bandung and the Villages of West Java*, Cambridge, Mass., Center for International Studies, M.I.T., 1974; M.I. Pereira de Queiroz, *Cultura, sociedade rural, sociedade urbana no Brasil*, São Paolo, Editora da Universidade de São Paolo, 1978; M.J. Swartz, ed., *Local-Level Politics: Social and Cultural Perspectives*, Chicago, Aldine Press, 1968; and S. Tarrow, *Peasant Communism in Southern Italy*, New Haven, Conn., Yale University Press, 1967. In Sicily and other regions the overlapping and intermingling of occupational roles and identities can hamper the formation of broad categorical commitments. For Sicily, see J. Schneider, 'Family Patrimonies and Economic Behaviour in Western Sicily', *Anthropological Quarterly*, 42:3 (1969), 109–29; and A. Blok, *The Mafia of a Sicilian Village 1860–1960*, Oxford, Basil Blackwell, 1974. See also notes 32 to 36 in chapter 4.

5 On bilateral kinship and its societal implications, see R.H. Pehrson, 'Bilateral Kin Groupings as a Structural Type', *Journal of East Asiatic Studies*, 3 (1954), 199–202; W. Davenport, 'Nonunilineal Descent and Descent Groups., *American Anthropologist*, 6 (1959), 557–72; O. Blehr, 'Action Groups in a Society with Bilateral Kinship: A Case Study of the Faroe Islands', *Ethnology*, 3:3 (1963), 269–75; J. Pitt-Rivers, 'The Kith and the Kin'; C.H. Landé, 'Kinship and Politics in Pre-Modern and Nonwestern Societies', in J.T. McAlister, Jr, ed., *Southeast Asia: The Politics of National Integration*, New York, Random House, 1973, pp. 219–33; and *idem*, 'Networks and Groups in Southeast Asia'. On the structure of kinship in the clientelistic societies, see E. Swanson, *Rules of Descent: Studies in the Sociology of Parentage*, Ann Arbor, University of Michigan Museum of Anthropology, Anthropological Papers, 1969; G.P. Murdock, 'Cognatic Forms of Social Organizations', in *idem*, ed., *Social Structure in Southeast Asia*, Viking Fund Publications in Anthropology, No.29, Chicago, Quadrangle Books, 1960, pp. 1–14; M.M. Khaing, *Burmese Family*, Bombay, Longman–Green, 1947; E. Wolf, 'Society and Symbols in Latin Europe and the Islamic Near East: Some Comparisons', *Anthropological Quarterly*, 42:3 (1969), 287–301; L.W. Moss and W.H. Thompson, 'The South Italian Family: Literature and Observations', *Human Organization*, 18:1 (1959), 35–41; O. Lewis, *The Children of Sanchez: An Autobiography of a Mexican Family*, New York, Random House, 1961; B.G. Hoffman, *The Structure of Traditional Moroccan Society*; and F.L. Hsu, *Kinship and Culture*, Chicago, Aldine Press, 1971. Even in the Middle East, the realities of kinship differed widely from the images of supposed strong, corporative lineages and extended kinship units. See B.G. Hoffman, *The Structure*; and J. Davis, *People of the Mediterranean*.

6 For a broad treatment of those concepts, see S.N. Eisenstadt and M. Curelaru, *Macro-Sociology; idem, The Form of Sociology;* and S.N. Eisenstadt, 'Cultural Orientations, Institutional Entrepreneurs, and Social Change: Comparative Analysis of Traditional Civilizations', *American Journal of Sociology,* 85:4 (1980), 840–69. On the above conceptions, see E. Wolf, 'Society and Symbols in Latin Europe and in the Islamic Middle East'; S.A. Hahha and G.H. Gardner, eds., *Arab Socialism,* Leiden, E.J. Brill, 1969; A.J.D. Matz, 'The Dynamics of Change in Latin America', *Journal of Inter-American Studies,* 9:1 (1966), 66–76; C.F. Gallagher, 'The Shaping of the Spanish Intellectual Tradition', *American Universities Field Staff Reports,* 9:8 (1976); D.E. Worcester, 'The Spanish–American Past: Enemy of Change', *Journal of Inter-American Studies,* 11:1 (1969), 66–75; K. Silvert, 'Latin America and its Alternative Future', *International Journal,* 24:3 (1969), 403–44; H.D. Evers, *Kulturwandel in Ceylon,* Baden-Baden, Verlag Lutzeyer, 1964; R. Sarkisyanz, *Buddhist Backgrounds of the Burmese Revolution,* The Hague, M. Nijhoff, 1965; C.F. Gallagher, 'Contemporary Islam: A Frontier of Communalism. Aspects of Islam in Malaysia', *American Universities Field Staff Reports,* Southeast Asia Series, 14:10 (1966); J. Peacock, *Rites of Modernization: Symbols and Social Aspects of Indonesian Proletarian Drama,* Chicago, Ill., University of Chicago Press, 1968; and R.N. Milton, 'The Basic Malay House', *Journal of the Royal Asiatic Society, Malay Branch,* 29:3 (1965), 145–55.

7 See for instance C.F. Keyes, *The Golden Peninsula: Culture and Adaptation in Mainland Southeast Asia,* New York, Macmillan; London, Collier Macmillan, 1977; B. Lewis, *Islam in History: Ideas, Men and Events in the Middle East,* London, Alcove, 1973; E. Gellner and C. Micaud, *Arabs and Berbers;* J. O'Dea *et al., Religion and Man: Judaism, Christianity and Islam,* New York, Harper and Row, 1975; and S.N. Eisenstadt, 'Cultural Orientations, Institutional Entrepreneurs, and Social Change'.

8 B.F. Hoselitz, *Sociological Aspects of Economic Growth,* New York, Free Press, 1960, pp. 85–114. For the concepts employed in this section, see K.E. Polanyi *et al.,* eds., *Trade and Market in Early Empires,* New York, The Free Press, 1957; G. Dalton, ed., *Primitive, Archaic and Modern Economies: Essays of Karl Polanyi,* New York, Anchor Books, 1968. On the economic structure and process in these societies, see S.N. Eisenstadt, *Traditional Patrimonialism and Modern Neopatrimonialism,* Beverly Hills, Sage Research Papers in the Social Sciences, 1973; for illustrative materials, see B. Rivlin and J.S. Szyliowicz, eds., *The Contemporary Middle East: Traditions and Innovations,* New York, Random House, 1965, especially pp. 297–324, 368–74; F.H. Golay *et al.,* eds., *Underdevelopment and Economic Nationalism in Southeast Asia,* Ithaca, N.Y., Department of Asian Studies, Cornell University, 1967; Soedjatmoko, *Economic Development as a Cultural Problem,* Ithaca, N.Y., Cornell University, Department of Asian Studies, 1968; T.H. Silock, ed., *Readings in Malayan Economics,* Singapore, Eastern Universities Press, 1961; H. Jaguaribe, *Desenvolvimento economico e desenvolvimento politico,* Rio de Janeiro, Fundo de Cultura, 1962; and J. Schneider and P. Schneider, *Culture and Political Economy in Western Sicily.*

9 On these polities, see S.N. Eisenstadt, *The Political System of Empires*, New York, The Free Press, 1963, especially chapter 7; and *idem, Political Sociology*.

10 See I.M. Wallerstein, ed., *Social Change: The Colonial Structure*, New York, John Wiley and Sons, 1969. S.N. Eisenstadt, *Traditional Patrimonialism and Modern Neopatrimonialism*, contains detailed bibliographical notes on these topics. On illustrations specifically from the literature on patron–client relations, see, for instance, J. Schneider and P. Schneider, *Culture and Political Economy in Western Sicily*; F. Snowden, 'On the Social Origins of Agrarian Fascism in Italy', *Archives Européennes de Sociologie*, 13:2 (1972), 268–95; J. Schneider, 'Family Patrimonies and Economic Behaviour in Western Sicily'; H. Hess, *Mafia and Mafiosi*; E. Feder, *Violencia y despojo del campesino: el latifundismo en América Latina*, Mexico, Siglo XXI, 1975 (1971); R. Stavenhagen, 'Social Aspects of Agrarian Structure in Mexico', *Social Research*, 33:3 (1966), 463–85; M. Rossi-Doria, 'The Land Tenure System and Class in Southern Italy'.

11 P.T. Bauer and B.S. Yamey, *The Economics of Underdeveloped Countries*, Cambridge, Cambridge University Press, 1957; C.S. Belshaw, 'Approaches to Articulation in the Economy', in *idem, Traditional Exchange and Modern Markets*, Englewood Cliffs, N.J., Prentice-Hall, 1965, pp. 84–107; G.W. Skinner and A.T. Kirsch, eds., *Change and Persistence in Thai Society: Essays in Honor of Lauristan Sharp*; F. Derossi, *El empresario mexicano*, Instituto de Investigaciones Sociales, Mexico, U.N.A.M., 1977.

12 The concept of dual character of these economies in colonial settings was formulated originally by J.H. Boeke, *Tropisch–Koloniale Staathuishoudkunde*, 1910. For its treatment, see J.S. Furnivall, *Netherlands India: A Study of Plural Economy*, Cambridge, Cambridge University Press, 1939; J.H. Boeke, *The Structure of Netherlands Indian Economy*, New York, Institute of Pacific Relations, 1942; and *idem, Economics and Economic Policy of Dual Societies*, New York, Institute of Pacific Relations, 1953. For the discussion of extractive mechanisms of the externally-oriented sectors of the economy see R. Stavenhagen, 'Seven Fallacies about Latin America', in J. Petras and M. Zeitlin, eds., *Latin America: Reform or Revolution?*, New York, Faucett Publications, 1968, pp. 13–31. For the renewed appreciation of such duality in industrialised societies see S. Berger and M.J. Piore, *Dualism and Discontinuity in Industrial Societies*, Cambridge, Cambridge University Press, 1980.

13 On the structuring of social hierarchies in some societies, see M. Sarfatti and A.E. Bergman, *Social Stratification in Peru*, Berkeley, University of California Institute of International Studies, Politics of Modernization Series No.5, 1969, pp. 43 and 52–4; B.G. Burnett and R.F. Johnson, eds., *Political Forces in Latin America*, Belmont, Mass., Wadsworth, 1968; J. Graciarena, *Poder y clases sociales en el desarrollo de América Latina*, Buenos Aires, Paidós, 1968; D.B. Heath and R. Adams, eds., *Contemporary Cultures and Societies in Latin America*, New York, Random House, 1965, especially part III; F. Bourricaud, 'Structure and Function of the Peruvian Oligarchy', *Studies in Comparative International Development*, 2:2 (1966), 17–31; A. Touraine, 'Social Mobility, Class Relations, and Nationalism in Latin America', *ibid.*, 1:3 (1965), 19–25; J.A. Fernandez, *The Political Elite in Argentina*, New

York, New York University Press, 1970; A. Touraine and D. Pecaut, 'Working Class Consciousness and Economic Development', *Studies in Comparative International Development*, 3:4 (1967–8), 71–84; H.J. Benda, 'Political Elites in Colonial Southeast Asia: i.e. an Historical Analysis', *Comparative Studies in Society and History*, 7:2 (1965), 233–51; and *idem*, 'Non-Western Intelligentsia as Political Elites', in S.N. Eisenstadt, ed., *Political Sociology*, pp. 437–45; M.R. Singer, *The Emerging Elite: A Study of Political Leadership in Ceylon*, Cambridge, Mass., M.I.T. Press, 1964; and M. Lissak, *A Socio-Political Hierarchy in a Loose Social Structure: The Structure of Stratification in Thailand*, Jerusalem, Academic Press, 1973.

14 See on these societies in greater detail S.N. Eisenstadt, *Revolution and the Transformation of Societies*, especially chapters 4, 5 and 9.

15 See J. Pitt-Rivers, *The Fate of Schechem or the Politics of Sex*; J. Davis, *People of the Mediterranean: An Essay in Comparative Social Anthropology*, London, Henley and Boston, Routledge and Kegan Paul, 1976; J.G. Peristiany, ed., *Honour and Shame*; and W. Herzfeld, 'Honour and Shame: Problems in the Comparative Analysis of Moral Systems', *Man* (N.S.), 15 (1980), 339–51.

16 On *giri* conceptions see references in note 7 in chapter 5.

17 R. Paine, 'A Theory of Patronage and Brokerage', in *idem*, ed., *Patrons and Brokers in the East Arctic*, Newfoundland Social and Economic Papers, No.2, Memorial University of Newfoundland, 1971, pp. 3–21. In the following paragraph we refer to this work.

18 C.P. Perreira de Camargo *et al.*, *São Paulo 1975: Crescimento e pobreza*, São Paulo, Loyola, 1981; G. Velho, ed., *O desafio da cidade*, Rio de Janeiro, Campus, 1980. For a broader treatment of such developments in Latin America, see the volume of the *Revista Mexicana de Sociología*, dealing with marginality, urbanisation and population in Latin America, 1978.

19 S.T. Freeman, *Neighbors: The Social Contract in a Castilian Hamlet*, Chicago, University of Chicago Press, 1970.

20 W.T. Stuart, 'On the Nonoccurrence of Patronage in San Miguel de Serna', in A. Strickon and S.M. Greenfield, eds., *Structure and Process in Latin America*, pp. 211–36.

Chapter 7

1 For a full description of the cases mentioned in this chapter, see chapter 4 above.

2 P.A. Allum, *Politics and Society in Postwar Naples*, Cambridge, Cambridge University Press, 1973.

3 See note 98 in chapter 4 above.

4 On the term and its application in Latin America, see S.E. Finer, *Comparative Government*, London and Harmondsworth, Allen Lane–The Penguin Press, 1970.

5 On such coalitions, see among others A. Hennessy, 'Latin America', in G. Ionescu and E. Gellner, eds., *Populism: Its Meanings and National Characteristics*, London, Duckworth, 1969, pp. 28–61; O. Ianni, *O Colapso do Populismo no Brasil*, Rio de Janeiro, Civilização Brasileira, 1975 (c. 1968); and A.E. Van

Niekerk, *Populism and Political Development in Latin America*, Rotterdam University Press, 1974.

6 See chapter 4, as well as L.O. Dare, 'Patron–Client Relations and Military Rule in Nigeria', MS, University of Ife, Nigeria, 1978; S.P. Huntington and C.H. Moore, *Authoritarian Politics in Modern Society*, New York and London, Basic Books, 1970; and C.H. Moore, *Politics in North Africa, Algeria, Morocco and Tunisia*, Boston, Mass., Little, Brown, 1970.

7 L. Guasti, 'Clientelism in Decline: A Peruvian Regional Study', in S.N. Eisenstadt and R. Lemarchand, eds., *Political Clientelism, Patronage and Development*, pp. 217–48.

8 J.D. Powell, *Political Mobilization of the Venezuelan Peasant*, Cambridge, Mass., Harvard University Press, 1971; *idem*, 'Peasant Society and Client-elist Politics', *American Political Science Review*, 64:2 (1970), 411–25.

9 R. Sandbrook, 'Patrons, Clients and Factions: New Dimensions of Conflict Analysis in Africa', *Canadian Journal of Political Science*, 5:1 (1972), 104–19; *idem*, 'Patrons, Clients, and Unions: The Labour Movement and Political Conflict in Kenya', *Journal of Commonwealth Political Studies*, 10:1 (1972), 3–27.

10 S. Tarrow, *From Center to Periphery: Alternative Models of National–Local Policy Impact and an Application to France and Italy*, Cornell University Western Societies Program Occasional Papers No.4, New York, 1976.

11 C.H. Moore, 'Clientelist Ideology and Political Change: Fictitious Networks in Egypt and Tunisia', in E. Gellner and J. Waterbury, eds., *Patrons and Clients*, pp. 255–74.

12 E. Wolf, 'Kinship, Friendship, and Patron–Client Relationships'.

13 U. Almagor, *Pastoral Partners*; *idem*, 'Coevals and Competitors', MS, Jerusalem, The Hebrew University, 1980.

14 R. da Matta, *Carnavais, malandros e herois*, Rio de Janeiro, Zahar, 1979.

15 There are also differences in the institutional levels on which the conversion of such political and relational resources is focused. Here it is worthwhile to differentiate between patron–client relations found in traditional semi-isolated settings and those of peripheral or semi-peripheral ones which are already integrated within wider institutional frameworks and in which markets gain a wider scope. In the relations found in semi-isolated settings and having a 'localised' structure, the socio-political significance of resources generated through patron–client ties is fully operative only at the local level. In relations linked to wider frames of interaction, those resources are often used by patrons in political struggles and to gain eminence in those higher institutional levels.

16 J. Pitt-Rivers, *The People of the Sierra*.

17 See, for instance, J. Boissevain, 'When the Saints Go Marching Out'; *idem*, *Saints and Fireworks; Religion and Politics in Rural Malta*, London, Athlone Press, 1965; and G.M. Foster, 'The Dyadic Contract'.

Chapter 8

1 See, for instance, L.M. Verbrugge, 'Multiplexity in Adult Friendship', *Social Forces*, 57:4 (1979), 1286–1309; M.T. Hallinan, 'The Process of

Friendship Formation', *Social Networks*, 1:2 (1978), 193–210; M. Hammer, 'Social Access and the Clustering of Personal Connections', *ibid.*, 2 (1980), 305–25; E.O. Laumann, *Bonds of Pluralism: The Form and Substance of Urban Social Networks*, New York, John Wiley and Sons, 1973.

2 For a fuller treatment of these and the following characterisation of such tribal societies, see S.N. Eisenstadt, *From Generation to Generation*; and *idem*, *Political Sociology*, part II.

3 S.N. Eisenstadt, 'Ritualised Personal Relations'.

4 Y. Cohen, 'Patterns of Friendship'.

5 E. Leyton, ed., *The Compact*; T.M. Kiefer, 'Institutionalised Friendship and Warfare among the Tausug of Jolo', *Ethnology*, 7 (1968), 225–44; cf. S. Price, 'Reciprocity and Social Distance: A Reconsideration', *Ethnology*, 17:3 (1978), 339–50.

6 See the *Ethics of Aristotle*, trans. J.A.K. Thomson, Penguin Classics, Harmondsworth, Penguin Books, 1966, pp. 227–85; J. Annas, 'Plato and Aristotle on Friendship and Altruism', *Mind*, 86:344 (1977), 532–44; and R. Paine, 'Anthropological Approaches to Friendship', in E. Leyton, ed., *The Compact*, pp. 1–14.

7 See chapters 4 and 5 above.

8 L.W. Pye, *The Dynamics of Factions and Consensus in Chinese Politics*. The quoted passages are from pp. 6 and 8.

9 On patterns of friendship in such societies, see S. Piker, 'Friendship to the Death in Rural Thai Society', *Human Organization*, 27 (1968), 200–4; B.L. Foster, 'Friendship in Rural Thailand', *Ethnology*, 15:3 (1976), 251–67; and R.E. Reina, 'Two Patterns of Friendship in a Guatamalan Community', *American Anthropologist*, 61 (1959), 44–50.

10 E. Schwimmer, 'Friendship and Kinship: An Attempt to Relate Two Anthropological Concepts', in E. Leyton, ed., *The Compact*, pp. 49–70.

11 S. Gudeman, 'The Compadrazgo as a Reflection of the Natural and Spiritual Person', pp. 57 and 59. See also E. Litwak and I. Szelenyi, 'Primary Group Structures and their Functions: Kin, Neighbors, and Friends', *American Sociological Review*, 34:4 (1969), 465–81; and R.A. Millner, 'The Golden Chain: A Study of the Structure, Function, and Patterning of *Comparatico* in a South Italian Village', *American Ethnologist*, 5:1 (1978), 116–36.

12 C.D. Schneider, *Shame, Exposure, and Privacy*, Boston, Mass., Beacon Press, 1977, p. 41. On privacy and the attitudes towards it in modern societies see *ibid.*, chapter 5: 'Vulnerability, Violation, and the Private', pp. 40–55; E.A. Shils, 'Privacy: Its Constitution and Vicissitudes', *Law and Contemporary Problems*, 31 (1966), 281–306; A. Simmel, 'Privacy', in *International Encyclopaedia of the Social Sciences*, volume 12, pp. 480–7; H. Arendt, 'The Public and the Private Realm', in *The Human Condition*, Chicago, Ill., University of Chicago Press, 1958, pp. 22–78; *Journal of Social Issues*, 33:3 (1977); and J.R. Pennock and J.W. Chapman, eds., *Privacy*, New York, Atherton Press, 1971.

13 On the German youth movements, see among others H. Kohn, 'Youth Movements', in *International Encyclopaedia of the Social Sciences*, volume 15,

pp. 516–20; W.Z. Laqueur, *Young Germany: A History of the German Youth Movement*, London, Routledge and Kegan Paul, 1962; P.D. Stachura, *The German Youth Movement 1900–1945: An Interpretative and Documentary History*, London, Macmillan, 1981; and G.L. Mosse, 'Friendship and Nationhood: About the Promise and Failure of German Nationalism', *Journal of Contemporary History*, 17 (1982), 351–67. On Russian friendship, see V.C. Nahirny, 'The Russian Intelligentsia'.

14 On these informal friendships and acquaintances, see among others D. Jacobson, 'Fair-Weather Friend: Label and Context in Middle-Class Friendships', *Journal of Anthropological Research*, 31 (1975), 225–31; E. Liebow, *Tally's Corner: A Study of Negro Streetcorner Men*, Boston, Mass., Little, Brown, 1967, pp. 161–207; R.L. Burgess and T.L. Huston, *Social Exchange in Developing Relationships*, New York, Academic Press, 1979; M.T. Hallinan, 'The Process of Friendship Formation', *Social Networks*, 1:2 (1978), 193–210; and M. Hammer, 'Social Access and the Clustering of Personal Connections', *ibid.*, 2 (1980), 305–25.

15 For an example of such attitudes, see I. Lepp, *The Ways of Friendship: A Psychological Exploration of Man's Most Valuable Relationship*, New York, Macmillan, 1966. See in connection to this the remarks of Z. Rubin on the possibility that such tendency should be anchored in a 'European' style of interaction characterised by being individualistic and exclusive – i.e. conducive to the establishment of closely-linked dyadic patterns of friendship among children – in Z. Rubin, *Children's Friendships*, Cambridge, Mass., Harvard University Press, 1980, pp. 133ff.

16 See on these points L.J. Miller, 'Intimacy', in A. Blum and R. McHugh, eds., *Friends, Enemies, and Strangers: Theorizing in Art, Science, and Everyday Life*, Norwood, N.J., Ablex, 1979, pp. 157–73.

17 See among others V. Aubert and O. Aner, 'On the Social Structure of the Ship', *Acta Sociologica*, 3 (1959), 200–19; R. Heberle and J.R. Gusfield, 'Social Movements', in *International Encyclopaedia of the Social Sciences*, volume 14, pp. 438–52.

18 O. Ramsøy, 'Friendship', p.14.

19 See, for instance, the material adduced by E. Goffman, *Asylums: Essays on the Social Situation of Mental Patients and Other Inmates*, New York, Doubleday, 1961.

20 See on some such relationships P. Stringer and D. Bannister, eds., *Constructs of Sociality and Individuality*, New York, Academic Press, 1979.

21 See, for instance, C.D. Schneider, *Shame, Exposure, and Privacy*; A. Simmel, 'Privacy'; and R.J. Lifton, *Thought Reform and the Psychology of Totalism: A Study of Brainwashing in China*, New York, Norton, 1961.

Index

addendum types of patron–client
relations, 173–200
age group, 4–5, 40–1, 286–7
aghas: in Turkey, 84–7; in Iraq 88–9
Aichhorn, A., 31
Allum, P. A., 230
Almagor, U., 246–7
ambivalence towards the institutional
order, 1–28, 276–301
amicitia: in Ancient Rome, 61–2
amity, 33
Argentina, patron–client relations in,
113–14
Aristotle, 277
ascriptive hierarchical systems, 173–84,
276–8

balance of power in patron–client
relations, 213–14, 217, 250–63
banditry, 68–70, 75, 200–2
bapakism, bapak–anak buah: in Indonesia
122–7
Bateson, G., 40
Blau, P. M., 33
Bloch, M., and S. Guggenheim, 13–4
Bolivia, patron–client relations in, 111–13
bossism, political: in U.S.A. 155–7; in
Japan 159–62. *See also* linked clientelistic
networks
Bowlby, J., 31
Brazil, patron–client relations in, 104–7,
216–17
brokerage, 228–45
Buber, M., ix, 40
Buddhism, 117–27, 130–8, 206–8, 261–3
buhake: in Rwanda, 153–4
Burma, patron–client relations in, 137–8
Burridge, K. O. L., 12

caciques, caciquismo, 72–3, 114–17

camarillas: in Mexico 116
Campbell, J. K., 80
'captive' clienteles, 225–7
Catholicism, 50–2, 64–71, 99–117, 206–8,
261–3 *passim*
caudillos, 102–3, 114–15. *See also* Latin
America
centre–periphery relations in clientelistic
societies, 204–6, 228–46
changes in clientelistic relations,
225–8, 263–8. *See also* patron–client
relations.
China, patron–client relations in,
139–45
clientelae: see patrocinium
clientelism, 166–219; in comparative
perspective, 166–73
coalitions 37–9, 234–41; populistic, 238;
authoritarian, 238–41. *See also* elites in
clientistic societies
Cohen, Y., 5, 7, 11, 274
Coleman, J., 4, 33–4
Colombia, patron–client relations in,
102–4
Communist systems, 157–9; and
favouritism, 186–91
compadrazgo, 13–6, 76–7, 109, 128, 248–50,
278–81
consociational systems, 170–2, 195–200,
290–1
coronéis, coronelismo, 105–6
corporatist systems, 170–2
Cyrenaica, southwestern, patron–client
relations in, 154–5

Davis, K., 21–3
discretion in patron–client relations,
259–63
Du Bois, C., 5, 7
Durkheim, E., 20–1, 34

341

Index

ecologico-social organisational matrix and patron–client relations, 216–18
Egypt, patron-client relations in, 89–91
Eisenstadt, S. N., 5–12, 273
elites, 37–9; in clientelistic societies, 207–11, 228–45
entitlements, 35–7

Fortes, M., 33, 36
Foster, G. M., 27
Frankenstein, C., 31
friendship, 2, 6–12, 15–18, 33, 269–93
futuwwat: in Egypt, 90–1

gamonales: in Colombia, 102–4
gauchos: in South America, 113–14
Gellner, E., 164
generalised exchange, 32–42; modes of structuring, 166–73
Goffman, E., 25–6, 175
Graziano, L., 66
Greece, patron–client relations in, 77–81
Guasti, L., 240
Gudeman, S., 13, 280–1
Guggenhaim, S., 13–14

hierarchical social systems, 169–70; and patron–client relations, 173–84
Homans, G. C., 33
honour, 15, 70, 74–7, 210–14

India, patron–client relations in 150–3, 178–84
Indonesia, patron–client relations in, 122–7
instability of patron–client relations, 229–42, 248–50, 263–7
interpersonal relations: the study of 1–28; contexts of variation of, 269–301
Iraq, northern, patron–client relations in, 88–9
Islamic societies and patron–client relations, 229–43, 248–50, 263–7
interpersonal relations, 81–99, 204–7
Israel, patron–client relations and countervailing forces in, 195–200
Italy, patron–client relations in, 64–71

jajmani relations: in India 150–3, 178–83
Japan, patron–client relations in, 145–50, 174–8; patron–client relationships in modern, 159–62, 248–50
Jordan, patron–client relations in, 87–8

kan-ch'ing relations: in China 139–42, 144–5, 276–8
Kenny, M., 73, 75
kinship, 15–18, 29–33, 272–81; bilateral,

206; corporate, 169–70; *dozoku*, 147–8, 247–8, *and see also* 176–7 on the Japanese family system; fictive, ritual: *see* ritualised relations, *compadrazgo*, *oyakun–kobun*

Latin America, patron–client relations in, 99–117
Lebanon, patron–client relations in, 91–5
Lévi-Strauss, C., 34–6
Leyton, E., 5, 185
liminality, 18
linked clientelistic networks, 228–34, 243–5

McNeill, W. H., 79
mafiosi: in western Sicily, 68–70
marginality, 117. *See also* Latin America
markets and personal relations, 29–42 *passim*; and patron–client relations, 43–50 *passim*, 252–68
Marx, K., 20–1
Mauss, M., 33–6
meaning in society, 24–42, 294–301. *See also* symbolic domain of human relations
Merton, R. K., 21–3
Mexico, patron–client relations in, 114–17
Mezzogiorno, patron–client relations in, 64–8
Middle East, (Muslim), patron–client relations in, 81–99
Moore, W. E., 21–3
mu-fu system: in China, 142–3
Muqata'ji: in Lebanon, 91–5

Naegele, K. D., 4, 7, 16
Nāi–phrai relations: in Thailand, 131–3
Nakane, C., 177

organisational clientelistic brokerage, 228–45
oyabun–kobun relations: in Japan, 146–50, 161–2, 174–8, 248–50

Paget, J., 4
Paine, R., x, 5, 16, 213–14
panelinhas, 107
Parsons, T., 4, 21–6, 33–4
patrocinium and *clientelae*: in Ancient Rome 52–64
patron-brokerage, 228–45
patron–client relations, 2, 43–268; as addenda to hierarchical models of generalised exchange, 173–84; as addenda to universalistic models of generalised exchange, 184–200; basic characteristics of, 43–50; clientelistic

342

Index

exchanges in, 250–63; conditions of emergence of, 203–19; continuities, discontinuities and instability in, 263–8, *and see also* changes in clientelistic relations; and countervailing forces in clientelistic societies, 200–2; and countervailing forces in universalistic societies, 185–200; organisational aspects of, 228–45; roles and role taking in, 245–58; styles of installation in, 248–50; variations in, 162–5, 220–68. *See also* balance of power in patron–client relations, discretion in patron–client relations, reciprocity in patron–client relations, socio-moral restraints in patron–client relations, subversion in patron–client relations

pelegos: in Brazil 106
Peru, patron–client relations in, 107–11
Philippines, patron–client relations in, 127–30
Pitt-Rivers, J., 2, 5–6, 15, 211
Poland, patron–client relations in, 200
Powell, J. D., 241
privacy and interpersonal relations, 282–93
Pye, L. W., 278

qabadayat: in Lebanon, 91–5

Ramsøy, O., 5–6, 11, 286
reciprocity in patron–client relations, 252–6, 256–63 *passim*
Republican Rome, patron–client relations in, 52–64
Riggs, F. W., 134–5
ritualised relations, 5, 8–11, 248–50, 269–82
ritual kinship: *see* ritualised relations, *compadrazgo, oyabun–kobun*
roles and role taking in patron–client relations, 245–8
Rwanda, patron–client relations in, 153–5

Scott, J. C., 231
sectarian and oppositionary orientations and interpersonal relations, 275–301
shillal: in Egypt and tunisia, 91
Shils, E., 21–3
Sicily, western, patron–client relations in, 68–70
Silverman, S., 71
Simmel, G., 2
Smelser, N., 21–3
social division of labour, 19–28, 224–5
social exchange, 33–42; and patron–client relations, 43–50, 250–63

social hierarchies in clientelistic societies, 205–10
socialisation, 11, 29–33, 39–40
sociology: criticisms, 23–6, 308–9; Founding Fathers and the study of social solidarity 19–28; sociological theory and the problem of trust 19–28; structural–functionalist approach 21–3
socio-moral restraints in patron–client relations 43–550, 259–63
solidarity, 19–28, *and see also* trust; and patron–client relations, 250–63
southeast Asia, patron–client relations in, 117–38
southern Europe, patron–client relations in, 50–81
Spain, patron–client relations in, 71–7
structure of power, 224–5
subversion in patron–client relations, 200–2, 259–68
symbolic domain of human relations, 4–5, 13–18, 269–301 *passim. See also* meaning in society

Tarrow, S., 67
Thailand, patron–client relations in, 130–7
Tönnies, F., 20
traditional patronage, 225–34
trust: construction, breakdown and extension of, 19–42, 213–15, 272–4, 278–9, 294–301
tselingas: in Greece 80–1
Turkey, patron–client relations in, 84–7
Turner, V., 18, 285

unconditionalities, 35–7
universalistic societies, 169–71; and patron–client relations, 184–200; and other interpersonal relations, 276–8, 282–93
U.S.A.: patron–client relations in, 155–7; countervailing forces to patron–client relations in, 191–5
U.S.S.R.: patron–client relations in, 157–9; countervailing forces to patron–client relations in, 186–91

wastah: in Jordan 87–8; in Lebanon 94. *See also* Middle East (Muslim), patron–client relations in
Waterbury, J., 164
Weber, M., 20–1
Weingrod, A., 231
Wolf, E., 5, 164, 246

yuryokusha in Japan, 159–62, 175

zuʿama: in Lebanon, 91–5

343

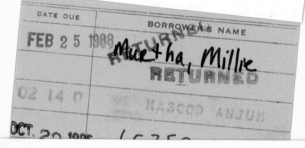